Blackstone's
POLICE MANUAL

GENERAL POLICE DUTIES

Blackstone's
POLICE MANUAL

GENERAL POLICE DUTIES

2000 edition

Fraser Sampson LLB, LLM, MBA

BLACKSTONE
PRESS LIMITED

First edition published in Great Britain 1998 by Blackstone Press Limited,
Aldine Place, London W12 8AA. Telephone (020) 8740 2277
www.blackstonepress.com

First edition 1998
Second edition 1999

ISBN: 1 85431 913 2

British Library Cataloguing in Publication Data
A CIP catalogue record for this book is available from the British Library.

Typeset by Style Photosetting Ltd, Mayfield, East Sussex
Printed by Ashford Colour Press, Gosport, Hampshire

CONTENTS

CONTENTS

CONTENTS

CONTENTS

PREFACE

There is a widely held public view that police officers are the guardians of the law. The assumption is that officers know the law. It is therefore surprising that, given this view, the average police officer is ill equipped when it comes to law books. Many police officers will remember with affection the old *Consolidated Guide*. Some will even remember the much loved works of Moriarty and Baker & Wilkie. Interestingly, none of these books were official books but they became the *vade-mecum* of many police officers.

Police officers have not only to know the law, they have to understand it. In the past police officers and support staff have had to choose between books written for lawyers which have too much law on too many pages and books supposedly written for police officers which have too little law on too many pages.

Blackstone's Police Manuals are designed for all police officers. They have been written by police officers who understand the problems that confront officers on a daily basis. They are designed to be read by probationers, sergeants and inspectors, and it is assumed that even more senior police officers will find them useful.

The Manuals are fully indexed and cross-referenced and will be published each year to keep them up to date, thus doing away with the need for inserts or supplements. More importantly for OSPRE candidates, if the law isn't in the latest edition of the Manual, it won't be in the exam. This edition contains one chapter (chapter 13) where the text appears with a vertical rule in the margin. This is to signify that the material has only been included for completeness and will NOT be tested in the promotion examination syllabus.

With a number of key pieces of legislation having taken their place on the statute books, this Manual seemed to fall naturally into three parts: Part 1 addressing the police, their management constitution and their powers, Part 2 the rapidly growing area of community safety and Part 3 what have become known as general police duties.

Many of the topics covered in this Manual form the basis of some of the most hard-won constitutional battles our courts have seen. Maintaining the balance between the exercise of necessarily wide powers by those entrusted with them and the legitimate expectations of those who are subjected to them is no mean feat. The increase in legal powers given to the police and public pressure to use them make it tempting to see recourse to the law as the best, or even the only option on many occasions. It is perhaps worth remembering, now more than ever, Lord Scarman's observation from his report into the Brixton disorders that *discretion* is critical in maintaining that balance — and that the exercise of discretion is a police officer's daily task.

While every care has been taken to ensure the accuracy of the contents of this manual, neither the author nor the publishers can accept any responsibility for any actions taken, or not taken, on the basis of the information contained in this manual.

ACKNOWLEDGEMENTS

Writing the first edition of this book to meet the needs of the varied readership was a challenge in itself; to have done it within the many other constraints and pressures that surrounded the project in its first year made the task a little more challenging than I would have liked. The many and varied contributions from police officers, Force Training Managers, trainers, lawyers and others have helped shape this second edition.

I would particularly like to thank: Suart Fairclough of No 1 Area Training Unit, Metropolitan Police: Paul Murphy of Greater Manchester Police; George Cooper from Northamptonshire Police and David Anson for their painstaking work and (relatively) painless feedback. I would also like to thank the Rastafari Universal Zion, Hugh Dent at National Police Training, Harrogate and the Crown Prosecution Service for permission to reproduce the Public Order Charging Standards.

Thanks also to Alistair, Heather, Mandy and Richard at Blackstone and, of course, to CC, TA, TJL and now AC for their patience and support in this as in all things.

TABLE OF CASES

TABLE OF CASES

TABLE OF CASES

TABLE OF STATUTES

TABLE OF STATUTES

TABLE OF STATUTORY INSTRUMENTS

European secondary legislation

PART ONE

POLICE

CHAPTER ONE

POLICE

1.1 The Police Act 1996

The Police Act 1996 is the principal piece of legislation affecting the maintenance and operation of police forces in England and Wales. It sets out, among other things, force areas (see sch. 1), the requirements for membership of police authorities (schs 2 and 3) and the affirmation to be taken by constables when they are sworn in (sch. 4). It imposes requirements for the submission of local policing plans and gives the Secretary of State wide powers in relation to the setting of performance targets, budgetary provisions and alteration of police areas. The 1996 Act also contains several key offences relating to police officers and is — since April 1999 — the source of the regulation of efficiency, conduct and complaints.

1.1.1 Home Secretary's Objectives

Under s. 37(1) of the Police Act 1996, the Secretary of State may set objectives for the policing of the areas of police authorities.

The latest order setting out those objectives is (at the time of writing) Police (Secretary of State's Objectives) (No. 2) Order 1999 (SI 1999 No. 1415) which lists those objectives as:

- to deal speedily and effectively with young offenders and to work with other agencies to reduce offending/re-offending by young people;

- to identify and reduce local problems of crime and disorder in partnership with local authorities, other local agencies and the public;

- to target and reduce drug-related crime in partnership with other local agencies, in particular local Drug Action Teams or Drug and Alcohol Teams, and having regard to the paper 'Tackling Drugs to Build a Better Britain; the Government's Ten-Year Strategy for Tackling Drugs Misuse'; and

- to increase trust and confidence in policing amongst minority ethnic communities.

For the objectives of the National Criminal Intelligence Service and the National Crime Squad, **see para. 1.5**.

1.1.2 Crime and Disorder Strategies

Sections 5 and 6 of the Crime and Disorder Act 1998 place a statutory responsibility on police forces and local authorities to formulate and implement crime and disorder strategies for their respective areas. These sections sought to build upon the work that had already been done in the area of crime prevention before the 1998 Act was passed and follow some of the proposals put forward in the report commissioned by the Home Office Standing Conference on Crime Prevention, 'Safer Communities; The Local Delivery of Crime Prevention through the Partnership Approach 1991' (the Morgan Report).

Responsibility under the 1998 Act is given jointly to police forces and local authorities with neither having primacy. Together, these 'responsible authorities' have a further duty to act in co-operation with every police authority, probation committee and health authority for the relevant area, together with any other person or body prescribed by the Secretary of State (s. 5(2)). Those bodies and agencies, which will include

- schools and educational institutions
- the Crown Prosecution Service
- youth services and
- local stakeholder groups

are similarly under an obligation to co-operate with the responsible authorities in exercising these functions.

Before formulating their strategies, the responsible authorities must have carried out a review of the levels and patterns of crime and disorder, taking into account the knowledge and experience of people in the area (s. 6(2)). They must then have published a report of that review and taken account of the views of any bodies and individuals prescribed by the Secretary of State on its contents.

The strategy must contain at least:

- objectives to be pursued

- long-term performance targets and

- short-term performance targets

(s. 6(4)).

The strategy must be published within the relevant area and must be kept under review with a view to monitoring its effectiveness, making any changes that appear necessary or expedient. Under s. 7 the Secretary of State may require the responsible authorities to submit — and publish — a report on specified matters connected with the exercise of their functions under s. 6.

1.1.3 Jurisdiction

Home Office Forces

Police officers in Home Office forces in England and Wales derive their jurisdiction from the Police Act 1996, s. 30 which provides that:

> *(1)   A member of a police force shall have all the powers and privileges of a constable throughout England and Wales and the adjacent United Kingdom waters.*

Keynote

Section 29 requires that every 'member of a police force' maintained for a police area (as set out in sch. 1) must be attested as a constable by making the appropriate declaration. Special constables are appointed under s. 27 and are also required to be attested (sworn in) in the same way as members of a police force.

Under s. 28, cadets may be appointed by a chief officer to undergo training with a view to their becoming members of that police force.

Note that the Criminal Justice and Public Order Act 1994 provides for cross-border enforcement of powers of arrest and the execution of warrants (**see chapter 2**).

Other Police Forces

There are several other full-time police forces in Great Britain with statutory policing functions. These include:

- British Transport Police (BTP) — see the British Transport Commission Act 1949 and the Transport Act 1962.

- Ministry of Defence Police (MDP) — see the Ministry of Defence Act 1987.

- UK Atomic Energy Authority Police — see the Atomic Energy Authority Act 1954.

- Ports police — see, e.g., the Port of London Act 1968 and the Harbour, Docks and Piers Clauses Act 1847.

Special Constables

The terms under which special constables may be appointed and deployed are also set out in s. 30. Section 30(2) provides that:

> *(2)   A special constable shall have all the powers and privileges of a constable in the police area for which he is appointed and, where the boundary of that area includes the coast, in the adjacent United Kingdom waters.*

Keynote

Special constables have all the powers and privileges of constables in other force areas to which they are sent as part of a mutual aid scheme. They also have jurisdiction in areas contiguous, i.e., next to their own. In the case of special constables in the City of London police, this includes areas contiguous to the Metropolitan Police District.

1.1.4 Vicarious Liability of Chief Officer

Section 88 of the Police Act 1996 provides that a chief officer will be vicariously liable for the 'torts' (civil wrongs) of his/her officers committed in the performance (or purported performance) of their duties. This means that the chief officer will be responsible for the payment of any damages arising out of a civil action in respect of such a tort. Section 88 does not apply in the case of officers seconded to central services such as the National Crime Squad or National Police Training (in such cases liability rests with the relevant Director General or the Home Secretary). For the law regulating such national 'authorities', **see para. 1.5.**

1.1.5 The Police Federation and Trade Union Membership

Part III of the Police Act 1996 makes provision for the establishment and maintenance of police representative institutions.

Section 59 provides for the continued existence of the Police Federation and specifies that it may represent a police officer in any proceedings brought under Regulations made under s. 50(3) (e.g. efficiency and conduct; see below) or an appeal from such proceedings.

The Secretary of State may make Regulations in relation to matters concerning the Federation (s. 60(1)), e.g., the Police Federation Regulations 1969 (SI 1969 No. 1787) as amended.

Provision is made under s. 61 for a Police Negotiating Board to represent the interests of police authorities and members in relation to:

- hours of duty
- leave
- pay and allowances
- pensions
- clothing, equipment and accoutrements.

The Police Act 1996, s. 64 provides that:

> *(1) Subject to the following provisions of this section, a member of a police force shall not be a member of any trade union, or of any association having for its objects, or one of its objects, to control or influence the pay, pensions or conditions of service of any police force.*

Keynote

Where a person was a member of a trade union before becoming a member of a police force, he/she may, with the consent of the chief officer of police, continue to be a member of that union during the time of his/her service in the police force (s. 64(2)).

Whether any body is a trade union or an association to which s. 64 applies will be determined by the chief registrar of friendly societies (s. 64(3)).

Section 64(5) provides that:

> *(5) Nothing in this section applies to membership of the Police Federations, or of any body recognised by the Secretary of State for the purposes of this section as representing members of police forces who are not members of those Federations.*

1.2 Performance, Conduct and Complaints

From 1 April 1999 a number of very significant changes were made to the procedures governing the performance and conduct of, and complaints against, police officers. These changes amended some previously existing procedures and processes but also introduced some entirely new ones.

Under s. 83 of the Police Act 1996, the Secretary of State may issue guidance to police authorities, chief officers and the members of their police forces in respect of the discharge of their functions in these matters. The Home Office has issued forces with such guidance.

The sources of the changes are to be found mainly within the Police Act 1996 and the various Regulations made under them. What follows is an attempt to steer a path through many of those new pieces of legislation. To this end, this part of the chapter is set out in four sections:

- unsatisfactory performance
- misconduct
- complaints
- appeals.

For a more detailed explanation of these new procedures and their practical application, see *Police Conduct, Complaints and Efficiency*, to be published by Blackstone Press Ltd.

1.2.1 Unsatisfactory Performance

The new Regulations give police managers an objective structure by which to evaluate and address any suspected failures to meet the required standard of performance by their police staff.

Who?

These procedures are generally set out in the Police (Efficiency) Regulations 1999 (SI 1999 No. 732). They do not apply to:

- officers above the rank of superintendent
- probationers
- cadets
- non-warranted (civilian) staff

each of whom has their own specific procedures. For the provisions relating to probationary constables and their dismissal, see the Police Regulations 1995 (SI 1995 No. 215), reg. 15. In its Report on Police Training and Recruitment the Home Affairs Committee (1999) recommended that probationer constables are not sworn in (or 'attested') until they have completed six months' service. This recommendation was made as a result of evidence received by the Committee to the effect that it was often difficult to deal with newly-appointed officers who showed themselves to be unsuited to or unfit for service. For special constables, see the Police Act 1996, s. 27(2) and the Special Constables Regulations 1965 (SI 1965 No. 536), as amended. For cadets, see the Police Act 1996, s. 28(2) and the Police Cadets Regulations 1979 (SI 1979 No. 1727), as amended.

Why?

Although there are procedures for dealing with allegations of *misconduct* against police officers (**see para. 1.2.2**), there has been a lack of any formal structure by which police managers can address issues of perceived poor *performance*. The distinction here between conduct and performance is an important one. The complaints system is generally inadequate and often inappropriate in helping police managers tackle issues of performance and it was clear for some time that another, separate mechanism similar to those used by many other employers, was needed.

Even under the new Code of Conduct (**see para. 1.2.2**) the focus is still on enforcement and punishment and the process follows more of a straight, linear path. In matters of perceived poor performance however, the process is a cycle. The emphasis needs to be on the early identification of problems followed by discussion and agreement on action and an opportunity to improve. There should then be a monitoring period followed by a review of performance and further agreement and action as appropriate. This notion of providing the under-performing officer with opportunities to improve is a key feature of this new process and can be found right up until after any formal inefficiency hearing has started. In other words, from the point of view of the officer, it is rarely 'too late' to show a sufficient improvement. Clearly there needs to be an end to the process somewhere and that final stage may well involve sanctions but the general tenor of the process is ultimately developmental.

What?

Unlike several of the other Regulations covered in this chapter, the Police (Efficiency) Regulations 1999 have no equivalent predecessor. Made under s. 50 of the Police Act 1996, the Regulations establish procedures for the management — and ultimately the punishment — of officers whose performance is felt to be unsatisfactory. In the majority of cases, general managerial discretion and appropriate words of guidance will probably suffice. In other cases, however, there may be a need to invoke the formal procedures set out below.

The Regulations came into force on 1 April 1999.

The Police (Efficiency) Regulations 1999

Regulation 4 states:

> *Where the reporting officer for a member of a Police force is of the opinion that the performance of that member is unsatisfactory, he may require the member concerned to attend an interview (in these Regulations referred to as a first interview) to discuss the performance of the member concerned.*

Keynote

Throughout the Regulations, the officer whose performance is in question is referred to as the 'member concerned', i.e. the member of a police force in respect of whom proceedings are, or are proposed to be taken (reg. 3(1)).

Although the expression 'member of a police force' is not itself defined anywhere in the Regulations, nor in the parent Act, its use throughout both pieces of legislation (especially in s. 29) would suggest that it refers only to a sworn police constable (as it does in the Police Pensions Act 1976). This interpretation, which also finds support in the Home Office guidance to chief officers, is used throughout this chapter.

The 'reporting officer' will be a police officer and is the person having immediate supervisory responsibility for the 'member concerned' (reg. 3(1)). In most instances involving constables, the 'reporting officer' will therefore be their sergeant. Where the officer's immediate supervisor is a civilian member of staff, a police officer having supervisory responsibility for the 'member concerned' will need to be identified — although he/she will probably need to consult closely with the civilian supervisor.

The Regulations only require that the reporting officer be *of the opinion* that the performance of the member concerned is unsatisfactory. However, single instances of poor performance would not generally be enough to invoke these Regulations and, as discussed above, the instigation of formal proceedings would not normally happen before day-to-day supervisory discretion had been applied. Although the Regulations do not say so, it would seem fair that, in assessing the 'performance' of the member concerned, nothing done before April 1999 is taken into account.

The source of the reporting officer's 'opinion' may be from internal observations and reports but it may also arise from members of the public. Although the procedures for performance improvement and the investigation of complaints (**see para. 1.2.3**) are quite separate, there may be cases where there is an overlap.

Arranging First Interview

Regulation 5 states:

> (1)   If the reporting officer decides to require a member of a police force to attend a first interview, he shall—
> (a)   send a notice in writing to the member concerned—
> (i)   requiring him to attend, at a specified time and place, an interview with the reporting officer or, if the member concerned so requests, the countersigning officer;
> (ii)   stating the reasons why his performance is considered unsatisfactory;
> (iii)   informing him that he may seek advice from a representative of his staff association and be accompanied at the interview by a member of a police force selected by him; and
> (b)   send a copy of the notice to the countersigning officer,
> (2)   A member of a police force who receives a notice pursuant to paragraph (1) may, not later than 7 days (or such longer period as the reporting officer may permit when sending the notice under paragraph (1)(a)) after the date on which the notice was received by him, request by notice in writing that the interview be conducted by the countersigning officer; and if the member concerned so requests the interview shall be conducted by the countersigning officer.

Keynote

The 'countersigning officer' will be a police officer and is the person having supervisory responsibility and who is senior in rank to the reporting officer (as to which see reg. 4 above). In many cases the countersigning officer will be an inspector although the wording of reg. 5 does not require that officer to have any particular responsibility *for the member concerned*. Again, if the relevant line manager for the member concerned is a civilian member of staff, the countersigning officer will probably have to liaise closely with him/her.

It is important to note that any superintendent or Assistant Chief Constable/Commander who attends or *is otherwise involved in* the first interview is barred from appearing on the panel of any later inefficiency hearing involving the member concerned (**see below**).

The 'first interview' will be with the reporting officer unless the member concerned asks for it to be with the countersigning officer. There is however a general time limit on making that request (reg. 5(2)).

Unlike some of the other procedures in this chapter, there does not appear to be any restriction on the timing of the first interview.

The responsibility for sending out the notice containing the details set out at reg. 1(a)(i) to (iii) falls to the reporting officer. The notice, which must be copied to the countersigning officer, must advise the member concerned that he/she may seek advice from the relevant staff association representative *and* that he/she may select another officer, from any force, to accompany him/her to the interview. This 'friend' is able to advise and assist the member concerned, to speak on the officer's behalf and to produce witnesses and exhibits where appropriate. The notice must also set out the *reasons* why the member's performance is considered to be unsatisfactory.

Procedure at First Interview

Regulation 6 states:

> *(1) The following provisions of this regulation apply to the procedure to be followed at the first interview.*
> *(2) The interviewing officer shall—*
> *(a) explain to the member concerned the reasons why the reporting officer is of the opinion that the performance of that member is unsatisfactory; and*
> *(b) provide the member concerned, or the member of a police force who has accompanied him to the interview, or both of them, with an opportunity to make representations in response.*
> *(3) If, after considering any representations made in accordance with paragraph (2)(b), the interviewing officer is satisfied that the performance of the member concerned has been unsatisfactory, he shall—*
> *(a) inform the member concerned in what respect his performance is considered unsatisfactory;*
> *(b) warn the member concerned of any specific action which he is required to take to achieve an improvement in his performance; and*
> *(c) warn the member concerned that, if a sufficient improvement is not made within such reasonable period as the interviewing officer shall specify, he may be required to attend a second interview in accordance with regulation 9.*
> *(4) The interviewing officer may, if he considers it appropriate, recommend that the member concerned seek assistance in relation to any matter affecting his health or welfare.*
> *(5) The interviewing officer may adjourn the interview to a specified later time or date if it appears to him necessary or expedient to do so.*

Keynote

The 'interviewing officer' is the person conducting the first interview (reg. 3(1)) and could be either the reporting officer or the countersigning officer.

Having explained the reasons why the member's performance is unsatisfactory, the interviewing officer must provide the member, his/her 'friend' *or both*, with an opportunity to make representations in response. This suggests that a reasonable amount of time must be allowed for the making of such representations.

Those representations must be 'considered' by the interviewing officer, not simply acknowledged or dismissed. The interviewing officer, having so considered the representations made, must carry out the actions set out in reg. 6(3)(a) to (c), provided he/she is 'satisfied' that the member's performance has been unsatisfactory.

The expression 'warn' at reg. 6(3)(b) seems odd in this context, particularly when the word 'inform' is used at the next stage (**see below**), but the 'warning' is referred to later in reg. 8. Whatever the terminology, the interviewing officer must tell the member concerned what he/she must do to achieve an improvement in his/her performance.

Under reg. 6(3)(c) the interviewing officer must specify a 'reasonable period' during which this improvement is to take place. This would appear to be normally no less than three, and probably no more than six months.

Regulation 6 says nothing about what must be done if the interviewing officer is *not* satisfied that the member's performance was unsatisfactory. Presumably the issue comes to a halt at this stage, although the reporting requirements under reg. 7 (**see below**) appear to apply irrespective of the outcome of the first interview.

After First Interview

Regulation 7 states:

> (1)   The interviewing officer shall, not later than 7 days after the date of the conclusion of the first interview—
>
> (a)   cause to be prepared a written record of the substance of the matters discussed at the interview; and
>
> (b)   send one copy or, where the member concerned was accompanied at the interview by a member of a police force selected by him, two copies of that record to the member concerned together with a notice in writing informing him that he may submit written comments, or indicate that he has no comment to make, not later than 7 days after the date on which the copy is received by him.
>
> (2)   Subject to paragraph (3), the member concerned shall be entitled to submit written comments in relation to the record of the interview to the interviewing officer not later than 7 days after the date on which the copy is received by him.
>
> (3)   The interviewing officer may, on the application of the member concerned, extend the period specified in paragraph (2) if he is satisfied that it is appropriate to do so.

Keynote

The written record need not be a verbatim account of all that took place at the first interview but it must summarise the 'substance' of the matters discussed. If the member concerned does not agree with the record, he/she may raise this in the form of written comments submitted under reg. 7(2).

The requirement under reg. 7(1)(b), to *send* the member and his/her 'friend' a copy of the record suggests that there is no need for personal service. The seven-day period for responding to the service of the documents begins when the copy of the record *is received by the officer*. This would mean that, if the officer were on annual leave or was otherwise unable to receive the posted documents at the place to which they were sent, he/she may not have 'received' them. If so the time limit should not begin until he/she physically receives the documents. If the member concerned applies for the time period to be extended, the interviewing officer may do so if it seems appropriate. The interviewing officer cannot extend the time period of his/her own volition.

The interviewing officer *may* make a recommendation that the member concerned seeks help in relation to his/her health or welfare.

Any written comments received by the interviewing officer must be retained with the record of interview (reg. 7(5)). Records of any stage of the unsatisfactory performance procedures will be expunged from an officer's personal record after two years have elapsed since the last action was taken (or the last review/appeal was heard (**see below**)).

Other Copies

Regulation 7 goes on to state:

> *(4)   The interviewing officer shall send a copy of the record of the interview, and of any written comments of the member concerned, to—*
> > *(a)   the senior manager;*
> > *(b)   the personnel officer; and*
> > *(c) (i)   if the interview was conducted by the reporting officer, the countersigning officer; or*
> > > *(ii)   if the interview was conducted by the countersigning officer, the reporting officer.*

Keynote

'Senior manager' means the officer who is for the time being the supervisory officer of the countersigning officer (reg. 3(1)(a)). Although the Regulations do not specify that this person must be a police officer, this will generally be a chief inspector or superintendent. Where the member concerned is a superintendent, the 'senior manager' will be his/her supervising officer but again there is no stipulation that this must be a police officer (reg. 3(1)(b)).

'Personnel officer' means a person employed under s. 15 of the Police Act 1996 (a civilian) or a police officer who, in either case, has responsibility for personnel matters relating to members of the force to which the member concerned belongs (reg. 3(1)).

Second Interview

Regulation 8 states:

> *(1)   Where the reporting officer is of the opinion that a member of a police force who was warned under regulation 6(3)(b) that he was required to improve his performance has, at the end of the period specified by the interviewing officer under regulation 6(3)(c), failed to make a sufficient improvement in his performance, he may refer the case to the countersigning officer.*
> *(2)   Where a case is referred under paragraph (1), the countersigning officer may, after consulting with the personnel officer, require the member concerned to attend a further interview (in these Regulations referred to as a second interview) to discuss the performance of the member concerned.*

Keynote

It is not mandatory for the reporting officer to refer the case back to the countersigning officer if the member concerned has failed to make sufficient improvement. Regulation 8(1) says that he/she *may* do so.

All that is necessary in order to make such a referral is that the reporting officer *is of the opinion* that there has been insufficient improvement in the member's performance. This broadly drafted requirement gives the reporting officer a considerable degree of latitude but again the importance of general supervisory discretion should perhaps be reinforced here. Such a referral can only be made at the end of the specified period.

Although the process is started by the reporting officer, the decision to hold a second interview will be made by the countersigning officer. Once again, there is no requirement to hold such an interview and the wording of reg. 8(2) is permissive rather than mandatory. What is mandatory however is that, in reaching his/her decision, the countersigning officer consult with the personnel officer (as defined above).

Regulation 9 states:

> If the countersigning officer decides to require a member of a police force to attend second interview, he shall—
> (a)   send a notice in writing to the member concerned—
>   (i)   requiring him to attend, at a specified time and place, an interview with the countersigning officer and the personnel officer;
>   (ii)   stating the reasons why his performance is considered unsatisfactory and that further action will be considered in the light of the interview; and
>   (iii)   informing him that he may seek advice from a representative of his staff association and be accompanied at the interview by a member of a police force selected by him; and
> (b)   send a copy of the notice to the reporting officer, the senior manager and the personnel officer.

Keynote

Once the decision is reached by the countersigning officer to hold a second interview, the responsibility to comply with the requirements of reg. 9 falls to him/her.

Again the notice must set out the reasons why the member's performance is considered unsatisfactory and must remind the member of his/her entitlement to consult the relevant staff association and to be accompanied by a 'friend' (police officer).

It is important to note that any superintendent or Assistant Chief Constable/Commander who attends *or is otherwise involved in* the second interview is barred from appearing on the panel of any later inefficiency hearing involving the member concerned (**see below**).

Regulation 10 states:

> (1)   The following provisions of this Regulation shall apply to the procedure to be followed at a second interview.
> (2)   The interview shall be conducted by the countersigning officer and the personnel officer.
> (3)   The countersigning officer shall—
>   (a)   explain to the member concerned the reasons why the reporting officer is of the opinion that the member concerned has failed to make a sufficient improvement in his performance or, as the case may be, that his performance is unsatisfactory and the conditions specified in regulation 8(2) are satisfied; and

(b)   provide the member concerned, or the member of a police force who has accompanied him to the interview, or both of them, with an opportunity to make representations in response.

Keynote

The personnel officer (as defined above) takes part in the second interview although it is clear from reg. 10(3) that the countersigning officer takes the lead in running the proceedings.

The countersigning officer must explain the grounds for the second interview and must provide the opportunity for the member, his/her 'friend' *or both* to make representations in response.

As with the first interview (**see above**) there will be an option of 'no further action', in which case any note of the procedure followed will be expunged from the member's personal record after two years have elapsed.

Regulation 10(4) goes on to state:

(4)   If, after considering any representations made under paragraph (3), the countersigning officer is satisfied that the performance of the member concerned has been unsatisfactory during the period specified by the interviewing officer under regulation 6(3)(c) or, as the case may be, the period specified in regulation 8(2), he shall—

(a)   inform the member concerned in what respect his performance is considered unsatisfactory;

(b)   warn the member concerned that he is required to improve his performance in any such respect;

(c)   inform the member concerned of any specific action which he is required to take to achieve such an improvement; and

(d)   warn the member concerned that, if a sufficient improvement is not made within such reasonable period as the countersigning officer shall specify, he may be required to attend an inefficiency hearing at which the officers conducting the hearing will have the power, if appropriate, to require the member concerned to resign from the force or to order reduction in rank.

Keynote

Once again, the representations made under reg. 10(3)(b) must be considered by the countersigning officer (and presumably, though it does not say so, the personnel officer).

The member must be told of any specific action that he/she is required to take to achieve the necessary improvement in performance. He/she must also be warned at this stage that failure to achieve sufficient improvement by the set date *may* result in a further hearing and that such a hearing would have the power to require the member to resign or to reduce him/her in rank. The warning will also contain a timescale for improvement which, as with the first interview, will not normally be less than three or more than six months from the time of the interview.

The countersigning officer may adjourn the second interview to a later time or a later date if it appears necessary or expedient to do so (reg. 10(5)).

After Second Interview

Regulation 11 states:

(1)   The countersigning officer shall, not later than 7 days after the conclusion of the second interview—

(a) in consultation with the personnel officer, prepare a written record of the substance of the matters discussed during the interview; and

(b) send one copy or, where the member concerned was accompanied at the interview by a member of a police force selected by him, two copies of that record to the member concerned together with a notice in writing—

(i) if a warning was given under regulation 10(4), confirming the terms of that warning; and

(ii) informing him that he may submit written comments, or indicate that he has no such comments, not later than 7 days after the date on which the copy is received by him.

(2) Subject to paragraph (3), the member concerned shall be entitled to submit written comments in relation to the record of the interview to the countersigning officer not later than 7 days after the date on which it was received by him.

(3) The countersigning officer may, on the application of the member concerned, extend the period specified in paragraph (2) if he is satisfied that it is appropriate to do so.

(4) If the countersigning officer receives any written comments under paragraph (2), he shall ensure that they are retained with the record of the interview.

(5) The countersigning officer shall send a copy of the record of the interview, and of any written comments by the member concerned, to the reporting officer, the personnel officer and the senior manager.

Keynote

The written record must be prepared *in consultation with* the personnel officer. The written record of the interview again appears to a summary of the substance rather than a verbatim account of what took place. The record must be accompanied by a written notice confirming the 'warning' if one was given under reg. 10(4). As the requirement refers to a singular warning (there are in fact *two* warnings under reg. 10(4)), that warning seems to be the one given in relation to the consequences of failing to improve (i.e. the warning at reg. 10(4)(d)). In practice, such a warning may only be given twice within a period of two years before resulting in a hearing. Once again, as with the first interview, there are requirements relating to the sending of copies to the relevant people concerned, together with the notice of opportunity to submit written comments within seven days. There are also similar requirements in relation to the retention of written responses and the countersigning officer may, on the application of the member concerned, extend the seven-day deadline.

Assessment of Performance

Regulation 12 states:

(1) Not later than 14 days after the date on which the period specified under regulation 10(4)(d) ends—

(a) the countersigning officer shall, in consultation with the reporting officer, assess the performance of the member concerned during that period; and

(b) the countersigning officer shall inform the member concerned in writing whether the reporting officer and the countersigning officer are of the opinion that there has been a sufficient improvement in performance during that period.

(2) If the countersigning officer is of the opinion that there has been an insufficient improvement, the member concerned shall also, within the period of 14 days mentioned in paragraph (1), be informed in writing that he may be required to attend, at a time (being not sooner than 21 days, but not later than 56 days, after the date on which the notification under this paragraph is received by him) to be notified separately, a hearing (in these Regulations referred to as an inefficiency hearing) to consider his performance.

(3) The countersigning officer shall refer any case in which the member concerned has been informed in accordance with paragraph (2) to the senior manager, who shall, if he thinks it appropriate to do so, direct that an inefficiency hearing be arranged under regulation 13.

Keynote

The countersigning officer, *in consultation with* the reporting officer must assess the performance of the member concerned and this must be done no later than 14 days after the period set out in the warning under reg. 10(4)(d). The assessment must relate to the member's performance *during that period*. Following this assessment, the countersigning officer must inform the member in writing whether or not he/she considers that there has been a sufficient improvement in the member's performance. If there *has* been a sufficient improvement however, there does not appear to be a specific requirement as to when the member must be so informed. Given the requirement at reg. 12(2) — to inform the member within the 14 day period that he/she may have to attend an inefficiency hearing — it would seem that, if the member has not heard anything from the countersigning officer within 14 days of the assessment period ending, he/she can assume that there must have been sufficient improvement in his/her performance.

If the countersigning officer feels that there has not been a sufficient improvement, he/she must refer the case to the 'senior manager' (as defined above) who then has the discretion to direct an inefficiency hearing to be held. As with the other stages of the process so far, this element is *discretionary* and there is no compulsion on the senior manager to direct that a hearing be held.

Inefficiency Hearing

Regulation 13 states:

> *(1)   The personnel officer shall, not less than 21 days before the date fixed for the hearing, send a notice in writing to the member concerned—*
> > *(a)   requiring him to attend an inefficiency hearing at a specified time and place;*
> > *(b)   stating the reasons why his performance is considered unsatisfactory;*
> > *(c)   informing him that he may be represented at the hearing—*
> > > *(i)   either by counsel or a solicitor; or*
> > > *(ii)   by a member of a police force selected by him; and*
> > *(d)   warning him of the powers under regulation 17 which are available to the officers conducting the inefficiency hearing in the event that they find that the performance of the member concerned has been unsatisfactory.*
> *(2)   If the member concerned wishes to call any witnesses other than the person representing him at the inefficiency hearing, he shall, not later than seven days before the hearing, give notice in writing to the personnel officer of the names and addresses of those witnesses.*
> *(3)   In paragraph (2), the reference to the hearing includes a reference to any hearing under regulation 15; and in relation to such a hearing the period within which notice is to be given under that paragraph shall be such period as the chairman of the hearing may direct when he postpones or, as the case may be, adjourns the hearing.*

Keynote

The responsibility for sending out the relevant notice here falls to the personnel officer. Such a notice must be *sent* — though not necessarily received — not less than 21 days before the proposed date of the hearing.

The notice will advise the member that he/she may be represented at the hearing by a solicitor/counsel *or* a police officer. This right emanates from s. 84 of the Police Act 1996 which provides that an officer (of the rank of superintendent or below) may not be dismissed, required to resign or reduced in rank as a result of a hearing unless he/she has been given an opportunity to elect to be legally represented.

The requirement under reg. 13(2) is important as only those witnesses that are mentioned in the member's notification are *entitled* (under reg. 14(7)) to give evidence at the hearing (though the chair may admit them under his/her discretion even if they were not specified above). Notification of which witnesses the member wishes to call must be made to the *personnel officer*.

The inefficiency hearing must be conducted by three officers, one of whom will be:

- in the case of a provincial police force — an Assistant Chief Constable
- in the case of the Metropolitan Police — a Commander in that force
- in the case of the City of London Police — a Commander in that force

(reg. 14).

This officer will chair the hearing (reg. 14(1)).

In practice the hearing will comprise any two superintendents (subject to the rule under reg. 14(2) below) plus the chair.

Where the member concerned is a Metropolitan Police officer, the superintendents will be Metropolitan Police officers (reg. 14(3)(b)).

Where the member concerned is a superintendent, the hearing will comprise two Assistant Chief Constables from outside the member's own force, together with an Assistant Chief Constable from the member's own force who will chair the hearing.

Where the member concerned is a Metropolitan Police superintendent, the hearing will be chaired by a Commander from the member's own area with two Commanders from another area/other areas.

Where the member is concerned is a City of London Police superintendent, the hearing will be chaired by a City of London Police Commander or the Assistant Commissioner, with two Assistant Chief Constables or Metropolitan Police Commanders.

In any case, the chair and any of the officers assisting him/her must not have attended or otherwise been involved with the first or second interview held in relation to the member concerned (reg. 14(2)).

Regulation 14 goes on to state:

> *(4)   As soon as the chief officer of police has appointed the chairman, the personnel officer shall arrange for a copy of any document—*
> *(a)   which was available to the interviewing officer in relation to the first interview;*
> *(b)   which was available to the countersigning officer in relation to the second interview; or*
> *(c)   which was prepared or submitted under regulation 11, 12 or 13,*
> *to be made available to the chairman; and a copy of any such document shall be sent to the member concerned.*

Keynote

The personnel officer must collate copies of any documents which were available to the interviewing officer and the countersigning officer at the first and second interview respectively and also copies of any document prepared or submitted under regs 11 to 13. The personnel officer must arrange to make these copies available to the chair of the hearing as soon as one has been appointed. These copies must also be sent to the member concerned, though there does not appear to be a specific time limit on this requirement.

Subject to the other provisions in reg. 14, the chair will determine the procedure to be followed at the inefficiency hearing (reg. 14(5)). As such, the chair might decide the 'batting order' for the respective parties and may call witnesses to the proceedings. This apparently wide discretion will, however, also be subject to the general principles of natural justice.

The inefficiency hearing will be held in private but may be in public *if both the chair and the member concerned agree* (reg. 14(6)).

The member concerned must be given the opportunity to make representations in relation to the matters referred to in the notice sent out by the personnel officer under reg. 13 (reg. 14(7)). A further effect of reg. 14(7) is that the member concerned is *entitled* to call any witnesses that he/she named in the notification to the personnel officer under reg. 13(2). There may be good reasons why the member failed to include details of potential witnesses in the reg. 13(2) notification and it would seem that the general discretion given to the chair under reg. 14(5) above would allow for other witnesses not previously named to be called.

Unlike the procedure to be followed at the first and second interview stages, a verbatim record must be made of the proceedings (reg. 14(8)).

Postponement and Adjournment

In addition to the general power to adjourn the proceedings under reg. 15(7), the chair may adjourn or postpone the hearing in a number of specified circumstances.

Additional Period for Assessment

The chair of the hearing may adjourn the proceedings if, having heard the representations from the member concerned, he/she considers it appropriate to allow a further period for assessment of the member's performance. Therefore, even after the hearing has begun, the member concerned may still be given the opportunity to address his/her shortcomings. Any further period under this regulation must not exceed three months. The time and date for the resumed hearing must be fixed by the chair and, within 14 days of the end of that period, the reporting officer and countersigning officer will prepare a report containing an assessment of the member's performance over that time (reg. 15(3)).

When the hearing resumes, the member concerned will be allowed to make representations on the matters referred to *in that latest report* and may call any of the original witnesses set out in the notification under reg. 13(2).

Reg. 15(6) makes provision for the situation where the chair of the inefficiency hearing is absent, incapacitated or suspended from duty when the hearing resumes. In such cases, if the chair is likely to be so absent, incapacitated or suspended for more than 28 days, the chief officer must arrange for a person eligible under the provisions of reg. 14 (**see above**) to chair the resumed hearing and to carry out the relevant functions thereof.

Non-attendance

If the member concerned does not attend the inefficiency hearing and gives what the chair considers to be a 'good reason' for that non-attendance, the chair *must* postpone or adjourn the hearing (reg. 15(1)).

If the member concerned informs the chair that he/she will be unable to attend the hearing, it must also be postponed or adjourned. A strict reading of the wording of reg. 15(1) suggests that the requirement for a 'good reason' to be given is confined to cases of *non-attendance* rather than a prospective *inability* to attend. The result of such an interpretation however, would allow for any number of stalling tactics to be used to avoid the hearing and may hold up what is supposed to be a quicker process for dealing with poor performance.

The hearing may proceed in the absence of the member concerned under reg. 14(9) but that option is 'subject to' the provisions of reg. 15(1) above.

Where any of the requirements under regs 14 or 15 cannot be complied with owing to the absence of the member concerned, the case may be proceeded with as if they had been complied with (reg. 14(10)). Again, this is intended to prevent the procedure from being obstructed or held back by the absence of the member concerned.

Ill Health

Home Office guidance suggests that the provisions of reg. 35 of the Police Regulations 1995 (SI 1995 No. 215) relating to absence from duty owing to sickness, do not apply to attendance at an inefficiency hearing. Therefore, an officer who is on sick leave may still appear at such a hearing. Nevertheless, if the state of the officer's health means that he/she is incapacitated to the extent that attendance at the hearing is not possible, the hearing is likely to be postponed (under reg. 15(1) above).

It is unlikely that such postponement would continue indefinitely. Guidance from the Home Office to chief officers points out that the unsatisfactory performance procedures should not prevent or delay the retirement of an officer who, in the circumstances, would normally have been retired on medical grounds.

The Finding

Regulation 16 states:

> *(1)   Subject to paragraph (2), at the conclusion of the inefficiency hearing, the officers conducting the hearing shall reach a decision whether the performance of the member concerned—*
> *(a)   in the period referred to in regulation 10(4)(d); or*

(b)   where the hearing was adjourned under regulation 15(2), over the whole of the period comprising the period referred to in regulation 10(4)(d) and the further period specified by the chairman under regulation 15(3)(a),

has been satisfactory or not.

(2)   The chairman may, at the conclusion of the hearing, defer reaching a decision until a later time or date if it appears necessary or expedient to do so.

(3)   The decision of the officers conducting the hearing shall state the finding and, where they have found that the performance of the member concerned has not been satisfactory, their reasons as well as any sanction which they impose under regulation 17.

(4)   The chairman shall record the decision in writing, and shall, not later than three days after the finding is stated under paragraph (3), send a copy of it to—

(a)   the member concerned;

(b)   the senior manager; and

(c)   the personnel officer;

and the copy sent to the member concerned shall be accompanied by a notice in writing informing him of his right to request a review under regulation 19.

Keynote

Unless the chair decides to defer the decision under reg. 16(2), the officers conducting the hearing must reach a conclusion as to whether the member's performance in the relevant period has been satisfactory or not. That decision — or a decision under reg. 17 below — need not be unanimous and may be based on a simple majority but this will not be indicated in the finding (reg. 16(5)). This appears to give the officers an equal say in the judgment with no special 'casting' vote being held by the chair.

Their decision must state their finding and, if the member's performance is found not to have been satisfactory, the decision must give reasons. The decision must also state the relevant sanction to be imposed. Although it is not explicit, there may of course be a finding that the member's performance has been satisfactory in which case there will be no further action and the records relating to the alleged poor performance will be removed from the member's personal file.

The record of the decision must be sent to the relevant parties no later than three days *after the finding is stated.* The copy sent to the member must also be accompanied by a notice in relation to the member's right to ask for a review under reg. 19.

Sanctions

Regulation 17 states:

(1)   If the officers conducting the inefficiency hearing make a finding that the performance of the member concerned during the relevant period has been unsatisfactory, they may—

(a)   require the member concerned to resign from the force either one month after the date on which a copy of the decision sent under regulation 16(4) is received by him or on such later date as may be specified;

(b)   order reduction in his rank with immediate effect and issue a written warning to the member concerned that unless a sufficient improvement in his performance is made within such period as the chairman shall specify, he may, following consideration of his performance during that period in accordance with regulation 18, be required to attend a first interview in respect of that performance; or

(c)   issue such a written warning as is mentioned in sub-paragraph (b).

(2)   Where the sanction under paragraph (1)(a) is imposed and where the member concerned has not resigned from the force in accordance with the requirement, then the effect of the decision shall be to dismiss the member concerned from the force as from the time referred to

Keynote

Any requirement for the member to resign cannot take effect before one month after the notice of the finding *was received* by the member. It may take effect at some later date. If the member has not resigned as required by the specified date, he/she will automatically be dismissed as of that date (reg. 17(2)).

Any reduction in rank must take effect 'immediately', an expression which presumably means immediately the finding is made as opposed to it being sent to, or received by, the member concerned. The instant effect of this finding will not be held up or deferred by any review or appeal process. In accordance with the developmental and ongoing nature of this process, a reduction in rank must be accompanied by a warning that a sufficient improvement is still required with a specified period. This indicates that the process is by no means over and that, under reg. 18 below, further reports as to the member's performance will be assessed.

A similar procedure involving a written warning followed by a further report is available as a third sanction without any reduction in rank.

Any sanction imposed under reg. 17 shall be expunged after two years if that period was free from any such sanction (see reg. 17 of the Police Regulations 1995).

Further Period of Assessment

Regulation 18 states:

> *(1)   This regulation applies where the member concerned has been given a written warning under paragraph (1)(b) or (c) of regulation 17.*
> *(2)   Not later than 14 days after the end of the period specified in the warning, the reporting officer shall—*
> *(a)   assess the performance of the member concerned during that period*
> *(b)   cause to be prepared a report on the performance; and*
> *(c)   send a copy of the report to the member concerned.*
> *(3)   Where the report prepared under paragraph (2)(b) concludes that the performance of the member concerned has been satisfactory during the period specified in the warning, no further action shall be taken in respect of that performance during that period.*
> *(4)   Where the report prepared under paragraph (2)(b) concludes that, in the opinion of the reporting officer, the performance of the member concerned has been unsatisfactory during that period, the reporting officer shall request the member concerned to attend a first interview in accordance with regulation 4; and these Regulations shall have effect for the purposes of the performance of the member concerned during that period as if he had been invited to a first interview under regulation 4.*

Keynote

Unlike the other stages in the process, this next stage makes specific provision for occasions where the member's performance is found to have been satisfactory. In such cases there is to be no further action in respect of *that* performance during *that* period. This does not necessarily mean that there can be no further action in relation to any performance during any other stage of the whole process.

If the 'reporting officer' is of the opinion that the member's performance during this most recent assessment period has been unsatisfactory, the reporting officer *must* request a 'first interview' and the whole cycle begins again. Unlike the original 'first interview' (**see above**), the wording of reg. 18 does not leave the request of the 'first interview' to the reporting officer's discretion.

The Review

Regulation 19 states:

> *(1) Where the officers conducting the inefficiency hearing have imposed a sanction under regulation 17, the member concerned shall be entitled to request the chief officer of the police force concerned, or where the member concerned is a member of the metropolitan police force the Assistant Commissioner, ('the reviewing officer') to review the finding or the sanction imposed, or both the finding and the sanction.*
>
> *(2) A request for a review must be made to the reviewing officer in writing within 14 days of the date on which a copy of the decision sent under regulation 16(4) is received by the member concerned unless this period is extended by the reviewing officer.*
>
> *(3) The request for a review shall state the grounds on which the review is requested and whether a meeting is requested.*

Keynote

'Sanction' here would appear to mean any of the three options set out under reg. 17(1)(a) to (c). Therefore, the member concerned may request a review where the hearing only imposes a written warning without any further punishment.

The request will be made to the member's chief officer or, in the case of a Metropolitan Police officer, to the Assistant Commissioner for the time being authorised under s. 8 of the Metropolitan Police Act 1856 (see reg. 3(1)). This person is referred to as the 'reviewing officer'.

Regulation 22 makes special provisions for situations where the chief officer or assistant commissioner is an 'interested party' or where there is an assistant chief officer deputising under s. 12 of the Police Act 1996.

For some reason the Regulations do not define 'interested party' but reg. 4 of the Police (Conduct) Regulations 1999 (**see para. 1.2.2**) define it as '. . . a witness or any person involved in the conduct which is the subject of the case or who otherwise has a direct interest in the case'. In cases falling under reg. 22, the review will be carried out by the Assistant Chief Constable designated under s. 12(4) of the Police Act 1996. Where that Assistant Chief Constable is absent or is an interested party, the review will be carried out by the chief officer of another force.

Where the member concerned is a Metropolitan Police officer and the review officer is absent or an interested party, the review will be carried out by the Commander designated under para. 4(7) of sch. 6 to the Police Regulations 1995. If that Commander is absent or an interested party, the review may be carried out by another Assistant Commissioner (reg. 22(3)).

Where the member concerned is a City of London Police officer and the Commissioner is absent or an interested party, the review will be carried out by the chief officer of another force or an Assistant Commissioner in the Metropolitan Police (reg. 22(4)).

The request must be made to the reviewing officer in writing within 14 days of the date on which the member *receives* the notification sent out under reg. 16(4). The period may be extended by the reviewing officer without the need for the member to apply for such an extension.

The purpose of the review can be to consider the finding, the sanction or both. The reviewing officer may confirm the decision of the hearing or he/she may impose a different sanction. However, the reviewing officer may not impose a sanction greater than that imposed at the hearing (reg. 21(2)).

The request must state the grounds on which it is made and whether a meeting is requested. If a meeting is requested, the reviewing officer must hold one (reg. 20(1)). However, a review can be carried out without holding such a meeting. Where a meeting is held, the member may be accompanied by a 'friend' (police officer) and a solicitor/counsel (reg. 20(2)).

The Finding of the Review

The member concerned must be informed of the finding of the reviewing officer in writing and within three days of the completion of the review (reg. 21(1)).

The reviewing officer's decision is substituted for that of the hearing and takes effect from the same date (reg. 20(3)). If there is a finding that the performance of the member concerned had not been unsatisfactory the original sanction will be expunged forthwith.

If the reviewing officer's decision results in the member concerned being required to resign or his/her reduction in rank, the member must be notified of the right to appeal to a Police Appeals Tribunal (reg. 20(4)) (**see para. 1.2.4**).

1.2.2   Misconduct

In addition to performance management, it is also an important supervisory and managerial function to be alert to the way in which individuals conduct themselves. As with issues of performance (**see para. 1.2.1**), a great deal of supervisory and managerial discretion is called for in dealing with information concerning the conduct of individual officers. The exercise of supervisory and managerial discretion is generally a matter for local and organisational policy. Any such policy relating to the alleged misconduct of police officers is however subject to the legislative provisions discussed in this chapter.

Who?

The new legislative provisions relating to allegations of misconduct can be found in the Police (Conduct) Regulations 1999 (SI 1999 No. 730). These Regulations apply to all police officers other than those above superintendent and, subject to the provisions below, revoke the previous Police (Discipline) Regulations 1985 and their respective amendments. As well as setting out the procedures to be followed in cases of alleged misconduct, the 1999 Regulations also introduce a new Code of Conduct which replaces the former Discipline Code (**see below**).

When?

The 1999 Regulations came into force on 1 April 1999.

Where a report, complaint or allegation has been received in respect of conduct that occurred or began *before 1 April 1999*, the Regulations will not apply and the former 1985 Regulations will apply (reg. 2(2)).

If the report, complaint or allegation in respect of conduct that occurred or began before 1 April 1999 is *received on or after 1 April 2000*, the conduct will be treated as if it had occurred or begun after 1 April 1999 (reg. 2(3)).

In other words, where the conduct reported or complained of took place before the starting date of these Regulations, the former Regulations will apply unless that report or complaint was itself received on/after 1 April 2000.

The Code of Conduct

Schedule 1 of the 1999 Regulations states:

1. Honesty and integrity
It is of paramount importance that the public has faith in the honesty and integrity of police officers. Officers should therefore be open and truthful in their dealings; avoid being improperly beholden to any person or institution; and discharge their duties with integrity.

2. Fairness and impartiality
Police officers have a particular responsibility to act with fairness and impartiality in all their dealings with the public and their colleagues.

3. Politeness and tolerance
Officers should treat members of the public and colleagues with courtesy and respect, avoiding abusive or deriding attitudes or behaviour. In particular, officers must avoid: favouritism of an individual or group; all forms of harassment, victimisation or unreasonable discrimination; and overbearing conduct to a colleague, particularly to one junior in rank or service.

4. Use of force and abuse of authority
Officers must never knowingly use more force than is reasonable, nor should they abuse their authority.

5. Performance of duties
Officers should be conscientious and diligent in the performance of their duties. Officers should attend work promptly when rostered for duty. If absent through sickness or injury, they should avoid activities likely to retard their return to duty.

6. Lawful orders
The police service is a disciplined body. Unless there is good and sufficient cause to do otherwise, officers must obey all lawful orders and abide by the provisions of Police Regulations. Officers should support their colleagues in the execution of their lawful duties, and oppose any improper behaviour, reporting it where appropriate.

7. Confidentiality
Information which comes into the possession of the police should be treated as confidential. It should not be used for personal benefit and nor should it be divulged to other parties except in the proper course of police duty. Similarly, officers should respect, as confidential, information about force policy and operations unless authorised to disclose it in the course of their duties.

8. Criminal offences
Officers must report any proceedings for a criminal offence taken against them. Conviction of a criminal offence may of itself result in further action being taken.

9. Property
Officers must exercise reasonable care to prevent loss or damage to property (excluding their own personal property but including police property).

10. Sobriety
Whilst on duty officers must be sober. Officers should not consume alcohol when on duty unless specifically authorised to do so or it becomes necessary for the proper discharge of police duty.

11. Appearance

Unless on duties which dictate otherwise, officers should always be well turned out, clean and tidy whilst on duty in uniform or in plain clothes.

12. General conduct

Whether on or off duty, police officers should not behave in a way which is likely to bring discredit upon the police service.

Notes

(a) *The primary duties of those who hold the office of constable are the protection of life and property, the preservation of the Queen's peace, and the prevention and detection of criminal offences. To fulfil these duties they are granted extraordinary powers; the public and the police service therefore have the right to expect the highest standards of conduct from them.*

(b) *This Code sets out the principles which guide police officers' conduct. It does not seek to restrict officers' discretion: rather it aims to define the parameters of conduct within which that discretion should be exercised. However, it is important to note that any breach of the principles in this Code may result in action being taken by the organisation, which, in serious cases, could involve dismissal.*

(c) *This Code applies to the conduct of police officers in all ranks whilst on duty, or whilst off duty if the conduct is serious enough to indicate that an officer is not fit to be a police officer. It will be applied in a reasonable and objective manner. Due regard will be paid to the degree of negligence or deliberate fault and to the nature and circumstances of an officer's conduct. Where off duty conduct is in question, this will be measured against the generally accepted standards of the day.*

Keynote

Although many of the new paragraphs had a corresponding 'offence' under the former discipline code, there is not an exact overlap. For a table showing what went where, **see below**. The former offence of being an accessory to a disciplinary offence has gone, but such conduct is probably subsumed under paras 6 and 12. The former protection against double jeopardy has gone (see the Police Act 1996, sch. 9, part II).

The rule (under the now repealed s. 104 of the Police and Criminal Evidence Act 1984) provided that, where an officer had been convicted or acquitted of a criminal offence, he/she would not be liable to be charged with a general disciplinary offence which was in substance the same as the criminal offence.

In relation to 'sobriety' at item 10 above, Home Office guidance suggests that superintendents will be classed as being 'on duty' while they are formerly 'on call'. They will not be 'on duty' by reason only of their general 24 hour responsibility for their own area of command or department. The guidance further provides that an officer who is *unexpectedly* called out for duty should be able, at no risk of discredit, to say that he/she has had too much to drink.

What Went Where

	The 'Discipline Code'	The New 'Code of Conduct'
1.	Discreditable conduct	General conduct
2.	Misconduct towards a member of a police force	Politeness and tolerance. Fairness and impartiality
3.	Disobedience to orders	Lawful orders

The 'Discipline Code'	The New 'Code of Conduct'
4. Neglect of duty	Performance of duties
5. Falsehood or prevarication	Honesty and integrity
6. Improper disclosure of information	Confidentiality
7. Corrupt or improper practice	Honesty and integrity
8. Abuse of authority	Use of force and abuse of authority
9. Racially discriminatory behaviour	Politeness and tolerance. Fairness and impartiality
10. Neglect of health	Performance of duties
11. Improper dress or untidiness	Appearance
12. Damage to police property	Property
13. Drunkenness	Sobriety
14. Drinking on duty or soliciting drink	Sobriety
15. Entering licensed premises	General conduct
16. Criminal conduct	Criminal offences

The Police (Conduct) Regulations 1999

Regulation 5 states:

> (1)   Where there has been a report, complaint or allegation which indicates that the conduct of a member of a police force does not meet the appropriate standard the chief officer of the force concerned may suspend the member concerned from membership of the force and from his office of constable whether or not the matter has been investigated.
>
> (2)   The chief officer concerned may exercise the power to suspend the member concerned under this regulation at any time from the time of the receipt of the report, complaint or allegation until—
>
> (a)   the supervising officer decides not to refer the case to a hearing,
>
> (b)   the notification of a finding that the conduct of the member concerned did not fail to meet the appropriate standard,
>
> (c)   the time limit under regulation 34 for giving notice of intention to seek a review has expired, or
>
> (d)   any review under regulation 35 has been completed.
>
> (3)   Where the member concerned is suspended under this regulation, he shall be suspended until there occurs any of the events mentioned in paragraph (2)(i) to (iv), or until the chief officer decides he shall cease to be suspended, whichever first occurs.
>
> (4)   Where the member concerned who is suspended is required to resign under regulation 31, he shall remain suspended during the period of his notice.
>
> (5)   The chief officer concerned may delegate his powers under this regulation to an officer of at least the rank of assistant chief constable or, where the member concerned is a member of the City of London or metropolitan police force, to an officer of at least the rank of commander.

Keynote

Many of the terms used within the 1999 Regulations are defined under reg. 4(1).

'Complaint' has the same meaning, as a complaint under s. 65 of the Police Act 1996 (**see para. 1.2.3**). Not every allegation of misconduct will amount to a 'complaint', particularly where the source of the allegation is internal. However, where there has been a 'complaint' so defined, the provisions under the 1996 Act will apply and, as with allegations of unsatisfactory performance (**see para. 1.2.1**) there will be occasions where there is some overlap.

'Appropriate standard' means the standard set out in the Code of Conduct (**see above**).

'Member concerned' means the officer in relation to whose conduct there has been a report, complaint, or allegation.

The 'supervising officer' is the person appointed under reg. 7 (**see below**) to supervise the investigation of the case.

For an explanation of regs 34 and 35 which relate to the review procedure, **see below**.

The power to suspend an officer appears to be very wide and applies whether or not the matter has been investigated (reg. 5(1)). Such a power must however be exercised in accordance with the general principles of law and will be subject to judicial review. The power under reg. 5 may be delegated to an Assistant Chief Constable or, in the case of Metropolitan Police or City of London Police officers, to a Commander (reg. 5(5)).

The effect of suspension is that the member is no longer a 'member' of his/her force and ceases to enjoy the powers and privileges of the office of constable. A further effect is that the officer will not, under the Rules of the Police Promotion Examinations Board, be able to sit the qualifying examination(s) for promotion unless his/her chief officer expressly authorises it.

Generally an officer who is suspended will continue to receive full pay unless his/her whereabouts are unknown or where he/she is in custody following conviction.

The power to suspend *may* be exercised at any time from the receipt of the allegation up until any of the circumstances set out at reg. 5(2)(a) to (d) *or* until the chief officer decides otherwise, whichever occurs first. Therefore, although a chief officer may end the member's suspension *before* any of the circumstances set out at (reg. 5(2)(a) to (d), he/she may not extend the suspension beyond the time when the first of those things occurs.

If a suspended officer is ultimately required to resign under reg. 31 (**see below**), he/she will remain suspended during his/her period of notice (reg. 5(4)).

Outstanding Criminal Proceedings

Regulation 6 states:

> *Where there are criminal proceedings outstanding against the member concerned, proceedings under these Regulations, other than exercise of the power to suspend under regulation 5, shall not take place unless the chief officer concerned believes that in the exceptional circumstances of the case it would be appropriate for them to do so.*

Keynote

Although as a general rule disciplinary proceedings other than suspension will not be brought against an officer while there are any outstanding criminal proceedings against him/her, reg. 6 leaves it open to the chief officer to do so. That discretionary power to institute disciplinary proceedings is limited to 'exceptional circumstances' where the chief officer *believes* it to be appropriate though there is no further requirement for that belief to be a 'reasonable' one.

Investigation Procedure

Supervising Officer

Regulation 7 states:

> *(1)   Subject to paragraph (2), where a report, complaint or allegation is received by the chief officer which indicates that the conduct of a member of a police force did not meet the appropriate standard, the case may be referred by him to an officer, who shall satisfy the conditions in paragraph (3), to supervise the investigation of the case.*
> *(2)   . . .*
> *(3)   The supervising officer shall be—*
>   *(a)   at least one rank above that of the member concerned;*
>   *(b)   of at least the rank of superintendent;*
>   *(c)   a member of the same force as the member concerned; and*
>   *(d)   not an interested party.*

Keynote

Regulation 7(1) does not apply where the case arises from a complaint the investigation of which *must* be supervised by the Police Complaints Authority (**see para. 1.2.3**).

The supervising officer must meet all of the criteria set out at reg. 7(3)(a) to (d).

The 'supervising officer' is not the same as the 'investigating officer' (**see below**).

An 'interested party' is 'a witness or any person involved in the conduct which is the subject of the case or who otherwise has a direct interest in the case' (reg. 4(1)).

Investigating Officer

Regulation 8 states:

> *(1)   The supervising officer may appoint an investigating officer to investigate the case.*
> *(2)   The investigating officer shall be—*
>   *(a)   a member of the same police force as the member concerned or, if at the request of the supervising officer the chief officer of some other force agrees to provide an investigating officer, a member of that other force;*
>   *(b)   of at least the rank of inspector or, if the member concerned is a superintendent, of at least the rank of assistant chief constable or, if the investigating officer is a member of the City of London or metropolitan police force, of at least the rank of commander;*
>   *(c)   of at least the same rank as the member concerned; and*
>   *(d)   not an interested party.*

Keynote

The investigating officer must meet all the criteria set out at reg. 8(2)(a) to (d).

He/she may be from a different force from the member concerned and must be at least of inspector rank. If the member concerned is a superintendent then the investigating officer must be of at least Assistant Chief Constable/Commander rank. Although reg. 7 does not specifically require it, it is likely that in cases where the investigating officer is a senior officer, the 'supervising officer' would also be of ACPO rank.

The provisions of reg. 8 are without prejudice to the powers of the Police Complaints Authority (**see para. 1.2.3**) to make requirements in relation to the appointment of investigating officers (reg. 8(3)).

Notice of Investigation

Regulation 9 states:

> The investigating officer shall as soon as is practicable (without prejudicing his or any other investigation of the matter) cause the member concerned to be given written notice—
> (a)   that there is to be an investigation into the case;
> (b)   of the nature of the report, complaint or allegation;
> (c)   informing him that he is not obliged to say anything concerning the matter, but that he may, if he so desires, make a written or oral statement concerning the matter to the investigating officer or to the chief officer concerned;
> (d)   informing him that if he makes such a statement it may be used in any subsequent proceedings under these Regulations;
> (e)   informing him that he has the right to seek advice from his staff association, and
> (f)   informing him that he has the right to be accompanied by a member of a police force, who shall not be an interested party, to any meeting, interview or hearing.

Keynote

The written notice must be given 'as soon as is practicable'. Practicable has been accepted as meaning 'possible to be accomplished with known means or resources' (see *Adsett* v *K & L Steelfounders* [1953] 1 All ER 97). However, the giving of such a notice must not be to the prejudice of the investigation of the matter — whether by the investigating officer or someone else — therefore there may be some justifiable delay in the provision of a reg. 9 notice.

The wording 'cause to be given' — as opposed to 'sent' — suggests that personal service is required.

The making of a statement in response to the receipt of a reg. 9 notice may have significant implications for the member concerned and serious consideration ought to be given to exercising the right to consult with a staff association representative.

Investigating Officer's Report

Regulation 10 states:

> (1)   At the end of his investigation the investigating officer shall submit a written report on the case to the supervising officer and, if the Authority are supervising the investigation, also to the Authority.

(2) If at any time during his investigation it appears to the investigating officer that the case is one in respect of which the conditions specified in Part I of Schedule 2 are likely to be satisfied, he shall, whether or not the investigation is at an end, submit to the supervising officer—

(a) a statement of his belief that the case may be one to which regulation 39 applies and the grounds for that belief, and

(b) a written report on the case so far as it has then been investigated.

Keynote

If the investigation is being supervised by the Police Complaints Authority (PCA) (**see below**), the investigating officer must submit two reports: one to the supervising officer and one to the PCA.

If it appears to the investigating officer that the case is a 'special case' as provided for under reg. 39 (i.e. involving a serious allegation of an imprisonable offence; **see below**), the investigating officer must submit a report stating his/her belief and setting out the current position of the investigation. Given the seriousness of 'special cases', this report would probably need to be submitted immediately and reg. 10(2) makes it clear that the report does not need to be delayed until the end of the investigation.

Regulation 11 states:

(1) Subject to paragraphs (2) and (3), on receipt of the investigating officer's report the supervising officer may refer the case to a hearing.

(2) Where—

(a) the chief officer has a duty to proceed under section 75(7) or 76(2) or (5) of the 1996 Act;

or

(b) the member concerned has received two written warnings about his conduct within the previous twelve months and has in a statement made under regulation 9 admitted that his conduct failed to meet the appropriate standard,

the supervising officer shall refer the case to a hearing.

Keynote

On receiving the report from the investigating officer, the supervising officer *may* refer the case to a hearing. Alternatively, he/she may decide not to refer the case and, where that happens, no reference to the case is to be made on the member's personal record (reg. 11(4)).

If the case comes under reg. 11(2)(a) or (b), the supervising officer *must* refer the case to a hearing (unless it is likely to be a 'special case').

The duties referred to at reg. 11(2)(a) (under s. 75(7) or 76(2) or (5) of the Police Act 1996) relate to the notification to, and supervision by, the Police Complaints Authority.

The circumstances at reg. 11(2)(b) require that the member has received two written warnings about his/her conduct in the last 12 months *and* that he/she has made a statement under reg. 9 above that his/her conduct failed to meet the required standard. It would seem that the written warnings must relate to the officer's *conduct* and not simply his/her *performance* (as to which **see para. 1.2.1**).

If it is the *supervising* officer's opinion that the case is *likely* to satisfy the 'special case' conditions (**see below**), he/she must refer the case to the 'appropriate' officer.

'Appropriate officer' means:

- where the member concerned is a member of the Metropolitan police or the City of London police, an Assistant Commissioner *in that force*
- in any other case, an Assistant Chief Constable

(reg. 4(1)).

The appropriate officer will then need to determine whether the conditions in relation to 'special cases' are satisfied or not. If they are not, he/she must return the case to the supervising officer. If the conditions are satisfied, the appropriate officer must then either certify the case as a 'special case' (under reg. 11(3)(b)(i) and refer it to a hearing or, if in his/her opinion it is not appropriate to make such a certification, refer it back to the supervising officer.

Any proceedings resulting from a referral under reg. 11 will be 'disciplinary proceedings' for the purposes of Part IV of the Police Act 1996 (reg. 11(5)).

No sanction may be imposed — under reg. 31 (**see below**) — unless a case has been referred to a hearing (reg. 14).

Withdrawal

Regulation 12 states:

> (1)   At any time before the beginning of the hearing the supervising officer may direct that the case be withdrawn, unless the chief officer has a duty to proceed under section 75(7) or 76(2) or (5) of the 1996 Act.
> (2)   Where a case is withdrawn it shall be treated as if the supervising officer had decided not to refer it to a hearing.

Keynote

For the 'duty to proceed' under the relevant sections of the Police Act 1996 **see para. 1.2.3**.

The effect of reg. 12(2) is that cases withdrawn before the beginning of a hearing will be treated as if they had never been referred in the first place and therefore no reference to them can be made on the member's personal record (see reg. 11(4) above).

Referral of Cases to Hearing

Regulation 13(1) states:

> (1)   The supervising officer shall ensure that, as soon as practicable, the member concerned is given written notice of a decision to refer the case to a hearing and that, not less than 21 days before the date of hearing, the member concerned is supplied with copies of—
> (a)   any statement he may have made to the investigating officer; and
> (b)   any relevant statement, document or other material obtained during the course of the investigation.

Keynote

Regulation 12(1) makes two requirements. The first is that the member be given written notice of the decision to refer the case to a hearing *as soon as practicable* (see also reg. 9). As with reg. 9 (**see above**), the wording suggests that the member must be served personally with the written notice here. This view is further reinforced by the modified wording used in reg. 13 in relation to 'special cases' (**see below**). This notice must specify the relevant conduct that allegedly failed to meet the appropriate standard, together with the relevant paragraph of the Code of Conduct (as to which **see above**) (reg. 13(2)).

The second requirement is that, not less than 21 days before the date of the hearing, the member concerned be supplied with copies of the documents set out at reg. 13(1)(a) and (b), including a copy of any account or statement given verbally (reg. 13(3)).

Notice of Hearing

Regulation 15 states:

> (1)   The supervising officer shall ensure that at least 21 days in advance the member concerned is notified of the time, date and place of the hearing.
>
> (2)   In a case to which this paragraph applies the hearing may, if the supervising officer considers it appropriate in the circumstances, take place before the expiry of the 21 days referred to in paragraph (1).
>
> (3)   Paragraph (2) applies where the member concerned is given a written notice under regulation 13(1) of a decision to refer the case to a hearing and—
>
> (a)   at the time he receives such a notice he is detained in pursuance of the sentence of a court in a prison or other institution to which the Prison Act 1952 applies, or has received a suspended sentence of imprisonment; and
>
> (b)   having been supplied under regulation 13 with the documents therein mentioned he does not elect to be legally represented at the hearing.

Keynote

Generally the member concerned must be given at least 21 days' notice of the time, date and place of any proposed hearing. However, in the (very unusual) circumstances set out at reg. 15(3)(a) and (b), the supervising officer may allow the hearing to take place earlier if he/she considers it appropriate in the circumstances.

If the supervising officer is of the opinion that the sanctions of

- dismissal
- requirement to resign, or
- reduction in rank

should be available to the hearing, he/she *must* make sure that any member concerned is given written notice that

- they are entitled to elect legal representation at the hearing, and
- that the hearing cannot reduce the member in rank, require them to resign or dismiss them unless they have been given the opportunity to elect such respresentation, and
- that unless they have so elected, they may only be represented at the hearing by a 'friend' (police officer)

(reg. 16).

This further notice must be given at the same time as the reg. 15 notice. Failure to notify the member of this entitlement will mean that the sanctions above will not be available and will also lead to the case being remitted under reg. 29 (**see below**). Practically, this means that, if the opportunity to be legally represented is not given to the member concerned, the only options open to the hearing are a fine, reprimand or caution (reg. 31(1)).

The member concerned will be 'invited' to state in writing:

- whether or not he/she accepts that his/her conduct did not meet the appropriate standard
- whether he/she wishes to be legally represented (if reg. 16 applies)
- whether he/she proposes to call any witnesses (and if so, their names and addresses so that the supervising officer may secure their attendance)

(reg. 17(1)).

Any such written response must be made within 14 days of the member being 'notified' that the last of the documents under reg. 13(1) have been supplied (reg. 17(1)).

Presumably, the documents must also have *been* supplied otherwise the member will not be in a position to make a full evaluation of the case against him/her.

As with a statement made under reg. 9 (**see above**), any admission made under reg. 17 may have significant consequences for the member concerned, particularly as an admission can, without more, amount to a finding against him/her (**see below**).

Any witnesses who are police officers will be ordered to attend the hearing (reg. 17(2)). The member concerned will also be ordered to attend the hearing (reg. 24(1)). If he/she fails to attend the hearing, it may proceed and be concluded in his/her absence (reg. 24(2)) and any requirement under these Regulations that cannot be complied with because the member is absent will be dispensed with (reg. 24(4)). In other words, the hearing does not *have* to be adjourned simply because the member concerned is prevented from attending — either by ill-health or any other cause — and may proceed to conclusion without him/her. If any requirement under the Regulations cannot be complied with because the member concerned has not attended the hearing, that does not mean that the procedure will be delayed; it means that the requirement is dispensed with.

If, however, the member informs the officer presiding over the hearing in advance that he/she is unable to attend as a result of ill-health, *or some other unavoidable reason*, the hearing *may* be adjourned (reg. 24(3)).

The supervising officer must cause any other witnesses to be notified that their attendance is required and to advise them of the time and place of the hearing (reg. 17(2)).

A hearing does not *have* to be adjourned simply because a witness is unable or unwilling to attend (reg. 17(3)). However, the officers conducting a hearing have a discretionary power to do so in the appropriate circumstances.

The Hearing

Regulation 18 requires that the hearing be conducted by three officers who are not 'interested parties' (as to which **see above**).

Subject to the regulation dealing with 'remission of cases' (**see below**), the 'presiding officer' at the hearing must be an Assistant Chief Constable or, in the case of a Metropolitan police or City of London police officer, a Commander (reg. 18(2)).

Generally, the other two assisting officers must be at least the rank of superintendent and must be from the same force as the member concerned (reg. 18(3)). However, where the member concerned is a superintendent, the assisting officers must be assistant chief constables (or Commanders in the case of Metropolitan and City of London officers) in different forces from that of the member concerned (reg. 18(4)).

Where the member concerned accepts, in accordance with reg. 17, that his/her conduct fell short of the 'appropriate standard' (i.e. the Code of Conduct), a summary of the facts of the case will be prepared and a copy supplied to the member at least 14 days before the hearing (reg. 19(1)). If the member disagrees with the summary, he/she may submit a response within seven days *of receiving it* (reg. 19(2)).

If the member has not accepted that his/her conduct fell short of the appropriate standard, there is no need for a summary (reg. 19(3)).

Where a summary of facts has been prepared, a copy of it will be supplied to the officers conducting the hearing in addition to a copy of the reg. 13 notice (reg. 20).

Unless the member has given notice (under reg. 17) that he/she wishes to be legally represented, the *supervising officer* must appoint another police officer to present the case (reg. 21(1)). This would generally be someone of at least inspector rank. Where the member concerned has elected to be legally represented, this regulation leaves it open for the case to be presented by a solicitor/counsel.

The member concerned may conduct his/her own case in person or by another police officer chosen by him/her. If the member has given notice under reg. 17, he/she may then be represented by a solicitor/counsel (reg. 21(2)).

The officers conducting the hearing may adjourn from time to time if it appears to them to be *necessary or expedient for the due hearing of the case* (reg. 22(1)).

Any decision of the officers need only be based on a simple majority but must not indicate whether it was so decided or whether it was reached unanimously (reg. 22(2)). No provision is made for the presiding officer to have any form of 'casting vote' or for his/her view to carry any more weight than the assisting officers.

Procedure at Hearing

The officers conducting the hearing will, subject to the provisions of the Regulations, determine their own procedure (reg. 23(1)). Any question as to whether any evidence is admissible, or whether any question should be put to a witness will also be determined by the officers conducting the hearing (reg. 28(1)). These widely drafted discretionary powers will however be subject to general principles of law (e.g. natural justice).

Additionally, the presiding officer may, *with the consent of the member concerned*, allow any document to be adduced in evidence, even though no copy of it was supplied to the member under reg. 13 (reg. 28(2)).

The job of the officers conducting the hearing (set out under reg. 23(2)) is threefold.

- they must first review the facts of the case and decide whether or not the member's conduct met the 'appropriate standard' (the Code of Conduct);

- if they decide that the member's conduct did not meet that standard, the officers must then decide whether, in all the circumstances, it would be reasonable to impose a sanction and, if so;

- they must determine which sanction to impose.

Therefore, a finding that the conduct fell short of the required standard does not automatically mean that any sanction must be imposed.

The officers conducting the hearing can only find that the member's conduct failed to meet the appropriate standard if:

- it is admitted by the member concerned, or
- it is proved by the person presenting the case *on the balance of probabilities*

(reg. 23(3)). Thus, the standard of proof required in such hearings has been reduced to that of an ordinary civil trial (and that required of a defendant where the burden of proof falls on him/her; **see Evidence and Procedure, chapter 11**). Although much attention has been given to this lowering of the standard of proof required, it is a general common law rule that the greater the consequences being faced by the defendant, the greater the degree of evidence that will be required to tip the balance of probabilities against him/her.

A verbatim record of the proceedings must be taken and, if the member concerned lodges notice of appeal (**see below**) and applies for a copy or transcript of the record within the time limit, it will be supplied to him or her (reg. 30).

Attendance of Others at Hearing

Generally, hearings will be conducted in private (reg. 26(1)). However, there are some exceptions.

- The member concerned may be accompanied by another police officer (reg. 26(3)).

- The presiding officer may allow witnesses to be accompanied by a friend or a relative (reg. 26(4)).

Where there has been a complaint made against the member concerned, whether directly or through the Police Complaints Authority (PCA) or some other person/body, the person who originated the complaint will generally be allowed to attend parts of the hearing. Regulation 25 provides that the originator of a complaint ('the complainant') will, as a general rule, be allowed to attend the hearing *while witnesses are being examined or cross-examined*. The complainant may also be accompanied by a friend or relative at the discretion of the presiding officer (reg. 25(2)). If the complainant or any accompanying friend/relative is to give evidence, neither will be allowed to attend the hearing before he/she gives evidence (reg. 25(3)).

If the member concerned gives evidence, he/she may be asked questions by the presiding officer on behalf of the complainant after the cross-examination. He/she may also be asked questions *by the complainant* at the presiding officer's discretion (reg. 25(4)).

Notwithstanding these provisions, the complainant and anyone accompanying him/her must not intervene in or interrupt the hearing. If any of these people misconduct themselves or behave in a disorderly or abusive manner, the presiding officer may exclude them from the hearing (reg. 25(5)).

If it appears to the presiding officer that a witness may disclose in evidence information which, in the public interest, ought not to be disclosed to the public, he/she must require any member of the public (including complainants and their accompanying friends) to withdraw while the evidence is given (reg. 27).

The presiding officer has discretion to allow the presence of any solicitor or other person that he/she considers desirable to attend the whole or part of the hearing *subject to the consent of all parties to the hearing* (reg. 26(2)).

Members of the PCA are entitled to attend hearings where there has been a complaint against the member concerned or where the case arose from a matter requiring the mandatory supervision of the investigation by the PCA (**see para. 1.2.3**) (reg. 26(2)). Home Office guidance also advises that members of the PCA be allowed to attend hearings where they have exercised their authority under s. 76 of the Police Act 1996 (recommending or directing that a chief officer bring proceedings against an officer).

Remission of Cases

Regulation 29 states:

> *(1)   The hearing of the case—*
> *(a)   shall, in the circumstances mentioned in paragraph (2); or*
> *(b)   may, in the circumstances mentioned in paragraph (5),*
> *be remitted by the presiding officer concerned to an officer of equivalent rank in the force concerned or to an officer of equivalent rank in another force who, at the presiding officer's request, has agreed to act as the presiding officer in the matter.*
> *(2)   A case shall be so remitted if—*
> *(a)   the presiding officer is an interested party otherwise than in his capacity as such; or*
> *(b)   there would not, because the member concerned was not given notice under regulation 16 of the opportunity to elect to be legally represented at the hearing, be available on a finding against him any of the sanctions referred to in that regulation, and it appears to the presiding officer concerned that those sanctions ought to be so available and that accordingly it would be desirable for there to be another hearing at which the member concerned could, if he so wished, be so represented.*

Keynote

Remission of a hearing really means passing it over to another officer of equivalent rank, either in the force concerned or of another force.

The hearing of a case *must* be remitted if:

- the presiding officer is an 'interested party'; or
- if the member was not given the opportunity to elect legal representation under reg. 16 (**see above**), thereby limiting the sanctions available to the hearing *and* the presiding officer feels that those sanctions ought to be available.

In addition, the hearing of a case *may* be remitted if, either before or during the hearing, the presiding officer considers it appropriate (reg. 29(5)).

If the case is remitted under the second item above, the member must be served in writing with a notice inviting him/her to elect *within 14 days of receipt*, to be legally represented. Further, in such cases, the officer remitting the case must not give any indication of his/her assessment of the case, nor of the sanction that might be imposed to the 'new' officer. This suggests that, in cases where the hearing is remitted under the first item above, or in cases where discretionary remission is adopted, the presiding officer *may* indicate his/her assessment of the case so far and also any sanctions that he/she thinks ought to be imposed.

The Sanctions

Regulation 31 states:

> *(1)   Subject to section 84(1) of the 1996 Act, the officers conducting the hearing may impose any of the following sanctions, namely—*
> *(a)   dismissal from the force;*
> *(b)   requirement to resign from the force as an alternative to dismissal taking effect either forthwith or on such date as may be specified in the decision;*
> *(c)   reduction in rank;*
> *(d)   fine;*
> *(e)   reprimand;*
> *(f)   caution.*

Keynote

The reference to s. 84(1) of the Police Act 1996 is to the general prohibition on imposing a reduction in rank, requirement to resign or dismissal without having first given the officer an opportunity to elect legal representation.

Any of the above sanctions *except a requirement to resign*, will have immediate effect (reg. 31(2)). This immediate effect will not be delayed by any appeal procedure.

If a fine is imposed it is subject to a maximum limit (set out under reg. 31(3)). To work out the maximum amount of the fine you must first assume that it is to be recovered from the member concerned by weekly deductions over the next 13 weeks. The overall sum — whether one fine or a number of fines— when spread across these 13 weeks must not exceed one-seventh of the member's weekly pay.

In other words, the fine(s) cannot exceed 13 days' pay — though reg. 31 does not say whether that is gross pay or net pay. Neither does reg. 31 appear to require the fine *to be paid* over the 13-week period following the imposition of the sanctions.

In considering what sanction to impose, the officers conducting the hearing *must* have regard to the member's service record (reg. 32(a)). In doing so, they *may* receive evidence from witnesses if the officers are of the opinion that such evidence would help them (reg. 32(a)).

The member concerned must be given the opportunity to make oral or written representations in respect of any sanction (either in person or through his/her representative (reg. 32(b)).

At the end of the hearing the member concerned must be informed *orally* of:

- the finding, and
- any sanction imposed.

He/she must also be provided with:

- *written notification*, and
- a *summary of the reasons*

within three days of the end of the hearing (reg. 33).

Chief officers must keep a book recording details of every case brought against a member of their force. The entry in that book must include details of the findings, together with any other decisions reached in proceedings connected with the case.

Review

As with the unsatisfactory performance process (**see para. 1.2.1**), the 1999 Regulations provide for a review of any sanction imposed under reg. 31 and for any sanction to be expunged if it is found that the member concerned had not failed to meet the appropriate standard.

The appropriate regulations here are regs 34 to 36. Generally, the provisions relating to a review are the same as those for unsatisfactory performance.

In misconduct cases, the time by which the request for a review must be made to the reviewing officer is 14 days from receipt of the written summary of reasons under reg. 33. The member concerned may be accompanied at any review meeting by a fellow officer but can only be additionally accompanied by a solicitor/counsel where reg. 16 (in relation to the availability of the sanctions of dismissal, requirement to resign or reduction in rank) applies (reg. 35(2)). This is in contrast to a review meeting in relation to unsatisfactory performance where there are no restrictions on the member concerned being accompanied by a solicitor/counsel.

Special Cases

Regulation 39 makes provision for 'special cases' involving allegations of misconduct. There are three elements to qualify as a 'special case':

- the report, complaint or allegation must indicate that the conduct of the member concerned did not meet the appropriate standard
- the conditions set out in part I of sch. 2 are satisfied (**see below**); and
- the appropriate officer (**see above**) has issued a certificate under reg. 11(3)(b)(i).

The Conditions

Part I of sch. 2 states:

> *(1)   The conditions referred to in regulation 39 are—*
>
> *(a)   the report, complaint or allegation indicates that the conduct of the member concerned is of a serious nature and that an imprisonable offence may have been committed by the member concerned; and*
>
> *(b)   the conduct is such that, were the case to be referred to a hearing under regulation 11 and the officers conducting that hearing were to find that the conduct failed to meet the appropriate standard, they would in the opinion of the appropriate officer be likely to impose the sanction specified in regulation 31(1)(a) (dismissal from the force); and*
>
> *(c)   the report, complaint or allegation is supported by written statements, documents or other material which is, in the opinion of the appropriate officer, sufficient without further evidence to establish on the balance of probabilities that the conduct of the member concerned did not meet the appropriate standard; and*
>
> *(d)   the appropriate officer is of the opinion that it is in the public interest for the member concerned to cease to be a member of a police force without delay.*
>
> *(2)   In this paragraph an 'imprisonable offence' means an offence which is punishable with imprisonment in the case of a person aged 21 or over.*

Keynote

All of the conditions set out under part I must be satisfied before a case can be designated a 'special case'.

The circumstances are such that any 'special case' will be very unusual and will be dealt with under legal advice at a very high organisational level. What constitutes conduct of a 'serious nature' is not clear but there must be an indication that the officer's alleged conduct involves an offence punishable with imprisonment (if commited by a person aged 21 years or over).

A further requirement for a case to be classified as 'special' is that, in the opinion of the appropriate officer, the officers conducting a hearing into the case would be likely to dismiss the member from the force if the case were found proved. 'Special cases' must also be supported by evidence which, again in the appropriate officer's opinion, is enough by itself to establish that the member's conduct did not meet the required standard (on the balance of probabilities).

The final requirement for a case to fall into this category is that, in the appropriate officer's opinion, it is in the public interest that the member concerned ceases to be a police officer without delay.

The times when all these criteria are most likely to be met is when an officer has been caught 'red-handed' in the commission of a serious offence.

Modifications for Special Cases

The important difference between 'special cases' and other cases involving allegations of misconduct is that the former will be subject to a 'fast track' procedure. That procedure, which is set out at part II of sch. 2, changes a number of the key regulations above. Where a case does meet the special case criteria but is subsequently returned to the supervising officer, the unchanged regulations will then apply once more (reg. 39(3)). A special case may be so returned at any time before the beginning of the hearing.

Generally, the modifications shift many of the administrative responsibilities to the 'appropriate officer'.

Remember that, under reg. 4, 'appropriate officer' means:

- where the member concerned is a member of the Metropolitan police or the City of London police, an Assistant Commissioner *in that force*;

- in any other case, an Assistant Chief Constable.

Broadly, the key differences in the regulations under the fast track procedure are:

- the setting of a *maximum* time limit (28 days) as well as a minimum for setting the hearing date;

- the notice informing the member of his/her opportunity to elect legal representation is mandatory in all cases;

- the provisions allowing oral testimony at the hearing are removed;

- the hearing must be heard/reviewed by a chief officer;

- the powers to adjourn the hearing are restricted in their duration and frequency;

- some of the restrictions on the attendance of a complainant at the hearing are removed;

- the time limits on notifying the finding of a hearing and of a review are reduced from three days to 24 hours.

The fast track procedure is designed to be completed within six weeks of the issuing of the relevant notice.

1.2.3 Complaints

Part IV of the Police Act 1996 sets out the provisions for the recording and investigation of complaints against police officers. Every police authority and the HMIC is under a statutory duty to 'keep themselves informed' as to the workings of the relevant sections of the Act relating to the recording and investigation of complaints (s. 77).

Provisions are also made for the making of regulations in respect of non-Home Office police forces under s. 78 of the 1996 Act.

Section 65 of the Police Act 1996 defines a complaint as:

> . . . *a complaint about the conduct of a member of a police force which is submitted—*
> *(a) by a member of the public, or*
> *(b) on behalf of a member of the public and with his written consent.*

Keynote

Therefore a complaint so defined must emanate from a member of the public and must be made about the conduct of a 'member of a police force'. As special constables and cadets are not members of a police force, the definition — and the attendant procedures — do not apply to them.

The definition allows for the reporting of complaints by third parties acting on behalf of the member of the public, e.g. MPs, Citizens Advice Bureaux or friends/family. If a complaint is made by another person/organisation, there must be some form of writing that indicates the complainant's willingness for that person/organisation to submit the complaint on their behalf. This would presumably include e-mails and other electronically-generated messages.

Clearly there will be occasions where there may be an overlap in the procedures relating to complaints, conduct and performance. Local advice should be sought in the recording and investigation of such incidents.

There is no requirement for the officer concerned to have been on duty at the time of the conduct complained of and again local guidance should be sought in relation to the recording and investigation of 'complaints' of off-duty police officers.

The definition does not extend to complaints in so far as they relate to the *direction or control* of a police force by the chief officer (s. 67(4)).

Where the conduct complained of is (or has been) wholly or partly the subject of criminal or disciplinary proceedings, none of the provisions relating to the recording and investigation of complaints under chapter 1 of Part IV of the 1996 Act applies (s. 67(5)).

Steps to be Taken

Section 67 of the Police Act 1996 states:

> *(1) Where a complaint is submitted to the chief officer of police for a police area, he shall take any steps that appear to him to be desirable for the purpose of obtaining or preserving evidence relating to the conduct complained of.*
> *(2) After complying with subsection (1), the chief officer shall determine whether he is the appropriate authority in relation to the member of a police force whose conduct is the subject of the complaint.*
> *(3) If the chief officer determines that he is not the appropriate authority, he shall—*
> *(a) send the complaint or, if it was submitted orally, particulars of it, to the appropriate authority, and*
> *(b) give notice that he has done so to the person by whom or on whose behalf the complaint was submitted.*

Keynote

The first duty to fall on a chief officer on receipt of a complaint is to obtain and preserve evidence. This duty is not dependent on the complaint having any *prima facie* foundation, neither is it dependent on the determination as to who is the 'appropriate authority'.

That 'authority' will be:

- in relation to a Metropolitan police officer — the Commissioner

- in relation to an officer above the rank of superintendent from another force — the police authority for that force
- in relation to an officer of superintendent rank or below from another force — the chief officer of that force

(s. 65).

The procedure to be followed in respect of officers over the rank of superintendent is set out in s. 68.

If the chief officer receiving the complaint determines that he/she is not the appropriate authority, he/she must follow the requirements set out at s. 67(3)(a) and (b) above.

Once these steps in relation to the preservation of evidence and determination of the appropriate authority have been completed, the complaint must be recorded (s. 69(1)).

After recording a complaint, the chief officer must decide whether it is suitable for informal resolution (**see below**) and may appoint another member of the force to assist (s. 69(2)). If the complaint is suitable for informal resolution, the chief officer must seek to resolve it informally and may appoint another officer from that force to do so (s. 69(4)).

If, after attempts to resolve a complaint informally, it appears to the chief officer that such informal resolution is 'impossible' or that the complaint is, for any other reason not suitable for informal resolution, he/she must appoint another officer of that, or some other force, to investigate it (s. 69(6)).

A complaint will not be suitable for informal resolution unless:

- the member of the public consents; and
- the chief officer is satisfied that the conduct complained of, even if proved, would not justify criminal *or disciplinary* proceedings

(s. 69(3)).

If the complaint is not suitable for informal resolution, the chief officer must appoint another member of that, or some other force, to investigate it (s. 69(5)).

Any request by a chief officer for the chief officer of another force to provide an officer to investigate a complaint (under ss. 69(5) or (6)) must comply with the request (s. 69(8)).

Any officer who has previously been appointed to resolve a complaint informally may not later investigate the complaint (s. 69(7)).

Unless the investigation of the complaint is supervised by the Police Complaints Authority under s. 72 (**see below**), the investigating officer must submit any report on the complaint to the chief officer who appointed him/her (s. 69(9)).

Informal Resolution

The informal resolution procedures are built on the principles of flexibility and simplicity and they are intended to prevent cases of a minor nature from receiving the full attentions of formal investigation. The procedure for the informal resolution of complaints is to be found mainly in the Police (Complaints) (Informal Resolution) Regulations 1985 (SI 1985 No. 671).

In addition to the restrictions placed on informal resolution under s. 69(3) of the Police Act 1996 above, a complaint that is supervised by the Police Complaints Authority, under its mandatory or discretionary remit, may not be informally resolved (reg. 3 of the 1985 Regulations).

Appointed Officers

If it is decided that informal resolution is appropriate, the officer initially deputed to handle the question may act as the 'appointed officer' (as defined in the 1985 Regulations) and seek an informal resolution. Alternatively, the case might be referred to another officer to undertake the role of appointed officer.

As soon as practicable after the decision to resolve the complaint informally, the appointed officer should seek the views of both the complainant and also the officer whose conduct has been complained of (reg. 4(1)). The officer should be allowed speak to a 'friend' about the matter first if he/she wishes.

At the same time, or thereafter, the appointed officer may take any steps that appear to be appropriate to resolve the complaint.

Early Resolution

Regulation 4(1) of the 1985 Regulations allows a supervisory officer of whatever rank to deal speedily with a complaint if it appears to them that it can be resolved in an informal manner at the time it is made.

Regulation 4 allows a supervisory officer to receive a complaint and, if the officer complained about is both present and willing to explain his/her understanding of the incident giving rise to the complaint, to deal with it at the time. In order to do this, the complainant must accept the explanation given or, if appropriate, any apology as a satisfactory outcome.

There is no requirement imposed on an officer to give an apology and the supervisor cannot do so on the officer's behalf unless he/she agrees that his/her conduct fell below the required standard. However, that does not prevent the supervisor apologising on behalf of the force.

If any explanation or apology is accepted, the supervisory officer should report the matter to the officer who has delegated responsibility for the informal resolution of complaints. If satisfied with the handling of the complaint, that officer may make a record in the complaints register and write to the complainant noting the way in which the complaint was handled and indicating the intention of recording it as having been informally resolved.

Where it appears to the appointed officer that the resolution of a complaint is likely to be assisted by a meeting between the complainant and the officer concerned — or also with any other person considered appropriate — then suitable arrangements may be made.

There will be no obligation on the officer who is the subject of the complaint to attend such a meeting.

A meeting may provide an opportunity for the complainant and the officer to exchange views and for any misunderstandings to be cleared up. It will also allow the officer, where there is an admission to the conduct complained of, to offer an explanation or an apology to the complainant.

If in the course of the informal resolution procedure evidence comes to light of a more serious complaint which might require a formal investigation, the informal procedures should be terminated and the matter reported to the chief officer immediately, whereupon the provisions of Part IV of the Act will apply.

Where there has been an attempted or a successful informal resolution of a complaint, no record must be made of it in the personal record of the officer concerned.

Where informal resolution appears to be impossible or it is apparent that the complaint is for any other reason not suitable to be so resolved, arrangements must be made for it to be investigated formally.

Admissibility of Statements

Generally a statement made for the purpose of an informal resolution of a complaint will not be admissible in any criminal, civil or disciplinary hearing (s. 86(1)). Where an officer makes a voluntary statement — oral or written — to the appointed officer, that officer must be told that this is the case. However, where the statement made consists of, or includes an admission relating to any matter that is not part of that complaint, s. 86(1) will *not* prevent it from being so used (s. 86(2)). Therefore informed consideration should be given by the officer before he/she makes any admissions in relation to the attempted informal resolution of a complaint.

The Police Complaints Authority

The Police Complaints Authority (PCA) is an independent body set up to oversee, among other things, the investigation of complaints against the police. Replacing the Police Complaints Board, the PCA was originally established under s. 83 of the Police and Criminal Evidence Act 1984. Its role has become increasingly important in ensuring the thorough and impartial investigation and supervision of sensitive and serious matters involving police conduct. If there is any doubt as to whether or not the PCA ought to be informed of any matter involving the conduct of police officers, local advice should be sought.

The PCA is made up of at least eight members plus a chair who is appointed by the Queen. Its constitution can be found in sch. 5 to the Police Act 1996.

Certain complaints made against police officers must be *referred* to the PCA. There are also provisions as to which investigations the PCA either may, or must, *supervise*.

Referral

Section 70(1)(a) of the Police Act 1996 requires that the following complaints be *referred* to the PCA, i.e. complaints alleging that the conduct complained of resulted in:

- the death of, or serious injury to, some other person
- assault occasioning actual bodily harm, bribery or a serious arrestable offence

(Police (Complaints) (Mandatory Referrals etc.) Regulations 1985 (SI 1985 No. 673)).

Section 70(2) allows the Police Complaints Authority to 'call in' any complaint not referred to them, irrespective of whether it meets the above criteria or not.

Section 71 allows chief officers to refer to the PCA other serious or exceptional matters not arising from a complaint but which indicate that an officer may have committed a criminal offence.

Supervision

It appears from the wording of s. 72 of the Police Act 1996 that any complaint involving the conduct set out above must be supervised by the Police Complaints Authority. It must also supervise any other complaint that is not within those criteria but which it determines is in the public interest for it to supervise.

Where the PCA supervise an investigation, it may place certain conditions on the appointment, or continued appointment, of an investigating officer (s. 72(3)). It may also make reasonable requirements in relation to the direction of the investigation and the resources committed to it. However, the PCA may not make any requirement relating to the obtaining and preserving of evidence in connection with a complaint where the possibility of criminal proceedings arises unless it has the consent of the Crown Prosecution Service. It must also seek the views of the relevant chief officer before making a requirement as to the commitment of his/her resources to an investigation.

At the end of a supervised investigation, the investigating officer must submit a report to the PCA as well as sending a copy to the 'appropriate authority' (the chief officer or police authority) (s. 73(1)).

After considering the report, the PCA will send a statement to the appropriate authority and, if it is practicable to do so, send a copy to the officer whose conduct is being investigated and to the complainant. That statement will say whether the investigation has been carried out to the PCA's satisfaction and specify any respect in which it has not been so carried out (s. 73(9)).

Ordinarily, no disciplinary proceedings or criminal proceedings may be brought until the PCA's statement has been submitted (s. 73(6) and (7)) but, in exceptional circumstances, the Director of Public Prosecutions may bring criminal proceedings before the statement has been submitted by the PCA if it is undesirable to wait (s. 73(8)).

Procedure After Investigation

At the end of any investigation, supervised or not, the chief officer must determine whether the report indicates that a criminal offence may have been committed by the officer. If he/she does conclude that a criminal offence may have been committed, the chief officer must send a copy of the report to the Director of Public Prosecutions s. 75(2) to (3) to the Police Act 1996).

Once the question of criminal proceedings has been dealt with, the chief officer will send a memorandum to the PCA stating whether or not it is proposed to bring disciplinary proceedings against the officer and if not, why not (s. 75(4)). This memorandum will be accompanied by a copy of the complaint and a copy of the report of the investigation.

Where a memorandum from the chief officer indicates that no disciplinary proceedings are to be brought, the PCA may 'recommend' to him/her that such proceedings *are* brought (s. 76(1)). If, having made such a recommendation and consulted with the chief officer, he/she still does not bring disciplinary proceedings, the PCA may *direct* him/her to do so, giving written reasons (s. 76(3) to (4)).

The chief officer must then:

- comply with this direction unless it is withdrawn (s. 76(5) to (6));
- advise the PCA of any action taken; and
- supply the PCA with such other information as it may reasonably require in discharging its functions

(s. 76(7)).

Withdrawn or Ill-founded Complaints

Although there is no specific legal remedy available against someone who makes a false complaint against a police officer, there are a number of options open to investigating officers in relation to withdrawn or ill-founded complaints.

If it is apparent from the outset that a complaint cannot or should not be investigated, dispensation from the requirement to investigate may be sought from the Police Complaints Authority (under reg. 3 of the Police (Dispensation from Requirement to Investigate Complaints) Regulations 1985 (SI 1985 No. 672)).

Cases where dispensation is sought will generally come under one or more of the following (D.I.S.P.) categories:

- **D**elay — where more than 12 months have elapsed between the incident giving rise to the complaint and its being reported *and* either no good reason is given for that delay or it would be unjust to the officer concerned to investigate it.

- **I**dentity — where there is an anonymous complainant who cannot reasonably be contacted or identified.

- **S**ame — in the case of repetitious complaints where the complainant has no fresh allegation/evidence but has made the same complaint before and it has been finalised.

- **P**racticable — where the investigation not reasonably practicable (e.g. because of the complainant's own conduct) or where complaint is vexatious, abusive or oppressive.

Even where a complaint falls into one of these categories, it might not receive dispensation, in which case a normal investigation would have to follow.

A complaint may be withdrawn at any time but should only be regarded as withdrawn when a signed statement is received from the complainant (or someone authorised to act on his/her behalf). Withdrawal of a complaint would not necessarily amount to an end to the investigation which might still be pursued under the internal conduct procedures (**see 1.2.2**).

In cases where it seems to the investigating officer that the complaint is ill-founded or that it would require a disproportionate amount of effort to investigate it, he/she may submit a report to the appropriate complaints department (or the Police Complaints Authority if supervised) to that effect.

1.2.4 Appeals

Where an officer has been:

- dismissed
- required to resign, or
- reduced in rank

following a hearing/chief officer's review in relation to unsatisfactory performance or misconduct, that officer has a right of appeal.

Police Appeals Tribunal

The Police Appeals Tribunal is a new feature for the police service. It is made up of a number of people drawn by the relevant police authority from a list maintained by the Home Office. The tribunal will comprise:

- a legally-qualified chair person
- a member of the police authority (or, in cases involving Metropolitan police officers, a member of the Metropolitan Police Committee)
- a serving or former chief officer (not from the appellant's force)
- a retired officer of appropriate rank (i.e. a superintendent/chief superintendent where the appellant was a superintendent, otherwise a chief inspector or below).

A tribunal does not need to have a hearing in all cases (Police Act 1996, sch. 6, para. 6). It may determine an appeal without the formality of a hearing, provided the appellant and respondent are given the opportunity to make representations as to the holding of a hearing and provided also that those representations have been considered.

The Rules

Section 85 of the Police Act 1996 empowers the Secretary of State to make regulations in respect of appeals from hearings. After consultation with the statutory body that oversees all tribunals, the Council on Tribunals, the Secretary of State made the Police Appeals Tribunals Rules 1999 (SI 1999 No. 818), which came into force on 1 April 1999.

Other than in cases brought under the old Police Discipline Regulations, the 1999 Rules revoke the former Police (Appeals) Rules 1985.

Any expression used in the Rules which also appears in the Police (Conduct) or Police (Efficiency) Regulations 1999 generally has the same meaning as it does in those Regulations (r. (2)).

Notice of Appeal

Rule 5 of the 1999 Rules states:

(1)   Subject to rule 7 and paragraph (2), the time within which notice of an appeal under section 85 of the Act shall be given is 21 days from the date on which the decision appealed against was notified to the appellant in pursuance of regulations made in accordance with section 50(3) of the Act.

(2)   In a case to which regulation 39 of the Police (Conduct) Regulations 1999 or regulation 25 of the Police (Conduct) (Senior Officers) Regulations 1999 applies where the decision appealed against was given in pursuance of those Regulations as modified by Part II of Schedule 2 or, as the case may be, by Part II of the Schedule to those Regulations, the time within which notice of an appeal under section 85 of the Act shall be given is 28 days from—

(a)   the conclusion of any criminal proceedings in which the appellant is charged with an offence in respect of the conduct to which the decision appealed against related; or

(b)   a decision that no such criminal proceedings will be instituted or taken over by the Director of Public Prosecutions has been communicated to the appellant.

Keynote

Notice of the appeal must be given within 21 days of the date *on which the decision appealed against was notified to the member concerned*. It would seem that this means the date on which the member concerned actually received the notification of the decision. This time limit may, however, be extended by the 'relevant police authority' under r. 7(1) (**see below**). The relevant police authority will be the police authority for the member's force. In the case of Metropolitan police officers, the authority will be the designated Home Office official of the Metropolitan Police Committee.

In 'special cases' (**see para. 1.2.3**) under reg. 39 of the Police (Conduct) Regulations 1999 — or its equivalent for senior officers — the time limit is 28 days from:

- the end of any related criminal proceedings against the appellant; or
- the date when a decision from the Director of Public Prosecutions not to institute any such proceedings has been communicated to the appellant.

The notice of appeal must be in writing and a copy must be sent to the 'respondent' (r. 5(3)).

The 'respondent' is simply the chief officer of the appellant's force (or, where the appellant is a senior officer, a person designated for that purpose by the relevant police authority) (r. 4).

Procedure

Rule 6 states:

(1)   As soon as practicable after receipt of a copy of the notice of appeal, the respondent shall provide to the relevant police authority—

(a)   a copy of the report of the person who made the decision appealed against;

(b)   the transcript of the proceedings at the original hearing; and

(c)   any documents which were made available to the person conducting the original hearing.

Keynote

The 'original hearing' is the conduct or inefficiency hearing which concluded that the appellant failed to meet the appropriate standard or that his/her performance was unsatisfactory (r. 3(1)).

A copy of the transcript referred to at r. 6(1)(b) must, at the same time, be sent to the appellant (r. 6(2)). Receiving this transcript provides the trigger for the 28-day time limit for the appellant to submit the various statements and documents under r. 6 (**see below**).

These copies must be provided/sent 'as soon as practicable' after the notification of appeal has been received.

Rule 6 goes on to state:

> *(3)* Subject to rule 7, the appellant shall, within 28 days of the date on which he receives a copy of the transcript mentioned in paragraph (1)(b), submit to the relevant police authority—
> > *(a)* a statement of the grounds of appeal;
> > *(b)* any supporting documents; and
> > *(c)* either—
> > > *(i)* any written representations which the appellant wishes to make under paragraph 6 of the Schedule 6 to the Act or, as the case may be, any request to make oral representations under that paragraph; or
> > > *(ii)* a statement that he does not wish to make any such representations as are mentioned in paragraph (i):
> > Provided that, in a case where the appellant submits a statement under sub-paragraph (c)(ii), nothing in this paragraph shall prevent representations under paragraph 6 of the Schedule 6 to the Act being made by him to the chairman of the tribunal.

Keynote

The appellant must, within the time limit, submit a statement setting out the grounds of his/her appeal and any supporting documentation to the relevant police authority. This time limit may also be extended by the 'relevant police authority' under r. 7(1) (**see below**).

He/she must also submit either:

- any written representations or a request to make oral representations (where there is to be no hearing); or
- a negative statement (i.e. that he/she does not wish to make any such representations).

Submission of a negative statement does not, however, prevent an appellant from making representations to the chair of the tribunal where it has been decided to proceed without a hearing (r. 6(3)).

The documents set out above must also be copied, as soon as practicable, to the members of the tribunal and to the 'respondent' (r. 6(4)).

Rule 6 goes on to state:

> *(5)* The respondent shall, not later than 21 days from the date on which he receives the copy documents sent to him under paragraph (4), submit to the relevant police authority—
> > *(a)* a statement of his response to the appeal;
> > *(b)* any supporting documents; and
> > *(c)* either—
> > > *(i)* any written representations which the respondent wishes to make under paragraph 6 of Schedule 6 to the Act or, as the case may be, any request to make oral representations under that paragraph; or

(ii)   a statement that he does not wish to make any such representations as are mentioned in paragraph (i):
    Provided that, in a case where the respondent submits a statement under sub-paragraph (c)(ii), nothing in this paragraph shall prevent representations under paragraph 6 of Schedule 6 to the Act being made by him to the chairman of the tribunal.

Keynote

The respondent must submit similar documents to those required of the appellant under r. 6(3) above and must do so no later than 21 days from the date on which he/she receives the copies of the appellant's documents.

The documents submitted by the respondent must also be copied to the members of the tribunal (r. 6(7)).

Only those documents set out in r. 6(5)(a) and (c) must be *copied* to the appellant but a list of any supporting documents must be sent to him/her (r. 6(6)).

Again, a negative statement in relation to the making of representations will not prevent the respondent from making representations to the chair of the tribunal where it has been decided to proceed without a hearing.

Extension of Time Limits

Rule 7 allows the police authority to extend the time limits under rr. 5 and 6(3) where:

- the appellant applies for an extension and
- the authority is satisfied that it is just to grant such an extension
- the special circumstances of the case require it.

Where an appellant makes a request for an extension and that request is turned down, the authority must give him/her written notice setting out the reasons (r. 7(2)). That notice must also advise the appellant of the right of appeal against this decision. The appellant can then appeal, within 14 days of receiving this notice, to the chair of the tribunal against the decision not to grant an extension. The chair may then grant an extension under r. 7.

Procedure at Hearing

Rules 8 to 10 regulate the procedure to be followed at a hearing.

Under r. 8 the appellant must generally be given at least 28 days' notice of the date of a hearing. However, this may be reduced provided both parties agree (r. 8(1)).

The provisions of the Local Government Act 1972 (giving powers in relation to local inquiries) are applied where relevant to hearings under these Rules.

There is no need for the appellant or the respondent to be present at the hearing which may proceed without either of them if it appears just and proper to do so (r. 8(3)).

The hearing may also be adjourned 'from time to time' as may appear necessary for the due hearing of the case (r. 8(3)).

Subject to the Rules (and also the general principles of law, the procedure at the hearing will be determined by the tribunal (r. 8(4)).

The hearing will be in private, though the tribunal has discretion to allow people it considers 'desirable' to attend the whole or part of the hearing (r. 9(1)).

A complainant (**see para. 1.2.3**) will be also allowed to attend the hearing where the appeal is not simply against the sanction imposed earlier. In cases where the complainant is allowed to be present, that entitlement only extends to occasions *while witnesses are being examined and cross-examined about the facts alleged* (r. 12). This would not appear to give a complainant any entitlement to be present during the giving of any antecedents, mitigation or extraneous background evidence relating to the appellant. The complainant may be allowed to be accompanied by a friend or relative *who is not going to be called as a witness* where appropriate (r. 12(3)).

If the complainant is going to give evidence, he/she must not attend before giving that evidence and, if the tribunal feels that a witness is going to give information that ought not to be disclosed to the public, it must require the complainant (and anyone accompanying him/her) to withdraw (r. 12(3)).

Generally, the respondent will 'open the batting' but the tribunal can determine otherwise (r. 10(1)). All oral evidence will be given under oath and the tribunal will decide what evidence is admissible or what questions can be put to a witness.

A verbatim record must be made of all evidence given at the hearing and this record must be kept for at least seven years after the end of the hearing (unless the chair asks for a transcript to be made) (r. 10(5)).

The tribunal may allow evidence to be submitted in a written statement in lieu of admissible oral evidence (r. 11).

Findings

A Police Appeals Tribunal may make an order which:

- appears to it to be *less* severe than the decision appealed against; and
- which could have been imposed by the person making that decision

(s. 85(2) of the Police Act 1996).

The chair of the tribunal must prepare a written statement of its findings, together with reasons (r. (13(1)). That statement must be submitted to the relevant police authority (and the Secretary of State where the appellant is a senior officer) 'within a reasonable period after the determination of the appeal. So too must a record of any order the tribunal makes under its powers under s. 85(2).

The relevant authority must copy the statement and record to the appellant and respondent as soon as practicable (r. 13(3)).

Where the decision appealed against arose from a complaint, the relevant police authority must also notify the complainant of the outcome of the appeal (r. 13(4)).

Although the Regulations relating to efficiency and misconduct specify that any decision may be reached by a simple majority (**see above**), the Appeals Rules make no such provision.

1.3   Other Regulations

1.3.1   Restrictions on Private Lives

The Police Regulations 1995 (SI 1995 No. 215) impose restrictions on the private lives of officers. Regulation 10 of the 1995 Regulations provides that the restrictions contained in sch. 2 shall apply to all members of a police force. It also provides that no restrictions other than those designed to secure the proper exercise of the functions of a constable shall be imposed by the police authority or the chief officer of police on the private lives of members of a police force except such as may temporarily be necessary or such as may be approved by the Secretary of State after consultation.

Schedule 2

Schedule 2 provides that a member of a police force:

- Shall at all times abstain from any activity which is likely to interfere with the impartial discharge of his/her duties or which is likely to give rise to the impression amongst members of the public that it may so interfere (this does not include serving as a school governor), and in particular a member of a police force shall not take any active part in politics.

- Shall not reside at premises which are not for the time being approved by the chief officer of police.

- Shall not, without the previous consent of the chief officer of police, receive a lodger in a house or quarters with which he/she is provided by the police authority, or sub-let any part of the house or quarters.

- Shall not, unless he/she has previously given written notice to the chief officer of police, receive a lodger in a house in which he/she resides and in respect of which he/she receives a rent allowance, or sub-let any part of such a house.

- Shall not wilfully refuse or neglect to discharge any lawful debt.

1.3.2   Business Interests

Regulation 10 of the Police Regulations 1995 provides that, if a member of a police force or a relative included in his/her family proposes to have, or has, a 'business interest', the member shall forthwith give written notice of that interest to the chief officer of police unless that business interest was disclosed at the time of the officer's appointment as a member of the force.

On receipt of such a notice, the chief officer shall determine whether or not the interest in question is compatible with the member concerned remaining a member of the force and shall notify the member in writing of his/her decision.

Within 10 days of being notified of the chief officer's decision (or within such longer period as the police authority may in all the circumstances allow), the member concerned may appeal to the police authority against that decision by sending written notice to the police authority.

If a business interest is felt to be incompatible, the chief officer may dispense with the member's services after giving them an opportunity to make representations.

For the purposes of reg. 11, a member of a police force or relative has a business interest if:

- the member holds any office or employment for hire or carries on any business;

- a shop is kept or a like business carried on by the member's spouse (not being separated) at any premises in the area of the police force in question or by any relative living with him/her; or

- the member, his/her spouse (not being separated) or any relative living with them has a pecuniary interest in any licence or permit granted in relation to liquor licensing, refreshment houses or betting and gaming or regulating places of entertainment in the area of the police force in question.

'Relative' includes a reference to a spouse, parent, son, daughter, brother or sister.

1.4   Offences

Offence — Malfeasance in a Public Office — Common Law
Triable on indictment. Imprisonment at large.
(*Arrestable offence*)

It is a misdemeanour at common law for the holder of a public office to do anything that amounts to a malfeasance or a 'culpable' misfeasance (*R* v *Wyatt* (1705) 1 Salk 380).

Keynote

It would appear that such offences can only be tried on indictment and the court has a power of sentence 'at large', that is, there is no limit on the sentence that can be passed (making this an arrestable offence, **see chapter 2**). The conduct can be separated into occasions of *mal*feasance and *mis*feasance. The first requires some degree of wrongful motive or intention on the part of the officer concerned while the second is more likely to apply where there has been some form of wilful neglect of duty. Although many of the earlier cases involved an element of corruption, this is not a requirement for the offence (*R* v *Dytham* [1979] 2 QB 722). This offence might be committed where a police officer wilfully neglects to prevent a criminal assault (as in *Dytham*), or possibly where a supervisory officer fails to intervene in a situation where one of his/her officers is carrying out an unlawful act. The neglect has to be 'wilful' (**see Crime, chapter 1**) and not simply inadvertent. It also has to be done without reasonable excuse or justification. The offence is a very serious one and therefore the conduct must have been sufficiently damaging to the public interest that it merits condemnation and criminal punishment.

Offence — Constables on Licensed Premises — Licensing Act 1964, s. 178
Triable summarily. Fine.
(No specific power of arrest)

The Licensing Act 1964, s. 178 states:

> *If the holder of a justices' licence—*
> *(a)   knowingly suffers to remain on the licensed premises any constable during any part of the time appointed for the constable's being on duty, except for the purposes of the execution of the constable's duty, or*
> *(b)   supplies any liquor or refreshment, whether by way of gift or sale, to any constable on duty except by authority of a superior officer of the constable, or*
> *(c)   bribes or attempts to bribe any constable,*
> *he shall be liable . . .*

Keynote

To prove the offence at s. 178(a), you must show that the licensee committed the offence 'knowingly'.

That knowledge must apply both to the fact that the person is a constable *and* that the constable was on duty.

That requirement does not explicitly apply to the other offences (but for state of mind generally, **see Crime, chapter 1**).

Offence — Impersonating a Police Officer — Police Act 1996, s. 90(1)
Triable summarily. Six months' imprisonment.
(No specific power of arrest)

The Police Act 1996, s. 90 states:

> *(1)   Any person who with intent to deceive impersonates a member of a police force or special constable, or makes any statement or does any act calculated falsely to suggest that he is such a member or constable, shall be guilty of an offence and liable . . .*

Keynote

This is a crime of 'specific intent' (**see Crime, chapter 1**). The intention to deceive must be proved.

Offence — Wearing or Possessing Uniform — Police Act 1996, s. 90(2) and (3)
Triable summarily. Fine.
(No specific power of arrest)

The Police Act 1996, s. 90 states:

> *(2)   Any person who, not being a constable, wears any article of police uniform in circumstances where it gives him an appearance so nearly resembling that of a member of a police force as to be calculated to deceive shall be guilty of an offence . . .*
> *(3)   Any person who, not being a member of a police force or special constable, has in his possession any article of police uniform shall, unless he proves that he obtained possession of that article lawfully and has possession of it for a lawful purpose, be guilty of an offence . . .*

Keynote

'Article of police uniform' means:

- any article of uniform or
- any distinctive badge or mark or
- any document of identification

usually issued to members of police forces or special constables (s. 90(4)).

Offence — Causing Disaffection — Police Act 1996, s. 91(1)

Triable either way. Two years' imprisonment on indictment; six months' imprisonment and/or a fine summarily.

(No specific power of arrest)

The Police Act 1996, s. 91(1) states:

> *(1) Any person who causes, or attempts to cause, or does any act calculated to cause, disaffection amongst the members of any police force, or induces or attempts to induce, or does any act calculated to induce, any member of a police force to withhold his services, shall be guilty of an offence . . .*

1.5 The Police Act 1997

The Police Act 1997 was passed in order to:

- make provisions for the National Criminal Intelligence Service and the National Crime Squad;

- make provision for the Police Information Technology Organisation;

- enable the entry on and interference with property and wireless telegraphy in the prevention or detection of serious crime;

- to provide for the issue of certificates about criminal records; and

- to make administrative provisions for the police.

1.5.1 National Criminal Intelligence Service

Part I of the Police Act 1997 provides for the continued operation of the National Criminal Intelligence Service (NCIS) under a 'service authority'. The NCIS Service Authority is made up of police service, police authority and independent members, together with a Home Office representative. It has a 'core membership' with the National Crime Squad (**see para. 1.5.2**) but, given its very wide geographical and professional boundaries, the Authority also includes representatives of the Secretaries of State for Scotland and Northern Ireland and HM Customs and Excise.

The 1997 Act sets out rules for the administration, organisation and funding of NCIS, together with provisions for the appointment of its Director General.

The statutory functions of NCIS are generally to gather, store and analyse information in order to provide criminal intelligence to police forces throughout the UK, as well as to other law enforcement agencies, domestically and internationally.

'Police members' of NCIS are either of ACPO rank or are engaged temporarily under s. 97 of the Police Act 1996 (or its Scottish and Northern Ireland equivalent). Many of the statutory conditions relating to police officers as members of their own force (e.g. pensions, membership of the Police Federation etc.) have been extended by the Act to include police officers seconded to NCIS. Officers seconded to central services under s. 97, although they remain constables in most instances, are not treated as 'members of a police force' and are not subject to the Regulations relating to discipline or conduct. Sections 37 to 40 of the Police Act 1997, however, make provision for discipline and complaints in relation to NCIS members and the relevant Regulations are to be found in the NCIS (Complaints) Regulations 1998 (SI 1998 No. 641 (as amended)).

For the Home Secretary's objectives in relation to NCIS, see the National Criminal Intelligence Service (Secretary of State's Objectives) Order 1999 (SI 1999 No. 822).

1.5.2 National Crime Squad

Part II of the Police Act 1997 creates an entirely new concept in British policing; a National Crime Squad (NCS). The squad will also operate under a 'service authority' headed by a Director General.

The 1997 Act merges the former Regional Crime Squads into a national investigative body to address major national and international crime.

The Act makes similar provisions in relation to the constitution of the NCS to those governing NCIS.

The NCS Service Authority consists of police service, police authority and independent members, together with a Home Office representative. Although it shares the 'core membership' with NCIS (**see para. 1.5.1**), the NCS authority membership does not extend beyond representatives from England and Wales.

The primary statutory function of the NCS is to prevent and detect serious crime which is of relevance to one or more police areas in England and Wales.

As with NCIS, the NCS has 'police members' who are either of ACPO rank or are seconded temporarily under s. 97 of the Police Act 1996 and the same comments in relation to their status as 'members of a police force' apply. However, NCS police members also have special provisions in relation to pensions, Federation membership and in relation to complaints and discipline — see the National Crime Squad (Complaints) Regulations 1998 (SI 1998 No. 638 (as amended)).

For the Home Secretary's objectives in relation to NCS, see the National Crime Squad (Secretary of State's Objectives) Order 1999 (SI 1999 No. 821).

1.5.3 Police Information Technology Organisation

The Police Information Technology Organisation (PITO) was set up in 1996 without statutory status. However, the increasingly demanding and diverse requirements of centralised IT support for all police agencies brought about the statutory provisions now to be found in Part IV of the Police Act 1997, makes PITO a non-departmental public body.

In this respect, PITO differs from NCIS and the NCS above. Whereas those two bodies are Service Authorities with special provisions as to their legal capacity and liability,

PITO is simply a 'body corporate' (see s. 109(1) of the 1997 Act) carrying out certain limited statutory functions.

Police officers seconded to PITO come under the provisions of s. 97 of the Police Act 1996 but there are no special provisions in relation to their conduct or the handling of complaints. Therefore, where an officer seconded to PITO is the subject of a complaint or the provisions of the Regulations relating to misconduct or efficiency, it would seem that he/she can only be dealt with on his/her return to force (see s. 97(6)).

1.5.4 Intrusive Surveillance

A further weapon in intelligence-led crime strategies is the use of surveillance techniques and Part III of the Police Act 1997 makes provision for interception of communications and other intrusive measures of evidence and intelligence gathering.

Part III provides for the appointment of a Chief Commissioner and other commissioners to oversee the operation of the powers under this Part of the Act.

It also identifies 'authorising officers' who may grant the relevant authority with the power to use intrusive surveillance techniques under the strict criteria set out in the Act. Those officers are:

- Chief constables of police forces maintained under the Police Act 1996, s. 2 (England and Wales) and the Police (Scotland) Act 1967, s. 1.

- The Commissioner and Assistant Commissioner(s) of the Metropolitan police.

- The Commissioner of the City of London police.

- The Chief Constable and Deputy Chief Constable of the Royal Ulster Constabulary.

- The Director General of NCIS and the NCS.

- The officer designated by the Commissioners of Customs and Excise.

In spite of these safeguards there is, perhaps unsurprisingly, a great deal of disquiet at the potential to infringe some fundamental rights and freedoms, particularly as the Human Rights Act 1998, which incorporates the European Convention on Human Rights into domestic law, is expected to come into force October 2000. In response, ACPO, NCIS, NCS and HM Customs and Excise have signed up to a Code of Practice governing covert law enforcement techniques. Issued under s. 101(3) of the 1997 Act, the Code is due to become effective as of October 1999 and is set out at **appendix 6**.

1.5.5 Criminal Records Certificates

Following the former government's White Paper, *On the Record*, together with the report into the murders by Thomas Hamilton (*Report of the Public Inquiry into the Shootings at Dunblane Primary School on 13 March 1996*, Cm 3386), there was a need to create a comprehensive national criminal record collection going beyond that held at New Scotland Yard (the National Identification Service).

Part V of the Police Act 1997 provides for the creation of a new Criminal Records Agency which is able to access the data on the Police National Computer and which will issue different types of criminal conviction certificate in response to 'searches' on certain individuals. Requests for such certificates in respect of individuals who have criminal records will not be restricted to police officers and are intended to help employers and others 'vet' applications for certain posts or positions.

The 1997 Act creates offences in relation to false information and provides for a Code of Practice but again the potential erosion of fundamental freedoms has created some anxiety among commentators.

CHAPTER TWO

POLICE POWERS

2.1 Introduction

In one of the most famous judgments concerning the freedoms enjoyed by people in England and Wales, Sir Robert Megarry pointed out that the UK is '. . . not a country where everything is forbidden except what is expressly permitted: it is a country where everything is permitted except what is expressly forbidden' (*Malone* v *Metropolitan Police Commissioner (No. 2)* [1979] 2 All ER 620 at 629).

The effect of the 'permissive' nature of our law means that the police, like anyone else, must be able to point to a specific authority or a power before they can interfere with the rights or freedoms of citizens. Such interference may come in the form of preventing people from going about their lawful business, entering their property or searching and seizing their belongings; ultimately, it may involve causing them injury or loss of life.

Police officers are entrusted with many powers and privileges. The most important of these powers, both practically and constitutionally, are the powers of arrest, search, entry and seizure. All of these powers can be separated into those authorised by warrant and those which can be executed without warrant.

These powers can come from a number of sources and this chapter sets out the main authorities. There are other sources of such powers, for instance those relating to drug trafficking and asset tracing which are not addressed in this Manual.

Using powers improperly can result in officers and their employers being liable, both at civil and criminal law; it can also lead to evidence being excluded and otherwise meritorious prosecutions being dropped. Even where police powers are exercised *lawfully*, the manner or frequency of their use might be perceived by the community as a source of oppression and discrimination, leading to a reduction in confidence in the police and the creation of an atmosphere of distrust. The risk of lawfully employed police powers being perceived in this way was highlighted very clearly in the Stephen Lawrence Inquiry (Cm 4262-I, see para. 46.31 and recommendation 61) (see also PACE Code A, Note 1AA).

It has been suggested that a further way to achieve even-handedness would be to adopt the key principles from the human rights legislation when deciding how and when to use such powers. These key principles require that any measures adopted:

- are proportionate and relevant to the threat or problem that the police officers are legitimately trying to address;

- involve the minimum number and extent of measures necessary to achieve their object;

- have a legal foundation and offer a form of remedy or redress to the person affected.

These principles, although not directly imposed upon the powers set out in this chapter, will become increasingly important once the Human Rights Act 1998 comes into force.

Where a police officer acts on the authority of a properly sworn warrant issued by a magistrate, he/she is protected against legal action by the Constables Protection Act 1750. This protection does not apply where the warrant has been issued by the High Court.

2.2   Acting Ranks

Many of the police powers considered in this — and subsequent — chapters are restricted to officers holding particular ranks. In particular, there are occasions where the Police and Criminal Evidence Act 1984 requires officers of certain ranks to perform roles. The 1984 Act recognises that there may be occasions where officers of the appropriate rank are not readily available and so in limited circumstances allows officers of a lower rank to perform their roles.

Section 107 of the Police and Criminal Evidence Act 1984 sets out occasions where an officer of a lower rank can perform the functions of that required by a higher rank.

Section 107 provides that:

> (1)   For the purpose of any provision of this Act or any other Act under which a power in respect of the investigation of offences or the treatment of persons in police custody is exercisable only by or with the authority of a police officer of at least the rank of superintendent, an officer of the rank of chief inspector shall be treated as holding the rank of superintendent if he has been authorised by an officer of at least the rank of chief superintendent to exercise the power or, as the case may be, to give his authority for its exercise.
> (2)   For the purpose of any provision of this Act or any other Act under which such a power is exercisable only by or with the authority of an officer of at least the rank of inspector, an officer of the rank of sergeant shall be treated as holding the rank of inspector if he has been authorised by an officer of at least the rank of chief superintendent to exercise the power or, as the case may be, to give his authority for its exercise.

The only mention of officers performing the higher rank of sergeant in the Police and Criminal Evidence Act 1984 is to be found in s. 36. Section 36 provides that:

> (3)   No officer may be appointed a custody officer unless he is of at least the rank of sergeant.
> (4)   An officer of any rank may perform the functions of a custody officer at a designated police station if a custody officer is not readily available to perform them.

However in *Vince and Another* v *Chief Constable of Dorset Police* [1993] 1 WLR 415 Steyn LJ made it clear that s. 36(4) should only be an exception:

For my part I would start from the provisional premise that the legislature intended to introduce an effective system for the care and protection of detained suspects by custody officers. And on this basis section 36(4), which allows an independent officer of any rank to perform the function of a custody officer at a designated police station 'if a custody officer is not readily available to perform them', can be viewed as a concession to practicality in the light of the problems which will inevitably occur in a busy police station. In other words, there is much to be said for the view that it was not intended that chief constables would be entitled to arrange matters so that as a matter of routine officers below the rank of sergeant performed the functions of custody officers.

2.2.1 Temporary Promotion

Regulation 8 of the Police (Promotion) Regulations 1996 (SI 1996 No. 1685) deals with temporary promotion. Regulation 8 provides that:

> *A member of a police force who is required to perform the duties of a higher rank may be promoted temporarily thereto, provided that, in the case of promotion to the rank of sergeant or inspector, he is qualified therefor under regulation 4.*

2.3 Stop and Search

In addition to the many specific powers provided under some Acts of Parliament (**see appendix 1**), the general power for police officers to stop and search people and vehicles comes from the Police and Criminal Evidence Act 1984 (PACE). Both the powers to stop and search below and those authorised by most other statutes must be carried out in accordance with Code A of the PACE Codes of Practice (**see appendix 1**). (There are exceptions for certain powers under the Aviation Security Act 1982 and those exercised by statutory undertakers.)

A number of important powers to stop and search people and vehicles are covered in other parts of this Manual.

2.3.1 Power to Stop and Search

One of the most controversial of all the powers available to police officers is probably the power to stop and search members of the community. As discussed above, the fact that a power is lawfully available does not necessarily mean that its use is appropriate in every case. Parliament has given these discretionary powers to constables and it is the responsibility of each individual officer to determine, not only whether a power *exists* in the circumstances, but also whether its use best serves the overall objectives of his/her police service. The law regulating these searches is set out under Part I of the Police and Criminal Evidence Act 1984 and Code A of the PACE Codes of Practice (**see appendix 1**).

Section 1 of the Police and Criminal Evidence Act 1984 provides that:

> *(1)   A constable may exercise any power conferred by this section—*
> *(a)   in any place to which at the time when he proposes to exercise the power the public or any section of the public has access, on payment or otherwise, as of right or by virtue of express or implied permission; or*
> *(b)   in any other place to which people have ready access at the time when he proposes to exercise the power but which is not a dwelling.*
> *(2)   Subject to subsection (3) to (5) below, a constable—*
> *(a)   may search—*

> (i)   any person or vehicle;
> (ii)   anything which is in or on a vehicle,
> for stolen or prohibited articles [or any article to which subsection (8A) below applies]; and
> (b)   may detain a person or vehicle for the purpose of such a search.

Keynote

The power is restricted to those places set out in s. 1(1)(a) or (b). This does not mean that the search itself must be carried out there, in fact Code A, para. 3.5 requires certain searches to be carried out away from public view.

Code A specifies that its provisions do not prevent the routine searching of people — with their consent or as a condition of entry — on their entering sports grounds (Note 1D). It also leaves open the possibility of conducting 'voluntary' searches in the street. Any such search, however, should be used with considerable caution given the general caveats on searching above. Moreover, where the person to be searched is a juvenile or other person incapable of giving informed consent, Code A, Note 1E states that a voluntary search should not be made.

The power only applies where the officer has 'reasonable grounds for suspecting' that he/she will find stolen or prohibited articles or articles falling under s. 139 of the Criminal Justice Act 1988 (bladed or sharply pointed articles; **see chapter 6**) (s. 1(3) of the 1984 Act).

Whether there were reasonable grounds for suspecting that the relevant articles would be found during the search is a question of fact to be decided in the light of all the circumstances. It must be shown that the grounds on which the officer acted would have been enough to give rise to that suspicion in a 'reasonable person' (*Nakkuda Ali* v *Jayaratne* [1951] AC 66). However, the existence of such circumstances or evidence is not enough. The officer must actually *have* a 'reasonable suspicion' that the relevant articles will be found. If, in fact the officer knows that there is little or no likelihood of finding the articles, the power cannot be used (*R* v *Harrison* [1938] 3 All ER 134).

'Suspicion' requires a lower degree of certainty than *belief*. The distinction between the two expressions has been held to be a significant one, intended by Parliament (see *Baker* v *Oxford* [1980] RTR 315). In that particular case — involving road traffic offences — the court held that the statutory requirement for a reasonable *belief* imposed a greater degree of certainty on the officers concerned. Accordingly, police officers using powers that impose such an extra requirement must be prepared to justify their belief. Suspicion has been described by Lord Devlin as '. . . a state of conjecture or surmise when proof is lacking' (*Shaaben Bin Hussein* v *Chong Fook Kam* [1970] AC 492).

That suspicion can be based on any evidence, even if the evidence itself would be inadmissible at trial (e.g. because it is hearsay (**see Evidence and Procedure, chapter 11**). Therefore it can arise from information given to the officer by a colleague, an informant or even anonymously (see *O'Hara* v *Chief Constable of the Royal Ulster Constabulary* [1997] 1 All ER 129). Very recently the Court of Appeal has reiterated the principle in *Hussein* (above) that an arrest of a person mistakenly thought to have been involved in an offence is not necessarily unlawful. It went on to say that a state of mind of 'being suspicious but uncertain' would provide reasonable grounds to support an arrest where reasonable suspicion was required (*Parker (Graham Charles)* v *Chief Constable of Hampshire Constabulary*, *The Times*, 25 June 1999; defendant seen in a car used in an earlier shooting incident in another part of the country).

Reasonable suspicion can never be founded on the basis of purely personal factors such as a person's colour, age or hairstyle (Code A, para. 1.7) and it is the duty of supervisory officers to be alert to this when checking stop and search records (see Code A, Note 4DA). However, Code A, para. 1.7AA makes provision for the searching of members of gangs or groups who habitually carry:

- knives unlawfully or
- weapons or
- controlled drugs

and wear a distinctive item of clothing or other means of identifying themselves with such a gang or group.

A person or vehicle may only be detained for such time as is reasonably necessary to permit a search to be carried out either at the place where the person or vehicle was first detained or nearby (s. 2(8) and Code A, para. 3.3).

The co-operation of the person must be sought in every case and, though force may ultimately be used, it should be viewed as a last resort and used only where the person has shown that he/she is unwilling to co-operate or he/she resists (Code A, para. 3.2).

If, in the course of a s. 1 search, the officer does find a stolen, prohibited or 'section 139' article, he/she may seize it (s. 1(6)).

If there are any grounds to suspect that the person has committed any offence, he/she must be cautioned before any questions are put to him/her about his/her involvement in the offence(s) if any answers, *or his/her silence*, is to be used in evidence (Code C, para. 10.1). For a full discussion of these provisions, **see Evidence and Procedure, chapter 11**).

The power under s. 1 does not authorise the officer to stop a vehicle (s. 2(9)(b)). For the power of police officers in uniform to stop vehicles, **see Road Traffic**. Compare this aspect of the stop and search power with that provided by s. 60 of the Criminal Justice and Public Order Act 1994 below.

Section 1 of the 1984 Act also states:

> (7)   *An article is prohibited for the purposes of this Part of this Act if it is—*
>   (a)   *an offensive weapon; or*
>   (b)   *an article—*
>   (i)   *made or adapted for use in the course of or in connection with an offence to which this sub-paragraph applies; or*
>   (ii)   *intended by the person having it with him for such use by him or by some other person.*
> (8)   *The offences to which subsection (7)(b)(1) above applies are—*
>   (a)   *burglary;*
>   (b)   *theft;*
>   (c)   *offences under section 12 of the Theft Act 1968 (taking motor vehicle or other conveyance without authority); and*
>   (d)   *offences under section 15 of that Act (obtaining property by deception).*
> (8A)   *This subsection applies to any article in relation to which a person has committed, or is committing or is going to commit an offence under section 139 of the Criminal Justice Act 1988.*
> (9)   *In this Part of this Act 'offensive weapon' means any article—*
>   (a)   *made or adapted for use for causing injury to persons; or*
>   (b)   *intended by the person having it with him for such use by him or by some other person.*

Keynote

For a full discussion on the law relating to offensive weapons and bladed/sharply pointed articles, **see chapter 6**.

For the offences listed at s. 1(8), **see Crime**.

Section 1 of the 1984 Act also states:

> (4)   If a person is in a garden or yard occupied with and used for the purposes of a dwelling or on other land so occupied and used, a constable may not search him in the exercise of the power conferred by this section unless the constable has reasonable grounds for believing—
>> (a)   that he does not reside in the dwelling; and
>> (b)   that he is not in the place in question with the express or implied permission of a person who resides in the dwelling.
> (5)   If a vehicle is in a garden or yard occupied with and used for the purposes of a dwelling or on other land so occupied and used, a constable may not search the vehicle or anything in or on it in the exercise of the power conferred by this section unless he has reasonable grounds for believing—
>> (a)   that the person in charge of the vehicle does not reside in the dwelling; and
>> (b)   that the vehicle is not in the place in question with the express or implied permission of a person who resides in the dwelling.

Keynote

If the person to be searched is in a garden, yard or other land occupied with and used as part of a dwelling, the power to search will not apply unless the officer has 'reasonable grounds for believing' that the person does not live there *and* that he/she is not there with the permission (express or implied) of any person who does live there.

If the garden or yard is attached to a house that is not so 'occupied', the restriction at s. 1(4) would not appear to apply.

Similar restrictions are placed on the searching of vehicles found in such places by s. 1(5). For the meaning of 'in charge' of a vehicle, **see Road Traffic, chapter** 1). For these purposes 'vehicle' include vessels, aircraft and hovercraft (s. 2(10) of the 1984 Act).

2.3.2   The Search

Section 2 of the Police and Criminal Evidence Act 1984 provides that:

> (1)   A constable who detains a person or vehicle in the exercise—
>> (a)   of the power conferred by section 1 above; or
>> (b)   of any other power—
>>> (i)   to search a person without first arresting him; or
>>> (ii)   to search a vehicle without making an arrest,
> need not conduct a search if it appears to him subsequently—
>>> (i)   that no search is required; or
>>> (ii)   that a search is impracticable.
> (2)   If a constable contemplates a search, other than a search of an unattended vehicle, in the exercise—
>> (a)   of the power conferred by section 1 above; or
>> (b)   of any other power, except the power conferred by section 6 below and the power conferred by section 27(2) of the Aviation Security Act 1982—
>>> (i)   to search a person without first arresting him; or

(ii)   to search a vehicle without making an arrest,
it shall be his duty, subject to subsection (4) below, to take reasonable steps before he commences the search to bring to the attention of the appropriate person—
   (i)   if the constable is not in uniform, documentary evidence that he is a constable; and
   (ii)   whether he is in uniform or not, the matters specified in subsection (3) below;
and the constable shall not commence the search until he has performed that duty.
   (3)   The matters referred to in subsection (2)(ii) above are—
   (a)   the constable's name and the name of the police station to which he is attached;
   (b)   the object of the proposed search;
   (c)   the constable's grounds for proposing to make it; and
   (d)   the effect of section 3(7) or (8) below, as may be appropriate.

Keynote

Having stopped a person for the purposes of searching them, there is no requirement for the officer to conduct the search if it appears that to do so is not necessary or that it is impracticable.

In searching:

- a person or a vehicle that has someone in charge of it

- under any power other than those available to 'statutory undertakers' or under the Aviation Security Act 1982, s. 27(2) and
- without first making an arrest

the officer carrying out the search must *take reasonable steps* to bring the matters at s. 2(3)(a) to (d) to the person's attention *before starting the search*. This information must be given whether it is requested or not. Whether reasonable steps have been taken to communicate information will ultimately be a question of fact for the court to decide and what is 'reasonable' will vary with the particular circumstances of each search (e.g. what is reasonable outside a busy city centre nightclub may well be different from that which is required on a rural public footpath). If there is any doubt as to the person's ability to understand what is being said, the guidance at Code A, para. 2.7 should be followed.

In enquiries related to the investigation of terrorism the requirement for an officer to give his/her name is removed (see Code A, para. 2.5).

The 'effect of section 3(7) or (8)' referred to in s. 2(3)(d) means the person's entitlement to a copy of any search record made.

If the person does not appear to understand what is being said, or there is *any doubt* about his/her ability to understand English, the officer must comply with the provisions of Code A, para. 2.7.

In carrying out a search, an officer is not authorised by s. 1 to require the person to remove any clothing in public other than his/her outer coat, jacket or gloves (s. 2(9)). However, for the power to require the removal of face coverings **see para. 2.3.5**. The powers of search under the Prevention of Terrorism (Temporary Provisions) Act 1989, ss. 13A and 13B (**see para. 2.3.6**) permit the removal of headgear and footwear (see also Code A, para. 3.5).

The 'appropriate person' is the person to be searched or the person in charge of the vehicle to be searched (s. 2(5)).

Unattended Vehicles

In the case of unattended vehicles, s. 2 of the Police and Criminal Evidence Act 1984 states:

> *(6) On completing a search of an unattended vehicle or anything in or on such a vehicle in the exercise of any such power as is mentioned in subsection (2) above a constable shall leave a notice—*
> *(a) stating that he has searched it;*
> *(b) giving the name of the police station to which he is attached;*
> *(c) stating that an application for compensation for any damage caused by the search maybe made to that police station; and*
> *(d) stating the effect of section 3(8) below.*
> *(7) The constable shall leave the notice inside the vehicle unless it is not reasonably practicable to do so without damaging the vehicle.*

2.3.3   Action After Search

Section 3 of the Police and Criminal Evidence Act 1984 makes certain requirements following any search of a person or vehicle (other than one not covered by s. 1 (**see para. 2.3.2**). The first requirement is that the officer makes a written record of the search, unless it is not practicable to do so (s. 3(1)). The word 'practicable', which is used in many statutes, has been accepted as meaning 'possible to be accomplished with known means or resources' (see *Adsett v K & L Steelfounders* [1953] 1 All ER 97). If it is not practicable to make a written record (i.e. because the search is carried out as part of a large-scale public order operation or because the prevailing conditions do not allow it), the officer must make the record as soon as practicable after the search has been completed (s. 3(2)).

The search record should contain the person's name but, if the officer does not know the name of the person, he/she cannot detain that person simply to find it out (s. 3(3)) and a description should be recorded instead (s. 3(4)). The record must also contain the information set out at Code A, para. 4.5.

A record of a vehicle search must include a description of the vehicle (s. 3(5)) and, if a person is in a vehicle and both are searched, only one search record need be completed (Code A, para. 4.6). (Ordinarily there must be one record for every search made.)

It has been held that a failure to make a record of a search does not thereby render the search unlawful (*Basher v DPP* [1993] COD 372).

Note 4DA is particularly important in relation to the duties of police supervisors and managers. It states:

> *4DA   Supervising officers, in monitoring the exercise of officers' stop and search powers, should consider in particular whether there is any evidence that officers are exercising their discretion on the basis of stereotyped images of certain persons or groups contrary to the provisions of this code. It is important that any such evidence should be addressed. Supervising officers should take account of the information about the ethnic origin of those stopped and searched which is collected and published under section 95 of the Criminal Justice Act 1991.*

Section 3(6) of the Police and Criminal Evidence Act 1984 states:

> *(6) The record of a search of a person or a vehicle—*
> *(a) shall state—*
> *(i) the object of the search;*

(ii)   the grounds for making it;
(iii)   the date and time when it was made;
(iv)   the place where it was made;
(v)   whether anything, and if so what, was found;
(vi)   whether any, and if so what, injury to a person or damage to property appears to the constable to have resulted from the search; and
(b)   shall identify the constable making it.

Keynote

Where a search record has been made, the person searched, or the person who was in charge of any vehicle that was searched, will be entitled to a copy of the record if he/she requests one within 12 months (s. 3(7), (8) and (9)).

Under the provisions of s. 2(3) (**see para. 2.3.2**), a person must be advised of his/her entitlement to a copy of the relevant search record unless it appears to the officer searching that it will not be practicable to make the record (s. 2(4)).

The requirements of s. 3 will apply to the searches of vehicles, vessels, aircraft and hovercraft (s. 3(10)).

2.3.4   Road Checks

The power to stop vehicles generally is provided under s. 163 of the Road Traffic Act 1988 (officers exercising the power must be in uniform; **see Road Traffic, chapter 10**). Having caused a vehicle to stop, there are then certain other powers which may be employed by a police officer (or other authorised people).

Among those powers are the powers set out in PACE 1984, s. 4 in relation to 'road checks'.

A road check is where the power under s. 163 of the Road Traffic Act 198 8 is used in any locality in such a way as to stop all vehicles or vehicles selected by any criterion (s. 4(2) of the 1984 Act). That general power for uniformed officers to stop vehicles might be used in a particular geographical area to stop all vehicles on the road or all vehicles of a certain make, model or colour, or only those vehicles containing a certain number of adult occupants. In all these cases, there would be a 'road check' for the purposes of s. 4.

Section 4 states:

(1)   This section shall have effect in relation to the conduct of road checks by police officers for the purpose of ascertaining whether a vehicle is carrying—
(a)   a person who has committed an offence other than a road traffic offence or a vehicle excise offence;
(b)   a person who is a witness to such an offence;
(c)   a person intending to commit such an offence; or
(d)   a person who is unlawfully at large.
(2)   . . .
(3)   Subject to subsection (5) below, there may only be such a road check if a police officer of the rank of superintendent or above authorises it in writing.
(4)   An officer may only authorise a road check under subsection (3) above—
(a)   for the purpose specified in subsection (1)(a) above, if he has reasonable grounds—
(i)   for believing that the offence is a serious arrestable offence; and

    (ii)   for suspecting that the person is, or is about to be, in the locality in which vehicles would be stopped if the road check were authorised;
    (b)   for the purpose specified in subsection (1)(b) above, if he has reasonable grounds for believing that the offence is a serious arrestable offence;
    (c)   for the purpose specified in subsection (1)(c) above, if he has reasonable grounds—
    (i)   for believing that the offence would be a serious arrestable offence; and
    (ii)   for suspecting that the person is, or is about to be, in the locality in which vehicles would be stopped if the road check were authorised;
    (d)   for the purpose specified in subsection (1)(d) above, if he has reasonable grounds for suspecting that the person is, or is about to be, in that locality.

Keynote

Road checks may only be authorised for the purposes set out at s. 4(4) and for the duration set out at s. 4(11) (**see below**). They must, subject to s. 4(5) (**see below**), be authorised in writing by an officer of superintendent rank or above (s. 4(3)).

For the 'serious arrestable offences' **see para. 2.5.1**.

The locality in which vehicles are to be stopped must also be specified (s. 4(10)).

If it appears to an officer below the rank of superintendent that a road check is required as a matter of urgency for one of the purposes in s. 4(1), he/she may authorise such a road check (s. 4(5)). What amounts to 'urgency' is not defined, but it would appear to be a somewhat subjective requirement based on the apprehension of the officer concerned. Where such an urgent road check is authorised, the authorising officer must, *as soon as is practicable to do so*, make a written record of the time at which the authorisation is given and must cause an officer of superintendent rank or above to be informed of the authorisation (s. 4(6) and (7)). Where this occurs, the superintendent (or more senior officer) may authorise, *in writing*, that the road check continue (s. 4(8)). If the officer considers that the road check should not continue, he/she must make a written record that it took place as well as the purpose for which it took place (including the relevant 'serious arrestable offence' (s. 4(9) and (14)).

Every written authorisation for a road check must include:

* the name of the authorising officer
* the purpose of the road check — including any relevant 'serious arrestable offence'
* the locality in which vehicles are to be stopped.

(s. 4(13)).

Duration of Road Check

Section 4 of the 1984 Act goes on to state:

    (11)   An officer giving an authorisation under this section, other than an authorisation under subsection (5) above—
    (a)   shall specify a period, not exceeding seven days, during which the road check may continue; and
    (b)   may direct that the road check—
    (i)   shall be continuous; or
    (ii)   shall be conducted at specified times,
during that period.
    (12)   If it appears to an officer of the rank of superintendent or above that a road check ought to continue beyond the period for which it has been authorised he may, from time to time, in writing specify a further period, not exceeding seven days, during which it may continue.

Keynote

In recording the purpose for the road check under s. 4(13), the officer must specify a period not exceeding seven days during which the road check is to run.

The road check may run continuously through that specified period or it may be carried out at specific times.

The road check may be extended — in writing — a number of times for further periods up to a total of seven days by a superintendent if it appears to him/her that it 'ought' to continue. There is no restriction of 'reasonableness' or requirement for the existence of particular grounds here and it seems that the judgment may be an entirely subjective one by the superintendent.

Where a vehicle is stopped during a road check, the person in charge of it is entitled to a written statement of the purpose of that road check if he/she applies for one no later than the end of the 12 month period from the day on which the vehicle was stopped (s. 4(15)).

2.3.5 Criminal Justice and Public Order Act 1994

In addition to the powers above, police officers may stop and search vehicles under the Criminal Justice and Public Order Act 1994.

Section 60 of the 1994 Act provides that:

> (1) If a police officer of or above the rank of inspector reasonably believes—
>> (a) that incidents involving serious violence may take place in any locality in his area, and that it is expedient to give an authorisation under this section to prevent their occurrence, or
>> (b) that persons are carrying dangerous instruments or offensive weapons in any locality in his police area without good reason,
>
> he may give an authorisation that the powers conferred by this section shall be exercisable at any place within that locality for a specified period not exceeding 24 hours.
>
> (2) (repealed)
> (3) . . .
> (3A) . . .
> (4) This section confers on any constable in uniform power—
>> (a) to stop any pedestrian and search him or anything carried by him for offensive weapons or dangerous instruments;
>> (b) to stop any vehicle and search the vehicle, its driver and any passenger for offensive weapons or dangerous instruments.

Keynote

This power was formerly restricted to superintendents and above.

Section 60(1)(a) has a generally preventive function in relation to the apprehension of incidents that will involve serious violence. Section 60(1)(b) however, is a much broader provision triggered by the officer's 'reasonable belief' that people are carrying dangerous instruments or offensive weapons. Serious violence is not defined in the 1994 Act but, although violence could relate to property, the whole tenor of the section suggests that it is aimed at tackling violence against people.

'Dangerous instruments' are bladed or sharply pointed instruments, while offensive weapons have the same meaning as that under s. 1(9) of the Police and Criminal

Evidence Act 1984 (**see para 2.3.1**). For a full discussion of the law relating to weapons generally, **see chapter 6**.

Confusingly, for the purposes of s. 60, 'carrying' will mean 'having in your possession' (s. 60(11A)), a much wider meaning than carrying usually conveys (**see chapter 6 and also Crime, chapter 12**). Why the legislators did not simply use the term 'possession' is not clear.

The person authorising the exercise of the powers under s. 60(1)(a) must reasonably *believe* that it is expedient to do so in order to prevent the occurrence of the incidents involving serious violence.

If it appears to an officer of or above the rank of superintendent that:

- having regard to offences that have, or are reasonably suspected to have been, committed
- in connection with any activity falling within the authorisation and
- it is expedient to do so

he/she may authorise the continuation of the authority to exercise the powers under s. 60(1) for a further period of 24 hours (s. 60(3)).

If the authorisation is given by an inspector, he/she must cause an officer of or above the rank of superintendent to be informed *as soon as it is practicable to do so* (s. 60(3A)). Presumably this requirement does not apply to *chief* inspectors though there is no reason why the authorisation should not be reinforced in such a case by advising a superintendent of its existence.

The authorisation must be in writing, signed by the officer giving it, and must specify:

- the grounds on which it is given
- the locality in which it is to operate and
- the period during which the powers are exercisable

and any direction for the authorisation to continue must also be given in writing at the time or reduced into writing as soon as it is practicable to do so (s. 60(9)). Such a direction for the authorisation to continue may only be given once; thereafter a new authorisation must be sought (Code A, Note 1F).

If the power is to be used in response to a threat or incident that straddles police force areas, the relevant authority will have to be given by an officer from each of the forces concerned (Code A, Note 1G).

A significant difference between this power and the general powers of stop and search (which are not affected by the granting of this power (s. 60(12)) is that it does not require any grounds at all for the officer to suspect that the person/vehicle is carrying offensive weapons or dangerous instruments (s. 60(5)).

A further difference is that the power under s. 60 authorises officers in uniform to stop vehicles in order to search them and their occupants (but not in relation to the removal and seizure of face coverings; see below).

The power allows the stopping and searching of pedestrians, vehicles (including caravans, aircraft, vessels and hovercraft) and passengers. If a dangerous instrument or anything reasonably suspected to be an 'offensive weapon' (**see chapter 6**) is found during the search, the officer may seize it (s. 60(6)). It also allows for the removal and seizure of face coverings (see below). For the provisions governing the disposal of items seized under s. 60 see the easy to remember Police (Retention and Disposal of Items Seized under Section 60 of the Criminal Justice and Public Order Act 1994) Regulations 1999 (SI 1999 No. 269).

Failing to stop (or to stop a vehicle) when required to do so under this power is a summary offence punishable with one month's imprisonment and/or a fine (s. 60(8)). A power of arrest may be available under the legislation dealing with obstruction of a police officer (Police Act 1996, s. 89; **see Crime, chapter 8**).

Failing to comply with a requirement to remove a face covering (under s. 60(8)(b) is an arrestable offence (see below).

Where a vehicle is stopped under s. 60, the *driver* (as opposed to the person 'in charge'; **see paras 2.3.1 and 2.3.4**) is entitled to a written statement *that the vehicle was so stopped* (as opposed to the 'purpose' for which it was stopped; **see para. 2.3.4**). That statement must be provided if the driver applies for one no later than the end of the 12 month period from the day on which he/she was stopped (s. 60(10)). A person who is searched under this section is also entitled to a statement stating that he/she was so searched if he/she applies for one no later than the end of the 12-month period from the day on which he/she was stopped (s. 60(10A)).

Powers to Require Removal of Items Concealing Identity

Section 60(4A) of the Criminal Justice and Public Order Act 1994 states that:

> (4A)   This section also confers on any constable in uniform power—
> (a)   to require any person to remove any item which the constable reasonably believes that person is wearing wholly or mainly for the purpose of concealing his identity;
> (b)   to seize any item which the constable reasonably believes any person intends to wear wholly or mainly for that purpose.

Keynote

This section gives police officers in uniform two new powers once authorisation under s. 60 has been given. These are:

- the power to require the *removal* of any item that the constable reasonably believes is being worn wholly or mainly for the purpose of concealing identity; and

- the power to *seize* such an item if the constable reasonably believes that *any person intends* to wear it wholly or mainly for that purpose.

It does not provide a power to *search* for such items. This presents a potential problem if the person removes the mask or item and hides it about his/her person before it can be seized. Clearly if such an item is found during a lawful search for other articles (say under s. 60(4)) which does not require any 'reasonable belief' by the officer, face coverings and masks could then be seized under s. 60(4A)(b).

Unlike the other provisions in s. 60(4), the power under s. 60(4A) does not provide a specific power to stop vehicles and the general power under the Road Traffic Act 1988, s. 163 (**see Road Traffic, chapter 10**) must be used if necessary.

The wording of the power of seizure suggests that the item can be seized before it has been worn and that the intended wearer of the item need not be the same person who is in possession of it at the time.

Failing to comply with a requirement under this section is an arrestable offence under s. 24(2)(o) of the Police and Criminal Evidence Act 1984 (**see para. 2.5.1**).

The expression 'item' is very wide and would clearly include balaclavas, scarves and crash helmets. It is not specifically restricted to face coverings and would appear to extend to anything that could be worn wholly or mainly for the purpose of concealing identity (e.g. where offenders swap clothing after an offence). Although the purpose of the legislation is primarily to ensure that people are not allowed to commit offences anonymously in situations of public disorder, it is unclear whether other methods that hinder identification — such as face paint in the colours of football clubs or nations — would be caught by this new power.

As with many other such powers, discretion is given to police officers in how and when they exercise the powers under s. 60(4A). It may be that a person's reason for wishing to conceal his/her identity is not in order to commit offences anonymously; he/she may be involved in lawful picketing (**see chapter 7**) or in peaceful protest against some other activity such as fox hunting or vivisection but does not wish to be identified in the press. More sensitively, there may be religious or cultural reasons why a person is wearing a particular item the *effect*, rather than the *purpose* of which is to conceal his/her identity and great care will have to be taken by individual officers in using these powers under such circumstances (see Code A, Note 1AA).

Offence — Failing to Comply with Requirement to Remove Items — Criminal Justice and Public Order Act 1994, s. 60(8)(b)
Triable summarily. One month's imprisonment and/or fine.
(*Arrestable offence*)

Section 60 of the Criminal Justice and Public Order Act 1994 provides that:

> (8)   A person who fails—
>   (a)   . . .
>   (b)   to remove any item worn by him
> when required to do so by a constable in the exercise of his powers under this section [commits an offence]

Keynote

The wording of this offence is absolute. There is no requirement that the person failed *without reasonable excuse* or *without good reason* etc., simply that he/she failed to remove an item worn by him/her. However, it must be shown that:

- the requirement was made (and presumably understood)
- it was made by a police officer in uniform
- in the exercise of powers authorised under s. 60 and
- in the reasonable belief that the person was wearing the item wholly or mainly for the purpose of concealing his/her identity.

This offence is made an arrestable offence by s. 24(2)(o) of the Police and Criminal Evidence Act 1984 (**see para. 2.5.1**).

Retention and Disposal of Seized Articles

A new s. 60A is inserted into the Criminal Justice and Public Order Act 1994 (by s. 26 of the Crime and Disorder Act 1998) which empowers the Secretary of State to make regulations for the retention and disposal of 'any things' seized by a constable under s. 60 (see SI 1999 No. 269).

2.3.6   Terrorism

Other powers to stop and search are provided under the Prevention of Terrorism (Temporary Provisions) Act 1989, s. 13A. Where it appears to any officer of or above the rank of assistant chief constable/commander (in relation to provincial forces and the Metropolitan/City of London police respectively) that it is expedient to do so, in order to prevent certain acts of terrorism, he/she may authorise the use of stop and search powers in a locality for a period not exceeding 28 days (s. 13A(1)). The exercise of these powers may be extended by an officer of the specified rank(s) from time to time for a further period of up to 28 days (s. 13A(8)).

These powers are subject to the provisions of Code A. Where an officer gives authorisation under s. 13B (**see below**), he/she must take *immediate* steps to send a copy of the authorisation to the National Joint Unit, Metropolitan Police Special Branch who in turn will forward it to the Secretary of State. The Secretary of State will then, within 48 hours of the authorisation being made, decide whether the authorisation should be confirmed, cancelled or altered (Code A, Note 1I).

As with the powers under s. 60 of the Criminal Justice and Public Order Act 1994 (**see para. 2.3.5**), s. 13A allows officers in uniform to stop vehicles and search them and any occupants. The object of the search will be to find articles of a kind which could be used for a purpose connected with the commission, preparation or instigation of certain acts of terrorism.

The Prevention of Terrorism (Additional Powers) Act 1996 adds similar powers in these circumstances for the stopping and searching of pedestrians and anything carried by them (s. 13B).

Again, as with the powers under the Criminal Justice and Public Order Act 1994, there is no requirement that the officers carrying out the search have any reasonable grounds to suspect that they will find such articles.

Section 13A or 13B searches carry similar entitlements for people who have been stopped/searched under these powers to request a statement to that effect.

Failing to stop when required to do so, or obstructing an officer using this power, is a summary offence punishable with six months' imprisonment and/or a fine.

Authorisation may be given orally but, where this is done, it must be confirmed in writing as soon as practicable by the person giving the authority.

In addition, superintendents may impose cordons on specified areas; to require people to leave that area and to search premises and people found within that area (see sch. 6A to the 1989 Act).

2.4   Powers of Arrest

An arrest involves depriving a person of his/her liberty to go where he/she pleases (*Lewis* v *Chief Constable of South Wales Constabulary* [1991] 1 All ER 206). In a criminal context an arrest will usually be to answer an alleged charge, but occasionally arrests may be preventive (such as where a person is arrested in connection with a breach of the peace; **see chapter 4**), it may be to take samples or fingerprints (see **Evidence and Procedure, chapter 16**), or it may be to return someone to prison or bring them before a court.

Every arrest must be lawful, that is, the person carrying it out must be able to point to some legal authority which allows it; otherwise an arrest will be unlawful and actionable as an assault or a civil wrong (see *Spicer* v *Holt* [1977] AC 987).

The source of a power of arrest may come from:

- The nature of the offence (i.e. an 'arrestable offence'; **see para. 2.5.1**).

- The conditions at the time (allowing an arrest under PACE 1984, s. 25; **see para. 2.5.3**).

- The provisions of the particular Act (e.g. the Public Order Act 1986; **see chapter 4**).

- The provisions of an order (e.g. a court order or a warrant).

- Common law (e.g. breach of the peace; **see chapter 4**).

Merely being told to arrest someone by a more senior officer is *not* a reasonable ground for doing so (see *O'Hara* v *Chief Constable of the Royal Ulster Constabulary* [1997] 1 All ER 129).

Any lawful arrest must be made for a proper purpose. Such a purpose may be in order to bring the person to a police station to subject them to the formal atmosphere there (*Holgate-Mohammed* v *Duke* [1984] AC 437) or to obtain a confession even after a complainant has withdrawn his/her initial complaint (*Plange* v *Chief Constable of Humberside*, *The Times*, 23 March 1992). Occasionally, officers investigating one offence may find that they have insufficient evidence to arrest for that particular offence, but that the circumstances would allow them to arrest the person for some other offence.

The practice of arresting someone on a 'holding' offence was accepted by the Court of Appeal in *R* v *Chalkley* [1998] 3 WLR 146 *provided the arresting officers had reasonable grounds for suspecting that the person had actually committed that offence.* If that suspicion is present then the fact that the officers making the arrest are doing so with the intention of investigating another, more serious offence, does not render the arrest unlawful. If, however, there are no such grounds to suspect that the person had in fact committed the offence, or the officers know at the time of the arrest that there is no possibility of the person actually being charged with it, the arrest will be unlawful.

Section 30(7) of the Police and Criminal Evidence Act 1984 (in keeping with common law) requires that, if the grounds for detaining a person cease to exist before reaching a police station, the person must be released (**see below**). This is particularly important in relation to arrests made under the 'general' conditions under s. 25 (**see para. 2.5.3**).

Any unlawful arrest will also carry implications for the officer if he/she is assaulted during the course of making it (**see Crime, chapter 8**).

2.4.1 Reasonable Grounds

Many — though not all — powers of arrest carry some requirement that the arresting officer be acting on 'reasonable suspicion' or has 'reasonable cause' to suspect/believe the existence of certain facts. As those requirements relate to the suspected/believed existence of facts rather than the state of the law, a police officer's mistaken belief that he/she had a power of arrest where in fact he/she did not may make the subsequent arrest unlawful (see e.g. *Todd* v *DPP* [1996] Crim LR 344). An officer's reasonable cause to believe that he/she has a power of arrest is not the same as a reasonable cause to believe that someone has committed an offence which carries a power of arrest.

Tests of reasonableness impose an element of objectivity and the courts will consider whether, in the circumstances, a reasonable and sober person might have formed a similar view to that of the officer. Failing to follow up an obvious line of enquiry (e.g. as to the ownership of property found in the possession of the defendant) may well provide grounds for challenging the exercise of a power of arrest (see, e.g. *Castorina* v *Chief Constable of Surrey* (1988) 138 NLJ 180). There is no need, however, for the officer to exhaust every possible defence or to obtain conclusive *proof* of the relevant facts or circumstances before effecting an arrest (*Ward* v *Chief Constable of Avon & Somerset Constabulary, The Times*, 26 June 1986).

An arrest begins at the time when the arresting officer informs the person of it or when his/her words *or actions* suggest that the person is under arrest (*Murray* v *Ministry of Defence* [1988] 1 WLR 692).

Police officers are not under any general duty to arrest without warrant and should always consider the use of the summons procedure where appropriate. (However, see PACE 1984, ss. 29 and 31.)

2.4.2 Information to be Given on Arrest

Whether an arrest is made under PACE 1984 or not, s. 28 makes clear provision for the information that *must* be given to a person on arrest. Section 28 provides that:

> (1) Subject to subsection (5) below, where a person is arrested, otherwise than by being informed that he is under arrest, the arrest is not lawful unless the person arrested is informed that he is under arrest as soon as is practicable after his arrest.
> (2) Where a person is arrested by a constable, subsection (1) above applies regardless of whether the fact of the arrest is obvious.
> (3) Subject to subsection (5) below, no arrest is lawful unless the person arrested is informed of the ground for the arrest at the time of, or as soon as is practicable after, the arrest.
> (4) Where a person is arrested by a constable, subsection (3) above applies regardless of whether the ground for the arrest is obvious.
> (5) Nothing in this section is to be taken to require a person to be informed—
>   (a)   that he is under arrest; or
>   (b)   of the ground for the arrest,
> if it was not reasonably practicable for him to be so informed by reason of his having escaped from arrest before the information could be given.

Keynote

Section 28 clearly makes provision for situations when the person cannot be told or would not be capable of understanding the information. However, as the failure to comply with s. 28 makes any arrest unlawful (see e.g. *Dawes* v *DPP* [1994] Crim LR 604), it is perhaps better to 'err on the side of caution'.

The reasons given for the arrest must be the *real* reasons in the officer's mind at the time (see *Christie* v *Leachinsky* [1947] AC 573) and he/she must clearly indicate to the person the fact that he/she is being arrested. This requirement might be met by using a colloquialism, provided that the person is familiar with it and understands its meaning (e.g., 'you're locked up' or 'you're nicked'; see *Christie* v *Leachinsky* above). It does not matter that the words describe more than one offence (e.g. 'burglary' or 'deception'), provided that they adequately describe the offence for which the person has been arrested (*Abbassy* v *Metropolitan Police Commissioner* [1990] 1 WLR 385).

2.4.3 Caution

PACE Code of Practice, Code C, para. 10.3 (**see Evidence and Procedure**) requires that a person must be cautioned on arrest *for an offence*. This would not include arrests for non-offence matters such as a breach of the peace (which is a 'complaint'; **see chapter 4**) but, again it may be better to err on the side of 'caution' (sorry!). As with the requirements under s. 28 of the 1984 Act, there are exceptions to the requirement to administer the caution and these are:

- where it is impracticable to do so by reason of the condition or behaviour *of the person arrested*; or

- where he/she has already been cautioned immediately before the arrest in accordance with Code C, para. 10.1 (requirement to caution where there are grounds to suspect commission of an offence).

The wording of the caution is set out at Code C, para. 10.4 (**see Evidence and Procedure**) but Note 10C to that Code provides that, if a person does not appear to understand what the caution means, the officer who has given it should go on to explain it in his/her own words.

2.4.4 Force

Section 117 of PACE 1984 allows the use of reasonable force when making an arrest. The Criminal Law Act 1967, s. 3 also allows the use of such force as is reasonably necessary in the arrest of people and the prevention of crime.

Whether any force used is 'reasonable' will be determined by the court in the light of all the circumstances, including the circumstances as the arresting officer believed them to be at the time. Such force may even be lethal to the defendant. Where serious harm is caused by an arrest, the courts will consider the time that was available to the officer to reflect on his/her actions and whether or not he/she believed that the danger presented to others by failing to arrest the person outweighed the harm caused to the person by the arrest (see *Attorney-General for Northern Ireland's Reference (No. 1 of 1975)* [1977] AC 105).

For the general power of search on arrest **see para. 2.9.2**.

Use of excessive force, while amounting to possible misconduct (**see chapter 1**) and assault (**see Crime, chapter 8**), does not render an otherwise lawful arrest unlawful (*Simpson* v *Chief Constable of South Yorkshire, The Times*, 7 March 1991).

2.5 Arrest Without Warrant

As discussed above, there are a number of sources from which a power of arrest can be gained. The main sources of powers of arrest without warrant are ss. 24 and 25 of PACE 1984.

2.5.1 Arrestable Offences

The expression 'arrestable offence' often creates confusion. 'Arrestable offences' should not be confused with those offences *for which a power of arrest exists*, e.g. offences under the Public Order Act 1986 and some drink/driving offences (**see Road Traffic, chapter 5**). '*Arrestable offences*' are a very specific group of offences covered by the provisions of PACE 1984, s. 24(1)(c). Arrestable offences are offences:

- for which the sentence is fixed by law (murder),
- for which a person aged 21 or over (not previously convicted) can be sentenced to five years' imprisonment or more,
- listed under s. 24(2).

Section 24(2) provides that:

(2)   *The offences to which this subsection applies are—*
    (a)   offences for which a person may be arrested under the customs and excise Acts, as defined in section 1(1) of the Customs and Excise Management Act 1979;
    (b)   offences under the Official Secrets Act . . . 1920 that are not arrestable offences by virtue of the term of imprisonment for which a person may be sentenced in respect of them;
    (bb)   offences under any provision of the Official Secrets Act 1989 except section 8(1), (4) or (5);
    (c)   offences under section . . . 22 (causing prostitution of women) or 23 (procuration of girl under 21) of the Sexual Offences Act 1956;
    (d)   offences under section 12(1) (taking motor vehicle or other conveyance without authority, etc.) or 25(1) (going equipped for stealing, etc) of the Theft Act 1968; and
    (e)   any offence under the Football (Offences) Act 1991;
    (f)   an offence under section 2 of the Obscene Publications Act 1959 (publication of obscene matter);
    (g)   an offence under section 1 of the Protection of Children Act 1978 (indecent photographs and pseudo-photographs of children);
    (h)   an offence under section 166 of the Criminal Justice and Public Order Act 1994 (sale of tickets by unauthorised persons);
    (i)   an offence under section 19 of the Public Order Act 1986 (publishing, etc. material intended or likely to stir up racial hatred);
    (j)   an offence under section 167 of the Criminal Justice and Public Order Act 1994 (touting for hire car services);
    (k)   an offence under section 1(1) of the Prevention of Crime Act 1953 (prohibition of the carrying of offensive weapons without lawful authority or reasonable excuse);
    (l)   an offence under section 139(1) of the Criminal Justice Act 1988 (offence of having article with blade or point in public place);
    (m)   an offence under section 139A(1) or (2) of the Criminal Justice Act 1988 (offence of having article with blade or point (or offensive weapon) on school premises);
    (n)   an offence under section 2 of the Protection from Harassment Act 1997 (harassment);

(o)   an offence under section 60(8)(b) of the Criminal Justice and Public Order Act 1994 (failing to comply with requirement to remove mask etc.);

(p)   an offence falling within section 32(1)(a) of the Crime and Disorder Act 1998 (racially-aggravated harassment);

(q)   an offence under section 16(4) of the Football Spectators Act 1989 (failure to comply with reporting duty imposed by restriction order).

Keynote

For details of the majority of these offences, **see Crime** and the later chapters of this Manual.

The power of arrest (**see para. 2.5.2**) also applies to attempting to commit these offences (**see Crime, chapter 3**) other than the offence under the Theft Act 1968, s. 12 (attempting to take a vehicle without consent).

This list is regularly amended and the most recent copy of the 1984 Act should be consulted in cases of doubt.

The commission or suspicion of an arrestable offence brings with it a number of wide powers of entry, search and seizure, some of which are discussed below.

A further definition exists for some offences which are classified as 'serious arrestable offences'. This classification generally affects the application of wider powers (e.g. of detention, search and the taking of samples; **see Evidence and Procedure, chapter 16**).

Section 116(2) of PACE 1984 provides that the following offences will *always* be 'serious':

(a)   an offence (whether at common law or under any enactment) specified in Part I of Schedule 5 to this Act;

(aa)   . . .

(b)   an offence under an enactment specified in Part II of that Schedule, and

(c)   any of the offences mentioned in paragraphs (a) to (f) of section 1(3) of the Drug Trafficking Act 1994.

Schedule 5 specifies the serious arrestable offences:

PART I   OFFENCES MENTIONED IN SECTION 116(2)(A)

1. Treason.
2. Murder.
3. Manslaughter.
4. Rape.
5. Kidnapping.
6. Incest with a girl under the age of 13.
7. Buggery with a person under the age of 16.
8. Indecent assault which constitutes an act of gross indecency.

PART II   OFFENCES MENTIONED IN SECTION 116(2)(B)

Explosive Substances Act 1883 (c 3)

1. Section 2 (causing explosion likely to endanger life or property).

Sexual Offences Act 1956 (c 69)

2. Section 5 (intercourse with a girl under the age of 13).

Firearms Act 1968 (c 27)

3. Section 16 (possession of firearms with intent to injure).
4. Section 17(1) (use of firearms and imitation firearms to resist arrest).
5. Section 18 (carrying firearms with criminal intent).

Taking of Hostages Act 1982 (c 28)

7. Section 1 (hostage-taking).

Aviation Security Act 1982 (c 36)

8. Section 1 (hi-jacking).

Criminal Justice Act 1988 (c 33)

9. Section 134 (Torture).

Road Traffic Act 1988 (c 52)

10. Section 1 (causing death by dangerous driving).
10A. Section 3A (causing death by careless driving when under the influence of drink or drugs).

Aviation and Maritime Security Act 1990 (c 31)

11. Section 1 (endangering safety at aerodromes).
12. Section 9 (hijacking of ships).
13. Section 10 (seizing or exercising control of fixed platforms).

Channel Tunnel (Security) Order 1994 No. 570

14. Article 4 (hijacking of Channel Tunnel trains).
15. Article 5 (seizing or exercising control of the tunnel system).

Protection of Children Act 1978 (c 37)

14. Section 1 (indecent photographs and pseudo-photographs of children).

Obscene Publications Act 1959 (c 66)

15. Section 2 (publication of obscene matter).

Keynote

Some offences under the Prevention of Terrorism (Temporary Provisions) Act 1989 are also always classed as 'serious' (s. 116(5)).

Section 116(6) goes on to provides that *any other arrestable offence* will be serious if its commission would lead to, or it is intended to lead to:

(a) serious harm to the security of the State or to public order;
(b) serious interference with the administration of justice or with the investigation of offences or of a particular offence;
(c) the death of any person;
(d) serious injury to any person;
(e) substantial financial gain to any person; and
(f) serious financial loss to any person.

Keynote

These consequences or intended consequences should be borne in mind when considering arrestable offences that do no fall under s. 116(2) above.

'Loss' is serious if, having regard to all the circumstances, it is serious for the person who suffers it (s. 116(7)) — therefore the test is a *subjective* one based on the victim's circumstances.

'Injury' includes any disease and any impairment of a person's physical or mental condition (s. 116(8)).

2.5.2 Power of Arrest: Arrestable Offences

Section 24 of PACE 1984 goes on to provide that:

> *(4)   Any person may arrest without a warrant—*
> *(a)   anyone who is in the act of committing an arrestable offence;*
> *(b)   anyone whom he has reasonable grounds for suspecting to be committing such an offence.*
> *(5)   Where an arrestable offence has been committed, any person may arrest without a warrant—*
> *(a)   anyone who is guilty of the offence;*
> *(b)   anyone whom he has reasonable grounds for suspecting to be guilty of it.*
> *(6)   Where a constable has reasonable grounds for suspecting that an arrestable offence has been committed, he may arrest without a warrant anyone whom he has reasonable grounds for suspecting to be guilty of the offence.*
> *(7)   A constable may arrest without a warrant—*
> *(a)   anyone who is about to commit an arrestable offence;*
> *(b)   anyone whom he has reasonable grounds for suspecting to be about to commit an arrestable offence.*

Keynote

The first two powers (s. 24(4) and (5)) are exercisable under the appropriate conditions by anyone and are the powers most likely to be used by store detectives and security staff. The requirement for an arrestable offence to have been committed can cause problems as it applies retrospectively. Thus, if a person involved in an alleged incident of say, theft, was arrested under s. 24(5) and later acquitted, no arrestable offence would have *been committed*. Therefore the arrest would be unlawful but the person making it would not find this out until many months later when the case (or often the appeal) was decided (*R* v *Self* [1992] 3 All ER 476).

For these subsections it is not enough that the person making the arrest *suspects* that an arrestable offence has been committed, however strong that suspicion may be. For that reason, s. 24(6) specifically provides police officers with a power of arrest under those circumstances. Provided there are reasonable grounds to suspect that an arrestable offence has been committed, the power will apply — but only to police officers acting within their jurisdiction (**see chapter 1**).

The final power (s. 24(7)), again limited to police officers, provides for occasions where a person is *about* to commit an arrestable offence.

'Reasonable grounds for suspicion' are not defined but the police officer must be able to demonstrate what those grounds were. The source of those grounds may be information passed on by another officer or by a PNC operator; they may even come from an anonymous call (*DPP* v *Wilson* [1991] RTR 284) or an informant (*James* v *Chief Constable of South Wales* [1991] 6 CL 80).

Note the power to enter premises in order to arrest a person for an arrestable offence (**see para. 2.9.2**).

2.5.3 General Arrest Power: PACE 1984, s. 25

Section 25 of PACE 1984 provides that:

> *(1)   Where a constable has reasonable grounds for suspecting that any offence which is not an arrestable offence has been committed or attempted, or is being committed or attempted, he may arrest*

the relevant person if it appears to him that service of a summons is impracticable or inappropriate because any of the general arrest conditions is satisfied.

(2) In this section 'the relevant person' means any person whom the constable has reasonable grounds to suspect of having committed or having attempted to commit the offence or of being in the course of committing or attempting to commit it.

Keynote

There are three main elements to the power under s. 25.

The first element is the presence of:

- reasonable grounds for suspecting
- that *any* offence — other than 'arrestable offence' above — however minor
- *has been* committed/attempted or
- *is being* committed/attempted.

Although the power relates to any non-arrestable offence, some difficulty arises when dealing with 'attempts' to commit summary offences. As summary offences cannot be 'attempted' under the provisions of the Criminal Attempts Act 1981 (**see Crime, chapter 3**), there could be no likelihood of charging/summonsing a person with *attempting* to commit a summary offence at the time of any arrest. This would, on the basis of some authorities on 'arrest' (e.g. *Holgate-Mohammed* v *Duke* [1984] AC 437; *R* v *Chalkley* [1998] 1 WLR 146; **see para. 2.4**) make such an arrest unlawful unless some other *preventive* power could be found.

The second element is the 'relevant person'. This is *any* person whom the officer has reasonable grounds to suspect of:

- having committed/attempted to commit the offence or
- being in the course of committing/attempting to commit the offence.

Therefore the power will not be available in relation to people who are reasonably suspected of being *about* to commit a non-arrestable offence, nor those reasonably suspected of conspiring, inciting or aiding another to do so.

The third element is the appearance to the officer that the service of a summons is:

- impracticable or
- inappropriate
- *because any of the general arrest conditions are satisfied.*

The wording of s. 25 makes a presumption that the summons procedure will generally be used and it is only in the circumstances set out at s. 25(3) — the 'general arrest conditions' — (**see below**) that a person can be arrested under this section.

Section 25 of PACE 1984 goes on to provide that:

(3) The general arrest conditions are—

(a) that the name of the relevant person is unknown to, and cannot be readily ascertained by, the constable;

(b) that the constable has reasonable grounds for doubting whether a name furnished by the relevant person as his name is his real name;

(c) that—

(i) the relevant person has failed to furnish a satisfactory address for service; or

(ii)   the constable has reasonable grounds for doubting whether an address furnished by the relevant person is a satisfactory address for service;

(d)   that the constable has reasonable grounds for believing that arrest is necessary to prevent the relevant person—

(i)   causing physical injury to himself or any other person;

(ii)   suffering physical injury;

(iii)   causing loss of or damage to property;

(iv)   committing an offence against public decency; or

(v)   causing an unlawful obstruction of the highway;

(e)   that the constable has reasonable grounds for believing that arrest is necessary to protect a child or other vulnerable person from the relevant person.

(4)   For the purposes of subsection (3) above an address is a satisfactory address for service if it appears to the constable—

(a)   that the relevant person will be at it for a sufficiently long period for it to be possible to serve him with a summons; or

(b)   that some other person specified by the relevant person will accept service of a summons for the relevant person at it.

(5)   Nothing in subsection (3)(d) above authorises the arrest of a person under sub-paragraph (iv) of that paragraph except where members of the public going about their normal business cannot reasonably be expected to avoid the person to be arrested.

(6)   This section shall not prejudice any power of arrest conferred apart from this section.

Keynote

If a person refuses to give his/her details the conditions under s. 25(3)(a) and (b) do not amount to an offence themselves (unlike the provisions under the road traffic legislation, **see Road Traffic, chapters 4 and 11**); they simply create a power to arrest. Therefore the reason for the arrest is not simply that the person has failed to give his/her details; it is his/her suspected involvement in the original offence, together with that fact. If the officer knows the person from previous dealings, or knows his/her address, these conditions would not be satisfied.

The requirement under s. 25(3)(b) and (3)(c)(ii) is for the officer to have 'reasonable grounds for doubting', on the face of it a very wide expression. This, together with the expression 'reasonable grounds for suspecting' (as to which **see para. 2.3.1**) should be contrasted with the further general arrest conditions set out under s. 25(3)(d) and (e). The expression used there is a narrower one requiring the officer to have reasonable grounds to *believe* that the arrest is *necessary* — as opposed to simply desirable — in order to prevent the person from bringing about the consequences set out in those subsections.

If the grounds for detaining the arrested person cease to exist before he/she reaches a police station and there are no further grounds for detaining him/her, the officer must release the person (s. 30(7); **see para. 2.8**).

The condition as to a satisfactory address under s. 25(3)(c) does not necessarily mean the person's own address; any reasonable address would suffice. It is up to the officer to justify why he/she thought the address was not satisfactory and there is no specific power to detain a person while an address is being checked.

In relation to the other conditions, there must still have been an offence or an attempted offence; simply to present a danger to oneself or to be *likely* to commit an offence against public decency is not enough. For the law governing the areas of assault, indecency, children/vulnerable persons and damage, **see Crime**; for obstruction of the highway,

see Road Traffic. The circumstances set out at s. 25 are also referred to in relation to the power of arrest for offences involving importuning by men under s. 32 of the Sexual Offences Act 1956 (**see Crime, chapter 10**).

For the general offences and powers in relation to the obstruction of the highway, **see Road Traffic, chapter 8**).

2.5.4   Preserved Powers of Arrest

Section 26 of PACE 1984 provides that:

> (1)   Subject to subsection (2) below, so much of any Act (including a local Act) passed before this Act as enables a constable—
>   (a)   to arrest a person for an offence without a warrant; or
>   (b)   to arrest a person otherwise than for an offence without a warrant or an order of a court, shall cease to have effect.
> (2)   Nothing in subsection (1) above affects the enactments specified in Schedule 2 to this Act.

Schedule 2 specifies the preserved powers of arrest:

1892 c 43	Section 17(2) of the Military Lands Act 1892.
1911 c 27	Section 12(1) of the Protection of Animals Act 1911.
1920 c 55	Section 2 of the Emergency Powers Act 1920.
1936 c 6	Section 7(3) of the Public Order Act 1936.
1952 c 52	Section 49 of the Prison Act 1952.
1952 c 67	Section 13 of the Visiting Forces Act 1952.
1955 c 18	Sections 186 and 190B of the Army Act 1955.
1955 c 19	Sections 186 and 190B of the Air Force Act 1955.
1957 c 53	Sections 104 and 105 of the Naval Discipline Act 1957.
1959 c 37	Section 1(3) of the Street Offences Act 1959.
1969 c 54	Section 32 of the Children and Young Persons Act 1969.
1971 c 77	Section 24(2) of the Immigration Act 1971 and paragraphs 17, 24 and 33 of Schedule 2 and paragraph 7 of Schedule 3 to that Act.
1976 c 63	Section 7 of the Bail Act 1976.
1977 c 45	Sections 6(6), 7(11), 8(4), 9(7) and 10(5) of the Criminal Law Act 1977.
1980 c 9	Schedule 5 to the Reserve Forces Act 1980.
1981 c 22	Sections 60(5) and 61(1) of the Animal Health Act 1981.
1983 c 2	Rule 36 in Schedule 1 to the Representation of the People Act 1983.
1983 c 20	Sections 18, 35(10), 36(8), 38(7), 136(1) and 138 of the Mental Health Act 1983.
1984 c 47	Section 5(5) of the Repatriation of Prisoners Act 1984

Keynote

The effect of s. 26 is to repeal all other police powers of arrest without warrant which existed before PACE 1984, except those listed in sch. 2. It does not repeal statutory powers of arrest for people other than police officers, such as railway ticket inspectors (*Moberly* v *Alsop* (1991) 156 JP 154). There has been some uncertainty in relation to statutes which provide powers of arrest for 'any person' (e.g. the offence of being disorderly whilst drunk in a public place; **see chapter** 4). Such powers are not generally preserved under sch. 2 above, and there is Home Office guidance to the effect that police officers should revert to their general arrest powers under s. 25 (see Home Office Circular 88/85). However, in two cases it has been made clear that the expression 'any person' in relation to a power of arrest includes polices officers. The first case, *DPP* v *Kitching* (1989) 154 JP 293 related to the offence of being disorderly whilst drunk in a public place under the Criminal Justice Act 1967, s. 91, while the second, *Gapper* v *Chief Constable of Avon & Somerset* [1998] 4 All ER 248 concerned the general power of arrest attached to the Vagrancy Act 1824. In both cases it was held that the Police and Criminal Evidence Act 1984 had not removed the powers of arrest in respect of police officers and that such powers were therefore still available to the police.

A remaining oddity can be found in the offence of 'going equipped' under s. 25 of the Theft Act 1968 (**see Crime, chapter 12**) which is both an arrestable offence under s. 24(2)(d) of the Police and Criminal Evidence Act 1984 and also carries a power of arrest without warrant by 'any person' under certain circumstances (s. 25(4)).

Absentees and Deserters

Section 186 of the Army Act 1955 and the Air Force Act 1955 provide a power of arrest without warrant where a constable has reasonable cause to suspect a person has deserted or is absent without leave. The Acts also make provision for the issuing of arrest warrants in respect of absentees/deserters, and give a power of arrest to forces personnel in respect of absentees/deserters where no constable is available.

Similar provisions for arresting Royal Navy personnel exist under the Naval Discipline Act 1957, s. 105.

Where suspected absentees or deserters have been arrested, they must be taken directly to a magistrates' court and the appropriate service authority should be informed. Magistrates' courts may remand absentees or deserters until they can be collected by a service escort. If the escort is likely to be provided soon after the person's appearance at court, the magistrates may remand that person to a police station and must issue a certificate which must be given to the service escort. Most forces have local arrangements in respect of military personnel who surrender themselves to police stations as being absent without leave.

2.5.5 Fingerprinting

For the power of arrest under s. 27 of PACE 1984 to take a person's fingerprints, **see Evidence and Procedure, chapter 16**.

2.5.6 Failure to Answer Police Bail

Section 46A of PACE 1984 provides that:

> *(1) A constable may arrest without a warrant any person who, having been released on bail under this Part of this Act subject to a duty to attend at a police station, falls to attend at that police station at the time appointed for him to do so.*
> *(2) A person who is arrested under this section shall be taken to the police station appointed as the place at which he is to surrender to custody as soon as practicable after the arrest.*
> *(3) For the purposes of—*
>   *(a) section 30 above (subject to the obligation in subsection (2) above), and*
>   *(b) section 31 above,*
> *an arrest under this section shall be treated as an arrest for an offence.*

Keynote

The offence will be treated as if the person had been arrested for the original offence for which bail was granted. For a detailed discussion on bail, **see Evidence and Procedure, chapter 5**.

2.5.7   Arrest to Take Samples

Section 63A of PACE 1984 provides a power of arrest without warrant in respect of people:

- who have been charged with/reported for a recordable offence and who have not had a sample taken or the sample was unsuitable/insufficient for analysis;

- who have been convicted of a recordable offence and have not had a sample taken since conviction;

- who have been so convicted and have had a sample taken before or since conviction but the sample was unsuitable/insufficient for analysis.

This is simply a summary of s. 63A and reference should be made to the 1984 Act for the exact wording. For further detail, **see Evidence and Procedure, chapter 16**.

2.5.8   Cross-Border Arrest Without Warrant

The Criminal Justice and Public Order Act 1994 (ss. 136 to 140) makes provision for officers from one part of the UK to go into another part of the UK to arrest someone there in connection with an offence committed within their jurisdiction.

Under the 1994 Act an officer from a force in England and Wales may arrest a person in Scotland where the offence committed within their jurisdiction is an 'arrestable offence' or where it would be impracticable to serve a summons for the same reasons which would justify an arrest in England and Wales.

A Scottish officer may arrest someone suspected of committing an offence in Scotland who is found in England, Wales or Northern Ireland if it would have been lawful to arrest that person had he/she been found in Scotland. In such a case the officer must take the person to a designated police station in Scotland or to the nearest designated police station in England or Wales (see s. 137(7)).

The 1994 Act sets out where a person arrested outside the relevant country should be taken on arrest (see s. 137(7)). The Act also provides wide powers of search in connection with arrests (see s. 139).

2.5.9   Mentally Disordered People

There is a power to remove a person who is apparently suffering from a mental disorder from a public place to a place of safety (**see Crime, chapter 11**).

2.6   Arrest Under Warrant

Arrest warrants may be issued by magistrates (generally under the Magistrates' Courts Act 1980, s. 1) and the Crown Court (under the Supreme Court Act 1981, s. 80(2)) where the statute in question, together with the powers of the court allow. Warrants of arrest may also be issued to secure the attendance of witnesses (see the Magistrates' Courts Act 1980, s. 97 and the Criminal Procedure (Attendance of Witnesses) Act 1965, s. 4).

Magistrates' courts may generally only issue an arrest warrant for offences that are imprisonable or indictable or where the person's address is not sufficient for the service of a summons. They can only issue a warrant for failing to appear at court where the offence is imprisonable or where they intend to impose a disqualification from holding a licence having convicted the defendant. The police owe defendants a duty of care when drawing up and enforcing the contents of warrants. Therefore, where officers put the wrong date on an arrest warrant issued by a magistrates' court and, as a result, the defendant was not released by the Prison Service when he should have been, the police were liable in damages for the defendant's unlawful imprisonment (*Clarke* v *Chief Constable of Northamptonshire Police*, *The Times*, 14 June 1999).

Warrants issued in relation to an offence may be backed for bail in which case the person is then granted bail in accordance with the conditions on the warrant. If not backed for bail, the warrant will specify where the person is to be brought (i.e. before the next sitting of the court).

For bail generally, **see Evidence and Procedure, chapter 5.**

Warrants issued in England, Wales, Scotland or Northern Ireland may be executed by officers from the country where they are issued or in the country where the person is arrested (see the Criminal Justice and Public Order Act 1994, s. 136).

Warrants from the Republic of Ireland (provided they are not issued for political offences) may be executed in England and Wales if so endorsed (Magistrates' Courts Act 1980, s. 125), as indeed may warrants issued in the Isle of Man or the Channel Islands if so endorsed (Indictable Offences Act 1848, s. 13).

Warrants issued in connection with 'an offence' (or for some purposes concerning the armed forces and domestic proceedings; see PACE 1984, s. 33) do not need to be in the possession of the officer executing them at the time (Magistrates' Courts Act 1980, s. 125).

However, where the warrant is for non-payment of a fine, the officer must have the warrant with him/her as the defendant should have the opportunity to pay the outstanding amount (*R* v *Peacock* (1989) 153 JP 199).

The requirement under PACE 1984, s. 28 to tell a person why they are being arrested applies to arrests under warrant.

For the law relating to warrants generally, **see Evidence and Procedure, chapter 4.**

2.7 Voluntary Attendance at a Police Station

Section 29 of PACE 1984 provides that:

> *Where for the purpose of assisting with an investigation a person attends voluntarily at a police station or at any other place where a constable is present or accompanies a constable to a police station or any such other place without having been arrested—*
> *(a)   he shall be entitled to leave at will unless he is placed under arrest;*
> *(b)   he shall be informed at once that he is under arrest if a decision is taken by a constable to prevent him from leaving at will.*

Keynote

The person's attendance at a police station or other place must be for the purpose of 'assisting with an investigation', which would, on a strict interpretation, encompass witnesses and victims. The main principle behind s. 29 (and see also Code C, para. 3.15) is to avoid the situation where people find themselves at a police station (or any other place where there is a police officer present) and feel compelled to remain there but without the attendant procedural protection that follows a formal arrest. Section 29(b) is unusual in that it (along with s. 31 below) imposes an obligation on a police officer to make an arrest, an activity that is usually entirely within his/her discretion.

If such a person is cautioned (under PACE Code C, para. 10), they must also be told that they are free to leave the police station. Although not in police detention (see s. 118), voluntary attenders should be given the opportunity to seek legal advice if they wish and should be given the appropriate notice (see Code C).

Section 31 of PACE 1984 goes on to provide that:

> Where—
>> (a) a person—
>>> (i)   has been arrested for an offence; and
>>> (ii)   is at a police station in consequence of that arrest; and
>> (b) it appears to a constable that, if he were released from that arrest, he would be liable to arrest for some other offence,
> he shall be arrested for that other offence.

Keynote

The purpose of s. 31, which like s. 29 above, also imposes an obligation to make an arrest, is to avoid the situation where the person concerned is to all extents and purposes under arrest — in that he/she will not be allowed to leave if he/she tries — but he/she is unaware of that fact.

2.8   After Arrest

Section 30 of PACE 1984 provides for the procedure to be adopted after a person has been arrested.

> (1)   Subject to the following provisions of this section, where a person—
>> (a) is arrested by a constable for an offence; or
>> (b) is taken into custody by a constable after being arrested for an offence by a person other than a constable,
> at any place other than a police station, he shall be taken to a police station by a constable as soon as practicable after the arrest.
>
> (2)   Subject to subsections (3) and (5) below, the police station to which an arrested person is taken under subsection (1) above shall be a designated police station.
>
> (3)   A constable to whom this subsection applies may take an arrested person to any police station unless it appears to the constable that it may be necessary to keep the arrested person in police detention for more than six hours.
>
> (4)   Subsection (3) above applies—
>> (a) to a constable who is working in a locality covered by a police station which is not a designated police station; and
>> (b) to a constable belonging to a body of constables maintained by an authority other than a police authority.

(5) *Any constable may take an arrested person to any police station if—*

   (a) *either of the following conditions is satisfied—*

      (i) *the constable has arrested him without the assistance of any other constable and no other constable is available to assist him;*

      (ii) *the constable has taken him into custody from a person other than a constable without the assistance of any other constable and no other constable is available to assist him; and*

   (b) *it appears to the constable that he will be unable to take the arrested person to a designated police station without the arrested person injuring himself, the constable or some other person.*

(6) *If the first police station to which an arrested person is taken after his arrest is not a designated police station, he shall be taken to a designated police station not more than six hours after his arrival at the first police station unless he is released previously.*

Keynote

When arrested at a place other than a police station, the person must be taken to a designated police station unless the conditions under s. 30(5) and (6) apply.

As discussed above (**see para. 2.5.3**), under s. 30(7), the officer *must* de-arrest a person if he/she is satisfied, before reaching the police station, that there are no grounds for detaining that person. This may happen where the person has been arrested under one of the general arrest conditions and the particular condition has ceased to apply (e.g. the person gives a suitable name and address having originally failed to do so). An officer who releases a prisoner under s. 30(7) must record the fact that he/she has done so and must make that record as soon as practicable after the release (s. 30(8) and (9)).

Section 30(10) allows the officer to delay taking the arrested person to a police station where his/her presence elsewhere is *necessary in order to carry out such investigations as it is reasonable to carry out immediately*. Where there is such a delay, the reasons for it must be recorded when the person first arrives at the police station (s. 30(11)).

Other exceptions in the application of s. 1 to terrorism and immigration are made by s. 30(12).

The delay permitted under s. 30(10) and (11) will only apply if the matter requires *immediate* investigation; if it can wait, the exception will not apply and the person must be taken straight to a police station (*R* v *Kerrawalla* [1991] Crim LR 451).

Taking an arrested person to check out an alibi before going to a police station may be justified in some circumstances (see *Dallison* v *Caffery* [1965] 1 QB 348).

2.9 Entry, Search and Seizure

Police powers to enter premises, search them and seize evidence and property are governed mainly by PACE 1984 and Code B (**see appendix 2**). The 1984 Act covers entry, search and seizure both with and without a warrant.

It is always possible to seek the consent of the relevant person in entering and searching premises, or in searching people. However, where there is a *power* to search, its utilisation avoids the potential problems of any consent being limited or withdrawn.

Consent to something where no power exists in law is very different from *co-operation* with the exercise of a legal power (for guidance, see Code B).

Throughout PACE 1984 some evidence is described as 'material' and certain categories are subject to particular safeguards in the search procedure (**see para. 2.9.8**). If anything found during a search is to be used as evidence, it is critical that the officers conducting the search can point to the relevant authority under which they were acting at the time. If they cannot justify the search then, in addition to the risk of possible civil liability, there is a strong likelihood that any evidence found will be excluded under the relevant provisions available to the courts (**see Evidence and Procedure, chapter 13**).

2.9.1 Powers of Search and Seizure under Warrant

There are many statutes which make provision for a court to issue a search warrant to police officers, many of which are covered within this Manual under the relevant headings.

The application for and execution of all such warrants is governed by PACE 1984 and the Codes of Practice. (For a fuller discussion of summonses and warrants, **see Evidence and Procedure, chapter 4**.)

Section 15 of PACE 1984 provides that:

> *(1) This section and section 16 below have effect in relation to the issue to constables under any enactment, including an enactment contained in an Act passed after this Act, of warrants to enter and search premises; and an entry on or search of premises under a warrant is unlawful unless it complies with this section and section 16 below.*
> *(2) Where a constable applies for any such warrant, it shall be his duty—*
> > *(a) to state—*
> > > *(i) the ground on which he makes the application; and*
> > > *(ii) the enactment under which the warrant would be issued;*
> > *(b) to specify the premises which it is desired to enter and search; and*
> > *(c) to identify, so far as is practicable, the articles or persons to be sought.*
> *(3) An application for such a warrant shall be made ex parte and supported by an information in writing.*
> *(4) The constable shall answer on oath any question that the justice of the peace or judge hearing the application asks him.*
> *(5) A warrant shall authorise an entry on one occasion only.*
> *(6) A warrant—*
> > *(a) shall specify—*
> > > *(i) the name of the person who applies for it;*
> > > *(ii) the date on which it is issued;*
> > > *(iii) the enactment under which it is issued; and*
> > > *(iv) the premises to be searched; and*
> > *(b) shall identify, so far as is practicable, the articles or persons to be sought.*
> *(7) Two copies shall be made of a warrant.*
> *(8) The copies shall be clearly certified as copies.*

Keynote

Sections 15 and 16 (**see below**) apply to *all* warrants to enter and search premises. 'Premises' include vehicles, vessels and hovercraft (see s. 23).

If the provisions of these sections are not complied with, any entry and search made under a warrant will be unlawful. Although the officers executing the warrant may have some protection from personal liability where there has been a defect in the *procedure* by which the warrant was issued, failure to follow the requirements of ss. 15 and 16 may result in the exclusion of any evidence obtained under the warrant (**see Evidence**

and Procedure, chapter 13). The details of the extent of the proposed search should be made clear in the application and the officer swearing the warrant out must be prepared to answer *any* questions put to him/her on oath under s. 15(4). Many courts will go into background detail about the particular premises, or part of the premises, and who is likely to be present on the premises at the time the warrant is executed (e.g. children). The action to be taken in relation to the swearing out of a warrant is set out in Pace Code B, para. 2.

Applications for all search warrants must be made with the authority of an officer of at least the rank of inspector (Code B, para. 2.4). However, in cases of urgency where no such officer is 'readily available', the senior officer on duty may authorise the application.

If an application for a warrant is refused, no further application can be made unless it is supported by additional grounds.

Section 16 of PACE 1984 provides that:

(1)   A warrant to enter and search premises may be executed by any constable.

(2)   Such a warrant may authorise persons to accompany any constable who is executing it.

(3)   Entry and search under a warrant must be within one month from the date of its issue.

(4)   Entry and search under a warrant must be at a reasonable hour unless it appears to the constable executing it that the purpose of a search may be frustrated on an entry at a reasonable hour.

(5)   Where the occupier of premises which are to be entered and searched is present at the time when a constable seeks to execute a warrant to enter and search them, the constable—

(a)   shall identify himself to the occupier and, if not in uniform, shall produce to him documentary evidence that he is a constable;

(b)   shall produce the warrant to him; and

(c)   shall supply him with a copy of it.

(6)   Where—

(a)   the occupier of such premises is not present at the time when a constable seeks to execute such a warrant; but

(b)   some other person who appears to the constable to be in charge of the premises is present, subsection (5) above shall have effect as if any reference to the occupier were a reference to that other person.

(7)   If there is no person present who appears to the constable to be in charge of the premises, he shall leave a copy of the warrant in a prominent place on the premises.

(8)   A search under a warrant may only be a search to the extent required for the purpose for which the warrant was issued.

(9)   A constable executing warrant shall make an endorsement on it stating—

(a)   whether the articles or persons sought were found; and

(b)   whether any articles were seized, other than articles which were sought.

Keynote

Although s. 16 allows for other people to be included in the warrant, authorising them to accompany the officer, some warrants *require* the presence of other people when a warrant is executed (e.g. under the Mental Health Act 1983, s. 135; **see Crime, chapter 11**).

Failure to comply with the requirements under s. 16 will make the entry and subsequent seizure of property unlawful. Therefore, where officers failed to provide the occupier of the searched premises with a copy of the warrant (under s. 16(5)(c)), they were obliged to return the property seized during the search (*R v Chief Constable of Lancashire, ex parte Parker* [1993] Crim LR 204).

Very minor departures from the letter of the warrant, however, will not render any search unlawful (see *Attorney-General of Jamaica* v *Williams* [1998] AC 351).

If the execution of the warrant is likely to have an adverse effect on community relations, the community liaison officer must be informed unless the case is urgent, in which case that officer must be advised as soon as practicable after the search — see Code B, Note 2B.

Code B goes on to make further provisions for the execution of the warrant.

If a warrant itself is invalid for some reason, any entry and subsequent seizure made under it are unlawful (*R* v *Central Criminal Court and British Railways Board, ex parte AJD Holdings Ltd* [1992] Crim LR 669). After a warrant has been executed, or if it has not been used within one month from its date of issue, it must be returned to the justices' clerk or the court officer as appropriate (s. 16(10)). These returned warrants must then be kept by the respective people for a period of 12 months in order that the occupiers of the named premises may inspect them (s. 16(11) and (12)).

Search Warrants for Serious Arrestable Offences

Section 8 of PACE 1984 provides that:

(1)   If on an application made by a constable a justice of the peace is satisfied that there are reasonable grounds for believing—
    (a)   that a serious arrestable offence has been committed; and
    (b)   that there is material on premises specified in the application which is likely to be of substantial value (whether by itself or together with other material) to the investigation of the offence; and
    (c)   that the material is likely to be relevant evidence; and
    (d)   that it does not consist of or include items subject to legal privilege, excluded material or special procedure material; and
    (e)   that any of the conditions specified in subsection (3) below applies,
he may issue a warrant authorising a constable to enter and search the premises.
(2)   A constable may seize and retain anything for which a search has been authorised under subsection (1) above.
(3)   The conditions mentioned in subsection (1)(e) above are—
    (a)   that it is not practicable to communicate with any person entitled to grant entry to the premises;
    (b)   that it is practicable to communicate with a person entitled to grant entry to the premises but it is not practicable to communicate with any person entitled to grant access to the evidence;
    (c)   that entry to the premises will not be granted unless a warrant is produced;
    (d)   that the purpose of a search may be frustrated or seriously prejudiced unless a constable arriving at the premises can secure immediate entry to them.
(4)   In this Act 'relevant evidence', in relation to an offence, means anything that would be admissible in evidence at a trial for the offence.
(5)   The power to issue a warrant conferred by this section is in addition to any such power otherwise conferred.

Keynote

For 'serious' arrestable offences, **see para. 2.5.1**. The officer applying for a warrant under s. 8 must have reasonable grounds for believing that material which is *likely to be of substantial value to the investigation of the offence* is on the premises specified. Therefore, when executing such a warrant, the officer must be able to show that any material seized thereunder fell within that description (*R* v *Chief Constable of the Warwickshire Constabulary, ex parte Fitzpatrick* [1998] 1 All ER 65). These requirements mean that material which is solely of value for *intelligence* purposes may not be seized under a s. 8 warrant.

The conditions set out under s. 8(1)(e) are part of the *application* process, not part of the general execution process (which is set out at s. 16 above). Therefore the officer swearing out a s. 8 warrant will have to satisfy the court that any of those conditions apply.

Where the search includes information contained in a computer, the provisions of s. 20 apply (**see para. 2.9.7**).

The power to issue a warrant under s. 8 also applies to certain offences under the Immigration Act 1971, s. 4, offences which include illegal entry, obtaining leave to remain in the country by deception and staying beyond the time allowed (see Asylum and Immigration Act 1996, s. 7(3)).

2.9.2 Powers Without Warrant

Apart from a general power of entry to prevent a breach of the peace (**see chapter 4**), all common law police powers of entry were abolished by PACE 1984. The Act introduced wide powers of entry, search and seizure particularly when made in connection with an arrest.

Arrestable Offences

Section 18 of PACE 1984 provides that:

(1)   Subject to the following provisions of this section, a constable may enter and search any premises occupied or controlled by a person who is under arrest for an arrestable offence, if he has reasonable grounds for suspecting that there is on the premises evidence, other than items subject to legal privilege, that relates—
   (a)   to that offence; or
   (b)   to some other arrestable offence which is connected with or similar to that offence.
(2)   A constable may seize and retain anything for which he may search under subsection (1) above.
(3)   The power to search conferred by subsection (1) above is only a power to search to the extent that is reasonably required for the purpose of discovering such evidence.
(4)   Subject to subsection (5) below, the powers conferred by this section may not be exercised unless an officer of the rank of inspector or above has authorised them in writing.
(5)   A constable may conduct a search under subsection (1) above—
   (a)   before taking the person to a police station; and
   (b)   without obtaining an authorisation under subsection (4) above,
if the presence of that person at a place other than a police station is necessary for the effective investigation of the offence.
(6)   If a constable conducts a search by virtue of subsection (5) above, he shall inform an officer of the rank of inspector or above that he has made the search as soon as practicable after he has made it.
(7)   An officer who—
   (a)   authorises a search; or
   (b)   is informed of a search under subsection (6) above, shall make a record in writing—
      (i)   of the grounds for the search; and
      (ii)   of the nature of the evidence that was sought.
(8)   If the person who was in occupation or control of the premises at the time of the search is in police detention at the time the record is to be made, the officer shall make the record as part of his custody record.

Keynote

This power only applies where a person has been arrested for an 'arrestable offence' (**see para. 2.5.1**); it does not apply where the person has been arrested under the general arrest conditions (**see para. 2.5.3**).

For items that relate to legal privilege, **see para. 2.9.8.**

The premises must be occupied or controlled by the arrested person. This expression is not defined but it is a *factual* requirement, i.e. it is not enough that the officer suspects or believes that the premises are occupied or controlled by that person.

The search is limited to evidence relating to the arrestable offence for which the person has been arrested or another arrestable offence which is similar or connected; it does not authorise a general search for anything that might be of use for other purposes (e.g. for intelligence reports). The extent of the search is limited by s. 18(3). If you are looking for a stolen fridge-freezer, you would not be empowered to search through drawers or small cupboards. You would be able to, however, if you were looking for packaging, receipts or other documents relating to the fridge-freezer.

The search authority must be given by an inspector and in writing (see also Code B, para. 3). That authority is for a search which is lawful *in all other respects*, that is, the other conditions imposed by s. 18 must be met. An inspector cannot make an otherwise unlawful entry and search lawful simply by authorising it (*Krohn* v *DPP* [1997] COD 345).

The provision under s. 18(5) relates to cases where the presence of the person *is in fact necessary* for the effective investigation of the offence. This is a more stringent requirement than merely reasonable suspicion or grounds to believe on the part of the officer concerned. If such a search is made, the searching officer must inform an inspector (or above) as soon as practicable after the search.

If the person is in police detention after the arrest, the facts concerning the search must be recorded in the custody record. Where a person is re-arrested under s. 31 (**see para. 2.8**) for an arrestable offence, the powers to search under s. 18 begin again, that is, a new power to search is created in respect of each arrestable offence. Where the search includes information contained in a computer, the provisions of s. 20 apply (**see para. 2.9.7**).

Search after Arrest for Other Offences

Where a person is arrested for any other offence, PACE 1984, s. 32 provides a number of general powers of entry, search and seizure.

Section 32 provides that:

> (1) A constable may search an arrested person, in any case where the person to be searched has been arrested at a place other than a police station, if the constable has reasonable grounds for believing that the arrested person may present a danger to himself or others.
> (2) Subject to subsections (3) to (5) below, a constable shall also have power in any such case—
>   (a) to search the arrested person for anything—
>   (i) which he might use to assist him to escape from lawful custody; or

> *(ii)   which might be evidence relating to an offence; and*
> *(b)   . . .*
> (3)   *The power to search conferred by subsection (2) above is only a power to search to the extent that is reasonably required for the purpose of discovering any such thing or any such evidence.*
> (4)   *The powers conferred by this section to search a person are not to be construed as authorising a constable to require a person to remove any of his clothing in public other than an outer coat, jacket or gloves but they do authorise a search of a person's mouth.*
> (5)   *A constable may not search a person in the exercise of the power conferred by subsection (2)(a) above unless he has reasonable grounds for believing that the person to be searched may have concealed on him anything for which a search is permitted under that paragraph.*

Keynote

The power to search the arrested person under s. 32(1) is a general one relating to safety. For the power to search at a police station, **see Evidence and Procedure, chapter 15.**

Section 32(2)(a) then goes on to provide a power to search the person in relation to anything that the arrested person might use to escape from lawful custody and anything that 'might be' evidence relating to *an offence*. There are restrictions placed on the extent and circumstances of the search (s. 32(3) and (4)) and the officer must have reasonable grounds to *believe* (as opposed to mere suspicion) that the person may have such things concealed on him/her (s. 32(5)). Nevertheless, this is still a very wide power.

Section 32(9) provides that:

> (9)   *A constable searching a person in the exercise of the power conferred by subsection (2)(a) above may seize and retain anything he finds, other than an item subject to legal privilege, if he has reasonable grounds for believing—*
> (a)   *that he might use it to assist him to escape from lawful custody; or*
> (b)   *that it is evidence of an offence or has been obtained in consequence of the commission of an offence.*

Search of Premises after Arrest

Section 32 also provides that a constable shall have the power in such a case to enter and search any premises in which the person was when arrested or immediately before being arrested (s. 32(2)(b)). The search may be conducted for the purpose of finding evidence relating to the offence for which the person was arrested.

Section 32 goes on to provide that:

> (6)   *A constable may not search premises in the exercise of the power conferred by subsection (2)(b) above unless he has reasonable grounds for believing that there is evidence for which a search is permitted under that paragraph on the premises.*
> (7)   *In so far as the power of search conferred by subsection (2)(b) above relates to premises consisting of two or more separate dwellings, it is limited to a power to search—*
> (a)   *any dwelling in which the arrest took place or in which the person arrested was immediately before his arrest; and*
> (b)   *any parts of the premises which the occupier of any such dwelling uses in common with the occupiers of any other dwellings comprised in the premises.*
> (8)   *A constable searching a person in the exercise of the power conferred by subsection (1) above may seize and retain anything he finds, if he has reasonable grounds for believing that the person searched might use it to cause physical injury to himself or to any other person.*
> . . .

(10)   Nothing in this section shall be taken to affect the power conferred by section 15(3), (4) and (5) of the Prevention of Terrorism (Temporary Provisions) Act 1989.

Keynote

Both 'reasonable grounds' and 'immediately' are questions of fact for a court to determine. It has been held that the power under s. 32(2)(b) is one for use at the time of arrest and should not be used to return to the relevant premises some time after the arrest in the way that s. 18 (**see above**) may be used (*R v Badham* [1987] Crim LR 202).

Officers exercising their power to enter and search under s. 32 must have a genuine belief (i.e. more than mere suspicion) that there is evidence on the premises; it is not a licence for a general fishing expedition (*R v Beckford* [1991] Crim LR 918).

Code B sets out the procedure to be followed after searches have been carried out (para. 7).

2.9.3   Other Powers of Entry Without Warrant

Just as there are many statutes which provide the police (and others) with powers to apply for warrants, there are as many statutes which provide a power of entry without warrant (an example would be the Scrap Metal Dealers Act 1964, s. 6 of which allows a constable entry at all reasonable times, onto a scrap metal dealer's premises to inspect the register and any scrap metal). Other examples are the power to enter:

- any land other than a dwelling house in order to search for crossbows (under the Crossbows Act 1987) (**see chapter 6**);

- *any place* for the purpose of carrying out a search under s. 47 of the Firearms Act 1968 (**see chapter 5**); and

- school premises in connection with weapons under the Criminal Justice Act 1988 (**see chapter 6**);

- relevant premises in connection with a direction to leave and remove vehicles etc. under the Criminal Justice and Public Order Act 1994 (**see chapter 9**).

The only common law power of entry without warrant is for dealing with a breach of the peace (**see chapter 4**). This power is preserved by s. 17(6) and only applies where officers have a genuine and reasonable belief that a breach of the peace is happening or is about to happen in the immediate future (*McLeod* v *Commissioner of Police for the Metropolis* [1994] 4 All ER 423).

Where police officers enter premises *lawfully* (including where they are there by invitation), they are on the premises for *all lawful purposes* (see *Foster* v *Attard* [1986] Crim LR 627). This means that they can carry out any lawful functions while on the premises, even if that was not the original purpose for entry. For instance, if officers entered under a lawful power provided by the Misuse of Drugs Act 1971 (**see Crime, chapter 6**), they may carry out other lawful functions such as enforcing the provisions of the Gaming Act 1945.

If officers are invited onto premises by someone entitled to do so they are lawfully there unless and until that invitation is withdrawn. Once the invitation is withdrawn, the officers will become trespassers unless they have a power to be there and the person may remove them by force (*Robson* v *Hallett* [1967] 2 QB 939). If that invitation is terminated, the person needs to communicate that clearly to the officer; it has been held that merely telling officers to '*fuck off*' is not necessarily sufficient (*Snook* v *Mannion* [1982] RTR 321 (**see Road Traffic, chapter 5**).

Once officers are lawfully on premises they may exercise the powers of seizure under PACE 1984, s. 19 (**see para. 2.9.7**).

2.9.4 Power of Entry: PACE 1984, s. 17

Section 17 of PACE 1984 provides that:

> (1)   Subject to the following provisions of this section, and without prejudice to any other enactment, a constable may enter and search any premises for the purpose—
>   (a)   of executing—
>   (i)   a warrant of arrest issued in connection with or arising out of criminal proceedings; or
>   (ii)   a warrant of commitment issued under section 76 of the Magistrates' Courts Act 1980;
>   (b)   of arresting a person for an arrestable offence;
>   (c)   of arresting a person for an offence under—
>   (i)   section 1 (prohibition of uniforms in connection with political objects) . . . of the Public Order Act 1936;
>   (ii)   any enactment contained in sections 6 to 8 or 10 of the Criminal Law Act 1977 (offences relating to entering and remaining on property);
>   (iii)   section 4 of the Public Order Act 1986 (fear or provocation of violence);
>   (iv)   section 76 of the Criminal Justice and Public Order Act 1994 (failure to comply with interim possession order);
>   (ca)   of arresting, in pursuance of section 32(1A) of the Children and Young Persons Act 1969, any child or young person who has been remanded or committed to local authority accommodation under section 23(1) of that Act;
>   (cb)   of recapturing any person who is, or is deemed for any purpose to be, unlawfully at large while liable to be detained—
>   (i)   in a prison, remand centre, young offender institution or secure training centre, or
>   (ii)   in pursuance of section 53 of the Children and Young Persons Act 1933 (dealing with children and young persons guilty of grave crimes), in any other place;
>   (d)   of recapturing any person whatever who is unlawfully at large and whom he is pursuing; or
>   (e)   of saving life or limb or preventing serious damage to property.
> (2)   Except for the purpose specified in paragraph (e) of subsection (1) above, the powers of entry and search conferred by this section—
>   (a)   are only exercisable if the constable has reasonable grounds for believing that the person whom he is seeking is on the premises; and
>   (b)   are limited, in relation to premises consisting of two or more separate dwellings, to powers to enter and search—
>   (i)   any parts of the premises which the occupiers of any dwelling comprised in the premises use in common with the occupiers of any other such dwelling; and
>   (ii)   any such dwelling in which the constable has reasonable grounds for believing that the person whom he is seeking may be.
> (3)   The powers of entry and search conferred by this section are only exercisable for the purposes specified in subsection (1)(c)(ii) or (iv) above by a constable in uniform.
> (4)   The power of search conferred by this section is only a power to search to the extent that is reasonably required for the purpose for which the power of entry is exercised.
> (5)   Subject to subsection (6) below, all the rules of common law under which a constable has power to enter premises without a warrant are hereby abolished.
> (6)   Nothing in subsection (5) above affects any power of entry to deal with or prevent a breach of the peace.

Keynote

The warrants under the Magistrates' Courts Act 1980 are warrants in connection with failing to pay fines or compensation orders (**see para. 2.6**) or maintenance orders.

For the offences listed at s. 17(1)(c), **see chapters 4 and 9**).

'Unlawfully at large' does not have a particular statutory meaning; it can apply to someone who is subject to an order under the Mental Health Act 1983, or someone who has escaped from custody (however, 'escaping' is an arrestable offence anyway, **see Crime, chapter 15**). The pursuit of the person must be 'fresh', that is, the power will only be available while the officer is actually 'pursuing' the person concerned (*D'Souza* v *DPP* (1993) 96 Cr App 278). Force may be used in exercising the power of entry where it is necessary to do so. Generally, the officer should first attempt to communicate with the occupier of the premises, explaining by what authority and for what purpose entry is to be made, before making a forcible entry. Clearly though, there will be occasions where such communication is impossible, impracticable or even unnecessary; in those cases there is no need for the officer to enter into such an explanation (*O'Loughlin* v *Chief Constable of Essex* [1998] 1 WLR 374).

The officer must have reasonable grounds to *believe* that the person is on the premises in all cases except saving life and limb at s. 17(1)(e). This expression is narrower than 'reasonable cause to suspect' and you must be able to justify that belief before using this power (although see *Kynaston* v *DPP*, *The Times*, 4 November 1987 where the court accepted reasonable cause to *suspect*).

Note the requirement for an officer to be in uniform for the purposes of s. 17(1)(c)(ii) and (iv).

Code B regulates the way in which these powers of entry will be executed (see e.g. paras 5.4 to 5.6).

Again this section contains restrictions on the extent of any searches made (**see para. 2.3**).

2.9.5 Fire

The Fire Services Act 1947, s. 30(1) provides that, among others, a constable may enter and if necessary break into:

- any premises or place
- in which a fire has or is reasonably believed to have broken out.

The constable may also break into or enter:

- any premises or place
- which it is necessary to enter for the purposes of extinguishing a fire
- or of protecting the premises from acts done for firefighting purposes

and may do all such things as he/she deems necessary for extinguishing the fire or for protecting from fire any such premises or place, or for rescuing any person or property therein.

This is clearly a very wide power which extends to adjacent premises or other places in need of protection from the fire *or* from the effects of firefighting.

The reasonable belief that a fire has broken out does not appear to have to be the *officer's* belief and the wording of s. 30 appears to suggest that *anyone* holding such a belief may trigger the power.

2.9.6 Powers of Seizure under PACE 1984

PACE 1984 provides many powers for the seizure of property. These include property:

- discovered during a stop/search (s. 1(6)), **see para. 2.3.1**;

- discovered when executing a search warrant issued by a magistrates' court in connection with a serious arrestable offence (s. 8(2)), **see para. 2.9.1**;

- discovered when executing a warrant issued by a circuit judge under sch. 1, **see para. 2.9.8**;

- discovered during a search in connection with an arrestable offence (s. 18(2)), **see para. 2.9.2**;

- discovered while lawfully on premises (s. 19), **see para. 2.9.7**;

- discovered after a person's arrest at a place other than a police station (s. 32), **see para. 2.9.2**:

- discovered during a search at a police station/while in police detention (ss. 54(3) and 55(12)), **see Evidence and Procedure, chapter 15.**

2.9.7 General Power of Seizure under PACE 1984, s. 19

Section 19 of PACE 1984 provides that:

(1) The powers conferred by subsections (2), (3) and (4) below are exercisable by a constable who is lawfully on any premises.

(2) The constable may seize anything which is on the premises if he has reasonable grounds for believing—

(a) that it has been obtained in consequence of the commission of an offence; and

(b) that it is necessary to seize it in order to prevent it being concealed, lost, damaged, altered or destroyed.

(3) The constable may seize anything which is on the premises if he has reasonable grounds for believing—

(a) that it is evidence in relation to an offence which he is investigating or any other offence; and

(b) that it is necessary to seize it in order to prevent the evidence being concealed, lost, altered or destroyed.

(4) The constable may require any information which is contained in a computer and is accessible from the premises to be produced in a form in which it can be taken away and in which it is visible and legible if he has reasonable grounds for believing—

(a) that—

(i) it is evidence in relation to an offence which he is investigating or any other offence; or

(ii) it has been obtained in consequence of the commission of an offence; and

(b) that it is necessary to do so in order to prevent it being concealed, lost, or destroyed.

(5) The powers conferred by this section are in addition to any power otherwise conferred.

(6)   No power of seizure conferred on a constable under any enactment (including an enactment contained in an Act passed after this Act) is to be taken to authorise the seizure of an item which the constable exercising the power has reasonable grounds for believing to be subject to legal privilege.

Keynote

For this very wide power to apply, the officer concerned must be on the premises lawfully (**see para. 2.9.2**). If the officers are on the premises only with the consent of the occupier, they become trespassers once that consent has been withdrawn (**see para. 2.9.3**). Once the officers are told to leave, they are no longer 'lawfully' on the premises — even though they must be given a reasonable opportunity to leave — and cannot then seize any property that they may find. For this reason, it is far safer to exercise a power where one exists, albeit that the *co-operation* of the relevant person should be sought.

The power of seizure only applies where the officer has 'reasonable grounds for believing' that:

- the property has been obtained in consequence of the commission of an offence, or
- the property is *evidence* in relation to an offence, *and*

in each case, that its seizure is *necessary* to prevent the property being concealed, lost or destroyed.

Unless these elements are satisfied, the power under s. 19 will not apply. Therefore, the power does not authorise the seizure of property purely for intelligence purposes.

If the warrant under which entry or seizure was made is invalid, the officers will not be on the premises lawfully (**see para. 2.9**).

Section 20(1) provides that:

(1)   Every power of seizure which is conferred by an enactment to which this section applies on a constable who has entered premises in the exercise of a power conferred by an enactment shall be construed as including a power to require any information contained in a computer and accessible from the premises to be produced in a form in which it can be taken away and in which it is visible and legible.

(2)   This section applies—
   (a)   to any enactment contained in an Act passed before this Act;
   (b)   to sections 8 and 18 above;
   (c)   to paragraph 13 of Schedule 1 to this Act; and
   (d)   to any enactment contained in an Act passed after this Act.

Keynote

This provision applies to:

- powers conferred under pre-PACE statutes;
- powers exercised under a s. 8 warrant (for 'serious arrestable offences');
- powers exercised under s. 18 (following arrest for an arrestable offence);
- powers under sch. 1 ('excluded' or 'special procedure material');
- powers exercised under s. 19 (officers lawfully on premises).

At the time of writing the government had drafted the Electronic Commerce Bill which proposes to tackle, among other things, the increasing use of encrypted data files by criminals. Under the present law, many files and programs seized by the police cannot be accessed because they are coded. The Electronic Commerce Bill seeks to create new offences of refusing to decode materials when required by investigators.

Section 21 makes provision for the supplying of copies of records of seizure to certain people after property has been seized. If requested by the person who had custody or control of the seized property immediately before it was seized, the officer in charge of the investigation must allow that person access to it under police supervision. The officer must also make provisions to allow for the property be to photographed or copied by that person or to supply the person with photographs/copies of it within a reasonable time. Such a request need not be complied with if there are reasonable grounds to believe that to do so would prejudice any related investigation or criminal proceedings (s. 21(8)).

Section 22 makes provision for the retention of seized property. Section 22(1) provides that anything seized may be retained for as long as necessary in all the circumstances. However, s. 22(2) allows for property to be retained for use as evidence in a trial, forensic examination or further investigation *unless a photograph or copy would suffice*. Seized property may be retained in order to establish its lawful owner (s. 22(2)(b)). There is no specific provision under s.22 for the retention of property for purely intelligence purposes.

Property seized simply to prevent an arrested person from using it to escape or to cause injury, damage etc. cannot be retained for those purposes once the person has been released (s. 22(3)).

Information gained as a result of a lawful search may be passed on to other individuals and organisations for purposes of investigation and prosecution. It must not be used for private purposes (*Marcel* v *Commissioner of Police for the Metropolis* [1992] Ch 225; also **see chapter 1** for the requirements as to confidentiality in the Code of Conduct for police officers).

For the provisions regarding the disposal of property in police possession, see the Police (Property) Act 1897.

There is a power of seizure — although not apparently a power of *search* — under the Confiscation of Alcohol (Young Persons) Act 1997, together with a power of arrest for failing to comply (**see chapter 10**).

There is also a power of seizure for any radio scanning or other equipment under the Telecommunications Act 1984, s. 79(1)(ba) (**see chapter 3**).

In addition, there is also a *duty* of seizure for a constable (and a park keeper!) in uniform in respect of people under 16 years old who have tobacco and cigarette papers in a public place (Children and Young Persons Act 1933, s. 7(3)).

2.9.8 Protected Material

Some material cannot be seized, either under PACE 1984 or any other enactment; certain other material can only be seized under special circumstances set out in the 1984 Act.

Legally Privileged Material

Material which falls within the definition at PACE 1984, s. 10(1) is subject to legal privilege which means that it cannot be searched for or seized.

Section 10(1) provides that:

(1) Subject to subsection (2) below, in this Act 'items subject to legal privilege' means—
(a) communications between a professional legal adviser and his client or any person representing his client made in connection with the giving of legal advice to the client;
(b) communications between a professional legal adviser and his client or any person representing his client or between such an adviser or his client or any such representative and any other person made in connection with or in contemplation of legal proceedings and for the purposes of such proceedings; and
(c) items enclosed with or referred to in such communications and made—
(i) in connection with the giving of legal advice; or
(ii) in connection with or in contemplation of legal proceedings and for the purposes of such proceedings,
when they are in the possession of a person who is entitled to possession of them.

Keynote

Items held with the intention of furthering a criminal purpose are no longer subject to this privilege (s. 10(2)). However, when making an application for a warrant to search for and seize such material the procedure under sch. 1 should be used. Occasions where this will happen are very rare and would include instances where a solicitor's firm is the subject of a criminal investigation (see *R* v *Leeds Crown Court, ex parte Switalski* [1991] Crim LR 559). For further discussion in relation to the extent of legal privilege, **see Evidence and Procedure, chapter 10.**

Excluded Material

Access to 'excluded material' can generally only be gained by applying to a judge for a production order under the procedure set out in PACE 1984, sch. 1 and Code B.

Section 11 of the 1984 Act provides that:

(1) Subject to the following provisions of this section, in this Act 'excluded material' means—
(a) personal records which a person has acquired or created in the course of any trade, business, profession or other occupation or for the purposes of any paid or unpaid office and which he holds in confidence;
(b) human tissue or tissue fluid which has been taken for the purposes of diagnosis or medical treatment and which a person holds in confidence;
(c) journalistic material which a person holds in confidence and which consists—
(i) of documents; or
(ii) of records other than documents.
(2) A person holds material other than journalistic material in confidence for the purposes of this section if he holds it subject—
(a) to an express or implied undertaking to hold it in confidence; or
(b) to a restriction on disclosure or an obligation of secrecy contained in any enactment, including an enactment contained in an Act passed after this Act.
(3) A person holds journalistic material in confidence for the purposes of this section if—
(a) he holds it subject to such an undertaking, restriction or obligation; and
(b) it has been continuously held (by one or more persons) subject to such an undertaking, restriction or obligation since it was first acquired or created for the purposes of journalism.

Keynote

Medical records and dental records would fall into this category, as might records made by priests or religious advisers.

'Personal records' are defined under PACE 1984, s. 12 and include records relating to the physical or mental health, counselling or assistance given to an individual who can be identified by those records.

'Journalistic material' is defined under s. 13 as material acquired or created for the purposes of journalism.

Special Procedure Material

Special procedure material can be gained by applying for a search warrant or a production order under PACE 1984, sch. 1.

Section 14 of PACE 1984 provides that:

> *(1)   In this Act 'special procedure material' means—*
> *(a)   material to which subsection (2) below applies; and*
> *(b)   journalistic material, other than excluded material.*
> *(2)   Subject to the following provisions of this section, this subsection applies to material, other than items subject to legal privilege and excluded material, in the possession of a person who—*
> *(a)   acquired or created it in the course of any trade, business, profession or other occupation or for the purpose of any paid or unpaid office; and*
> *(b)   holds it subject—*
> *(i)   to an express or implied undertaking to hold it in confidence; or*
> *(ii)   to a restriction or obligation such as is mentioned in section 11(2)(b) above.*

Keynote

For items subject to 'legal privilege' and 'excluded material', **see the Keynote above**.

The person believed to be in possession of the material must have come by it under the circumstances set out at s. 14(2)(a) *and* must hold it under the undertakings or obligations set out at s. 14(2)(b).

PART TWO

COMMUNITY SAFETY

CHAPTER THREE

HARASSMENT, HOSTILITY AND ANTI-SOCIAL BEHAVIOUR

3.1 Introduction

In addition to the generic police powers considered in **chapter 2**, there are many other provisions that exist to help the police in their efforts to preserve the safety and quality of life of the community. This chapter, and the rest of Part Two, aims to set out the main areas of criminal law and procedure that address public and individual anxiety, threats to personal safety and anti-social behaviour.

3.2 Racially Aggravated Offences

Since the offence of inciting racial hatred was created by the Race Relations Act in 1965, various governments have tried to install an effective method by which the criminal law can address offending that is actuated by racism. That, and the many provisions which followed, were found to present a number of practical problems, many relating to the actual or perceived difficulties of proving the various elements of the offences. In addition to the racial hatred offences, there have been other attempts to single out criminal conduct that has an overtly racist element (for example the offences of 'racialist' chanting under the Football Offences Act 1991 (**see chapter 4**)).

For whatever reasons, the various measures introduced since 1965 had not succeeded in preventing a rise in the number of reported 'racial incidents' (as defined by ACPO). Although the Home Affairs Select Committee recommended the creation of a new offence of racially motivated violence, the most immediate response was the amendment of the Public Order Act 1986 (under s. 154 of the Criminal Justice and Public Order Act 1994), inserting a new s. 4A. This created a summary offence of intentionally causing harassment, alarm or distress (**see chapter 4**). Again there has been some dissatisfaction as to the extent to which this additional offence (s. 4A) has addressed the behaviour that it was aimed at curbing. More recently, the Stephen Lawrence inquiry focused a great deal of attention on the many potential sources of racism — particularly those that are not immediately apparent on the surface. The inquiry observed (at para. 45.17) that:

We believe that the use of the words 'racial' and 'racially motivated' are in themselves inaccurate because we all belong to one human race, regardless of our colour, culture or ethnic origin . . .

Consequently, the inquiry recommended (para. 45.17) a new definition of a *racist incident* namely 'any incident which is perceived to be racist by the victim or any other person.'

That definition does not yet appear in any legislation. However, the Crime and Disorder Act 1998 (passed before the report of the Stephen Lawrence inquiry) has re-visited the whole issue of racially aggravated crime. Although adopting the use of the expression 'racially aggravated', the Act seeks to address many of the issues of criminal law arising from the Stephen Lawrence inquiry. It sets out certain conditions under which specified offences will be deemed to be 'racially aggravated' and increases the powers available to the courts in the punishment of racist offenders.

The 1998 Act further allows the courts to take account of any element of racial aggravation in an offence coming before them by introducing a new requirement under s. 82. Although that section formalises an earlier sentencing decision (*R* v *Ribbans* (1995) 12 Cr App R (S) 698) in requiring a court to take any element of racial aggravation into account when passing sentence, the new statutory requirement means that the court must also state openly that such features of the offence have been taken into consideration.

The requirement under s. 82 applies to *any offence other than the new racially aggravated offences* created by the Act. It was felt by the legislators that, even though some offences carried a high enough maximum penalty under the existing legislation (examples of which might be arson (**see Crime, chapter 14**) or wounding with intent (**see Crime, chapter 8**), s. 82 would make the courts take account of, and draw attention to, any racial aggravation when determining the appropriate sentence in any particular case.

3.2.1   **The Offences**

Sections 28–33 of the Crime and Disorder Act 1998 do not so much create *new* offences, but rather take *existing* offences and set out circumstances under which those offences will be deemed to be 'aggravated'. Those offences are:

- wounding or grievous bodily harm — Offences Against the Person Act 1861, s. 20
- causing actual bodily harm — Offences Against the Person Act 1861, s. 47
- common assault — Criminal Justice Act 1988, s. 39

(s. 29; **see Crime, chapter 8**)

- 'simple' criminal damage — Criminal Damage Act 1971, s. 1(1)

(s. 30; **see Crime, chapter 14**)

- causing fear or provocation of violence — Public Order Act 1986, s. 4
- intentional harassment, alarm or distress — Public Order Act 1986, s. 4A
- causing harassment, alarm or distress — Public Order Act 1986, s. 5

(s. 31; **see chapter 4**)

- harassment — Protection from Harassment Act 1997, s. 2
- putting in fear of violence — Protection from Harassment Act 1997, s. 4

(s. 32; **see para. 3.4**).

In order to prove these offences there must be proof of the relevant, substantive offence (e.g. common assault) together with further proof of the aggravating circumstances. Once both conditions have been made out, the offences attract greater maximum penalties and powers. For that reason the specific effects of this legislation are dealt with under the relevant chapters in this Manual.

3.2.2   'Racially Aggravated'

The test for racial aggravation is set out at s. 28 of the Crime and Disorder Act 1998:

> (1)   An offence is racially aggravated for the purposes of sections 29 to 32 if—
>   (a)   at the time of committing the offence, or immediately before or after doing so, the offender demonstrates towards the victim of the offence hostility based on the victim's membership (or presumed membership) of a racial group; or
>   (b)   the offence is motivated (wholly or partly) by hostility towards members of a racial group based on their membership of that group.
>   (2)   In subsection (1)(a) above—
>   'membership', in relation to a racial group, includes; association with members of that group;
>   'presumed' means presumed by the offender.
>   (3)   It is immaterial for the purposes of paragraph (a) or (b) of subsection (1) above whether or not the offender's hostility is also based, to any extent, on—
>   (a)   the fact or presumption that any person or group of persons belongs to any religious group; or
>   (b)   any other factor not mentioned in that paragraph.
>   (4)   In this section 'racial group' means a group of persons defined by reference to race, colour, nationality (including citizenship) or ethnic or national origins.

Keynote

The aggravating factors for the purposes of s. 28 can be divided into:

- *demonstration* of hostility by the defendant
- *motivation* by hostility of the defendant.

The second type of situation, where the defendant is *motivated* by racial hostility, is the type at which the government's policies to tackle racism are aimed; it is also by far the harder of the two to prove, even though the relevant offence need only be *partly* motivated by racial hostility.

Hostility

Common to both factors under s. 28(1)(a) and (b) is the notion of hostility.

Hostility is not defined. However, in comparison to the problematic expression of 'racial hatred' used in the Public Order Act 1986 (**see para. 3.3**), hostility may well be much easier to identify and prove. The *Oxford English Dictionary* defines 'hostile' as 'of the nature or disposition of an enemy; unfriendly, antagonistic'. It would seem relatively straightforward to show that someone's behaviour in committing the relevant offences was 'unfriendly or antagonistic'. The difficult bit will come when trying to show that the hostility was *based on* the relevant person's membership of a racial group.

Racial groups

In each case the hostility must be based on the relevant person's membership of a racial group, i.e. membership of a group of people defined by reference to:

- race
- colour
- nationality (including citizenship)
- ethnic origins
- national origins

(s. 28(4)).

This definition is the same as that used in the Public Order Act 1986 (**see below**).

It is also very similar to that used in the Race Relations Act 1976.

In determining whether or not a group is defined by *ethnic origins*, the courts will have regard to the judgment in the House of Lords in *Mandla* v *Dowell Lee* [1983] 2 AC 548. In that case their Lordships decided that Sikhs were such a group (for the purposes of the Race Relations Act 1976) after considering whether they as a group had:

- A long shared *history*.
- A *cultural tradition* of their own, including family and social customs and manners, often, but not necessarily, associated with religious observance.
- Either a *common geographical origin* or descent from a small number of *common ancestors*.
- A *common language*, not necessarily peculiar to that group.
- A *common literature* peculiar to that group.
- A *common religion* different from that of neighbouring groups or the general community surrounding the group.
- The characteristic of being a *minority* or an *oppressed* or a *dominant* group within a larger community.

Lord Fraser's *dictum* suggests that the first two characteristics above are essential in defining an 'ethnic group', while the others are at least relevant.

His Lordship also approved a decision from New Zealand to the effect that Jews are a group with common ethnic origins (*Kings-Ansell* v *Police* [1979] 2 NZLR 531).

Religion

Although Lord Fraser's sixth point above refers to religion as a possible defining characteristic of an ethnic group, one notable omission from the ambit of *racial groups* as defined under s. 28(4) is religion. Despite some opposition during the passing of the Crime and Disorder Act 1998, the legislators decided not to include religion as a point of reference when classifying racial groups.

Therefore, a purely religious group such as Rastafarians (who have been held not to be members of an ethnic group *per se* (*Dawkins* v *Crown Suppliers (Property Services Agency)*, *The Times*, 4 February 1993)) are not covered by the definition of racial group. That is not to say, however, that an attack on a Rastafarian cannot be a racially aggravated offence under s. 28. Such an attack might be based on the defendant's hostility towards a *racial group* (e.g. African-Caribbeans) into which many Rastafarians fall. Alternatively, such an attack might be made on a white Rastafarian based on similar hostility towards a racial group to which the person belongs. In such cases, s. 28(3) (**see below**) would prevent the defendant from claiming that his/her hostility was based on the fact that the person was a Rastafarian.

This distinction seems to produce unfair treatment of behaviour that is essentially the same. An example given by several commentators is the contrast between deliberately sending pork to a Jew (clearly capable of being a racially aggravated form of harassment because Jews have been held to be a group with common ethnic origins) and deliberately sending beef to a Hindu, which would not be racially aggravated as Hindus are a *religious* group.

Muslims have also been held to be religious, but not racial groups (*J.H Walker* v *Hussain* [1996] ICR 291).

In practice, these distinctions are unlikely to arise as barriers to most pertinent prosecutions.

Other Racial Groups

Traditional 'gypsies' (as opposed to travellers) are capable of being a racial group on the basis of ethnic origin (*Commission for Racial Equality* v *Dutton* [1989] QB 783). English and Scottish people have been held to constitute groups defined by reference to national origins and thus as members of 'racial groups' in the broad sense as defined and protected from discrimination under the Race Relations Act 1976 (*Northern Joint Police Board* v *Power* [1997] IRLR 610). This decision ought logically to extend to Irish and Welsh people.

Membership

An important extension of 'racial groups' lies in the inclusion of people who associate with members of that group. 'Membership' *for the purposes of s. 28(1)(a)* will include *association* with members of that group (a slightly circular definition) (s. 28(2)). This means that a white man who has a black female partner would potentially fall within the category of a 'member' of her racial group — and vice versa. Moreover, people who work within certain racial groups within the community could also be regarded as members of those groups for these purposes.

For the purposes of s. 28(1)(a), 'membership' will also include anyone *presumed by the defendant* to be a member of a racial group. Therefore, if a defendant wrongly presumed that a person was a member of a racial group, say a Pakistani, and assaulted them as a result, the defendant's *presumption* would be enough to make his/her behaviour 'racially aggravated', even though the victim was in fact an Indian.

Such a presumption would not extend to the aggravating factors under s. 28(1)(b). The only apparent reason for this would seem to be that the s. 28(1)(a) offence requires hostility to be demonstrated towards a particular person ('the victim') while the offence under s. 28(1)(b) envisages hostility towards members of a racial group generally and does not require a specific victim.

As a concession to the pressure to include religion within the new laws on racial aggravation, s. 28(3) goes on to provide that it is immaterial whether the defendant's hostility (in either case under s. 28(1)) is also based to any extent on the relevant persons' membership/presumed membership of any *religious* group or on *any other factor*.

This concession in s. 28(3) only prevents the defendant pointing to another *factor* — including membership of a religious group — in order to explain his/her behaviour in committing the relevant offence (assault, criminal damage, etc.). Although it removes the opportunity for a defendant to argue that his/her behaviour was as a result of other factors (e.g. arising out of a domestic dispute), the subsection does not remove the burden on the prosecution to show that the defendant either demonstrated racial hostility or was motivated by it.

Demonstration of Hostility

Under s. 28(1)(a) it must be shown that the defendant *demonstrated* the required hostility:

- at the time of the offence
- immediately before or
- immediately after committing the offence.

No guidance is given as to how *immediately* will be interpreted. It is submitted that whether a defendant's demonstration of hostility came immediately before or after the relevant offence will be a question of fact to be decided in light of all the circumstances.

In deciding the issue of immediacy the courts will have to consider the degree of proximity between the defendant's demonstration of racial hostility and the relevant offence itself. It is submitted that the degree of proximity will have to be very high before the defendant's hostility could be shown to have been *immediately* before or after the *actus reus* of the offence. This might cause problems with offences that are said to be 'continuing' or 'ongoing'.

It is also necessary, for the purposes of s. 28(1)(a), to show that the defendant demonstrated his/her hostility *towards the victim of the offence*. Again this may be problematic in relation to certain offences e.g. criminal damage (**see Crime, chapter 14**).

3.3   Other Offences Involving Racism: Racial Hatred

In addition to the racially aggravated offences discussed above — and elsewhere in this Manual — there are still several former offences under earlier legislation. Few prosecutions took place under these headings before the passing of the Crime and Disorder Act 1998. How long they will continue as a significant feature of the criminal justice system's armoury in tackling racism remains to be seen and what follows is simply a summary of these offences.

The Public Order Act 1986 introduced several offences aimed at addressing incidents specifically motivated by racial hatred.

For these purposes 'racial hatred' means hatred against a group of persons in Great Britain defined by reference to colour, race, nationality (including citizenship) or ethnic or national origins (s. 17).

3.3.1   Use of Words, Behaviour or Display of Written Material

Offence — Use of Words or Behaviour or Display of Written Material — Public Order Act 1986, s. 18
Triable either way. Two years' imprisonment and/or a fine on indictment;
six months' imprisonment and/or a fine summarily.
(*Statutory power of arrest*)

The Public Order Act 1986, s. 18 states:

(1)   A person who uses threatening, abusive or insulting words or behaviour, or displays any written material which is threatening, abusive or insulting, is guilty of an offence if—
(a)   he intends thereby to stir up racial hatred, or
(b)   having regard to all the circumstances racial hatred is likely to be stirred up thereby.
(2)   An offence under this section may be committed in a public or a private place, except that no offence is committed where the words or behaviour are used, or the written material is displayed, by a person inside a dwelling and are not heard or seen except by other persons in that or another dwelling.

Keynote

This, and the other offences under this part of the Act, may not be prosecuted without the consent of the Attorney-General (or Solicitor-General).

Generally, in order to prove these offences, you must show that a defendant:

- *intended* to stir up racial hatred; or
- that he/she *intended* the relevant words, behaviour or material to be threatening, abusive or insulting; or
- that he/she *was aware* that the relevant words/behaviour/material might be threatening, abusive or insulting.

This offence does not apply to broadcasts in a programme (**but see below**) and there are exemptions in the case of fair and accurate reports of parliamentary or court proceedings.

Defence

The Public Order Act 1986, s. 18 states:

(4)   In proceedings for an offence under this section it is a defence for the accused to prove that he was inside a dwelling and had no reason to believe that the words or behaviour used, or the written material displayed, would be heard or seen by a person outside that or any other dwelling.

Power of Arrest

The Public Order Act 1986, s. 18 states:

(3)   A constable may arrest without warrant anyone he reasonably suspects is committing an offence under this section.

3.3.2 Publishing or Distributing Written Material

**Offence — Publishing or Distributing Written Material —
Public Order Act 1986, s. 19**
*Triable either way. Two years' imprisonment and/or a fine on indictment;
six months' imprisonment and/or a fine summarily.*
(*Arrestable offence*)

The Public Order Act 1986, s. 19 states:

> *(1)   A person who publishes or distributes written material which is threatening, abusive or insulting is guilty of an offence if—*
> *(a)   he intends thereby to stir up racial hatred, or*
> *(b)   having regard to all the circumstances racial hatred is likely to be stirred up thereby.*
> *(2) . . .*
> *(3)   References in this Part to the publication or distribution of written material are to its publication or distribution to the public or a section of the public.*

Defence

The Public Order Act 1986, s. 19 states:

> *(2)   In proceedings for an offence under this section it is a defence for an accused who is not shown to have intended to stir up racial hatred to prove that he was not aware of the content of the material and did not suspect, and had no reason to suspect, that it was threatening, abusive or insulting.*

3.3.3 Other offences under Part III

Other Public Order Act 1986 offences involving activities intended or likely to stir up racial hatred are:

- presenting or directing a public performance of a play — s. 20
- distributing, showing or playing recordings — s. 21
- providing, producing, directing or appearing in a programme service — s. 22
- possessing written material or recordings with a view to displaying, publishing, distributing and playing in a programme service — s. 23.

Each of these offences is triable either way and has its own specific statutory defence.

3.4   Protection from Harassment

Following a number of highly-publicised cases which illustrate the effects which 'stalking' and other forms of persistent harassment can have on victims, the Protection from Harassment Act 1997 was introduced. Some of the 1997 Act's most sweeping provisions have been brought into force by the Crime and Disorder Act 1998.

3.4.1 The Offences

Offence — Harassment — Protection from Harassment Act 1997, ss. 1 and 2
Triable summarily. Six months' imprisonment and/or a fine.
(*Arrestable offence*)

Offence — Racially Aggravated — Crime and Disorder Act 1998, s. 32(1)(a)

*Triable either way. Two years' imprisonment and/or a fine on indictment;
six months' imprisonment and/or a fine summarily.*
(*Arrestable offence*)

The Protection from Harassment Act 1997, ss. 1 and 2 state:

> 1.—(1) A person must not pursue a course of conduct—
>   (a) which amounts to harassment of another, and
>   (b) which he knows or ought to know amounts to harassment of the other.

> 2.—(1) A person who pursues a course of conduct in breach of section 1 is guilty of an offence.

Keynote

This offence is made an 'arrestable offence' (**see chapter 2**) by s. 2(3).

The racially-aggravated offence is made an arrestable offence by s. 32(2) of the Crime and Disorder Act 1998 which adds it to those offences listed under s. 24(2) of the Police and Criminal Evidence Act 1984 (**see chapter 2**).

Unlike some of the other racially-aggravated offences (**see below** and **Crime, chapters 8 and 14**), provisions are specifically made for alternative verdicts in relation to harassment (see s. 32(5)).

For a full explanation of the meaning of 'racially aggravated' **see para. 3.2**.

'Harassment' includes alarming the person or causing them distress (s. 7(1) of the 1997 Act).

The inclusion of alarm or distress is significant as it has been held by the Divisional Court that a person — in this case, a police officer — can be alarmed for the safety of another (*Lodge* v *DPP*, *The Times*, 26 October 1988).

'Course of conduct' must involve conduct on at least two occasions but it can involve speech (s. 7(3) and (4)). The issue of whether two acts of harassment against two different victims would suffice for an offence under s. 2 was raised in *DPP* v *Williams (Michael)*, unreported, 27 July 1998. In that case the defendant had reached in through an open bathroom window while one woman was taking a shower and had then climbed onto a roof to see the woman and a friend through a bedroom window. Unfortunately, the Divisional Court held that there was no need to construe the wording of the Act as one of the women had been involved in both incidents. It is arguable that, under the terms of the Interpretation Act 1978, s. 6, the requirements of the offence could be met where there are two separate victims but this will have to await clarification. What the court did decide in *Williams*, however, was that the offence was not restricted to acts of 'stalking'.

As this is new legislation, the way in which a court might separate conduct into different instances is not yet known. It may be that, in a case of 'stalking', simply following the same person on two occasions during the same day may be enough.

There is no specific requirement that the activity making up the course of conduct be of the same nature. Therefore two distinctly different types of behaviour by the defendant (e.g. making a telephone call on one occasion and damaging the victim's property on another) may suffice. In a case involving the racially-aggravated offence, the aggravating element will need to be proved in relation to both instances of the defendant's conduct.

Some behaviour will be sufficiently disturbing or alarming for two instances to suffice (e.g. the making of overt threats). If sufficiently alarming or distressing, the behaviour may also amount to an offence in itself under some other legislation (**see Crime, chapter 8**). Other behaviour, however, may not be sufficient to establish 'harassment' after only two occasions (e.g. the sending of flowers and gifts) and may require more than the bare statutory minimum of two occasions.

The repeated commission of other offences (say, public order offences or offences against property) involving the same victim may also amount to harassment. In such cases the advice of the Crown Prosecution Service should be sought as to which charge(s) to prefer.

In order to prove this offence you must show that:

- the defendant pursued a 'course of conduct'
- the course of conduct amounted to harassment as defined in s. 7(1), and
- the defendant knew, or ought to have known, that his/her conduct amounted to harassment.

In order to avoid the practical difficulties of proving the subjective *intention* of the defendant, the offence focuses on an objective test.

In addition, s. 1(2) provides that:

> (2)   For the purposes of this section, the person whose course of conduct is in question ought to know that it amounts to harassment of another if a reasonable person in possession of the same information would think the course of conduct amounted to harassment of the other.

If the person concerned in the course of conduct can show that he/she did so:

- for the purpose of preventing or detecting crime, or
- under any enactment or rule of law to comply with a particular requirement, or
- in circumstances whereby the course of conduct was reasonable

the offence under s. 1(1) will not apply (s. 1(3)).

The burden of proving any of these features or circumstances lies with the defendant (on the balance of probabilities, **see Evidence and Procedure, chapter 11**).

Examples might be police or DSS surveillance teams, or court officers serving summonses. (See also the defence under s. 12 below.)

Whether a course of conduct is 'reasonable' will be a question of fact for a court to decide in the light of all the circumstances. The wording of s. 1(2) suggests that such a test might be an *objective* one (i.e. as a reasonable bystander) and not one based upon the particular belief or perception of the defendant — otherwise the main effect of the 1997 Act would be considerably diluted.

For the powers of a court to issue a restraining order or injunction in relation to this offence, **see below**).

Under s. 3(1) conduct or apprehended conduct falling within s. 1 may be the subject of a civil claim by the victim/intended victim. This creates a 'statutory tort' of harassment in addition to the criminal offence.

Offence — Putting People in Fear of Violence — Protection from Harassment Act 1997, s. 4
Triable either way. Five years' imprisonment and/or a fine on indictment; six months' imprisonment and/or a fine summarily.
(Arrestable offence)

Offence — Racially Aggravated — Crime and Disorder Act 1998, s. 32(1)(b)
Triable either way. Seven years' imprisonment and/or a fine on indictment; six months' imprisonment and/or a fine summarily.
(Arrestable offence)

The Protection from Harassment Act 1997, s. 4 states:

(1)   A person whose course of conduct causes another to fear, on at least two occasions, that violence will be used against him is guilty of an offence if he knows or ought to know that his course of conduct will cause the other so to fear on each of those occasions.

Keynote

'Course of conduct' is discussed above.

You must show that the defendant knew, or ought to have known that their conduct would cause the other person to fear violence. This may be shown by any previous conversations or communications between the defendant and the victim, together with the victims' response to the defendant's earlier behaviour (e.g. running away, calling the police etc.).

The fear of violence being used against the victim must be present on both occasions. If it is present on one occasion but not the other, the offence under s. 2 above may be appropriate.

For a full explanation of the meaning of 'racially aggravated', **see para. 3.2**.

Unlike some of the other racially-aggravated offences (**see Crime, chapters 8 and 14**), provisions are specifically made for alternative verdicts in relation to harassment (see s. 32(6). Where the racially aggravated form of the offence is charged, the aggravating element of the defendant's conduct must be shown in relation to both instances.

As with the s. 2 offence, a single instance of behaviour may be enough to support a charge for another offence (e.g. assault **see Crime, chapter 8** or threats to kill, **see below**).

Again, this offence is not one of *intent* but one which is subject to a test of reasonableness against the standard of an ordinary person in possession of the same information as the defendant.

For the powers of a court to issue a restraining order or injunction in relation to this offence, **see below**.

Section 4 goes on to state that:

> (2)   For the purposes of this section, the person whose course of conduct is in question ought to know that it will cause another to fear that violence will be used against him on any occasion if a reasonable person in possession of the same information would think the course of conduct would cause the other so to fear on that occasion.

Defence

Section 4(3) provides that:

> (3)   It is a defence for a person charged with an offence under this section to show that—
> (a)   his course of conduct was pursued for the purpose of preventing or detecting crime,
> (b)   his course of conduct was pursued under any enactment or rule of law or to comply with any condition or requirement imposed by any person under any enactment, or
> (c)   the pursuit of his course of conduct was reasonable for the protection of himself or another or for the protection of his or another's property.

Keynote

There is a slight difference in the wording of the defence when compared to that under s. 1(3) above. There, the defendant may show that his/her conduct was reasonable in the particular circumstances. In relation to the more serious offence under s. 4, the defendant must show that his/her conduct was reasonable *for the protection of themselves, another person or their own/another's property*. These are the only grounds on which the defendant may argue reasonableness in answer to a charge under s. 4. He/she could not therefore argue, say, that the pursuit of the course of conduct was 'reasonable' in order to enforce a debt or to communicate with the victim.

In addition, s. 12 allows for the Secretary of State to certify that the conduct was carried out by a 'specified person' on a 'specified occasion' related to:

- national security
- the economic well-being of the UK, or
- the prevention or detection of serious crime

on behalf of the Crown. If such a certification is made, the conduct of the specified person will not be an offence under the 1997 Act.

3.4.2   Injunctions

Under the Protection from Harassment Act 1997, s. 3(1), the High Court or a county court may issue an injunction in respect of civil proceedings brought in respect of an actual or apprehended breach of s. 1. The effect of this is that a defendant may be made the subject of an injunction even though his/her behaviour has not amounted to an offence under the 1997 Act.

Section 3(3) provides

> *(3) Where—*
>   *(a) in such proceedings the High Court or a county court grants an injunction for the purpose of restraining the defendant from pursuing any conduct which amounts to harassment, and*
>   *(b) the [claimant] considers that the defendant has done anything which he is prohibited from doing by the injunction,*
> *the [claimant] may apply for the issue of a warrant for the arrest of the defendant.*

Keynote

Anyone arrested under such a warrant may be dealt with by the court at the time of his/her appearance. Alternatively, the court may adjourn the proceedings and release the defendant, dealing with him/her within 14 days of his/her arrest provided the defendant is given not less than two days' notice of the adjourned hearing (see the Rules of the Supreme Court 1998 (SI 1998 No. 1898) and the County Court (Amended) Rules 1998 (SI 1998 No. 1899)).

This is in contrast to some other injunctions (e.g. under the Family Law Act 1996 (**see chapter** 7) and the Housing Act 1996 (**see chapter 9**)). In a case involving an injunction restraining the actions of an anti-vivisection group, the Divisional Court held that the 1997 Act was not a means of preventing individuals from exercising their right to protest over issues of public interest. Eady J said that such an extension of the law had clearly not been Parliament's intention and that the courts would resist any attempts to interpret the Act widely (*Huntingdon Life Sciences Ltd* v *Curtin, The Times*, 11 December 1997).

Of far greater significance is the offence created by s. 3(6) of the Protection from Harassment Act 1997.

Offence — Breach of Injunction — Protection from Harassment Act 1997, s. 3(6)
Triable either way. Five years' imprisonment and/or a fine on indictment;
six months' imprisonment and/or a fine summarily.
(*Arrestable offence*)

The Protection from Harassment Act 1997, s. 3(6) states:

> *(6) Where—*
>   *(a) the High Court or a county court grants an injunction for the purpose mentioned in subsection (3)(a), and*
>   *(b) without reasonable excuse the defendant does anything which he is prohibited from doing by the injunction,*
> *he is guilty of an offence.*

Keynote

Civil injunctions generally will only involve the police where a power of an arrest has been attached (e.g. under s. 3(3) above). In these cases the role of the police will be to bring the defendant before the court in order that he/she can explain his/her behaviour. There is therefore no investigative or prosecuting function on the part of the officers. Section 3(6), however, creates a specific offence of breaching the terms of an injunction. Like the Anti-Social Behaviour Order (ASBO) (see below) and Sex Offender Order (SOO) (**see Crime, chapter 10**) this marks a new concept in the criminal law.

If a defendant breaches an injunction and commits the offence under s. 3(6) above, he/she will be dealt with in the way of any other prisoner brought into police detention and will face a prison sentence of five years.

It is important to distinguish the offence under s. 3(6), breaching an injunction, from the provisions of s. 5 which deal with restraining orders.

3.4.3   Restraining Orders

Section 5 of the Protection from Harassment Act 1997 provides that a court dealing with a person convicted of an offence under s. 2 or 4 may make an order (a restraining order). Such an order can only be made after a defendant's conviction for an offence under s. 2 or 4 of the 1997 Act. It is therefore much more limited than the injunction discussed above.

Section 5(2) goes on to provide that:

> (2)   *The order may, for the purpose of protecting the victim of the offence, or any other person mentioned in the order, from further conduct which—*
> (a)   *amounts to harassment, or*
> (b)   *will cause a fear of violence,*
> *prohibit the defendant from doing anything described in the order.*

Keynote

The purpose behind these orders is to empower the courts to restrain the conduct of offenders following their conviction — an area that was previously seen as one of particular weakness in the criminal justice system.

Unlike the injunction under s. 3(3), restraining orders can be made in criminal court.

The order may be made for the protection of the victim or anyone else mentioned and it may run for a specified period or until a further order.

The prosecutor, the defendant or anyone else mentioned in the order may apply to the court that made it to have the order varied or discharged (s. 5(4)).

Offence — Breach of Restraining Order — Protection from Harassment Act 1997, s. 5(5)
Triable either way. Five years' imprisonment and/or a fine on indictment; six months' imprisonment and/or a fine summarily.
(*Arrestable offence*)

The Protection from Harassment Act 1997, s. 5(5) states:

> (5)   *If without reasonable excuse the defendant does anything which he is prohibited from doing by an order under this section, he is guilty of an offence.*

Keynote

The fact that restraining orders can only be made after a conviction for one of the offences under s. 2 or 4 may affect decisions when selecting appropriate charges arising out of an incident. Substituting or failing to include a charge under s. 2 or 4, removes the court's powers to make a restraining order which may be the main remedy sought by a victim. In any cases of doubt the guidance of the Crown Prosecution Service should be sought.

3.5 Anti-Social Behaviour Orders

In aiming to create communities which are safer and which feel safer, the government has introduced a new form of restraint that can be imposed on the behaviour of some members of those communities — the Anti-Social Behaviour Order (ASBO) and the Sex Offenders Order (SOO); see **Crime, chapter 10**. (See also the remedies under the Protection from Harassment Act 1997, **para. 3.4**.)

A significant feature of these orders lies in the fact that they are civil complaints, made under the procedure set out in the Magistrates' Courts Act 1980. This means that the application process is governed by the civil burden of proof, i.e. on the balance of probabilities (**see Evidence and Procedure, chapter 11**). Given the fact that breach of an order can result in a sentence of imprisonment of five years, this is an important, and to some commentators, a worrying development in the criminal law. Although there are other occasions where failure to abide by what is effectively a civil order can lead to arrest (e.g. under the Family Law Act 1996, **see chapter** 7), the new orders introduced by the Crime and Disorder Act 1998 impose substantial restrictions on a person's freedom of movement, speech etc. It is uncertain how those restrictions will be reconciled with the European Convention on Human Rights and the Human Rights Act 1998 which is set to come into force in the year 2000.

3.5.1 The Anti-Social Behaviour Order (ASBO)

The Crime and Disorder Act 1998, s. 1 states:

(1) An application for an order under this section may be made by a relevant authority if it appears to the authority that the following conditions are fulfilled with respect to any person aged 10 or over, namely—
(a) that the person has acted, since the commencement date, in an anti-social manner, that is to say, in a manner that caused or was likely to cause harassment, alarm or distress to one or more persons not of the same household as himself, and
(b) that such an order is necessary to protect persons in the local government area in which the harassment, alarm or distress was caused or was likely to be caused from further anti-social acts by him;
and in this section 'relevant authority' means the council for the local government area or any chief officer of police any part of whose police area lies within that area.
(2) A relevant authority shall not make such an application without consulting each other relevant authority.
(3) Such an application shall be made by complaint to the magistrates' court whose commission area includes the place where it is alleged that the harassment, alarm or distress was caused or was likely to be caused.
(4) If, on such an application, it is proved that the conditions mentioned in subsection (1) above are fulfilled, the magistrates' court may make an order under this section (an 'anti-social behaviour order') which prohibits the defendant from doing anything described in the order.

Keynote

In order to apply for an ASBO, it must:

- appear to the relevant authority that

- a relevant person acted in a manner that caused, or was likely to cause harassment, alarm or distress to one or more people who are not of the same household as the relevant person, and

- that such an order is necessary to protect people in the local government area in which the consequences of that person's behaviour were caused/likely to be caused, from further anti-social acts by that person.

The 'relevant authority' for the purposes of an ASBO is the local authority or the chief officer of police, any part of whose police area lies within the area of that local authority. However, the requirement under subsection (2) means that both of these sources of authority will have to work together in bringing any application for an ASBO. This imposition of dual responsibility, which effectively enforces a collaborative approach between the police and local authorities, is another key feature of the 1998 Act (see also ss. 5 and 6, **chapter 1**).

For these purposes, the relevant local government areas are:

- in relation to England, a district or London borough, the City of London, the Isle of Wight and the Isles of Scilly;

- in relation to Wales, a county or county borough

(s. 1(12)).

It is the relevant authority who makes the application for an ASBO, thereby removing from the 'victim' of the conduct the burden of seeking a remedy themselves (contrast this with the new remedy using an injunction in cases of harassment; see **para. 3.4.2**).

An application may be made in respect of the behaviour of any person aged 10 or over. This is another significant departure from the earlier law and, together with the abolition of the presumption of *doli incapax* (**see Crime, chapter 4**), is consistent with the government's expressed intention to impose criminal responsibility on older children.

The application must be made before the local court that covers the area where the harassment, alarm or distress were caused/likely to be caused (s. 1(3)). This appears to suggest that it is the court in whose commission area the alleged or feared consequences took place which will not necessarily be the same place where the defendant's behaviour took place (for instance, where that behaviour involved the making of threatening communications).

Section 1(6) goes on to say that:

> *(6)   The prohibitions that may be imposed by an anti-social behaviour order are those necessary for the purpose of protecting from further anti-social acts by the defendant—*
> *(a)   persons in the local government area; and*
> *(b)   persons in any adjoining local government area specified in the application for the order; and a relevant authority shall not specify an adjoining local government area in the application without consulting the council for that area and each chief officer of police any part of whose police area lies within that area.*

Keynote

The proviso at s. 1(1)(a) — which excludes people from the same household — shows that the ASBO is not intended as a remedy for domestic disputes (as to which **see chapter 7**).

Section 1(5) provides that:

> *(5)   For the purpose of determining whether the condition mentioned in subsection (1)(a) above is fulfilled, the court shall disregard any act of the defendant which he shows was reasonable in the circumstances.*

Keynote

This requirement clearly places the burden of showing the reasonableness of his/her behaviour on the defendant.

The procedure for application for an ASBO is governed by the Magistrates' Courts (Sex Offenders and Anti-Social Behaviour Orders) Rules 1998 (SI 1998 No. 2682).

3.5.2   Duration of ASBO

An ASBO has a minimum period of two years' duration (s. 1(7)).

Under s. 1(8) of the 1998 Act, either the applicant or the defendant may apply to have the order varied or discharged but, under s. 1(9), no ASBO shall be discharged before the end of two years except with the consent of both parties.

**Offence — Breaching an Anti-Social Behaviour Order —
Crime and Disorder Act 1998, s. 1(10)**
*Triable either way. Five years' imprisonment and/or a fine on indictment;
six months' imprisonment and/or a fine summarily.*
(*Arrestable offence*)

The Crime and Disorder Act 1998, s. 1(10) states:

> *(10)   If without reasonable excuse a person does anything which he is prohibited from doing by an anti-social behaviour order, he shall be liable—*
> *(a)   on summary conviction, to imprisonment for a term not exceeding six months or to a fine not exceeding the statutory maximum, or to both; or*
> *(b)   on conviction on indictment, to imprisonment for a term not exceeding five years or to a fine, or to both.*

Keynote

As the punishment provided by a conditional discharge (under the Powers of Criminal Courts Act 1973) has the same general effect as an ASBO, a court cannot impose a conditional discharge on a defendant found guilty of committing an offence under s. 1(10) above (s. 1(11)).

Given the breadth of an ASBO, which may restrain a defendant from communicating with a particular person or from creating noise or nuisance, the behaviour required to commit this offence could be relatively minor. The advice of the Crown Prosecution Service may need to be sought in cases involving what appear to be innocuous but technical breaches of such an order.

It appears from the wording of the 1998 Act that a person might have an ASBO made against him/her in his/her absence. Although a magistrates' court has the power to issue a summons and then a warrant (under the Magistrates' Courts Act 1980) in order to compel the person to come to court when an application for an ASBO is being heard, it does seem that the court can go on to make an ASBO *ex parte* (in the absence of the other party). Again, if this is the case, there are serious human rights implications which may allow the procedure to be challenged.

3.5.3 Appeal

Section 4 of the Crime and Disorder Act 1998 states:

> *(1) An appeal shall lie to the Crown Court against the making by a magistrates' court of an anti-social behaviour order or sex offender order.*
> *(2) On such an appeal the Crown Court—*
> *(a) may make such orders as may be necessary to give effect to its determination of the appeal;* and
> *(b) may also make such incidental or consequential orders as appear to it to be just.*

Keynote

There is no right of appeal open to the local authority or chief officer against a decision of a court not to make an order. That would not preclude the applicant from requiring the court to 'state a case' for consideration by the Divisional Court in appropriate circumstances.

3.6 Nuisance

There are many forms of behaviour which, although not falling within some of the more 'serious' offences discussed elsewhere in this Manual, are nevertheless a source of annoyance or disquiet to the community. Some of these activities are usefully classified as 'nuisances'.

3.6.1 Public Nuisance

Although many of the activities dealt with in this chapter are described as 'nuisances', there is a specific offence of creating or being responsible for a public nuisance, an offence that overlaps with some other aspects of criminal behaviour.

The common law concept of nuisance is separated into public and private nuisance. Private nuisance is dealt with under civil law as a *tort* ('wrong'). Public nuisance, however, can also be dealt with under criminal law.

A public nuisance is an unlawful act or an omission to discharge a duty which, in either case, obstructs or causes inconvenience or damage to the public in the exercise of their common rights (see *Attorney-General* v *PYA Quarries Ltd* [1957] 2 QB 169).

Although there is no 'magic number' of people who must suffer from the annoyance or obstruction in order for it to amount to a *public nuisance*, you must show that the act or omission affected the public in general as opposed to a small group of people (such as the employees of a firm). Therefore, in *R* v *Madden* [1975] 1 WLR 1379, where a person made a hoax bomb call (**see para. 3.7.1**) to an organisation it was held that such behaviour could in theory amount to a public nuisance, although in *Madden* it did not as the annoyance/obstruction was limited in its effect.

People who entered school premises for the purpose of glue sniffing were held to have committed a public nuisance by unduly interfering with the comfortable and convenient enjoyment of the land, even though the school was empty (*Sykes* v *Holmes* [1985] Crim LR 791). (For offences and powers in relation to educational premises specifically, **see chapter 9**).

Given that the courts have unlimited sentencing power in relation to this offence, there may well be advantages in considering its application to cases where the only other offences disclosed would be summary offences. An example is the case of *R* v *Johnson* [1996] 2 Cr App R 434 where the defendant made several hundred obscene telephone calls to women across a county over a period of five years. As the only other available offence (before the offences of harassment were available), appeared to be the summary offence under the Telecommunications Act 1984 (as to which **see para. 3.7**), the availability of the offence of public nuisance gave the courts and the investigating officers far wider powers in dealing with the defendant.

Offence — Public Nuisance — Common Law
Triable either way. Unlimited powers of sentence on indictment; statutory maxima apply summarily.
(*Arrestable offence*)

It is an offence at common law for a person to cause a public nuisance.

Keynote

As this offence is a common law 'misdemeanour', a court may pass sentence at its discretion on indictment, that is, its sentencing powers are unlimited.

The behaviour of the defendant must interfere with the material rights enjoyed by a class of Her Majesty's subjects (*R* v *Johnson* [1996] 2 Cr App R 434).

It is not necessary to prove that every member within a class of people in the community has been affected by the defendant's behaviour; simply that a representative cross-section has been so affected (*Attorney-General* v *PYA Quarries Ltd*). Such a cross-section might include members of a housing estate or users of a public transport facility such as a main-line railway station.

In Lord Denning's view (also in the *PYA* case), a nuisance would need to be 'so widespread in its range or so indiscriminate in its effect' that it would not be reasonable to expect one person to bring proceedings on his/her own to put a stop to it.

There is no need to show that the defendant intended his/her actions or omission to cause a public nuisance and, as with the offence of harassment (**see para. 3.4**) it will be enough that he/she knew or ought to have known that the conduct would bring about a public nuisance (*R* v *Shorrock* [1994] QB 279).

Examples of criminal public nuisances have included:

- Allowing a rave to take place in a field (*R* v *Shorrock*).

- Making hundreds of nuisance telephone calls to at least 13 women (*R* v *Johnson*).

- Contaminating 30 houses with dust and noise from a quarry (*Attorney-General* v *PYA Quarries Ltd*).

- Selling meat which was unfit for consumption (*R* v *Stephens* (1866) LR 1 QB 702).

In addition, the Environmental Protection Act 1990, s. 79 sets out a list of 'statutory nuisances', any of which would potentially be capable of amounting to a criminal offence if they met the relevant conditions.

Defence

Statutory authorisation for a person's conduct (e.g. building a road or a railway), will be a defence provided the behaviour is specifically permitted by that statute (*Hammersmith and City Railway Co.* v *Brand and Louisa* (1868) LR 4 QB 171).

Enforcement

In addition to providing powers of arrest and sentencing for tackling public nuisance through the criminal process, there is always the preventive measure of a court injunction available. Historically the Attorney-General has sought injunctions on behalf of the public at large. However, local authorities have the power to apply for a public nuisance injunction under the Local Government Act 1972 (see *Stoke-on-Trent City Council* v *B & Q (Retail) Ltd* [1984] AC 754) and there appears to be no reason why chief officers should not do the same.

3.6.2   **Dangerous Activities on Highways**

**Offence — Dangerous Activity on Highways — Highways Act 1980,
ss. 161 to 162**
Triable summarily. Fine.
(***No specific power of arrest***)

The Highways Act 1980, ss. 161 to 162 state:

161.—(1)   If a person, without lawful authority or excuse, deposits any thing whatsoever on a highway in consequence of which a user of the highway is injured or endangered, that person is guilty of an offence . . .
   (2)   If a person, without lawful authority or excuse—
      (a)   lights any fire on or over a highway which consists of or comprises a carriageway; or
      (b)   discharges any firearm or firework within 15.24 metres (50 feet) of the centre of such a highway, and in consequence a user of the highway is injured, interrupted or endangered, that person is guilty of an offence . . .
   (3)   If a person plays at football or any other game on a highway to the annoyance of a user of the highway he is guilty of an offence . . .
   (4)   If a person, without lawful authority or excuse, allows any filth, dirt, lime or other offensive matter or thing to run or flow on to a highway from any adjoining premises, he is guilty of an offence . . .

161A.—(1)   If a person—
> *(a)   lights a fire on any land not forming part of a highway which consists of or comprises a carriageway; or*
> *(b)   directs or permits a fire to be lit on any such land,*

and in consequence a user of any highway which consists of or comprises a carriageway is injured, interrupted or endangered by, or by smoke from, that fire or any other fire caused by that fire, that person is guilty of an offence . . .

162.—A person who for any purpose places any rope, wire or other apparatus across a highway in such a manner as to be likely to cause danger to persons using the highway is, unless he proves that he had taken all necessary means to give adequate warning of the danger, guilty of an offence . . .

Keynote

For the definition of 'highway', **see Road Traffic, chapter 1.**

'Carriageway' means a way constituting or comprised in a highway, being a way (other than a cycle track) over which the public have a right of way for the passage of vehicles (s. 329 of the 1980 Act).

The offences at ss. 161(1), (2) and (3) and s. 161A(1) are all offences of 'consequence', that is, you must show the relevant consequence (e.g. injury, annoyance etc.).

Although no specific power of arrest exists, the general arrest condition under s. 25(3)(d)(v) of the Police and Criminal Evidence Act 1984 may apply (see **chapter 2**).

For more serious offences involving a threat to the safety of motorists, **see Road Traffic, chapter 8**.

Defence

There is a defence to s. 161A(1) if the defendant proves:

- that at the time the fire was lit he/she was satisfied on reasonable grounds that it was unlikely that users of any highway consisting of or comprising a carriageway would be injured, interrupted or endangered by, or by smoke from, that fire or any other fire caused by that fire *and*

that either:

- both before and after the fire was lit the defendant did all he/she reasonably could to prevent users of any such highway from being so injured, interrupted or endangered, or

- he/she had a reasonable excuse for not doing so.

3.6.3   Fireworks

Restrictions on the sale of gunpowder, including fireworks (s. 39), are imposed by the Explosives Act 1875, s. 30.

Section 31 of the 1875 Act provides a summary offence in respect of anyone selling gunpowder to a person who appears to be under 16 years old.

There are also restrictions on fireworks in the Fireworks (Safety) Regulations 1997 (SI 1997 No. 2294). Made under s. 11 of the Consumer Protection Act 1987, the Regulations describe virtually every conceivable type of firework and go on to place a number of restrictions on the supply of such items. As you would expect, the Regulations also make a number of concessions and exceptions, allowing the supply of certain fireworks by certain people under certain conditions.

Regulation 6(1) of the 1997 Regulations creates a summary offence of supplying any firework — or assembly that includes a firework — to any person apparently under the age of 18. The offence is charged under s. 12 of the Consumer Protection Act 1987 and is punishable with six months' imprisonment and/or a fine. The offence does not apply to the supply of any cap, cracker snap, novelty match, party popper, 'serpent' or 'throw down' (as defined in reg. 2) (reg. 6(2)).

Regulation 7 goes on to create a number of other summary offences — again chargeable under s. 12 — in relation to the supply of certain fireworks and in particular makes it an offence to supply a sparkler unless it is in a packet marked with the words, 'Warning: not to be given to children under 5 years of age'.

Regulation 8 creates a similar offence for any person who carries on a retail business involving, to whatever extent, the sale of fireworks, to supply a firework that has been removed from a 'primary' pack or selection pack.

Offence — Throwing Fireworks into Highway or Street — Explosives Act 1875, s. 80
Triable summarily. Fine.
(No specific power of arrest)

The Explosives Act 1875, s. 80 states:

> If any person throw, cast, or fire any fireworks in or into any highway, street, thoroughfare, or public place, he [shall be guilty of an offence and liable] . . .

Keynote

For other offences involving explosives, **see chapter 4.**

3.6.4   **Post Boxes**

Offence — Placing Substances in Post Boxes — Post Office Act 1953, s. 60(1)
Triable either way. 12 months' imprisonment on indictment; a fine summarily.
(No specific power of arrest)

The Post Office Act 1953, s. 60 states:

> (1)   A person shall not place or attempt to place in or against any post office letter box . . . any fire, match, light, explosive substance, dangerous substance, filth, noxious or deleterious substance, or fluid, and shall not commit a nuisance in or against any post office letter box and shall not do or attempt to do anything likely to injure the box, . . . or its appurtenances or contents.
> (2)   If any person acts in contravention of this section, he shall be liable . . .

Keynote

Many offences under s. 60 are also likely to involve criminal damage or articles intended for causing damage (**see Crime, chapter 14**) and such offences are 'arrestable' (**see chapter 2**).

Section 61(1) of the 1953 Act goes on to create a further summary offence of attaching anything to or causing disfigurement to post boxes.

3.6.5 Noise

The Noise Act 1996 provides powers to allow local authorities to tackle the problems of noise within their community. Sections 2 and 3 of the 1996 Act allow for the serving of warning notices in relation to 'excessive noise' emanating from one house which can be heard in another at night. Night is defined as being between 11 pm and 7 am (s. 2(6)).

The noise level must be measured using an 'approved device' (s. 6). Any warning must be served on the person who appears to be responsible for the noise or by leaving the warning notice at the 'offending dwelling' (s. 3(3)).

Offence — Exceeding Noise Level After Service of Notice — Noise Act 1996, s. 4(1)
Triable summarily. Fine.
(No specific power of arrest)

The Noise Act 1996, s. 4 states:

> *(1)   If a warning notice has been served in respect of noise emitted from a dwelling, any person who is responsible for noise which—*
> *(a)   is emitted from the dwelling in the period specified in the notice, and*
> *(b)   exceeds the permitted level, as measured from within the complainant's dwelling,*
> *is guilty of an offence.*
> *(2)   It is a defence for a person charged with an offence under this section to show that there was a reasonable excuse for the act, default or sufferance in question.*

Keynote

The 'permitted level' may be set or varied under regulations made by the Secretary of State (s. 5).

Sections 8 and 9 provide for the local authority to implement a 'fixed penalty procedure' whereby liability to prosecution under s. 4 above can be avoided by paying the fee (currently £100) within the prescribed period.

Section 10 provides powers of entry to local authority officers where a warning notice has been served in respect of a dwelling and excessive noise is still measured as having come therefrom. There is also a power to seize any sound equipment involved, together with a power to apply for a warrant for local authority officers to enter premises.

Obstruction of anyone exercising these powers is a summary offence (s. 10(8)) and the provisions for the seizure and disposal of any equipment are set out in the schedule to the 1996 Act.

3.6.6   Litter

The law regulating the roles of local authorities in controlling litter can be found in the Litter Act 1983. The 1983 Act makes allowances for actions by 'litter authorities' (i.e. local councils and park boards, see s. 10) to discourage the dropping of litter and for the provision of litter bins.

Removing or interfering with local authority litter bins or litter notices is a summary offence under s. 5(9).

The remainder of the provisions regulating the dropping of litter are in the Environmental Protection Act 1990.

Offence — Leaving Litter —Environmental Protection Act 1990, s. 87(1)
Triable summarily. Fine.
(*No specific power of arrest*)

The Environmental Protection Act 1990, s. 87 states:

> (1)   *If any person throws down, drops or otherwise deposits in, into or from any place to which this section applies, and leaves, any thing whatsoever in such circumstances as to cause, or contribute to, or tend to lead to, the defacement by litter of any place to which this section applies, he shall, subject to subsection (2) below, be guilty of an offence.*
>
> . . .
>
> (4)   *In this section 'public open place' means a place in the open air to which the public are entitled or permitted to have access without payment; and any covered place open to the air on at least one side and available for public use shall be treated as a public open place.*

Keynote

Under s. 87(3), the offence can be committed in any 'open space' and also relevant land belonging to:

- the principal litter authority (i.e. local council etc.)
- the Crown
- a designated statutory undertaker (e.g. a railway, tramway or dock company)
- a designated educational institution.

A telephone kiosk enclosed on all sides with a six inch gap around the bottom was held not to be a 'public open place' in *Felix* v *DPP, The Times*, 5 May 1998.

'Litter' can include animal droppings for this purpose (Litter (Animal Droppings) Order 1991 (SI 1991 No. 961)). Note also the powers given to local authorities to designate areas which must be kept free from dogs under the Dogs (Fouling of Land) Act 1996.

Section 88 of the 1990 Act makes provision for the payment of a 'fixed penalty' within the prescribed period in order to avoid liability under the s. 87 offence.

Under s. 91, a magistrates' court may act on a complaint of anyone who is aggrieved by the defacement by litter or refuse of any relevant road, highway or land occupied by relevant statutory undertakers or educational institutions. Before doing so, the court must notify the occupier of the complaint. The court may then issue a litter abatement order requiring the relevant person to remedy the situation and failure to comply with such an order is a summary offence under s. 91(9).

Section 99 and sch. 4 to the 1990 Act give local authorities powers to deal with problems involving the abandonment of shopping trolleys and luggage trolleys. Schedule 4 allows local authorities (after abiding by the procedure in s. 99) to seize, retain and ultimately dispose of such trolleys.

Section 87(2) provides that:

> (2)   No offence is committed under this section where the depositing and leaving of the thing was—
> (a)   authorised by law, or
> (b)   done with the consent of the owner, occupier or other person or authority having control of the place in or into which that thing was deposited.

3.7   Offences Involving Communications

The making of direct threats to people's lives or their property is covered by a number of statutes.

There are, however, specific offences which deal with the making of general threats and other communications which are intended to cause alarm or anxiety among people receiving them.

3.7.1   Bomb Threats

The fear and disquiet that can be generated by a single telephone call is considerable, as is the potential economic loss to businesses within the community. Those consequences are reflected in both the sentencing power and practices of the courts.

Offence — Placing or Sending Articles — Criminal Law Act 1977, s. 51(1)
Triable either way. Seven years' imprisonment on indictment; six months' imprisonment and/or a fine summarily.
(Arrestable offence)

The Criminal Law Act 1977, s. 51 states:

> (1)   A person who—
> (a)   places any article in any place whatever; or
> (b)   dispatches any article by post, rail or any other means whatever of sending things from one place to another,
> with the intention (in either case) of inducing in some other person a belief that it is likely to explode or ignite and thereby cause personal injury or damage to property is guilty of an offence.
> In this subsection 'article' includes substance.

Offence — Communicating False Information — Criminal Law Act 1977, s. 51(2)
Triable either way. Seven years' imprisonment on indictment; six months' imprisonment and/or a fine summarily.
(Arrestable offence)

The Criminal Law Act 1977, s. 51 states:

> *(2)   A person who communicates any information which he knows or believes to be false to another person with the intention of inducing in him or any other person a false belief that a bomb or other thing liable to explode or ignite is present in any place or location whatever is guilty of an offence.*

Keynote

The definitions above are very wide; the 'article' concerned in s. 51(1) can be anything at all, while the information communicated under s. 51(2) need not be specific. A message saying that there is a bomb somewhere has been held to be enough, even though no location was given (*R* v *Webb* (1995) *The Times*, 19 June 1995).

The wording of the offence is in the *present* tense which suggests that a message threatening to place a bomb etc. sometime in the *future* would not suffice.

The use of some form of code word is not a prerequisite of the offence but it does go towards proving the defendant's intention that the threat etc. be taken seriously; it may also be taken into account when passing sentence.

The 'communication' can be in any form (including, it would seem, on the Internet) and can be direct (e.g. to a railway station or department store where the bomb or device is alleged to be) or indirect (to a radio station switchboard).

There is no need for the person making the communication to have any particular person in mind at the time (s. 51(3)).

Both offences are offences of 'specific intent', **see Crime, chapter 1.**

3.7.2   Misuse of Postal Service

Offence — Unlawfully Taking or Opening Mail Bag — Post Office Act 1953, s. 53
Triable either way. Five years' imprisonment on indictment; six months' imprisonment and/or a fine summarily.
(*Arrestable offence*)

The Post Office Act 1953, s. 53 states:

> *If any person unlawfully takes away or opens a mail bag sent by any ship, vehicle or aircraft employed by or under the Post Office for the transmission of postal packets under contract, or unlawfully takes a postal packet in course of transmission by post out of a mail bag so sent, he shall be guilty of an offence . . .*

Keynote

To solicit or try to get someone else to commit an offence under this section is a similar offence under s. 68.

Keeping or detaining mail bags or postal packets is a summary offence under s. 55.

Offence — Sending Prohibited Articles by Post — Post Office Act 1953, s. 11(1)
Triable either way. Twelve months' imprisonment on indictment; a fine summarily.
(*No specific power of arrest*)

The Post Office Act 1953, s. 11 states:

> *(1)   A person shall not send or attempt to send or procure to be sent a postal packet which—*

(a) save as the Post Office may either generally or in any particular case allow, encloses any explosive, dangerous, noxious or deleterious substance, any filth, any sharp instrument not properly protected, any noxious living creature, or any creature, article or thing whatsoever which is likely to injure either other postal packets in course of conveyance or a person engaged in the business of the Post Office; or

(b) encloses any indecent or obscene print, painting, photograph, lithograph, engraving, cinematograph film, book, card or written communication, or any indecent or obscene article whether similar to the above or not; or

(c) has on the packet, or on the cover thereof, any words, marks or designs which are grossly offensive or of an indecent or obscene character.

(2) If any person acts in contravention of the foregoing subsection, he shall be liable . . .

Keynote

Whether an article is obscene etc. is a question of fact for the court to determine in each case. That test will not look at the particular views or frailties of the recipient but will be an objective test based on a reasonable bystander (*Kosmos Publications Ltd* v *DPP* [1975] Crim LR 345).

If the article in question is intercepted by the Royal Mail before it is delivered, that fact will not affect the commission of any offence (s. 11(4)).

As causing severe shock can amount to an assault, the relevant offences against the person may be considered (**see Crime, chapter 8**).

For the offences of harassment, **see para. 3.4**.

Offence — Placing Substances in Post Boxes — Post Office Act 1953, s. 60(1)
Triable either way. Twelve months' imprisonment on indictment; a fine summarily.
(*No specific power of arrest*)

The Post Office Act 1953, s. 60 states:

(1) A person shall not place or attempt to place in or against any post office letter box . . . any fire, match, light, explosive substance, dangerous substance, filth, noxious or deleterious substance, or fluid, and shall not commit a nuisance in or against any post office letter box . . . , and shall not do or attempt to do anything likely to injure the box, . . . or its appurtenances or contents.

(2) If any person acts in contravention of this section, he shall be liable . . .

Keynote

Many offences under s. 60 are also likely to involve criminal damage or articles intended for causing damage (**see Crime, chapter 14**).

For other offences involving fireworks, **see para. 3.6.3**.

Section 61(1) goes on to create a further offence of attaching anything to post boxes.

3.7.3 Malicious Communications

Offence — Malicious Communications — Malicious Communications Act 1988, s. 1(1)
Triable summarily. Fine.
(*No specific power of arrest*)

The Malicious Communications Act 1988, s. 1 states:

> (1)   Any person who sends to another person—
>   (a)   a letter or other article which conveys—
>   (i)   a message which is indecent or grossly offensive;
>   (ii)   a threat; or
>   (iii)   information which is false and known or believed to be false by the sender; or
>   (b)   any other article which is, in whole or part, of an indecent or grossly offensive nature,
> is guilty of an offence if his purpose, or one of his purposes, in sending it is that it should, so far as falling within paragraph (a) or (b) above, cause distress or anxiety to the recipient or to any other person to whom he intends that it or its contents or nature should be communicated.

Keynote

The offence is not restricted to threatening or indecent communications and can include giving false information provided that *one* of the senders' purposes in so doing is to cause distress or anxiety. 'Purposes' appears simply to be another way of stating intention in which case this an offence of 'specific intent' (**see Crime chapter 1**).

That distress or anxiety may be intended towards the recipient *or* any other person.

It is clear from s. 1(3) that the offence can be committed by using someone else to send or deliver a message. This would include occasions where a person falsely reports that someone has been a victim of a crime in order to cause anxiety or distress by the arrival of the police. (For wasting police time, **see Crime, chapter 15**.)

Section 1(1)(b) covers occasions where the article itself is indecent or grossly offensive (such as putting dog faeces through someone's letter box).

Defence

Section 1(2) of the 1988 Act provides that:

> A person is not guilty of an offence by virtue of subsection (1)(a)(ii) above if he shows—
>   (a)   that the threat was used to reinforce a demand which he believed he had reasonable grounds for making; and
>   (b)   that he believed that the use of the threat was a proper means of reinforcing the demand.

Keynote

Given the decisions of the courts in similarly-worded defences under the Theft Act 1968 (blackmail; **see Crime, chapter 12**), it is unlikely that any demand could be reasonable where agreement to it would amount to a crime.

The defence is intended to cover financial institutions and other commercial concerns who often need to send forceful letters to customers. However, for the offence of unlawfully harassing debtors, see the Administration of Justice Act 1970, s. 40.

3.7.4   Threats to Kill

Offence — Making a Threat to Kill — Offences Against the Person Act 1861, s. 16
Triable either way. Ten years' imprisonment on indictment; six months' imprisonment and/or a fine summarily.
(Arrestable offence)

132

The Offences Against the Person Act 1861, s. 16 states:

A person who without lawful excuse makes to another a threat, intending that that other would fear it would be carried out, to kill that other or a third person shall be guilty of an offence . . .

Keynote

The proviso that the threat must be made 'without lawful excuse' means that a person acting in self-defence or in the course of his/her duty in protecting life (e.g. an armed police officer) would not commit this offence (provided that his/her behaviour was 'lawful'; **see Crime, chapter 4**).

You must show that the threat was made (or implied (*R* v *Solanke* [1970] 1 WLR 1)) with the intention that the person receiving it would fear that it would be carried out. It is the intention of the person who makes the threat which is important in this offence. It does not matter whether the person to whom the threat is made *does* fear that the threat would be carried out, or that the person whose life is threatened so fears (unless that person is the same person to whom the threat is made). The threat may be to kill another person at some time in the future or it may be an immediate threat, but the threatened action must be directly linked with the defendant. Simply passing on a threat on behalf of a third person would probably be insufficient for this offence.

3.7.5 Telephone Calls

Offence — Improper Use of Public Telecommunication Systems — Telecommunications Act 1984, s. 43
Triable summarily. Six months' imprisonment and/or a fine.
(No *specific* power of arrest)

The Telecommunications Act 1984, s. 43 states:

(1) A person who—
(a) sends, by means of a public telecommunication system, a message or other matter that is grossly offensive or of an indecent, obscene or menacing character; or
(b) sends by those means, for the purpose of causing annoyance, inconvenience or needless anxiety to another, a message that he knows to be false or persistently makes use for that purpose of a public telecommunication system,
shall be guilty of an offence . . .

Keynote

This offence is designed to deal with 'nuisance' calls. It only applies to 'public' telecommunication systems which are those systems designated by the Secretary of State as such (s. 9(1)) and would therefore not include internal calls in a work place. It appears from the wording that this offence may apply to the sending of messages via the Internet (provided the system used comes within the definition under s. 9(1)).

Again this offence applies to calls which convey false information.

The wording of the offence suggests that there is no need to show a particular 'purpose' (intention) in the case of behaviour falling under s. 43(1)(a) and the offence is complete if the defendant sends the relevant message or other matter that is, as a matter of fact, indecent, obscene or menacing.

In the case of a charge under s. 43(1)(b) there is a need to prove that the defendant acted *for the purpose* of causing annoyance, inconvenience or needless anxiety to another.

Unlike the offence under the Criminal Law Act 1977, s. 51(2) (**see para. 3.7.1**), there is no need for any information passed to be 'false'.

Where a number of calls have been made to several different people within the community, the offence of public nuisance may also be considered (**see para. 3.6.1**).

3.7.6 Unsolicited Publications

It is a summary offence to send unsolicited material or advertising material which describes or illustrates human sexual techniques (Unsolicited Goods and Services Act 1971, s. 4). This offence cannot be prosecuted without the consent of the Director of Public Prosecutions.

3.7.7 Interception of Messages

Offence — Interception of Messages — Wireless Telegraphy Act 1949, s. 5(b)
Triable summarily. Fine.
(**No specific power of arrest**)

The Wireless Telegraphy Act 1949, s. 5 states:

> (a) . . .
> (b)   otherwise than under the authority of the Secretary of State or in the course of his duty as a servant of the Crown, either—
>   (i)   uses any wireless telegraphy apparatus with intent to obtain information as to the contents, sender or addressee of any message (whether sent by means of wireless telegraphy or not) which neither the person using the apparatus nor any person on whose behalf he is acting is authorised by the Secretary of State to receive; or
>   (ii)   except in the course of legal proceedings or for the purpose of any report thereof, discloses any information as to the contents, sender or addressee of any such message, being information which would not have come to his knowledge but for the use of wireless telegraphy apparatus by him or by another person,
> shall be guilty of an offence under this Act.

Keynote

This offence covers the receiving of police radio messages when not licensed to do so. You need only show that the defendant received the message and that he/she intended to do so. However, if a person inadvertently comes across the channel when tuning his/her radio and passes over it, he/she does not commit this offence as there is no intention to obtain any information (*DPP* v *Waite* [1997] Crim LR 123). If the defendant is found in possession of a receiver with pre-set channels, it must be proved that he/she programmed those pre-set channels himself/herself; simply possessing such a receiver that has been pre-set by someone is not enough to prove this offence (*McMeekin* v *McPhail* 1991 SCCR 432).

There is a power of seizure for any scanning or other equipment under the Telecommunications Act 1984, s. 79(1)(ba).

Subsection (a) of this offence applies to the sending of distress signals etc. and is triable either way.

Offence — Intentionally Intercepting Message — Interception of Communications Act 1985, s. 1

Triable either way. Two years' imprisonment and/or a fine on indictment; fine summarily.
(**No specific power of arrest**)

The Interception of Communications Act 1985, s. 1 states:

(1) Subject to the following provisions of this section, a person who intentionally intercepts a communication in the course of its transmission by post or by means of a public telecommunication system shall be guilty of an offence.

Keynote

This offence has two elements; the interception of a communication sent by post and the interception of a communication sent on a public telecommunication system.

Like the offence of receiving radio transmissions above, in each case here there must be an *intentional* act; simply opening someone's mail by mistake or listening in on a crossed line would not, without more, be enough.

As with the offence under the Telecommunications Act 1984, s. 43 (**see para. 3.7.5**), the telecommunication system must be a 'public' one. Therefore, where a person uses a cordless phone which sends a signal to the base set within his/her own home, any interception of that signal is not covered by the above offence (see *R v Effik* [1995] 1 AC 309).

Similarly, where the payphone in a police station was not connected directly with the public exchange but was routed via the internal system to the switchboard, an interception of a message sent on that payphone was not a contravention of this section (see *R v Ahmed* [1995] Crim LR 246. The Act is aimed at regulating the behaviour of 'officials' and therefore does not protect the communications of others being intercepted by private individuals (*R v Sargent*, unreported, 15 February 1999).

Interception of a police officer's calls made while at work has been held to be capable of violating Article 8 of the European Convention on Human Rights (see *Halford* v *UK* case no. 73/1996/692/884 (1997)).

The provisions of the 1985 Act do not apply where the interception is made with the consent of the subscriber and any information so obtained is admissible (see *R v Rasool* [1997] 1 WLR 1092).

Section 1 goes on to provide a defence for a person who is acting under the authority of a warrant issued by the Secretary of State under s. 4. (For guidance concerning the interception of communications in relation to investigations, the National Criminal Intelligence Service should be contacted.)

Section 1(3) provides specific defences for people working within the postal or telecommunications services or for those involved in the prevention or detection of offences involving wireless telegraphy.

CHAPTER FOUR

PUBLIC DISORDER AND TERRORISM

4.1 Introduction

Threats to public order or the 'normal state of society' can arise in many forms, from intimidating and anti-social behaviour to full scale riot. The law which appears in this chapter exists to protect some of the fundamental rights and freedoms of individuals — and groups — within the community, rights which in most other countries are enshrined in a written constitution. Freedoms such as the freedom from harassment (**see chapter 3**), freedom to associate with others, freedom to enjoy property and freedom of speech are currently protected by the civil and criminal law in the same way as any other legal 'right'. The coming into force of the Human Rights Act 1998 will bring about significant developments in this area.

When reading this chapter, regard should be had to the CPS Public Order Offences Charging Standard (**see appendix 3**).

4.2 Breach of the Peace

The lowest level of threat to public order is probably represented in the common law 'complaint' of a breach of the peace. Defined in *R* v *Howell* [1982] QB 416, a breach of the peace occurs when an act is done, or threatened to be done:

- which harms a person or, in his/her presence, his/her property; or
- which is likely to cause such harm; *or*
- which puts someone in fear of such harm.

A breach of the peace is not a criminal offence. Therefore someone who is arrested for a breach of the peace is not, strictly speaking, in police detention per the Police and Criminal Evidence Act 1984 (PACE) s. 118 (**see Evidence and Procedure, chapter 15**) and cannot be granted bail. They may be detained and placed before the next available sitting of a court or held until the likelihood of a recurrence of the breach of the peace has gone.

The punishment for a breach of the peace is binding over.

A breach of the peace may take place on private premises as well as in public places (*R v Chief Constable of Devon and Cornwall, ex parte Central Electricity Generating Board* [1982] QB 458). The police are entitled to enter premises to prevent a breach of the peace and to remain there in order to do so (*Thomas v Sawkins* [1935] 2 KB 249). This power has not been affected by the general powers of entry provided by PACE 1984 (**see chapter 2** and PACE 1984, s. 17(6)).

Although the police have a general duty to preserve the Queen's peace and enjoy common law powers to carry out that duty, they also have a wide discretion as to how they go about that function. The common law powers of the police allow them, where appropriate, to prevent people from travelling to certain locations (e.g. striking miners heading for a working coalfield where their presence would give reasonable grounds to apprehend a breach of the peace (*Moss v McLachlan* [1985] IRLR 76)). However, where the exercise of conflicting interests - such as the right to engage in lawful trade and a right to protest — threaten a breach of the peace, chief officers are required to balance the competing needs of the parties and the other policing needs of community at large. There is no rule that prevents the police from restraining lawful activity where to do so is the only realistic way of preventing a breach of the peace. In deciding what strategy to adopt in order to avoid a breach of the peace, not only are chief officers able to consider restraining lawful activities of others, they are also entitled to consider the financial resources available to them, together with the rights of others in their police area and the risk of injury to all concerned. Consequently, there is no absolute requirement for a chief officer to deploy his/her resources in order to protect a person's right to trade, even where the disruption of that trade is caused by unlawful conduct and under circumstances in which other chief officers had acted differently in the past (*R v Chief Constable of Sussex, ex parte International Trader's Ferry Ltd* [1999] 1 All ER 186).

4.2.1 Power of Arrest

A constable or any other person may arrest without warrant any person:

- who is committing a breach of the peace;
- who he/she reasonably believes will commit a breach of the peace in the immediate future; or
- who has committed a breach of the peace, where it is reasonably believed that a recurrence of the breach of the peace is threatened.

This power of arrest may be exercised on private premises, even where there is no other member of the public present (*McConnell v Chief Constable of Greater Manchester Police* [1990] 1 All ER 423), and it is not affected by the Public Order Act 1986 (see s. 40(4)).

Even if exercising the power under circumstances where a breach of the peace has not yet occurred, it is enough that a constable uses the wording 'I am arresting you for a breach of the peace' when arresting someone under this power (*R v Howell*).

4.3 Drunk and Disorderly

Offence — Drunk and Disorderly — Criminal Justice Act 1967, s. 91(1)
Triable summarily. Fine.
(*Statutory power of arrest*)

The Criminal Justice Act 1967, s. 91 states:

> *(1)   Any person who in any public place is guilty, while drunk, of disorderly behaviour may be arrested without warrant by any person and shall be liable . . .*

Keynote

To prove this offence you must show that the defendant was both drunk and disorderly. The drunkenness must be as a result of excessive consumption of *alcohol*; if the person's state is caused by some other intoxicant (e.g. glue solvents), the offence is not made out (*Neale* v *R. M. J. E. (a minor)* (1984) 80 Cr App R 20). The same ruling applies to a person 'found drunk' in a public place (*Lanham* v *Rickwood* (1984) 148 JP 737 (**see chapter 10**). This can be contrasted with the situation in relation to drink/driving cases (**see Road Traffic, chapter 5**) where unfitness to drive can arise from drugs as well as alcohol.

'Drunkenness' here means where the defendant has taken intoxicating liquor to an extent that affects his/her steady self-control (per Goff LJ in *Neale*).

Where there are *several* causes of a person's incapacitated state, one of which is alcohol, a court can find that the person was in fact 'drunk', even though some additional intoxicant had an exacerbating effect on his/her loss of 'steady self-control'.

Despite the effects of PACE 1984, s. 26(1) (**see chapter 2**), the Divisional Court has held that the statutory power of arrest still applies to constables (*DPP* v *Kitching* [1990] Crim LR 394). Nevertheless, the general power of arrest under PACE 1984 may well be available (see Home Office Circular 88/1985).

When a person is arrested for this offence by a constable, he/she may be taken to an approved treatment centre for alcoholism (a 'detoxification' centre) and he/she will be treated as being in lawful custody for the purposes of that journey (see Criminal Justice Act 1972, s. 34(1)).

4.4   The Public Order Acts

Many of the most common offences regulating public disorder and threats to public order were formerly contained in the Public Order Act 1936. This left several key offences, such as riot and affray to the common law. These provisions were felt to be inadequate and the Public Order Act 1986 was passed in an attempt to codify the law in this area.

4.5   Riot

Offence — Riot — Public Order Act 1986, s. 1
Triable on indictment. Ten years' imprisonment.
(*Arrestable offence*)

The Public Order Act 1986, s. 1 states:

> *(1)   Where 12 or more persons who are present together use or threaten unlawful violence for a common purpose and the conduct of them (taken together) is such as would cause a person of*

reasonable firmness present at the scene to fear for his personal safety, each of the persons using unlawful violence for the common purpose is guilty of riot.
> (2)   *It is immaterial whether or not the 12 or more use or threaten unlawful violence simultaneously.*
> (3)   *The common purpose may be inferred from conduct.*
> (4)   *No person of reasonable firmness need actually be, or be likely to be, present at the scene.*
> (5)   *Riot may be committed in private as well as in public places.*

Keynote

This offence requires the consent of the Director of Public Prosecutions before a prosecution can be brought. Although there may be occasions where 12 or more people behave in the way proscribed by s. 1, it still very rare for a charge of riot to be brought. This may have something to do with the provisions of the Riot Damages Act 1886 which enables people who have suffered loss or damage during a riot to claim compensation from the local police budget (s. 2).

It is not necessary that all 12 people concerned use or threaten unlawful violence at the same time. However, the courts have held that each defendant must be shown to have *used* unlawful violence and not merely threatened to do so (*R v Jefferson* [1994] 1 All ER 270). A defendant must be shown to have *intended* to use/threaten violence or to have *been aware* that his/her conduct may have been violent (s. 6(1)).

The offence may be committed in private as well as in a public place. There is no need to prove that a person of reasonable firmness was actually caused to fear for his/her safety; merely that such a person would be caused so to fear (although clearly one way to prove that element would be by the testimony of those witnessing the behaviour).

Although there must be a common purpose, this need not be part of a pre-determined plan, nor be unlawful in itself. A common purpose to get into a rock concert or even the January sales at a high street store could therefore be enough, provided all other elements are present.

4.5.1   Violence

Section 8 of the Public Order Act 1986 provides guidance on when conduct will amount to 'violence':

> *'violence' means any violent conduct, so that—*
> (a)   *except in the context of affray, it includes violent conduct towards property as well as violent conduct towards persons, and*
> (b)   *it is not restricted to conduct causing or intended to cause injury or damage but includes any other violent conduct (for example, throwing at or towards a person a missile of a kind capable of causing injury which does not hit or falls short).*

Keynote

It has been held that the use of the term 'unlawful' in the 1986 Act has been included to allow for the general defences — such as self-defence (**see Crime, chapter 4**) — to be applicable (see *R v Rothwell* [1993] Crim LR 626).

4.5.2   Drunkenness

The effect of drunkenness on criminal liability generally is discussed in **Crime, chapter 4**. However, parliament has specifically catered for self-induced intoxication, not just for the offence of riot, but in relation to other offences under the 1986 Act by s. 6 which states:

(5)   For the purposes of this section a person whose awareness is impaired by intoxication shall be taken to be aware of that of which he would be aware if not intoxicated, unless he shows either that his intoxication was not self-induced or that it was caused solely by the taking or administration of a substance in the course of medical treatment.

(6)   In subsection (5) 'intoxication' means any intoxication, whether caused by drink, drugs or other means, or by a combination of means.

4.6   Violent Disorder

Offence — Violent Disorder — Public Order Act 1986, s. 2
Triable either way. Five years' imprisonment and/or a fine on indictment; six months' imprisonment and/or a fine summarily.
(Arrestable offence)

The Public Order Act 1986, s. 2 states:

(1)   Where 3 or more persons who are present together use or threaten unlawful violence and the conduct of them (taken together) is such as would cause a person of reasonable firmness present at the scene to fear for his personal safety, each of the persons using or threatening unlawful violence is guilty of violent disorder.

(2)   It is immaterial whether or not the 3 or more use or threaten unlawful violence simultaneously.

(3)   No person of reasonable firmness need actually be, or be likely to be, present at the scene.

(4)   Violent disorder may be committed in private as well as in public places.

Keynote

In order to convict any defendant of this offence, you must show that there were three or more people using or threatening violence. If this is not proved then the court should acquit each defendant (*R v McGuigan* [1991] Crim LR 719). Ordinarily this will mean that, if there are only three defendants, the acquittal of one will mean the acquittal of all, unless you prove that there were others taking part in the disorder who were not charged (*R v Worton* (1989) 154 JP 201).

The requirements as to the hypothetical effects on an equally hypothetical person of reasonable firmness are the same as for the offence of riot. However, there is no requirement to prove a common purpose.

Again, a defendant must be shown to have *intended* to use/threaten violence or to have *been aware* that his/her conduct may have been violent (s. 6(2)) and the offence may be committed in private as well as in a public place. 'Violence' for these purposes can include violent conduct towards property (s. 8).

4.7   Affray

Offence — Affray — Public Order Act 1986, s. 3
Triable either way. Three years' imprisonment and/or a fine on indictment; six months' imprisonment and/or a fine summarily.
(Statutory power of arrest)

The Public Order Act 1986, s. 3 states:

> (1)   *A person is guilty of affray if he uses or threatens unlawful violence towards another and his conduct is such as would cause a person of reasonable firmness present at the scene to fear for his personal safety.*
> (2)   *Where 2 or more persons use or threaten the unlawful violence, it is the conduct of them taken together that must be considered for the purposes of subsection (1).*
> (3)   *For the purposes of this section a threat cannot be made by the use of words alone.*
> (4)   *No person of reasonable firmness need actually be, or be likely to be, present at the scene.*
> (5)   *Affray may be committed in private as well as in public places.*

Keynote

Formerly an offence requiring more than one person, this offence may now be committed by a single defendant although, if he/she acts with another, the conduct of them taken together will be the relevant factor in determining their criminal conduct (s. 3(2)).

Although the word affray comes from the French verb *afrayer* meaning to terrify, the test here will be whether or not the defendant's conduct would have caused a hypothetical person (not the actual person(s) present) to fear for his/her personal safety (*R* v *Sanchez* (1996) 160 JP 321).

The threat cannot be made by words alone (s. 3(3)), therefore there must be some action by the defendant (even if that 'action' consists of utilising something else such as a dog to threaten the violence (*R* v *Dixon* [1993] Crim LR 579).

Although violence is 'not restricted to conduct causing or intended to cause injury or damage but includes any other violent conduct' (s. 8), the expression does not include conduct towards property as it does with the offences under ss. 1 and 2.

Once more, a defendant must be shown to have *intended* to use/threaten violence or to have *been aware* that his/her conduct may have been violent (s. 6).

4.7.1   Power of Arrest

The Public Order Act 1986, s. 3 states:

> (6)   *A constable may arrest without warrant anyone he reasonably suspects is committing affray.*

Keynote

The power of arrest here is limited to the present tense, that is, to someone who is reasonably suspected of being in the process of committing an affray. This is the same as the power provided for offences under ss. 4 and 4A (**see below**). A preventive power can be found under the common law provisions in respect of an apprehended breach of the peace (**see para. 4.2**). Other powers may be available in relation to assaults or threats to cause damage (**see Crime, chapters 8 and 14**).

4.8   Fear or Provocation of Violence

Offence — Fear or Provocation of Violence — Public Order Act 1986, s. 4
Triable summarily. Six months' imprisonment and/or a fine.
(*Statutory power of arrest*)

Offence — Racially Aggravated — Crime and Disorder Act 1998, s. 31(1)(a)
*Triable either way. Two years' imprisonment and/or a fine on indictment;
six months' imprisonment and/or a fine summarily.*
(Statutory power of arrest)

The Public Order Act 1986, s. 4 states:

> *(1) A person is guilty of an offence if he—*
> *(a) uses towards another person threatening, abusive or insulting words or behaviour, or*
> *(b) distributes or displays to another person any writing, sign or other visible representation*
> *which is threatening, abusive or insulting,*
> *with intent to cause that person to believe that immediate unlawful violence will be used against him*
> *or another by any person, or to provoke the immediate use of unlawful violence by that person or*
> *another, or whereby that person is likely to believe that such violence will be used or it is likely that*
> *such violence will be provoked.*
>
> *(2) An offence under this section may be committed in a public or a private place, except that no*
> *offence is committed where the words or behaviour are used, or the writing, sign or other visible*
> *representation is distributed or displayed, by a person inside a dwelling and the other person is also*
> *inside that or another dwelling.*

Keynote

The term 'threatening, abusive or insulting' is not defined but it was interpreted by the courts under the Public Order Act 1936. Whether words or behaviour are threatening, abusive or insulting will be a question of fact for the magistrate(s) to decide in each case (see *Brutus* v *Cozens* [1973] AC 854).

It is not enough that conduct is 'offensive' but it has been held that masturbation towards a police officer in a public lavatory is capable of being insulting (*Parkin* v *Norman* [1983] QB 82).

'Immediate' unlawful violence does not have to be instantaneous but it must be shown that the defendant's conduct was likely to lead to more than some form of violence at some later date. Therefore publication of material by the author Salman Rushdie, however insulting it may have been to some people, was not enough to support a charge under s. 4 (*R* v *Horseferry Road Metropolitan Stipendiary Magistrate, ex parte Siadatan* [1991] 1 QB 260).

There are a number of ways in which this offence can be committed (**see below**). In all of these, however, there must be the use of threatening/abusive/insulting words or behaviour (or distribution/display of writing, signs etc.). This must be carried out with the requisite state of mind set out at s. 6(3) which states:

> *(3) A person is guilty of an offence under section 4 only if he intends his words or behaviour, or*
> *the writing, sign or other visible representation, to be threatening, abusive or insulting, or is aware*
> *that it may be threatening, abusive or insulting.*

In addition, it must be shown that the person further *intended* to bring about the consequences set out below (at (a) and (b)) or that the consequences (at (c) and (d)) were likely.

The offence was broken down into four component parts in *Winn* v *DPP* (1992) 156 JP 881. For each of these parts it must be shown:

(a) that the defendant:

- intended the person against whom the conduct was directed
- to believe
- that immediate unlawful violence would be used
- either against him/her or against anyone else
- by the defendant or anyone else; *or*

(b) that he/she:

- intended to provoke the immediate use of unlawful vilolence
- by that person or anyone else; *or*

(c) that:

- the person against whom the words or behaviour (or distribution/display of writing etc.) were directed
- was likely to believe
- that immediate unlawful violence would be used; *or*

(d) that:

- it was likely that immediate unlawful violence would be provoked.

In the case at (a) above, it does not have to be shown that the other person *actually believed* that immediate violence would be used; it has to be shown that the defendant *intended to cause* him/her to believe it (*Swanston* v *DPP* (1997) 161 JP 203).

The person in whom the defendant intends to create that belief must be the same person at whom the conduct is directed (*Loade* v *DPP* [1990] 1 QB 1052). Therefore, if the defendant uses threatening behaviour towards person A, intending that this will cause person B to believe that immediate unlawful violence will be used, the offence under s. 4 is not, without more, made out.

The inclusion of this offence within the provisions of the Crime and Disorder Act 1998 attracts a higher maximum sentence (under s. 31(4) of the 1998 Act) where the offence is racially aggravated.

For a full explanation of the meaning of 'racially aggravated', **see chapter 3**).

Unlike some of the other racially-aggravated offences (**see Crime, chapters 8 and 14**), provisions are specifically made for alternative verdicts in relation to the above public order offence (see s. 31(6) of the 1998 Act).

Under the Public Order Act 1986, s. 8, dwelling is defined as:

> . . . *any structure or part of a structure occupied as a person's home or as other living accommodation (whether the occupation is separate or shared with others) but does not include any part not so occupied, and for this purpose 'structure' includes a tent, caravan, vehicle, vessel or other temporary or movable structure.*

Keynote

Given that the offence at s. 4 can be committed in private (under the restrictions in relation to dwellings by s. 4(2) above), it appears that the offence could be committed by a person sending out e-mails or other forms of communication from his/her house to other non-dwellings or from his/her place of work to people's houses.

Communal landings which form access routes to separate dwellings have been held not to constitute part of a dwelling even though they could only be entered by way of an entry phone system (*Rukwira* v *DPP* [1993] Crim LR 882).

4.8.1 Power of Arrest

The Public Order Act 1986, s. 4 states:

> *(3)   A constable may arrest without warrant anyone he reasonably suspects is committing an offence under this section.*

Keynote

For the effect of this and alternative powers of arrest, **see para 4.7.1**.

The Crime and Disorder Act 1998, s. 31(2) provides a constable with a power of arrest without warrant in respect of anyone whom he/she reasonably suspects to be committing an offence under this section which is racially aggravated.

4.9   Intentional Harassment, Alarm or Distress

**Offence — Intentionally Causing Harassment, Alarm or Distress —
Public Order Act 1986, s. 4A**
Triable summarily. Six months' imprisonment and/or a fine.
(Statutory power of arrest)

Offence — Racially Aggravated — Crime and Disorder Act 1998, s. 31(1)(b)
*Triable either way. Two years' imprisonment and/or fine on indictment;
six months' imprisonment and/or fine summarily.*
(Statutory power of arrest)

The Public Order Act 1986, s. 4A states:

> *(1)   A person is guilty of an offence if, with intent to cause a person harassment, alarm or distress, he—*
>> *(a)   uses threatening, abusive or insulting words or behaviour, or disorderly behaviour, or*
>> *(b)   displays any writing, sign or other visible representation which is threatening, abusive or insulting,*
> *thereby causing that or another person harassment, alarm or distress.*

Keynote

The inclusion of this offence within the provisions of the Crime and Disorder Act 1998 attracts a higher maximum sentence (under s. 31(4) of the 1998 Act) where the offence is racially aggravated.

For a full explanation of the meaning of 'racially aggravated', **see chapter 3**.

Unlike some of the other racially-aggravated offences (**see Crime, chapters 8 and 14**), provisions are specifically made for alternative verdicts in relation to the above public order offence (see s. 31(6) of the 1998 Act).

In order to prove this offence you must show that the defendant *intended* to cause harassment, alarm or distress and, it seems, that by so doing, the defendant actually caused some harassment, alarm or distress.

Harassment, alarm or distress are not defined and it would appear that they are to be given their ordinary everyday meaning. A police officer can be caused such harassment, alarm or distress (*DPP* v *Orum* [1989] 1 WLR 88), and he/she can feel that harassment, alarm or distress for someone else present (e.g. a child — see *Lodge* v *DPP*, *The Times*, 26 October 1988).

Posting a threatening, abusive or insulting letter through someone's letter box is not an offence under this section (*Chappell* v *DPP* (1988) 89 Cr App R 82). It may, however, amount to an offence under the Malicious Communications Act 1988 (**see chapter 3**).

Section 4A states:

> (2)   *An offence under this section may be committed in a public place or a private place, except that no offence is committed where the words or behaviour are used, or the writing, sign or other visible representation is displayed, by a person inside a dwelling and the person who is harassed, alarmed or distressed is also inside that or another dwelling.*

4.9.1   Defence

The Public Order Act 1986, s. 4A provides a specific defence:

> (3)   *It is a defence for the accused to prove—*
> (a)   *that he was inside a dwelling and had no reason to believe that the words or behaviour used, or the writing, sign or other visible representation displayed, would be heard or seen by a person outside that or any other dwelling, or*
> (b)   *that his conduct was reasonable.*

Keynote

If is for the defendant to prove that one of the elements existed at the time of the offence. The standard of proof here will be that of the balance of probabilities, i.e. that it was more likely than not.

4.9.2   Power of Arrest

The Public Order Act 1986, s. 4A states:

> (4)   *A constable may arrest without warrant anyone he reasonably suspects is committing an offence under this section.*

Keynote

For the effect of this and alternative powers of arrest, **see para. 4.7.1**.

The Crime and Disorder Act 1998, s. 31(2) provides a constable with a power of arrest without warrant in respect of anyone whom he/she reasonably suspects to be committing an offence under this section which is racially aggravated.

4.10 Harassment, Alarm or Distress

Offence — Harassment, Alarm or Distress — Public Order Act 1986, s. 5
Triable summarily. Fine.
(*Statutory power of arrest*)

Offence — Racially Aggravated — Crime and Disorder Act 1998, s. 31(1)(c)
Triable summarily. Fine.
(*Statutory power of arrest*)

The Public Order Act 1986, s. 5 states:

> (1)   *A person is guilty of an offence if he—*
> (a)   *uses threatening, abusive or insulting words or behaviour, or disorderly behaviour, or*
> (b)   *displays any writing, sign or other visible representation which is threatening, abusive or insulting,*
> *within the hearing or sight of a person likely to be caused harassment, alarm or distress thereby.*

Keynote

Unlike the other racially aggravated forms of public order offences, the offence under s. 5 remains triable summarily, even if aggravated by the conditions set out in the Crime and Disorder Act 1998, s. 28 (s. 31(5)). (For a full explanation of the meaning of 'racially aggravated', **see chapter 3**.)

The racially-aggravated circumstances set out at s. 28(1)(a) of the Crime and Disorder Act 1998 deal with situations where the defendant demonstrates racial hostility at the time of (or immediately before or after) committing the offence, towards the *victim*. To clarify such situations in relation to the racially aggravated form of the above offence, s. 31(7) provides that the person 'likely to be caused harassment, alarm or distress' will be treated as the 'victim'. This appears to be a more useful provision than its counterpart in relation to the Criminal Damage Act 1971 (**see Crime, chapter 14**).

Provision is also specifically made for alternative verdicts in relation to the above public order offence (see s. 31(6)).

Note that 'disorderly' is not defined and ought to be given its ordinary everyday meaning. It need not be shown that the disorderly behaviour is itself threatening, abusive or insulting, nor that it brought about any feelings of apprehension in the person to whom it was directed (*Chambers* v *DPP* [1995] Crim LR 896). The wording of s. 5 is not limited to rowdy behaviour and will extend to any behaviour that could be construed as threatening, abusive or insulting. 'Insulting' has been held by the Divisional Court to include the actions of a market trader who installed a hidden video camera to film women trying on swimwear (*Vigon* v *DPP* (1998) 162 JP 115).

The discussion above (**see para. 4.9**) in relation to intentional harassment, alarm or distress also applies to this offence, except here there needs to be a person within whose sight or hearing the conduct takes place.

Section 5 states:

> (2)   *An offence under this section may be committed in a public or a private place, except that no offence is committed where the words or behaviour are used, or the writing, sign or other visible*

representation is displayed, by a person inside a dwelling and the other person is also inside that or another dwelling.

4.10.1 State of Mind

The Public Order Act 1986, s. 6 states:

> *(4)   A person is guilty of an offence under section 5 only if he intends his words or behaviour, or the writing, sign or other visible representation, to be threatening, abusive or insulting, or is aware that it may be threatening, abusive or insulting or (as the case may be) he intends his behaviour to be or is aware that it may be disorderly.*

4.10.2 Defence

The Public Order Act 1986, s. 5 provides a specific defence:

> *(3)   It is a defence for the accused to prove—*
> *(a)   that he had no reason to believe that there was any person within hearing or sight who was likely to be caused harassment, alarm or distress, or*
> *(b)   that he was inside a dwelling and had no reason to believe that the words or behaviour used, or the writing sign or other visible representation displayed, would be heard or seen by a person outside that or any other dwelling, or*
> *(c)   that his conduct was reasonable.*

Keynote

It is for the defendant to prove that one of the elements existed at the time of the offence. The standard of proof here will be that of the balance of probabilities, i.e. that it was more likely than not.

In deciding whether a defendant's conduct was reasonable under s. 5(3)(c) an objective test will be applied (*DPP* v *Clarke* (1991) 94 Cr App R 359).

4.10.3 Power of Arrest

The Public Order Act 1986, s. 5 states:

> *(4)   A constable may arrest a person without warrant if—*
> *(a)   he engages in offensive conduct which a constable warns him to stop, and*
> *(b)   he engages in further offensive conduct immediately or shortly after the warning.*

The Crime and Disorder Act 1998, s. 31(3) states:

> *(3)   A constable may arrest a person without warrant if—*
> *(a)   he engages in conduct which a constable reasonably suspects to constitute an offence falling within subsection (1)(c) above;*
> *(b)   he is warned by that constable to stop; and*
> *(c)   he engages in further such conduct immediately or shortly after the warning.*
> *The conduct mentioned in paragraph (a) above and the further conduct need not be of the same nature.*

Keynote

It is no longer necessary that the warning be given by the same officer who later arrests the defendant (Public Order (Amendment) Act 1996, s. 1). For a warning to be sufficient, the words must convey to the defendant that to continue with his/her conduct will amount to an offence (*Groom* v *DPP* [1991] Crim LR 713).

4.11 Wearing of Political Uniforms in Public Places

Section 1 of the Public Order Act 1936 prohibits the wearing of uniforms signifying association with any political organisation in a public place or at a public meeting and creates a summary offence to that effect. A chief officer of police may, with the consent of the Secretary of State, permit the wearing of such uniforms under certain circumstances.

Section 2 of the 1936 Act outlaws quasi-military organisations which are trained or organised to usurp the functions of the police or the armed forces, or to display physical force in promoting any political object.

Although the 1936 Act (s. 7(3)) creates a power of arrest without warrant by a constable in relation to any person he/she reasonably suspects to be committing an offence under s. 1, no prosecution can be brought under either s. 1 or 2 without the consent of the Attorney-General (or Solicitor-General).

4.12 Public Processions and Assemblies

4.12.1 Procession Organiser

The Public Order Act 1986 places certain obligations on the organisers of public processions that are intended:

- to demonstrate support for, or opposition to, the views or actions of any person or body
- to publicise a cause or campaign, or
- to mark or commemorate an event.

If a public procession is to be held for any of these purposes, the organisers must give written notice — by delivering it to a police station in the relevant police area — unless it is not reasonably practicable to do so (s. 11(1) and (4)).

In the case of a procession that is to begin in Scotland but will cross over into England, the notice must be delivered to a police station in the first police area in England on the proposed route (s. 11(4)(b)).

The notice must specify:

- the date and time of the proposed procession
- the proposed route, and
- the name and address of the person(s) proposing to organise it

(s. 11(3)).

If such a procession is held without compliance with these requirements or, if a procession takes place on a different date, time or route, each of the people organising it commits a summary offence (s. 11(7)).

Defence

The Public Order Act 1986, s. 11 states:

(8)   It is a defence for the accused to prove that he did not know of, and neither suspected nor had reason to suspect, the failure to satisfy the requirements or (as the case may be) the difference of date, time or route.

(9)   To the extent that an alleged offence turns on a difference of date, time or route, it is a defence for the accused to prove that the difference arose from circumstances beyond his control or from something done with the agreement of a police officer or by his direction.

4.12.2   Imposing

Section 12 of the Public Order Act 1986 allows for conditions to be imposed on public processions. These conditions may be imposed by 'the senior police officer' in each case. For the purposes of s. 12, the 'senior police officer' is:

- in relation to a procession being held or intended to be held where people are assembling to take part in it, *the most senior rank present at the scene*;

- in relation to any other intended procession, the chief officer of police.

Therefore, where advance notice of a procession is given, the chief of police may impose conditions on it as set out below. Where the procession has already begun, or where people are gathering to take part in it, the most senior officer present at the scene may impose those conditions.

The chief officer's directions must be in writing (s. 12(3)); the directions of other officers may be given orally, though it will be far easier to prove the relevant offences of failing to comply with those directions if there is some permanent and reliable record of them.

If the senior police officer, having regard to:

- the time or place of the procession *and*
- the conditions in which it is to be held *and*
- its route/proposed route

'reasonably believes' (**see chapter 2**) that it may result in:

- serious public disorder
- serious damage to property *or*
- serious disruption to the life of the community

he/she may give directions imposing such conditions as appear to him/her to be necessary to prevent such disorder, damage or disruption on the organisers or the people taking part (s. 12(1)).

The senior police officer (as defined above) may also give those directions where he/she reasonably believes that the purpose of the person(s) organising the procession is the intimidation of others with a view to compelling them either:

- not to do an act they have a right to do *or*

- to do an act they have a right not to do.

In any of the cases above, the directions may include directions as to the route of the procession or a prohibition on it entering certain public places (s. 12(1)).

Offences

There are three summary offences created in relation to these directions under s. 12(4), (5) and (6).

The first two are:

- organising or
- taking part in

a public procession and, in doing so, *knowingly* (**see Crime, chapter 1**) failing to comply with a condition imposed under s. 12.

The third offence is inciting another (**see Crime, chapter 3**) to take part in a public procession in a way which the person incited knows is failing to comply with an imposed condition.

Power of Arrest

The Public Order Act 1986, s. 12 states:

> *(7)   A constable in uniform may arrest without warrant anyone he reasonably suspects is committing an offence under subsection (4), (5) or (6).*

Keynote

This power of arrest, limited to a constable in uniform, is drafted in the present tense, that is, it will only apply where there is a reasonable suspicion that the person is in the act of committing one of the relevant offences. For a further general power of arrest relating to obstructing a police officer, **see Crime, chapter 8**.

For a discussion of 'reasonable suspicion', **see chapter 2**.

4.12.3   Prohibited Processions

The Public Order Act 1986, s. 13, allows for a public procession to be prohibited, either by the district council on application from the chief constable (outside the City of London or the Metropolitan Police District) or the Commissioner with approval of the Secretary of State.

As with the conditions imposed under s. 12 above, there are three summary offences created in relation to prohibited public processions. The first two offences are committed by people who either organise a public procession which they *know* has been prohibited under s. 13 or who take part in such a procession *knowing* that it has been so prohibited (s. 13(7) and (8)). There is also an offence of a person inciting another to take part in a procession which he/she knows has been prohibited (s. 13(9)).

Power of Arrest

The Public Order Act 1986, s. 13 states:

> *(10) A constable in uniform may arrest without warrant anyone he reasonably suspects is committing an offence under subsection (7), (8) or (9).*

Keynote

This power of arrest is limited to officers in uniform. It is drafted in the present tense, that is, it will only apply where there is a reasonable suspicion that the person is in the act of committing one of the relevant offences.

For a discussion of 'reasonable suspicion', **see chapter 2**.

4.12.4 Public Assemblies

Section 14 of the Public Order Act 1986 allows for the 'senior police officer' (as defined above) to impose conditions on public assemblies in the same way as public processions.

A public assembly is an assembly of 20 or more people in a public place that is wholly or partly open to the air (s. 16).

The circumstances under which such conditions may be imposed are the same as for public processions with the added provision that the officer may direct:

- the maximum duration or
- the maximum number of people

as appears necessary to him/her in order to avoid disorder, damage, disruption or intimidation (s. 14(1)).

The chief officer's directions must be given in writing but, as with the offences relating to public processions, it will be easier to prove the offences under s. 14 if there is a reliable record of any directions given by the senior officer.

Summary offences are again created in relation to the organising, taking part or inciting others to take part in a public assembly in each case where the person knowingly fails to comply with a condition imposed under s. 14 (s. 14(4), (5) and (6)). In the cases of people organising or taking part in such an assembly, there is a statutory defence available if the defendant can prove that the failure to comply with the relevant condition arose from circumstances beyond his/her control.

Power of Arrest

The Public Order Act 1986, s. 14 states:

> *(7) A constable in uniform may arrest without warrant anyone he reasonably suspects is committing an offence under subsection (4), (5) or (6).*

Keynote

See keynote above.

4.12.5   Trespassory Assemblies

The provisions of s. 14 above apply to public assemblies. However, occasions have arisen where the assembly has been *trespassory*, that is, on land which is either private or where there is only a limited right of public access and the permission of the relevant landowner has not been granted. In such instances, s. 14A of the Public Order Act 1986 provides the police with certain powers.

Section 14A allows a chief officer of police (including the Commissioners of the City of London and Metropolitan Police) to apply to the relevant district council for an order prohibiting the holding of trespassory assemblies.

The conditions under which a chief officer may make such an application are where he/she reasonably believes that an assembly is to be held in any district at a place on land to which the public has no right/limited rights of access and that the assembly:

- is likely to be held without the permission of the occupier of the land *or*
- to conduct itself in such a way as to exceed the limits of the public's right of access

and that the assembly may result:

- in serious disruption to the life of the community or
- where the land (or a building/monument on it) is of historical, architectural, archaeological or scientific importance, significant damage to the land, building or monument.

The classic example of such a situation can be found at sites such as Stonehenge.

On receiving the application, the council may — *with the consent of the Secretary of State* — make an order either in the terms of the application or with such modifications as may be approved by the Secretary of State (s. 14A(2)(a)). The order must be in writing or reduced into writing as soon as practicable after being made (s. 14A(8)).

If such an order is made it must not last for more than four days nor must it apply to an area beyond a radius of five miles from a specified centre (s. 14A(6)).

As with a 'public' assembly, an assembly for these purposes means 20 or more people; 'land' means land in the open air; and 'public' includes a section of the public (s. 14A(9)).

Offences

There are three summary offences in relation to trespassory assemblies in respect of which an order has been passed. These offences, under s. 14B(1), (2) and (3) apply to people who:

- organise or
- take part in

an assembly that they *know* is prohibited by an order under s. 14A *or*

- who incite another to take part in such an assembly.

Even where an order has been passed, there will be a need to show that the assembly was obstructive of the highway or at least that it exceeded the public's general right of access (*DPP* v *Jones*, *The Times*, 5 March 1999).

Power of Arrest

The Public Order Act 1986, s. 14B states:

> (4)   *A constable in uniform may arrest without a warrant anyone he reasonably suspects to be committing an offence under this section.*

Keynote

This power of arrest, which is restricted to officers in uniform, is drafted in the present tense, that is, it will only apply where there is a reasonable suspicion that the person is in the act of committing one of the relevant offences. For a further general power of arrest relating to obstructing a police officer, **see Crime, chapter 8.**

For a discussion of 'reasonable suspicion', **see chapter 2.**

Police Powers

Section 14C of the 1986 Act provides:

> (1)   *If a constable in uniform reasonably believes that a person is on his way to an assembly within the area to which an order under section 14A applies which the constable reasonably believes is likely to be an assembly which is prohibited by that order, he may, subject to subsection (2) below—*
>   (a)   *stop that person, and*
>   (b)   *direct him not to proceed in the direction of the assembly.*
> (2)   *The power conferred by subsection (1) may only be exercised within the area to which the order applies.*
> (3)   *A person who fails to comply with a direction under subsection (1) which he knows has been given to him is guilty of an offence.*
> (4)   *A constable in uniform may arrest without a warrant anyone he reasonably suspects to be committing an offence under this section.*

Keynote

This power allows officers to stop people, though not, it would seem, vehicles (in which case the general power under the Road Traffic Act 1988 must be used; **see Road Traffic, chapter 10**). For the more general powers to stop people and vehicles, **see chapter 2.** As with the other powers of arrest in relation to processions and assemblies, this power applies only to someone reasonably suspected of being in the act of committing an offence under this section. There seems to be no requirement that the officer exercising the power of arrest is the same officer as the officer who issued the direction not to proceed (which would dilute the efficacy of the power).

4.12.6   Public Meetings

It is an offence to attempt to break up a public meeting.

Offence — Trying to Break up a Public Meeting — Public Meeting Act 1908, s. 1
Triable summarily. Six months' imprisonment and/or a fine.
(**No specific power of arrest**)

Section 1 of the Public Meeting Act 1908 provides:

(1) Any person who at a lawful public meeting acts in a disorderly manner for the purpose of preventing the transaction of the business for which the meeting was called together shall be guilty of an offence and shall on summary conviction be liable to imprisonment for a term not exceeding six months or to a fine not exceeding level 5 on the standard scale or to both . . .

(2) Any person who incites others to commit an offence under this section shall be guilty of a like offence.

Keynote

If a constable reasonably suspects any person of committing this offence, he/she may, *if requested by the person chairing the meeting*, require the offender to declare his/her name and address immediately. Failing to comply with such a request or giving false details is a summary offence (s. 1(3)).

'Public meeting' is not defined in the 1908 Act. There appears to be no requirement for the meeting to be lawfully assembled.

This offence does not apply to meetings held in relation to the Representation of the People Act 1983, s. 97 (meetings concerned with public elections) (s. 1(4)). In the case of people acting or inciting others to act in a disorderly way at such meetings, there is a specific summary offence under s. 97(1) of the 1983 Act.

4.13 Sporting Events

In addition to the more general offences regulating public order, there are several offences which are specifically aimed at tackling disorder and anti-social behaviour at sporting events. The Government has recently introduced the Football (Offences and Disorder) Act which addresses a number of the areas discussed below. The Act received the Royal Assent on 27 July 1999 and is expected to come into force within the next three months.

4.13.1 Offences under the Football (Offences) Act 1991

Offence — Misbehaviour at Designated Football Match —
Football (Offences) Act 1991, ss. 2, 3 and 4
Triable summarily. Fine.
(**Arrestable offence**)

The Football (Offences) Act 1991, ss. 2, 3 and 4 state:

2. It is an offence for a person at a designated football match to throw anything at or towards—
(a) the playing area, or any area adjacent to the playing area to which spectators are not generally admitted, or
(b) any area in which spectators or other persons are or may be present, without lawful authority or lawful excuse (which shall be for him to prove).

3.—(1) It is an offence to take part at a designated football match in chanting of an indecent or racialist nature.

(2)   For this purpose—

(a)   'chanting' means the repeated uttering of any words or sounds in concert with one or more others; and

(b)   'of racialist nature' means consisting of or including matter which is threatening, abusive or insulting to a person by reason of his colour, race, nationality (including citizenship) or ethnic or national origins.

4.   *It is an offence for a person at a designated football match to go onto the playing area, or any area adjacent to the playing area to which spectators are not generally admitted, without lawful authority of lawful excuse (which shall be for him to prove).*

Keynote

These offences can be separated into those affecting the playing area and adjacent parts of the ground (ss. 2 and 4) and the offence of indecent or 'racialist' chanting (s.3).

In the case of the first offence (s. 2), throwing anything at or towards the playing area etc., there is a defence of having lawful authority or reasonable excuse. Presumably this would cover someone returning the ball after it has been kicked into the stands but, that apart, there seem to be few occasions on which a defendant would have lawful authority/reasonable excuse for the behaviour prohibited by s. 2.

Section 4 makes the same savings in relation to lawful authority/reasonable excuse and, in both cases, the burden of proof falls on the defendant. (The *standard* of proof will be that of the balance of probabilities; **see Evidence and Procedure, chapter 11**.)

For the offence under s. 3, the defendant must be shown to have repeated the words — or sounds — with at least one other person before it can be classed as 'chanting'.

'Indecent' is not defined but whether such chanting was indecent will be a question of fact for the court to decide in all the circumstances.

'Racialist' is a slightly outdated term and requires matter that is threatening, abusive or insulting to a person by reason of his/her colour, race, nationality or ethnic/national origins. This wording requires that the chanting *is* rather than might potentially be, threatening, abusive or insulting (compare with the wording under the other general public order offences above). Therefore, although there is no express requirement for a 'victim' of the offence under this section, the best way to prove that element of the offence would be to find someone who was so threatened, abused or insulted by the behaviour.

As with the racially aggravated offences created by the Crime and Disorder Act 1998, religion is not included in the definition. For a full discussion on racist behaviour generally, **see chapter 3**.

Designated Football Match

A 'designated football match' is an association football match designated, or of a description designated, for the purposes of the 1991 Act by the Secretary of State. The Football (Offences) (Designation of Football Matches) Order 1991 (SI 1991 No. 1565), as amended, has been made for this purpose. It covers any UEFA club or national team competition played at either a sports ground designated under the Safety of Sports Grounds Act 1975 or the ground of a member of the Football League or the Football Association Premier League.

References to things done at a designated football match include anything done at the ground:

- within the period beginning two hours before the start of the match or (if earlier) two hours before the time at which it is advertised to start and ending one hour after the end of the match,

- where the match is advertised to start at a particular time on a particular day but does not take place, within the period beginning two hours before and ending one hour after the advertised starting time (s. 1(2) of the 1991 Act).

4.13.2 Offences under the Football Spectators Act 1989

The Football Spectators Act 1989 was passed as a measure to:

- control the admission of spectators to designated football matches in England and Wales;
- provide for the safety of those spectators; and
- provide for the making and enforcing of orders imposing restrictions on certain people in order to prevent violence and disorder at/in connection with designated matches played outside England and Wales.

Many of the licensing provisions in the 1989 Act have not been brought into force.

Restriction Orders

Under s. 15 of the 1989 Act a court may make a restriction order on a person who it has convicted of a 'relevant offence' if the court is satisfied that making such an order would help prevent violence and disorder at/in connection with 'designated football matches'.

'Designated football matches' are those designated by the Secretary of State (see e.g. the Football Spectators (Designation of Football Matches outside England and Wales) Order 1990 (SI 1990 No. 732), as amended).

The relevant offences are set out at sch. 1 to the 1989 Act (**see appendix 4**). They include offences relating to drunkenness, violence or threats of violence or public order offences committed on journeys to or from designated matches or during the period of such a match.

The effect of a restriction order is that the person initially has to report to the police station specified in it within five days (s. 16(2)). Thereafter, he/she must report to any police station in England or Wales on the occasion of certain designated matches in accordance with the restriction order.

The National Criminal Intelligence Service (**see chapter 1**) have responsibility for monitoring the movement of football spectators and should be consulted in cases involving restriction orders and the movement /offending of spectators generally.

For further guidance on restriction orders, see Home Office Circular 70/1997.

Offence — Failing to Comply with Restriction Order — Football Spectators Act 1989, s. 16(4)
Triable summarily. Six months' imprisonment and/or a fine.
(*Arrestable offence*)

Section 16 of the Football Spectators Act 1989 provides:

> *(4)   A person who, without reasonable excuse, fails to comply with the duty to report imposed by a restriction order commits an offence.*

Keynote

This offence was made an 'arrestable offence' (**see chapter 2**) by the Crime and Disorder Act 1998, s. 84(2), the idea being to give the police greater powers to deal with *potential* offenders travelling away to matches. However, given that the only *preventive* power in relation to arrestable offences relates to a person who is reasonably suspected of being 'about to commit' an arrestable offence, it is difficult to see how this new power helps. The restriction order can only require the person to report to a police station *on the occasion* of designated matches (s.16(2)(b)). Whereas the offence clearly gives wide powers *once the person has failed* to report under the conditions of a restriction order, it would be difficult to argue that a person waiting to board a train or ferry many hours or even days before a football match is 'about' to commit the arrestable offence set out above.

Where the person convicted of a relevant (sch. 1) offence is sentenced to imprisonment taking immediate effect, any restriction order imposed will last for five years. (There are special provisions made for reporting times in respect of people serving prison sentences during part of the restriction period (s. 16(3).)

In any other case, a restriction order lasts for two years, though once it has run for a year, the person may apply to the court to have it terminated (ss. 16(1)(b) and 17(1)).

A number of exemptions are provided for under s. 20. These allow, among other things, for the person on whom a restriction order has been passed to apply for exemption from the duties of the order under special circumstances.

In addition to having the power to make a restriction order where a person is convicted of a sch. 1 offence, the court may also make such an order where the person has been convicted of a 'corresponding offence, (specified by Order in Council) in another country (s. 22(2)). An example of this can be found in the Football Spectators (Corresponding Offences in France) Order 1998 passed in connection with the World Cup.

In order to bring a person to court for the purpose of making a restriction order following a conviction abroad, magistrates may issue a summons or, where appropriate, a warrant of arrest.

Exclusion Orders

Whereas restriction orders are available in relation to designated matches being played outside England and Wales, *exclusion* orders can be made to prohibit a person from entering any premises for the purpose of attending any 'prescribed football match'. The power to make these exclusion orders comes from s. 30 of the Public Order Act 1986. Section 2 of the Football Spectators Act 1989 was supposed to repeal the relevant sections relating to exclusion orders but, at the time of writing, s. 2 has not been brought into force and the power to impose such an exclusion order still exists.

The prescribed football matches are association football matches prescribed by order by the Secretary of State (s. 36). (See e.g. the Public Order (Football Exclusions) Order 1987 (SI 1987 No. 853).)

Under s. 37, the Secretary of State may prescribe some other sporting events as well.

The conditions that must exist before an exclusion order can be made are that the offence:

- was committed during any period relevant to a prescribed football match while the offender was at, entering or leaving (or trying to enter/leave) the ground concerned; or

- was committed while the offender or the victim was on a journey to/from an association football match (*whether prescribed or not*) and involved the use or threat of violence towards another person, property or involved an offence under the Public Order Act 1986, s. 5 or Part III (racial hatred); or

- was committed under the Sporting Events (Control of Alcohol etc.) Act 1985, ss. 1(3), (4), 1A(3) or (4).

An exclusion order lasts for not less than three months and for as long as is specified in the order (s. 32).

As with restriction orders above, an exclusion order may only be made if the court is satisfied that making it would help to prevent violence or disorder at/in connection with prescribed football matches (s. 30).

Copies of the order will be sent to the appropriate chief officer of police and, if the prosecution make an application, the court may order the offender to have a photograph taken and deliver it to a police station within seven days (s. 35).

It is a summary offence to enter premises in breach of an exclusion order (s. 32(3)).

Power of Arrest

The Public Order Act 1986, s. 32 states:

> *(4)   A constable who reasonably suspects that a person has entered premises in breach of an exclusion order may arrest him without warrant.*

Keynote

There is no requirement for the officer to be in uniform for this power. However, the power only applies 'after the fact', that is, the person must have entered the relevant premises before the power becomes available.

'Premises' is not defined but, given the wording of s. 30(1) which allows a court to make an order prohibiting the person from entering *any premises for the purposes of attending any prescribed football match there*', the expression must refer to a relevant football ground.

4.13.3   Offences under the Sporting Events (Control of Alcohol etc.) Act 1985

Offence — Alcohol on Coaches and Trains — Sporting Events (Control of Alcohol etc.) Act 1985, s. 1
Triable summarily. Three months' imprisonment and/or a fine (s. 1(3)); fine (s. 1(2) and (4)).
(Statutory power of arrest)

The Sporting Events (Control of Alcohol etc.) Act 1985, s. 1 states:

> (1) This section applies to a vehicle which—
> (a) is a public service vehicle or railway passenger vehicle, and
> (b) is being used for the principal purpose of carrying passengers for the whole or part of a journey to or from a designated sporting event.
> (2) A person who knowingly causes or permits intoxicating liquor to be carried on a vehicle to which the section applies is guilty of an offence—
> (a) if the vehicle is a public service vehicle and he is the operator of the vehicle or the servant or agent of the operator, or
> (b) if the vehicle is a hired vehicle and he is the person to whom it is hired or the servant or agent of that person.
> (3) A person who has intoxicating liquor in his possession while on a vehicle to which this section applies is guilty of an offence.
> (4) A person who is drunk on a vehicle to which this section applies is guilty of an offence.

Keynote

Section 1 creates a number of offences in relation to public service vehicles and trains being used principally (though not exclusively) to carry passengers for the whole or part of a journey, to or from a designated sporting event.

The offences can be committed by the vehicle operator/hirer or his/her servant or agent provided there is evidence of *knowingly* causing or permitting the carrying of intoxicating liquor (for 'cause and permit', **see Road Traffic, chapter 1**).

The other offences are committed by people who have intoxicating liquor in their 'possession' (as to which **see Crime, chapter 6**) and by people who are drunk on a relevant vehicle. Generally, any mature and competent witness may give evidence as to drunkenness (**see Evidence and Procedure, chapter 11**).

Section 7(3) provides a power for a police officer to stop a public service vehicle in order to search it where he/she has reasonable grounds to suspect an offence under this section *is being or has been committed* in respect of that vehicle. It also provides a power to search a railway carriage (though not to stop the train) under the same circumstances. The power to search people in those vehicles comes from s. 7(2).

Offence — Alcohol on Other Vehicles — Sporting Events (Control of Alcohol etc.) Act 1985, s. 1A
Triable summarily. Three months, imprisonment and/or a fine (s. 1A(3)); fine (s. 1A(2) and (4))
(Statutory power of arrest)

Section 1A of the Sporting Events (Control of Alcohol etc.) Act 1985 provides:

(1)   This section applies to a motor vehicle which—
(a)   is not a public service vehicle but is adapted to carry more than 8 passengers, and
(b)   is being used for the principal purpose of carrying two or more passengers for the whole or part of a journey to or from a designated sporting event.
(2)   A person who knowingly causes or permits intoxicating liquor to be carried on a motor vehicle to which this section applies is guilty of an offence—
(a)   if he is its driver, or
(b)   if he is not its driver but is its keeper, the servant or agent of its keeper, a person to whom it is made available (by hire, loan or otherwise) by its keeper or the keeper's servant or agent, or the servant or agent of a person to whom it is so made available.
(3)   A person who has intoxicating liquor in his possession while on a motor vehicle to which this section applies is guilty of an offence.
(4)   A person who is drunk on a motor vehicle to which this section applies is guilty of an offence.

Keynote

This section creates similar offences to those set out under s. 1 but these relate to mechanically propelled vehicles that are intended or adapted for use on roads and that are adapted to carry more than eight passengers (not being PSVs). For an explanation of each of these terms, **see Road Traffic, chapter 1.**

For the purposes of the above offences, a vehicle's 'keeper' is the person having the duty to take out a vehicle excise licence for it (**see Road Traffic, chapter 12**) (s. 1A(5)).

The power to stop and search vehicles and their occupants under s. 7(3) above also applies to an offence under this section.

Designated Sporting Event

A 'designated sporting event' means an event or proposed event which has been designated or is part of a class designated by order made by the Secretary of State. It also includes events designated under comparable Scottish legislation. Events which are to be held outside Great Britain can also be designated.

Power of Arrest

Section 7(2) provides that a constable may search a person he/she has reasonable grounds to suspect is committing or has committed an offence under the 1985 Act, and may arrest such a person.

Offence — Alcohol at Sports Grounds —
Sporting Events (Control of Alcohol etc.) Act 1985, s. 2
Triable summarily. Three months' imprisonment and/or a fine (s. 2(1)); fine (s. 2(2))
(Statutory power of arrest)

The Sporting Events (Control of Alcohol etc.) Act 1985, s. 2 states:

(1)   A person who has intoxicating liquor or an article to which this section applies in his possession—
(a)   at any time during the period of a designated sporting event when he is in any area of a designated sports ground from which the event may be directly viewed, or

(b) while entering or trying to enter a designated sports ground at any time during the period of a designated sporting event at that ground, is guilty of an offence.

(2) A person who is drunk in a designated sports ground at any time during the period of a designated sporting event at that ground or is drunk while entering or trying to enter such a ground at any time during the period of a designated sporting event at that ground is guilty of an offence.

Keynote

The articles to which s. 2 applies are:

- articles capable of causing injury to a person struck by them, being
- bottles, cans or other portable containers (including ones that are crushed or broken), which
- are for holding any drink, and
- are of a kind which are normally discarded or returned to/left to be recovered by the supplier when empty

and include parts of those articles. Any such article that is for holding any medicinal product (within the meaning of the Medicines Act 1968) is excluded from this definition (s. 2(3)).

Section 7(1) provides a power for a constable to enter any part of a ground during a designated sporting event for the purpose of enforcing the provisions of the Act.

Offence — Having Fireworks, Flares etc. — Sporting Events (Control of Alcohol etc.) Act 1985, s. 2A
Triable summarily. Three months' imprisonment and/or a fine.
(*Statutory power of arrest*)

Section 2A of the Sporting Events (Control of Alcohol etc.) Act 1985 provides:

(1) A person is guilty of an offence if he has an article or substance to which this section applies in his possession—
(a) at any time during the period of a designated sporting event when he is in any area of a designated sports ground from which the event may be directly viewed, or
(b) while entering or trying to enter a designated sports ground at any time during the period of a designated sporting event at the ground.
(2) . . .
(3) This section applies to any article or substance whose main purpose is the emission of a flare for purposes of illuminating or signalling (as opposed to igniting or heating) or the emission of smoke or a visible gas; and in particular it applies to distress flares, fog signals, and pellets and capsules intended to be used as fumigators or for testing pipes, but not to matches, cigarette lighters or heaters.
(4) This section also applies to any article which is a firework.

Keynote

There is a defence under s. 2A(2) for the person to prove that he/she had possession of the article with lawful authority. 'Possession' is quite a broad concept going beyond 'carrying' (**see Crime, chapter 6**).

For other offences involving fireworks **see chapter 3** and for explosives offences generally **see below**.

As with all other offences under the 1985 Act, the powers of entry, search and arrest under s. 7 apply to this offence.

Designated Sports Ground

Under s. 9 of the 1985 Act, a 'designated sports ground' means:

> (2) . . . any place—
> (a) used (wholly or partly) for sporting events where accommodation is provided for spectators, and
> (b) for the time being designated, or of a class designated, by order made by the Secretary of State,
> and an order under this subsection may include provision for determining for the purposes of this Act the outer limit of any designated sports ground.

The period of a 'designated sporting event' is also covered by s. 9:

> (4) The period of a designated sporting event is the period beginning two hours before the start of the event or (if earlier) two hours before the time at which it is advertised to start and ending one hour after the end of the event, but—
> (a) where an event advertised to start at a particular time on a particular day is postponed to a later day, the period includes the period in the day on which it is advertised to take place beginning two hours before and ending one hour after that time, and
> (b) where an event advertised to start at a particular time on a particular day does not take place, the period is the period referred to in paragraph (a) above.

4.13.4 Ticket Touts

Offence — Ticket Touts — Criminal Justice and Public Order Act 1994, s. 166
Triable summarily. Fine.
(Arrestable offence)

The Criminal Justice and Public Order Act 1994, s. 166 states:

> (1) It is an offence for an unauthorised person to sell, or offer or expose for sale, a ticket for a designated football match in any public place or place to which the public has access or, in the course of a trade or business, in any other place.

Keynote

Unless a person has written authorisation from the home club or by the match organisers, he/she is 'unauthorised'.

'Ticket' will include anything which purports to be a ticket (s. 166(2)).

This offence is split into two categories, the first being capable of commission by anyone who sells, offers/exposes for sale a ticket in any public place or place to which the public has access. The second category applies to people who are selling, offering or exposing for sale any ticket in the course of a trade or business. In such cases, there is no restriction of the place of sale/offering for sale. There appears to be no need for the trade or business to be the defendant's own and selling tickets on behalf of someone else's business would appear to meet the requirements of the second part of this offence.

This offence was classified as an arrestable offence under PACE 1984, s. 24(2).

The power to search on arrest under s. 32 of PACE 1984 (**see chapter 2**) extends to vehicles that it is believed are being used by ticket touts.

4.14 Terrorism

The Prevention of Terrorism (Temporary Provisions) Act 1989 creates many offences; it also provides (in its amended form) a number of powers aimed at curbing the activities of terrorists (**see chapter 2**). For a full discussion on these provisions see *Blackstone's Criminal Practice*, 1999, section B.10. Many of the offences relate only to 'proscribed organisations' as opposed to terrorist organisations generally. Section 1 of the 1989 Act provides that the only 'proscribed organisations' are those listed in sch. 1 to the Act and, at the time of writing, the only organisations referred to in sch. 1 are:

- the Irish Republican Army (IRA); and
- the Irish National Liberation Army (INLA).

Some offences, however, refer to the organisations proscribed under the equivalent legislation in Northern Ireland. These include:

- the Ulster Freedom Fighters (UFF);
- the Ulster Volunteer Force (UVF);
- the Irish People's Liberation Organisation (IPLO); and
- the Ulster Defence Association (UDA).

(See the Northern Ireland (Emergency Provisions) Act 1996.)

The significance of these other organisations may increase following the recent political developments in Northern Ireland.

4.14.1 Exclusion Orders

Under s. 5 of the 1989 Act, the Secretary of State may make an order excluding certain people from entering Great Britain (or, under ss. 6 and 7, Northern Ireland and the United Kingdom respectively). The Secretary of State can also make an order under sch. 2 to the Act requiring a person to leave Great Britain.

Before the Secretary of State can make such an order, he/she must be satisfied that the person:

- is, or has been, concerned in the commission, preparation or instigation of acts of terrorism; or
- is attempting, or may attempt to enter Great Britain for those purposes.

Exclusion orders cannot be made against a British citizen who is, at the time, ordinarily resident in Great Britain and who has been so for the last three years (s. 5(4)).

Offence — Failing to Comply with Exclusion Order — Prevention of Terrorism (Temporary Provisions) Act 1989, s. 8
Triable either way. Five years' imprisonment and/or a fine on indictment; six months' imprisonment and/or a fine summarily.
(*Serious arrestable offence*)

The Prevention of Terrorism (Temporary Provisions) Act 1989, s. 8 states:

(1)   A person who is subject to an exclusion order is guilty of an offence if he fails to comply with the order at a time after he has been, or become liable to be, removed under Schedule 2 to this Act.

(2)   A person is guilty of an offence—

(a)   if he is knowingly concerned in arrangements for securing or facilitating the entry into Great Britain, Northern Ireland or the United Kingdom of a person whom he knows; or has reasonable grounds for believing, to be an excluded person; or

(b)   if he knowingly harbours such a person in Great Britain, Northern Ireland or the United Kingdom.

Keynote

An 'excluded person' is generally someone who is subject to an exclusion order and who (under the relevant section) is liable to be removed from the country.

The offence under s. 8(2) requires a high degree of *mens rea* (**see Crime, chapter 1**) in that the person must be shown to have acted with the relevant 'knowledge' in each case.

A prosecution for this offence may only be brought by the Attorney-General (or Solicitor-General) (s. 19).

It is summary offence for a person who fails without reasonable excuse to comply with directions given to him/her under sch. 2 to the 1989 Act (sch. 2, para. 6(8)).

4.14.2   Proscribed Organisations

Offence — Membership of, Support for Proscribed Organisation — Prevention of Terrorism (Temporary Provisions) Act 1989, s. 2

Triable either way. Ten years' imprisonment and/or fine on indictment; six months' imprisonment and/or a fine summarily.
(*Serious arrestable offence*)

The Prevention of Terrorism (Temporary Provisions) Act 1989, s. 2 states:

(1)   Subject to subsection (3) below, a person is guilty of an offence if he—

(a)   belongs or professes to belong to a proscribed organisation;

(b)   solicits or invites support for a proscribed organisation other than support with money or other property; or

(c)   arranges or assists in the arrangement or management of, or addresses, any meeting of three or more persons (whether or not it is a meeting to which the public are admitted) knowing that the meeting is—

(i)   to support a proscribed organisation;

(ii)   to further the activities of such an organisation; or

(iii)   to be addressed by a person belonging or professing to belong to such an organisation.

Keynote

There are a number of offences relating to proscribed organisations included under s. 2. These briefly are:

* belonging to/professing to belong
* soliciting/inviting support
* arranging/assisting in arrangement, managing/assisting in management of, or addressing a meeting (of three or more people) to support, further the activities or to be addressed by a member of a proscribed organisation (or person professing so to belong).

Where a person is charged with the offence under s. 2(1)(a) above (belonging/professing to belong to a proscribed organisation), s. 2A and 2B make further provisions in relation to proving that offence. These sections were inserted by the Criminal Justice (Terrorism and Conspiracy) Act 1998. Section 2A allows a police officer of the rank of superintendent or above to give oral evidence that, in his/her opinion, a defendant belongs to a specified organisation or did belong to such an organisation at a particular time. Although the statement is admissible, it will not be conclusive as to the fact of the person's membership of a proscribed organisation and a defendant will not be liable to be committed for trial in England and Wales, nor to be convicted solely on the basis of such a statement — s. 2A(3).

Section 2A goes on to allow certain inferences to be drawn from a defendant's failure to mention certain material facts when questioned or charged by the police. (For the law relating to inferences from silence generally, **see Evidence and Procedure, chapter 11.**)

Section 2(3) provides a specific defence to the offence of belonging to a proscribed organisation if the person can show that he/she became a member when the organisation was not proscribed and that he/she has not taken part in any of its activities at any time while it has been proscribed.

A prosecution for this offence may only be brought by the Attorney-General (or Solicitor-General) (s. 19).

Offence — Display of Support in Public for Proscribed Organisation — Prevention of Terrorism (Temporary Provisions) Act 1989, s. 3
Triable summarily. Six months' imprisonment and/or a fine.
(No specific power of arrest)

The Prevention of Terrorism (Temporary Provisions) Act 1989, s. 3 states:

(1) Any person who in a public place—
(a) wears any item of dress; or
(b) wears, carries or displays any article,
in such a way or in such circumstances as to arouse reasonable apprehension that he is a member or supporter of a proscribed organisation, is guilty of an offence.

Keynote

'Public place' for these purposes includes any highway and any premises to which, at the material time, the public have access, whether on payment or otherwise (s. 3(3)).

There is no need to show any intention on the part of the defendant to arouse any such apprehension that he/she is a member or supporter of a proscribed organisation.

4.14.3   Possession of Articles

Offence — Possession of Articles for Terrorism — Prevention of Terrorism (Temporary Provisions) Act 1989, s. 16A
Triable either way. Ten years' imprisonment and/or a fine on indictment; six months' imprisonment and/or a fine summarily.
(Serious arrestable offence)

The Prevention of Terrorism (Temporary Provisions) Act 1989, s. 16A states:

(1)   A person is guilty of an offence if he has any article in his possession in circumstances giving rise to a reasonable suspicion that the article is in his possession for a purpose connected with the commission, preparation or instigation of acts of terrorism to which this section applies.
(2)   The acts of terrorism to which this section applies are—
(a)   acts of terrorism connected with the affairs of Northern Ireland; and
(b)   acts of terrorism of any other description except acts connected solely with the affairs of the United Kingdom or any part of the United Kingdom other than Northern Ireland.

Keynote

This offence requires the consent of the Director of Public Prosecutions before it can be prosecuted (s. 19). The Divisional Court has held recently that, in deciding whether or not to bring a prosecution under this legislation the Director of Public Prosecutions must take account of the provisions of the Human Rights Act 1998. As and when that Act comes into force, there is every likelihood that convictions under the above legislation will be challenged. The court also held that the wording of the offences under ss. 16A and 16B (**see below**) allowed a jury to convict even though they had a reasonable doubt as to whether or not the defendant had the articles or information for a terrorist purpose. As this violated the fundamental principle of the presumption of innocence, making the offences at ss. 16A and 16B inconsistent with the Human Rights Act 1998, the courts could expect the legislation to be challenged on those grounds (*R v DPP, ex parte Kebilene, The Times*, 31 March 1999).

'Possession' is a broad term which goes beyond immediate custody or control (**see Crime, chapter 6**). 'Article' is not defined but would potentially extend to any inanimate object.

This offence is not restricted to the activities of 'proscribed organisations'.

There is a specific defence under s. 16A(3) for a person to prove that the article in question was not in his/her possession for the purpose alleged.

4.14.4   Collection of Information

Offence — Collection of Information — Prevention of Terrorism (Temporary Provisions) Act 1989, s. 16B
Triable either way. Ten years' imprisonment and/or a fine on indictment; six months' imprisonment and/or a fine summarily.
(*Serious arrestable offence*)

The Prevention of Terrorism (Temporary Provisions) Act 1989, s. 16B states:

(1)   No person shall, without lawful authority or reasonable excuse (the proof of which lies on him)—
(a)   collect or record any information which is of such a nature as is likely to be useful to terrorists in planning or carrying out any act of terrorism to which this section applies; or
(b)   have in his possession any record or document containing any such information as is mentioned in paragraph (a) above.

Keynote

The acts of terrorism to which this offence applies are those set out under s. 16A(2) above.

As to the possible effects of the Human Rights Act 1998 on this offence, **see above**.

'Recording' information will include taking photographs or any other means of recording (s. 16B(3)). Courts are empowered to order the confiscation of any documents or records found in the possession of a defendant convicted of this offence.

4.14.5 Soliciting Funds for Terrorism

Offence — Soliciting Funds for Terrorism — Prevention of Terrorism (Temporary Provisions) Act 1989, s. 9
*Triable either way. Fourteen years' imprisonment and/or a fine on indictment; six months'
imprisonment and/or a fine summarily.*
(Serious arrestable offence)

The Prevention of Terrorism (Temporary Provisions) Act 1989, s. 9 states:

> *(2)   A person is guilty of an offence if he—*
>   *(a)   gives, lends or otherwise makes available to any other person, whether for consideration or not, any money or other property, or*
>   *(b)   enters into or is otherwise concerned in an arrangement whereby money or other property is or is to be made available to another person,*
> *knowing or having reasonable cause to suspect that it will or may be applied or used [for the commission of, or in furtherance of, or in connection with 'acts of terrorism'].*

Keynote

Section 9 of the 1989 Act creates a further serious arrestable offence in relation to providing money or other property (or soliciting others to do so), intending that the money or property be used in connection with 'acts of terrorism'. Such 'acts of terrorism' are not restricted to the activities of 'proscribed organisations' and, in addition to acts connected with the affairs of Northern Ireland, include ' . . . acts of terrorism of any other description except acts connected solely with the affairs of the United Kingdom or any part of the United Kingdom other than Northern Ireland' (s. 9(3)(b)).

In proving this offence, it must be shown that the defendant knew or had reasonable cause to suspect that the property would or might be used for the purposes set out. Property includes real or personal property, things in action and intangible property (s. 20).

Sections 10 and 11 of the 1989 Act also create serious arrestable offences of being involved with soliciting, giving or retaining funds or property. These offences apply to funds or property intended for the benefit of 'proscribed organisations'. To complicate matters however, 'proscribed organisations' here includes those organisations named in the Northern Ireland (Emergency Provisions) Act 1996.

The courts have extensive powers to seize funds and property connected with terrorism (see s. 13 and sch. 4 to the 1989 Act).

Section 12 enables a person to pass on any suspicions he/she may have about property being derived from terrorist funds irrespective of any other restriction imposed on the disclosure of information.

In addition, s. 12 provides a number of specific defences to the offences above, most of which are based on lack of knowledge or the proper reporting of any suspicions to the appropriate authorities. Section 12 goes on to provide a defence for police officers acting in the course of their duties in combating terrorism.

The offences under ss. 9, 10 and 11 can only be prosecuted with the consent of the Attorney-General (or Solicitor-General).

4.14.6 Failure to Disclose Information

Sections 18 and 18A of the 1989 Act create further arrestable offences (carrying five years' imprisonment and/or fine on indictment and six months' imprisonment and/or a fine summarily) of failing to inform the police or other appropriate authority of:

- information which the person knows/believes might be of material assistance in preventing an act of terrorism connected with the affairs of Northern Ireland or securing the apprehension, prosecution or conviction of a person for such an offence (s. 18); or

- information which the person comes by on the course of his/her employment or business which causes him/her to know or suspect that another person is providing financial assistance for terrorism (s. 18A).

The first offence (s. 18) is a general one which presents difficulties of proof, while the second offence (s. 18A) applies to people such as employees of financial institutions or accountants who come across information *in their capacity as such*. In each case, the person is required to pass on the information as soon as is reasonably practicable.

Section 18A(3) provides a specific defence to the offences of failing to advise the authorities of information. In addition, information received by a legal adviser in the course of his/her duties is covered by 'legal privilege' (**see Evidence and Procedure, chapter 10**) and, as such, does not need to be disclosed.

Section 17 creates other arrestable offences carrying a maximum of five years' imprisonment in relation to the obstruction or prejudicing of a terrorist investigation.

4.14.7 Explosives

Offence — Causing Explosion likely to Endanger Life or Property — Explosive Substances Act 1883, s. 2
Triable on indictment. Life imprisonment.
(***Serious arrestable offence***)

The Explosive Substances Act 1883, s. 2 states:

> *A person who in the United Kingdom or (being a citizen of the United Kingdom and Colonies) in the Republic of Ireland unlawfully and maliciously causes by any explosive substance an explosion of a nature likely to endanger life or to cause serious injury to property shall, whether any injury to person or property has actually been caused or not, be guilty of an offence. . . .*

Keynote

The consent of the Attorney-General (or Solicitor-General) is required before prosecuting this offence (s. 7(1) of the 1883 Act).

'Explosive substance' includes any materials for making any explosive substance; any implement or apparatus used, or intended or adapted to be used for causing or aiding any explosion (s. 9(1)).

The definition of 'explosive' under the Explosives Act 1875 (**see chapter 3**) also applies to this offence (see *R* v *Wheatley* [1979] 1 WLR 144). Therefore fireworks and petrol bombs will be covered (*R* v *Bouch* [1983] QB 246). For offences involving fireworks generally, **see chapter 3**; for offences involving fireworks at sporting events, **see above**.

Other articles which have been held to amount to 'explosive substances' include:

* shotguns (*R* v *Downey* [1971] NI 224);
* electronic timers (*R* v *Berry (No. 3)* [1994] 2 All ER 913);
* gelignite with a fuse and detonator (*R* v *McCarthy* [1964] 1 WLR 196).

You must prove that the act was carried out 'maliciously' (**see Crime, chapter 1**).

Sections 73–75 of the Explosives Act 1875 provide powers to search for explosives in connection with the above offence.

Offence — Attempting to Cause Explosion or Keeping Explosive with Intent — Explosive Substances Act 1883, s. 3
Triable on indictment. Life imprisonment.
(*Arrestable offence*)

The Explosive Substances Act 1883, s. 3 states:

(1)   A person who in the United Kingdom or a dependency or (being a citizen of the United Kingdom and Colonies) elsewhere unlawfully and maliciously—
(a)   does any act with intent to cause, or conspires to cause, by an an explosive substance an explosion of a nature likely to endanger life, or cause serious injury to property, whether in the United Kingdom or the Republic of Ireland, or
(b)   makes or has in his possession or under his control an explosive substance with intent by means thereof to endanger life, or cause serious injury to property, whether in the United Kingdom or the Republic of Ireland, or to enable any other person so to do,
shall, whether any explosion does or does not take place, and whether any injury to person or property is actually caused or not, be guilty of an offence . . .

Offence — Making or Possessing Explosive under Suspicious Circumstances — Explosive Substances Act 1883, s. 4
Triable on indictment. Fourteen years' imprisonment.
(*Arrestable offence*)

The Explosive Substances Act 1883, s. 4 states:

(1)   Any person who makes or knowingly has in his possession or under his control any explosive substance under such circumstances as to give rise to a reasonable suspicion that he is not making it or does not have it in his possession or under his control for a lawful object, shall, unless he can show that he made it or had it in his possession or under his control for a lawful object, be guilty of [an offence] . . .

Keynote

The offence under s. 3 is one of specific intent (**see Crime, chapter 1**).

Both of the above offences require the consent of the Attorney-General (or Solicitor-General) before a prosecution can be brought.

It would seem that the wording of these offences requires the prosecution — in cases of 'possession' — to prove that a defendant *had* the relevant article in his/her possession and that he/she *knew* the nature of it (see *R* v *Hallam* [1957] 1 QB 569). This should be contrasted with the usual approach to offences involving 'possession' where the second part (knowledge of the 'quality' of an item) does not need to be shown; **see Crime, chapter 6**.

'Reasonable suspicion' in this case will be assessed *objectively*, that is, you must prove that the circumstances of the possession or making of the explosive substance would give rise to suspicion in a reasonable and objective bystander (*R* v *Fegan* (1971) 78 Cr App R 189).

Whether a person's purpose in having the items prohibited by these offences is a 'lawful object' will need to be determined in each case (*Fegan*).

Sections 73–75 of the Explosives Act 1875 provide powers to search for explosives in connection with the above offence.

Gunpowder

Sections 28–30 of the Offences Against the Person Act 1861 create arrestable offences of exploding gunpowder to cause bodily injury; throwing or placing gunpowder or corrosive fluid with intent to cause bodily harm; and placing gunpowder or explosives near buildings or vessels with intent to cause bodily injury. The 1861 Act also creates an offence of possessing or making gunpowder or explosives (or other noxious things) with intent to enable any other person to commit an offence under the Act (s. 64). This offence is triable on indictment and carries two years' imprisonment.

4.14.8 Other Offences Connected with Terrorism

Other terrorist activity may be covered by one or more of the offences listed below, all of which carry life imprisonment:

- Hijacking of aircraft (Aviation Security Act 1982, s. 1) — serious arrestable offence.

- Destroying, damaging or endangering aircraft (Aviation Security Act 1982, ss. 2 and 3) — arrestable offence.

- Endangering safety at aerodromes (Aviation and Maritime Security Act 1990, s. 1) — serious arrestable offence.

- Hijacking of ships (Aviation and Maritime Security Act 1990, s. 9) — serious arrestable offence.

- Hostage taking (Taking of Hostages Act 1982, s. 1) — serious arrestable offence (**see Crime, chapter 9**).

- Kidnapping (common law) — serious arrestable offence (**see Crime, chapter 9**).

- Endangering safety on railways (Offences Against the Person Act 1861) — arrestable offence (**see chapter 13**).

- Hijacking channel tunnel trains or seizing control of the tunnel system (Channel Tunnel (Security) Order 1994 — serious arrestable offence.

See also chapters 5 and 6 for offences involving weapons and firearms respectively.

CHAPTER FIVE

FIREARMS

5.1 Introduction

The law regulating the possession, transfer and use of firearms remained largely unchanged between the passing of the main Firearms Act in 1968 and the introduction of the Firearms (Amendment) Act in 1988. During 1997, however, the law underwent significant amendment and what were already fairly stringent controls were reinforced by further restrictions on the ownership and use of firearms generally.

In addition to the primary legislation, s. 53 of the Firearms Act 1968 allows the Secretary of State to make rules in relation to the 1968 Act's implementation (see e.g. the Firearms Rules 1989 (SI 1989 No. 854), as amended. The Home Office has also issued guidance to chief officers on the control and licensing of firearms.

5.2 The 'This' Checklist

When considering any situation involving firearms legislation, whether practically or for the purposes of study, it is useful to apply the 'this' checklist.

The 'this' checklist, which is also useful in other areas of law (**see Road Traffic**), means asking whether:

- **this** certificate/exemption
- covers **this** person
- for **this** activity
- involving **this** firearm/ammunition
- for **this** purpose.

5.2.1 This Certificate/Exemption

The Firearms Act 1968 provides for people to be authorised by certificate to hold, transfer or buy firearms under specified conditions.

The 1968 Act — and the amending legislation — also contains many exemptions, some generally applicable and others very specific.

In each case, whether considering a certificate or other authority, or a possible exemption, it is critical that you establish what conditions apply.

5.2.2 This Person

Certificates will authorise the *holder* to do certain things (e.g. to buy firearms); other authorities will allow a wider group of people to do things (e.g. borrow the rifle of a certificate holder). In considering offences it is important to establish exactly which person is authorised or is exempt from any liability.

5.2.3 This Activity

Certificates and exemptions never grant unlimited authority to undertake any activity with every firearm or ammunition. Certificates will usually specify whether the holder can have a firearm in his/her '*possession*'; which firearms or ammunition he/she can possess; and whether he/she can *sell* or *transfer* firearms *or* ammunition. Exemptions are the same in that they will not apply to everyone in respect of all activities.

5.2.4 This Firearm/Ammunition

In addition to the restrictions on the activity, certificates and exemptions will only apply to particular firearms and/or ammunition. A person authorised to possess a shotgun is not thereby permitted to have an automatic rifle. Similarly, a person who runs a mini rifle range is not thereby given authority to possess mortar shells!

5.2.5 This Purpose

Certificates and exemptions will specify the precise purposes for which they apply. For instance, if a certificate allows a person to possess a firearm for slaughtering animals while at the slaughterhouse, that does not permit the possession of the firearm by the slaughterer while at home or travelling to work.

Similarly, some of the general exemptions apply only to the people concerned while they are involved in *the ordinary course of their business*, whether they are registered firearms dealers or members of the armed forces; possession or use of a firearm outside the particular circumstances will not be covered.

5.3 Firearms Generally

Section 57 of the Firearms Act 1968 provides that:

> *(1)   In this Act, the expression 'firearm' means a lethal barrelled weapon of any description from which any shot, bullet or other missile can be discharged, and includes—*
> *(a)   any prohibited weapon, whether it is such a lethal weapon as aforesaid or not; and*
> *(b)   any component part of such a lethal or prohibited weapon; and*
> *(c)   any accessory to any such weapon designed or adapted to diminish the noise or flash caused by firing the weapon.*

Keynote

'Lethal barrelled weapon' is not defined under the 1968 Act.

The way in which the courts have determined whether or not something amounts to such a weapon is by asking:

- Can any shot, bullet or other missile be discharged from the weapon?, or
- Could the weapon be adapted so that any shot, bullet or other missile can be discharged?
- If so, is the weapon a 'lethal barrelled' weapon?

(See *Grace v DPP* (1989) 153 JP 491.)

A weapon is a lethal barrelled weapon if it is capable of causing injury, irrespective of the intentions of its maker (*Read v Donovan* [1947] KB 326). In determining whether a firearm is in fact a lethal barrelled weapon from which missiles can be discharged a court need not consider any specific evidence of someone who has seen the effects of it being fired. Therefore, where magistrates had heard evidence from a gun shop assistant that an air rifle was in working order, they were entitled to conclude that it fell within the definition even though no evidence was given as to the actual effects of the gun being fired (*Castle v DPP*, *The Times*, 3 April 1998).

Air pistols (*R v Thorpe* [1987] 1 WLR 383), imitation revolvers (*Cafferata v Wilson* [1936] 3 All ER 149) and signalling pistols (*Read v Donovan*, above) have all been held to be lethal barrelled weapons. That is not to say, however, that they will always be so and each case must be determined in the light of the evidence available.

Component parts, such as triggers or barrels, are also included in the definition, as are silencers and accessories to hide the muzzle flash of a weapon. This expression does not include telescopic sights.

A weapon may cease to be a firearm if it is de-activated in line with the provisions of the Firearms (Amendment) Act 1988, s. 8 which provides that:

> *For the purposes of the principal Act and this Act it shall be presumed, unless the contrary is shown, that a firearm has been rendered incapable of discharging any shot, bullet or other missile, and has consequently ceased to be a firearm within the meaning of those Acts, if—*
>
> *(a) it bears a mark which has been approved by the Secretary of State for denoting that fact and which has been made either by one of the two companies mentioned in section 58(1) of the principal Act or by such other person as may be approved by the Secretary of State for the purposes of this section; and*
>
> *(b) that company or person has certified in writing that work has been carried out on the firearm in a manner approved by the Secretary of State for rendering it incapable of discharging any shot, bullet or other missile.*

Keynote

For the 'two companies' referred to, **see para. 5.4.2.**

5.4 Definitions

The law regulating firearms classifies weapons into several categories, each of which is specifically defined. As with offences under road traffic legislation (**see Road Traffic,**

chapter 1), it is critical that the relevant definition is considered before deciding upon a particular charge or offence.

5.4.1 Prohibited Weapon

A prohibited weapon is defined under the Firearms Act 1968, s. 5. The definition formerly covered the more powerful or potentially destructive firearms — and their ammunition — such as automatic weapons and specialist ammunition.

Since the Firearms (Amendment) Acts of 1997, however, s. 5 also covers many small firearms which were formerly covered by other parts of the 1968 Act.

The test as to whether a weapon is a 'prohibited' weapon is a purely objective one and is not affected by the intentions of the defendant. Therefore, where a firearm was capable of successively discharging two or more missiles without repeated pressure on the trigger, that weapon was 'prohibited' irrespective of the intentions of the firearms dealer who was in possession of it (*R* v *Law (Richard Andrew)*, *The Times*, 4 February 1999).

Whereas a firearms certificate is usually needed in order to possess, buy or acquire firearms and ammunition, the authority of the Secretary of State is needed if the firearm or ammunition is a 'prohibited weapon'.

The full list of prohibited weapons and ammunition under the Firearms Act 1968, s. 5, is as follows:

(1) . . .
   (a) *any firearm which is so designed or adapted that two or more missiles can be successively discharged without repeated pressure on the trigger;*
   (ab) *any self-loading or pump-action rifled gun other than one which is chambered for 0.22 rim-fire cartridges;*
   (aba) *any firearm which either has a barrel less than 30 centimetres in length or is less than 60 centimetres in length overall, other than an air weapon, a muzzle-loading gun or a firearm designed as signalling apparatus;*
   (ac) *any self-loading or pump-action smooth-bore gun which is not an air weapon or chambered for 0.22 rim-fire cartridges and either has a barrel less than 24 inches in length or is less than 40 inches in length overall;*
   (ad) *any smooth-bore revolver gun other than one which is chambered for 9 mm rimfire cartridges or a muzzle-loading gun;*
   (ae) *any rocket launcher, or any mortar, for projecting a stabilised missile, other than a launcher or mortar designed for line-throwing or pyrotechnic purposes or as signalling apparatus;*
   (b) *any weapon of whatever description designed or adapted for the discharge of any noxious liquid, gas or other thing;*
   (c) *any cartridge with a bullet designed to explode on or immediately before impact, any ammunition containing or designed or adapted to contain any such noxious thing as is mentioned in paragraph (b) above and, if capable of being used with a firearm of any description, any grenade, bomb (or other like missile), or rocket or shell designed to explode as aforesaid.*
   (1A) . . .
   (a) *any firearm which is disguised as another object;*
   (b) *any rocket or ammunition not falling within paragraph (c) of subsection (1) of this section which consists in or incorporates a missile designed to explode on or immediately before impact and is for military use;*
   (c) *any launcher or other projecting apparatus not falling within paragraph (ae) of that subsection which is designed to be used with any rocket or ammunition falling within paragraph (b) above or with ammunition which would fall within that paragraph but for its being ammunition falling within paragraph (c) of that subsection;*

(d)   any ammunition for military use which consists in or incorporates a missile designed so that a substance contained in the missile will ignite on or immediately before impact;

(e)   any ammunition for military use which consists in or incorporates a missile designed, on account of its having a jacket and hard-core, to penetrate armour plating, armour screening or body armour;

(f)   any ammunition which incorporates a missile designed or adapted to expand on impact;

(g)   anything which is designed to be projected as a missile from any weapon and is designed to be, or has been, incorporated in—

(i)   any ammunition falling within any of the preceding paragraphs; or

(ii)   any ammunition which would fall within any of those paragraphs but for its being specified in subsection (1) of this section.

Keynote

Therefore the firearms which will require the authority of the Secretary of State before they can be possessed, acquired, bought, sold or transferred will include:

- automatic weapons
- most self-loading or pump-action weapons
- any firearm which is less than 60 cms long *or* which has a barrel less than 30 cms long (other than an air weapon or signalling apparatus)
- most smooth bore revolvers
- any weapon — of whatever description — designed or adapted for the discharge of any noxious liquid, gas or other thing
- military weapons and ammunition including grenades and mortars.

Taking empty washing-up liquid bottles and filling them with a noxious fluid such as hydrochloric acid does not amount to 'adapting' them, neither is such a thing a 'weapon' for the purposes of s. 5(2) (*R* v *Formosa* [1991] 2 QB 1).

An electric 'stun gun' has been held to be a prohibited weapon as it discharges an electric current (*Flack* v *Baldry* [1988] 1 WLR 393) and it continues to be such even if it is not working (*R* v *Brown*, *The Times*, 27 March 1992).

The Secretary of State may amend the list above.

Note that s. 5A of the Firearms Act 1968 creates exemptions under the European Council Directive (91/477/EEC) which allows people from member States to possess some prohibited weapons under certain circumstances (**see para. 5.7.1**).

5.4.2   **Shotguns**

A shotgun is defined under the Firearms Act 1968, s. 1(3)(a). Section 1 provides that:

(3)   . . .

(a)   a shotgun within the meaning of this Act, that is to say a smooth-bore gun (not being an airgun) which—

(i)   has a barrel not less than 24 inches in length and does not have any barrel with a bore exceeding 2 inches in diameter;

(ii)   either has no magazine or has a non-detachable magazine incapable of holding more than two cartridges; and

(iii)   is not a revolver gun. . . .

(3A)   A gun which has been adapted to have such a magazine as is mentioned in subsection (3)(a)(ii) above shall not be regarded as falling within that provision unless the magazine bears a *mark approved by the Secretary of State for denoting that fact and that mark has been made, and the adaptation has been certified in writing as having been carried out in a manner approved by him, either by one of the two companies mentioned in section 58(1) of this Act or by such other person as may be approved by him for that purpose.*

Keynote

A barrel's length is measured from the muzzle to the point at which the charge is exploded on firing the weapon (s. 57(6)(a) of the 1968 Act).

The 'two companies' referred to are the Society of the Mystery of Gunmakers of the City of London and the Birmingham proof house.

5.4.3 Air Weapons

Air weapons are defined under the Firearms Act 1968, s. 1 (3)(b) as being 'an air rifle, airgun or air pistol', including a rifle, pistol or gun powered by compressed carbon dioxide (see the Firearms (Amendment) Act 1997, s. 48).

Some air weapons are deemed to be specially dangerous and therefore subject to stricter control than conventional air weapons. Those which are subject to this stricter control are those declared to be so by the Secretary of State. Listed in the Firearms (Dangerous Air Weapons) Rules 1969 (SI 1969 No. 47), r. 2, they include:

2.—(1)   [any] air rifle, air gun or air pistol—
(a)   which is capable of discharging a missile so that the missile has, on being discharged from the muzzle of the weapon, kinetic energy in excess, in the case of an air pistol of 6ft lb or, in the case of an air weapon other than an air pistol, of 12 ft lb. [other than one designed for use when submerged in water, or]
(b)   which is disguised as another object.

5.4.4 Section 1 Firearm

There is a group of firearms which, although not a category defined in the 1968 Act, are subject to a number of offences including s. 1 (see below). Firearms which fall into this group are often referred to as 'section 1 firearms' and include all firearms except shotguns (**see para. 5.4.2**) and conventional air weapons (**see para. 5.4.3**). Shotguns which have been 'sawn off' (i.e., had their barrels shortened) are section 1 firearms, as are air weapons declared to be 'specially dangerous'.

Section 1 ammunition includes any ammunition for a firearm except:

- cartridges containing five or more shot, none of which is bigger than 0.36 inch in diameter;
- ammunition for an airgun, air rifle or air pistol; and
- blank cartridges not more than one inch in diameter

(s. 1(4)).

5.4.5 Conversion

Some weapons which began their life as section 1 firearms or prohibited weapons will remain so even after their conversion to a shotgun, air weapon or other type of firearm (see the Firearms (Amendment) Act 1988, s. 7).

5.4.6 Imitation Firearms

Some, though not all, offences which regulate the use of firearms will also apply to *imitation* firearms. Whether they do so can, be found either in the specific wording of the offence, or by virtue of the Firearms Act 1982.

Put simply there are two types of imitation firearms:

- general imitations — those which have the appearance of firearms (which are covered by the Firearms Act 1968, s. 57); and

- imitations of section 1 firearms — those which both have the appearance of a *section 1 firearm* and which can be readily converted into such a firearm (which are covered by the Firearms Act 1982, ss. 1 and 2).

Where 'imitation firearms' are referred to *in the wording of the offence*, that offence will apply to the first category above, that is, 'anything which has the appearance of being a firearm'. Note that this category does not include anything which resembles a prohibited weapon *under s. 5(1)(b)*. Prohibited weapons under s. 5(1)(b) are those which are designed or adapted to discharge noxious liquid etc. (**see para. 5.4.1**).

In some other offences, *the definition of the 1982 Act is applicable*. These offences are all offences which involve section 1 firearms, except those under ss. 4(3) and (4), 16 to 20 and 47 of the 1968 Act.

If an offence does not come within either of the circumstances above, it will not apply to an imitation firearm.

Whether or not something has the appearance of being a firearm will be a question of fact for the jury/magistrate(s) to decide in each case.

5.5 Possessing etc. Firearm or Ammunition without Certificate

**Offence — Possessing etc. Firearm or Ammunition without Certificate —
Firearms Act 1968 s. 1**
*Triable either way. Sentence: see sch. 6, **appendix 5***
(*Arrestable offence*)

The Firearms Act 1968, s. 1 states:

> *(1)   Subject to any exemption under this Act, it is an offence for a person—*
> *(a)   to have in his possession, or to purchase or acquire, a firearm to which this section applies without holding a firearm certificate in force at the time, or otherwise than as authorised by such a certificate;*
> *(b)   to have in his possession, or to purchase or acquire, any ammunition to which this section applies without holding a firearm certificate in force at the time, or otherwise than as authorised by such a certificate, or in quantities in excess of those so authorised.*

Keynote

This offence relates to those firearms described above as section 1 firearms.

179

If the firearm involved is a sawn-off shotgun, the offence becomes 'aggravated' (under s. 4(4)) and attracts a maximum penalty of seven years' imprisonment (see sch. 6 at **appendix 5**.

The Firearms Act 1982 applies to this section and therefore the second definition of 'imitation firearms' at **para. 5.4.6** above applies here.

The certificate referred to is issued by the chief officer of police under s. 26. Such certificates may carry significant restrictions on the types of firearms which the holder is allowed, together with the circumstances under which he/she may have them (see the Firearms (Amendment) Act 1997, s. 44(1)).

The purpose of the legislation regulating the licensing of firearms is to provide certainty and consistency in the effective control of such weapons. Therefore the issue of whether a certificate covers a particular category of weapon is a matter of law for the judge to decide and cannot be affected by the intentions or misunderstanding of the defendant (*R* v *Paul (Benjamin)*, *The Times*, 17 September 1998).

For the forms to be used in relation to the grant of certificates and permits, see the Firearms Rules 1998 (SI 1998 No. 1941).

A person may hold a European firearms pass or similar document, in which case he/she will be governed by the provision of the Firearms Act 1968, ss. 32A to 32C.

If a person has such a certificate which allows the possession etc. of the firearm in question and under the particular circumstances encountered, no offence is committed.

5.5.1 Possession

As in other areas of criminal law (**see Crime, chapter 6**), the meaning of possession is wider here than actual physical custody of the firearm in question. A person can remain in possession of a firearm even if someone else has custody of it (*Sullivan* v *Earl of Caithness* [1976] QB 966).

Possession for the purposes of this offence does not require any specific knowledge on the part of the defendant. For example, if X knows he is in possession of *something* (e.g. a box), then X is in possession of its contents, *even though X does not know what those contents are* (*R* v *Hussain* [1981] 1 WLR 416).

Therefore there is no need to prove that the defendant knew the nature of the thing which he/she possessed in order to prove this offence (and the offence under s. 19, **see para. 5.8.7**). If a defendant is carrying a rucksack and that rucksack turns out to contain ammunition for a section 1 firearm, the defendant is 'in possession' of that ammunition irrespective of his/her knowledge — or ignorance — of its presence in the rucksack (see *R* v *Waller* [1991] Crim LR 381). (For a discussion of the situation in respect of drugs, **see Crime, chapter 6**.)

5.5.2 Acquire

Acquire will include hiring, accepting as a gift and borrowing (Firearms Act 1968, s. 57(4)).

5.5.3 Exemptions

The offence specifies that it is subject to any exemptions under the 1968 Act.

There are three main categories of exemption under the firearms legislation:

- General exemptions — listed below.

- European exemptions — these are made under s. 5A to reflect the European weapons directive (**see para. 5.7.1**).

- Special exemptions — which apply to the provisions affecting prohibited weapons under s. 5 (**see para. 5.7.1**).

Many of the exemptions overlap as they follow a fairly common sense approach to the necessary possession and use of firearms/ammunition in the course of work and leisure.

5.5.4 General Exemptions

The general exemptions, which apply to the provisions of ss. 1 to 5 of the Firearms Act 1968 are mainly concerned with the various occupations of people whom you might expect to be in contact with firearms in one form or another. They include:

Police Permit Holders

Under s. 7(1) of the 1968 Act, the chief officer of police may grant a permit authorising the possession of firearms or ammunition under the conditions specified in the permit.

Clubs, Athletics and Sporting Purposes

Section 11 of the 1968 Act provides exemptions for a person:

- borrowing the firearm/ammunition from a certificate holder *for sporting purposes only* (s. 11(1));

- possessing a firearm at an athletic meeting for the purposes of starting races (s. 11(2));

- in charge of a miniature rifle range buying, acquiring or possessing miniature rifles and ammunition, and using them at such a rifle range (s. 11(4));

- who is a member of an approved rifle club, miniature rifle club or pistol club to possess a firearm or ammunition *when engaged as a club member in target practice* (Firearms (Amendment) Act 1988, s. 15(1));

- borrowing a shotgun from the occupier of private premises and using it on those premises in the occupier's presence (s. 11(5) of the 1968 Act);

- using a shotgun at a time and place approved by the chief officer of police for shooting at artificial targets (s. 11(6)).

FIREARMS

Borrowed Rifle on Private Premises

Section 16 of the Firearms (Amendment) Act 1988 allows a person to borrow a rifle from the occupier of private premises, provided the person is on those premises and in the presence of the occupier (or his/her servant), as long as the occupier holds a certificate and that the borrowing of the rifle complies with that certificate. The person borrowing the rifle may buy or acquire ammunition for it in accordance with the certificate's conditions.

Visitors' Permits

Section 17 of the Firearms (Amendment) Act 1988 provides for issuing of a visitors' permit by a chief officer of police and for the possession of firearms and ammunition by the holder of such a permit.

Visitors' permits will not be issued to anyone without a European firearms pass. It is a summary offence (punishable with six months' imprisonment) to make a false statement in order to get a visitors' permit, and it is a similar offence to fail to comply with any conditions within such a permit (see s. 17(10)).

Antiques as Ornaments or Curiosities

Section 58(2) of the 1968 Act allows for the sale, buying, transfer, acquisition or possession of antique firearms *as curiosities or ornaments*. Whether a firearm is such an antique will be a question of fact to be determined by the court in each case. Mere belief in the fact that a firearm is an antique will not be enough (*R* v *Howells* [1977] QB 614).

Authorised Firearms Dealers

Section 8(1) of the 1968 Act provides for registered firearms dealers (or their employees) to possess, acquire or buy firearms or ammunition in the ordinary course of their business without a certificate. If the possession etc. is not in the ordinary course of their business, the exemption will not apply.

Auctioneers, Carriers or Warehouse Staff

Section 9(1) of the 1968 Act allows auctioneers, carriers, warehousemen or their employees to possess firearms and ammunition in the ordinary course of their business without a certificate.

Section 14(1) of the Firearms (Amendment) Act 1988 makes it a summary offence (punishable by six months' imprisonment) for such people to fail to take reasonable precautions for the safe custody of the firearms and ammunition in their possession, or to fail to report the theft of those firearms and ammunition.

Again, if the possession of the firearm or ammunition is in circumstances which do not fall within the ordinary course of their business, the exemption will not apply.

Licensed Slaughterers

Section 10 of the 1968 Act allows licensed slaughterers to have in their possession a slaughtering instrument (or ammunition for it) in any *slaughterhouse* or knackers' yard in which they are employed.

The exemption will only apply to slaughtering instruments and ammunition while in the places specified. If these conditions are not met, the exemption will not apply.

Theatrical Performers

Section 12 of the 1968 Act allows people taking part in theatrical performances or films to possess firearms without a certificate, *during, and for the purpose of*, the performance, rehearsal or production. If performers do anything which falls outside this strict definition, they will not be exempt.

Ships or Aircraft Equipment

Section 13(1) of the 1968 Act provides for the possession of signalling equipment and firearms/ammunition for that purpose when on board ships or at aerodromes, or when removing the equipment from such places.

Section 13(1)(c) provides for the removal of firearms or signalling apparatus from ships, aircraft and aerodromes where authorised by a police permit to do so. The removal to or from such a place must only be done under the authority of police permit and must only be for the purpose specified therein (e.g. to get the firearm or signalling apparatus repaired).

Crown Servants

The effect of s. 54(1) of the 1968 Act is to exclude Crown servants from some of the provisions of the Act relating to possession. This general exemption applies to police officers, members of Her Majesty's armed forces (including cadet corps) and visiting forces from other countries. The exemptions are restricted to certain conditions and again only operate where the relevant person is acting in his/her official capacity.

This exemption extends to people employed by a police authority under the direction and control of a chief officer (e.g. civilian crime scene examiners) and also to members of NCIS and the National Crime Squad (**see chapter 1**).

People on service premises may possess a firearm or ammunition if they are supervised by a member of HM armed forces (Firearms (Amendment) Act 1988, s. 16A(1)). This provision does not include civilian guards who are engaged in the protection of service premises.

Proof Houses

Under s. 58(1) of the 1968 Act, members of the Mystery of Gunmakers of the City of London and the guardians of the Birmingham proof house and the Small Heath range at Birmingham have certain statutory duties involving firearms (**see, e.g., para. 5.4.2**). They are therefore exempt from those provisions of the Act which interfere with their statutory functions.

Museums Licence

Section 19 of the Firearms (Amendment) Act 1988 provides for people involved in the management of certain museums to hold a museums firearms licence which allows them to possess, buy or acquire firearms and ammunition under certain circumstances.

There are several summary offences involved in the fraudulent application for such licences and the failure to comply with their conditions (see para. 4 to the schedule to the 1988 Act).

5.6 Shotgun Offences

Offence — Possessing Shotgun without Certificate — Firearms Act 1968, s. 2(1)
*Triable either way. Sentence: see sch. 6, **appendix 5**.*
(Arrestable offence)

The Firearms Act 1968, s. 2 states:

> *(1) Subject to any exemption under this Act, it is an offence for a person to have in his possession, or to purchase or acquire, a shotgun without holding a certificate under this Act authorising him to possess shotguns.*

Keynote

For the definition of 'shotgun', **see para. 5.4.2**.

The relevant exemptions above will also apply to shotguns.

A shotgun certificate is granted by a chief officer of police under s. 26 of the 1968 Act and will have certain conditions attached to it. A person failing to comply with those conditions commits the following offence:

Offence — Failing to Comply with Conditions of Shotgun Certificate — Firearms Act 1968, s. 2(2)
*Triable summarily. Sentence: see sch. 6, **appendix 5**.*
(No specific power of arrest)

The Firearms Act 1968, s. 2 states:

> *(2) It is an offence for a person to fail to comply with a condition subject to which a shotgun certificate is held by him.*

5.7 Possessing or Distributing Prohibited Weapons or Ammunition

Offence — Possessing or Distributing Prohibited Weapons or Ammunition — Firearms Act 1968, s. 5
*Triable either way. Sentence: see sch. 6, **appendix 5**.*
(Arrestable offence)

The Firearms Act 1968, s. 5 states:

> *(1) A person commits an offence if, without the authority of the Secretary of State, he has in his possession, or purchases, or acquires, or manufactures, sells or transfers [a prohibited weapon or ammunition] . . .*

Keynote

See para. 5.4.1 for keynote on prohibited weapons. For 'possession', **see para. 5.5.1**.

'Self-loading' and 'pump-action' mean designed or adapted so that the weapon is either automatically reloaded, or is reloaded by manual operation of the fore-end or forestock (s. 57 of the 1968 Act).

Section 5(7) provides guidance in determining whether certain arms and ammunition will fall within the descriptions in s. 5, including the fact that any folding or detachable butt-stock of a firearm will not count when measuring the weapon's overall length.

5.7.1 Exemptions

The first set of exemptions were discussed in relation to the offence under s. 1 (**see para. 5.5.3**); the second and third set are relevant to the offences under s. 5.

Those remaining exemptions are:

- European exemptions — exemptions to conform with the European weapons directive.

- Special exemptions.

European Weapons Directive

The European Weapons Directive (91/477/EEC) was brought into effect in order to adjust our domestic legislation in line with the expansion of the European internal market. Its effect is to create certain additional savings and exemptions in relation to the possession of, or some transactions in, specified firearms and ammunition by people who have the relevant certificates or who are recognised as collectors under the law of another country.

To this end, s. 5A of the Firearms Act 1968 provides for a number of occasions where the authority of the Secretary of State will not be required to possess or deal with certain weapons under certain conditions.

The main areas covered by s. 5A are:

- authorised collectors and firearms dealers possessing or being involved in transactions of weapons and ammunition;

- authorised people being involved in transactions of particular ammunition used for lawful shooting and slaughtering of animals, the management of an estate or the protection of other animals and humans.

Section 57(4A) of the Firearms Act 1968 makes other provisions in relation to the European directive as an authority for certain uses of firearms.

Special Exemptions

The list of general exemptions to the offences involving firearms under s. 5(1)(aba) focuses largely on people in jobs where they will need to come into contact with firearms mainly in connection with animals or leisure activities.

The exemptions include:

- **Slaughterers** — A slaughterer, if entitled under s. 10 of the 1968 Act (**see para. 5.5.4**), may possess a slaughtering instrument. In addition, persons authorised by certificate to possess, buy, acquire, sell or transfer slaughtering instruments are exempt from the provisions of s. 5 (Firearms (Amendment) Act 1997, s. 2). This is the most common exemption.

- **Humane killing of animals** — A person authorised by certificate to possess, buy or acquire a firearm solely for use in connection with the humane killing of animals may possess, buy, acquire, sell or transfer such a firearm (Firearms (Amendment) Act 1997, s. 3). When determining whether a firearm falls within the meaning of a 'humane killer', the definition of a 'slaughtering instrument' under s. 57(4) may be referred to (*R* v *Paul (Benjamin)*, *The Times*, 17 September 1998.

- **Shot pistols for vermin** — A person authorised by certificate to possess, buy or acquire a 'shot pistol' solely for the shooting of vermin, may possess, buy, acquire, sell or transfer such a pistol (Firearms (Amendment) Act 1997, s. 4(1)). A 'shot pistol' is a smooth-bored gun chambered for .410 cartridges or 9mm rim-fire cartridges (s. 4(2)).

- **Treatment of animals** — A person authorised by certificate to possess, buy or acquire a firearm for use in connection with the treatment of animals may possess, buy, acquire, sell or transfer any firearm or ammunition designed or adapted for the purpose of tranquillising or treating any animal (Firearms (Amendment) Act 1997, s. 8). This exemption also applies to offences involving firearms under s. 5(1)(b) and (c) (**see para. 5.4.1**).

- **Races at athletic meetings** — A person may possess a firearm at an athletic meeting for the purpose of starting races at that meeting (Firearms (Amendment) Act 1997, s. 5(1)). Similarly, a person authorised by certificate to possess, buy or acquire a firearm solely for the purposes of starting such races may possess, buy, acquire, sell or transfer a firearm for such a purpose (s. 5(2)).

- **Trophies of war** — A person authorised by certificate to do so may possess a firearm which was acquired as a trophy before 1 January 1946 (Firearms (Amendment) Act 1997, s. 6).

- **Firearms of historic interest** — Some firearms are felt to be of particular historical, aesthetic or technical interest. Section 7(4) of the Firearms (Amendment) Act 1997 makes detailed provision for the exemption of such firearms, exemptions which exist in addition to the general exemptions under s. 58 of the Firearms Act 1968 (**see para. 5.5.4**). These provisions are set out in the Firearms (Amendment) Act 1997 (Firearms of Historic Interest) Order 1997 (SI 1997 No. 1537) and the Firearms (Amendment) Act 1997 (Transitional Provisions and Savings) Regulations 1997 (SI 1997 No. 1538).

5.8 Further Offences

5.8.1 Possession with Intent to Endanger Life

Offence — Possession with Intent to Endanger Life — Firearms Act 1968, s. 16
*Triable on indictment. Sentence: see sch. 6, **appendix 5**.*
(***Serious arrestable offence***)

The Firearms Act 1968, s. 16 states:

> *It is an offence for a person to have in his possession any firearm or ammunition with intent by means thereof to endanger life or to enable another person by means thereof to endanger life whether any injury has been caused or not.*

Keynote

There is no reference to imitation firearms in the wording of the offence, neither does the 1982 Act apply, therefore this offence cannot be committed by possessing an imitation firearm (**see para. 5.4.6**).

The offence involves 'possession' (**see para. 5.5.1**); there is no need for the firearm to be produced or shown to another.

This is a crime of 'specific intent' (**see Crime, chapter 1**). You will have to show an intention by the defendant to behave in a way that he or she knows will in fact endanger the life of another (*R v Brown* [1995] Crim LR 328).

That intent does not have to be an immediate one and it may be conditional (e.g. an intent to shoot someone if they do not do as they are asked) (*R v Bentham* [1973] QB 357).

The life endangered must be the life of 'another', not the defendant's (*R v Norton* [1977] Crim LR 478) but that other person may be outside the UK (*R v El-Hakkoui* [1975] 1 WLR 396).

The firearm must provide the means by which life is endangered; it is not enough to have a firearm at the time when life is endangered by some other means (e.g. by dangerous driving).

There may be occasions where self-defence can be raised in answer to a charge under s. 16 of the 1968 Act but these circumstances will be very unusual (see *R v Georgiades* [1989] 1 WLR 759).

5.8.2 Possession with Intent to Cause Fear of Violence

Offence — Possession with Intent to Cause Fear of Violence — Firearms Act 1968, s. 16A
*Triable on indictment. Sentence: see sch. 6, **appendix 5**.*
(***Arrestable offence***)

The Firearms Act 1968, s. 16A states:

> It is an offence for a person to have in his possession any firearm or imitation firearm with intent—
> (a) by means thereof to cause, or
> (b) to enable another person by means thereof to cause,
> any person to believe that unlawful violence will be used against him or another person.

Keynote

This offence includes imitation firearms in the general sense (**see para. 5.4.6**).

This is a crime of 'specific intent' (**see Crime, chapter 1**).

As with the offence under s. 16, the offence is committed by possession, accompanied by the required intent; there is no need for the firearm to be produced or shown to anyone. The firearm must provide the 'means' for the threat; possession of a firearm while making a general threat to someone who does not know of its presence is unlikely to fall within this section.

5.8.3 Using Firearm to Resist Arrest

Offence — Using Firearm to Resist Arrest — Firearms Act 1968, s. 17(1)
*Triable on indictment. Sentence: see sch. 6, **appendix 5**.*
(*Serious arrestable offence*)

The Firearms Act 1968, s. 17 states:

> (1) It is an offence for a person to make or attempt to make any use whatsoever of a firearm or imitation firearm with intent to resist or prevent the lawful arrest or detention of himself or another person.

Keynote

If the defendant has the firearm or imitation firearm with them at the time of resisting or preventing an arrest, they commit the offence under s. 18 (**see para. 5.8.6**).

The 'firearm' to which s. 17 refers is that defined at **para. 5.3**, *except* component parts and silencers/flash diminishers (s. 17(4)).

This offence includes imitation firearms in the general sense (**see para. 5.4.6**) but not imitation component parts, etc.

This is a crime of 'specific intent' (**see Crime, chapter 1**). It requires proof, not of possession, but of evidence that the defendant made some actual use of the firearm and did so intending to resist/prevent the arrest of themselves or someone else. Any arrest which the defendant intended to prevent/resist must have been 'lawful'.

5.8.4 Possessing Firearm while Committing a Schedule 1 Offence

Offence — Possessing Firearm while Committing or being Arrested for Schedule 1 Offence — Firearms Act 1968, s. 17(2)
*Triable on indictment. Sentence: see sch. 6, **appendix 5**.*
(*Arrestable offence*)

The Firearms Act 1968, s. 17 states:

> *(2) If a person, at the time of his committing or being arrested for an offence specified in schedule 1 to this Act, has in his possession a firearm or imitation firearm, he shall be guilty of an offence under this subsection unless he shows that he had it in his possession for a lawful object.*

Keynote

This offence may be committed in two ways; either by being in possession of the weapon at the time of committing the sch. 1 offence or by being in possession of it *at the time of being arrested* for such an offence. Clearly in the second case, there may be some time between actually committing the sch. 1 offence and being arrested for it.

Nevertheless, if the defendant is in possession of the firearm at the time of his/her arrest, the offence is committed (unless he/she can show that it was for a lawful purpose).

It is for the defendant to prove that the firearm was in his/her possession for a lawful purpose, presumably on the balance of probabilities (**see Evidence and Procedure, chapter** 7).

This offence includes imitation firearms in the general sense (**see para. 5.4.6**).

Schedule 1 Offences

The *main* offences listed in sch. 1 are:

* **D**amage — Criminal Damage Act 1971, s. 1

* **A**ssaults and woundings — Offences Against the Person Act 1861, (ss. 20 and 47); assault police (Police Act 1996, s. 89) and civilian custody officers (Criminal Justice Act 1991, s. 90(1) and the Criminal Justice and Public Order Act 1994, s. 13(1).

* **R**ape and 'taking out of possession' — Sexual Offences Act 1956, ss. 1, 17, 18 and 20.

   Child Abduction Act 1984, Part I.

* **T**heft, robbery, burglary, blackmail and taking a conveyance — Theft Act 1968.

(**D.A.R.T.**).

Although covering several types of assault, sch. 1 does not extend to wounding/causing grievous bodily harm with intent. Schedule 1 also covers the aiding, abetting or attempting to commit such offences.

5.8.5   **Trespassing with Firearms**

Offence — Trespassing with Firearm in Building — Firearms Act 1968, s. 20(1)
Triable either way (unless imitation firearm or air weapon).
*Sentence: see sch. 6, **appendix 5**.*
(*Arrestable offence unless imitation firearm or air weapon*)

The Firearms Act 1968, s. 20 states:

>   *(1)   A person commits an offence if, while he has a firearm or imitation firearm with him, he enters or is in any building or part of a building as a trespasser and without reasonable excuse (the proof whereof lies on him).*

Keynote

This offence includes a specific reference to imitation firearms (**see para. 5.4.6**).

If the relevant firearm is an imitation or an air weapon, the offence is triable summarily (**see appendix** 5).

This offence can be committed either by entering a building/part of a building or simply by *being* in such a place, in each case as a trespasser while having the firearm. As there is no need for the defendant to have 'entered' the building as a trespasser in every case, the offence might be committed after the occupier has withdrawn any permission for the defendant to be there. (Contrast the offence of trespassing with a weapon of offence; **see chapter 6.**)

For a discussion of the elements of entering a building/part of a building as a trespasser, **see Crime, chapter 12.**

For the interpretation of 'has with him', **see para. 5.8.6.**

It will be for the defendant to prove that he/she had reasonable excuse and the standard of that proof will be judged against the balance of probabilities.

The power of entry and search under s. 47 of the 1968 Act applies to this offence (**see para. 5.10**).

Offence — Trespassing with Firearm on Land — Firearms Act 1968, s. 20(2)
*Triable summarily. Sentence: see sch. 6, **appendix 5.***
(***No specific power of arrest***)

The Firearms Act 1968, s. 20 states:

>   *(2)   A person commits an offence if, while he has a firearm or imitation firearm with him, he enters or is on any land as a trespasser and without reasonable excuse (the proof whereof lies on him).*

Keynote

The elements of this offence are generally the same as those for the s. 20(1) offence above.

As with the s. 20(1) offence, there is no requirement that the defendant had the firearm/imitation firearm with him/her when entering onto the land (compare with the offence of aggravated burglary under the Theft Act 1968; **see Crime, chapter 12**).

'Land' for these purposes will include land covered by water (s. 20(3)).

Although this section does not have a specific power of arrest, there is a power of arrest for a police officer in uniform in relation to a person reasonably suspected of trespassing with a weapon of offence which may be appropriate (**see chapter 6**).

5.8.6 **Having Firearm with Intent to Commit Indictable Offence or Resist Arrest**

Offence — Having Firearm with Intent to Commit an Indictable Offence or Resist Arrest — Firearms Act 1968, s. 18(1)
*Triable on indictment. Sentence: see sch. 6, **appendix 5**.*
(*Serious arrestable offence*)

The Firearms Act 1968, s. 18 states:

> *(1) It is an offence for a person to have with him a firearm or imitation firearm with intent to commit an indictable offence, or to resist or prevent the arrest of another, in either case while he has a firearm or imitation firearm with him.*

Keynote

This offence, which overlaps with that under s. 17(1) (**see para. 5.8.3**), requires the defendant to have the firearm 'with him'. This is a more restrictive expression than 'possession' (as to which, **see para. 5.5.1**), and requires that the firearm is 'readily accessible' to the defendant (e.g. in a car nearby) (*R* v *Pawlicki* [1992] 1 WLR 827).

Despite this narrower meaning, the defendant does not have to be shown to have been 'carrying' the firearm (*R* v *Kelt* [1977] 1 WLR 1365), a decision which now conflicts with the situation relating to identical statutory expressions under the Theft Act 1968 (**see Crime, chapter 12**) and also under the legislation relating to weapons (**see chapter 11**).

This is a crime of 'specific intent' (**see Crime, chapter 1**) and, in proving that intent, s. 18(2) provides that:

> *(2) In proceedings for an offence under this section proof that the accused had a firearm or imitation firearm with him and intended to commit an offence, or to resist or prevent arrest, is evidence that he intended to have it with him while doing so.*

It is not necessary to show that the defendant intended to *use* the firearm to commit the indictable offence or to prevent/resist the arrest (*R* v *Duhaney*, *The Times*, 9 December 1997). (Contrast the offence under s. 17(1); **see para. 5.8.3**.)

An indictable offence includes an offence triable either way (Interpretation Act 1978).

Section 18 does not appear to require that any arrest be 'lawful' and it may be that parliament intended for this offence to be broader in that respect than the offence under s. 17.

This offence includes imitation firearms in the general sense (**see para. 5.4.6**).

The power of entry and search under s. 47 of the 1968 Act applies to this offence (**see para. 5.10**).

5.8.7 **Having Loaded Firearm in Public Place**

Offence — Having Loaded Firearm in Public Place — Firearms Act 1968, s. 19
*Triable either way. Sentence: see sch. 6, **appendix 5**.*
(***Arrestable offence unless air weapon***)

The Firearms Act 1968, s. 19 states:

> *A person commits an offence if, without lawful authority or reasonable excuse (the proof whereof lies on him), he has with him in a public place a loaded shotgun or loaded air weapon, or any other firearm (whether loaded or not) together with ammunition suitable for use in that firearm.*

Keynote

Public place includes any highway and any other premises or place to which the public have access at the material time, or to which the public are permitted access at the material time whether on payment or otherwise (see s. 57(4) of the 1968 Act).

'Loaded' here means if there is ammunition in the chamber or barrel (or in any magazine or other device) whereby the ammunition can be fed into the chamber or barrel by the manual or automatic operation of some part of the weapon (see s. 57(6)(b)).

If the weapon is a firearm other than an air weapon or a shotgun, the offence is committed by having suitable ammunition with it; there is no requirement for it to be loaded.

If the weapon is an air weapon the offence is only triable summarily (**see appendix 5**).

The Firearms (Amendment) Act 1982 does not apply here, neither is there any mention of imitation firearms in the wording of the section. Therefore the offence does not apply to imitation firearms.

For the meaning of 'has with him', **see para. 5.8.6**.

This offence is an 'absolute' offence like s. 1 (**see para. 5.5**). Therefore, if you can show that the defendant (X) knew he had something with him and that the 'something' was a loaded shotgun/airweapon (or other firearm with ammunition), the offence is complete (*R* v *Vann* [1996] Crim LR 52).

It is for the defendant to show lawful authority or reasonable excuse; possession of a valid certificate does not of itself provide lawful authority for having the firearm/ammunication in a public place (*Ross* v *Collins* [1982] Crim LR 368).

5.9 Possession or Acquisition of Firearms by Certain People

Sections 21 to 24 of the Firearms Act 1968 place further restrictions on the people who can possess, acquire, receive or otherwise have involvement with firearms. Section 21 deals with people who have been convicted of certain offences while ss. 22–24 set out minimum ages in respect of certain firearms and transactions.

Section 21 generally provides that any person who has been sentenced to:

- custody for life, or
- to preventive detention, imprisonment, corrective training, youth custody or detention in a young offender institution for three years or more

must not, *at any time*, have a firearm or ammunition in his/her possession.

Section 21 goes on to provide that any person who has been sentenced to imprisonment, youth custody detention in a young offender institution or a secure training order for three months or more, *but less than three years*, must not have a firearm or ammunition in his/her possession at any time before the end of a five year period beginning on the date of his/her release.

Date of release means, for a sentence partly served and partly suspended, the date on which the offender completes the part to be served and, in the case of a person subject to a secure training order, the date on which he/she is released from detention (under the various relevant statutes) or the date halfway through the total specified by the court making the order, whichever is the latest (s. 21(2A)).

A person holding a licence under the Children and Young Persons Act 1933 or a person subject to a recognisance to keep the peace or be of good behaviour with a condition relating to the possession of firearms, must not, *at any time during the licence or the recognisance*, have a firearm or ammunition in his/her possession (s. 21(3)).

Where sentences or court orders are mentioned, their Scottish equivalents will also apply and a person prohibited in Northern Ireland from possessing a firearm/ammunition will also be prohibited in Great Britain (s. 21(3A)).

Section 21 does not apply to imitation firearms as there is no express reference to them in the section and because the reference in the Firearms Act 1982 does not apply (**see para. 5.4.6**).

If the person who has been sentenced as set out in s. 21 contravenes the provisions above (e.g. by possessing etc. any firearm), he/she commits an either way offence punishable with a maximum of five years' imprisonment (thereby making it an arrestable offence).

5.9.1 Supplying Firearm to Person Prohibited by Section 21

Offence — Selling or Transferring Firearm to Person Prohibited by Section 21 — Firearms Act 1968, s. 21(5)
*Triable either way. Sentence: sch. 6, **appendix 5**.*
(*Arrestable offence*)

The Firearms Act 1968, s. 21 states:

> (5)   *It is an offence for a person to sell or transfer a firearm or ammunition to, or to repair, test or prove a firearm or ammunition for, a person whom he knows or has reasonable ground for believing to be prohibited by this section from having a firearm or ammunition in his possession.*

Keynote

Given that all people are presumed to know the law once it is published, it would seem that the knowledge or belief by the defendant would apply to the *convictions of* the other person, not the fact that possession by that person was an offence.

What you must show is knowledge by the defendant or at least *reasonable ground for believing*; this latter requirement is stronger than mere cause to *suspect* (**see chapter 2**).

5.9.2 Other Restrictions on Possession or Acquisition

In addition to the general provisions relating to possession, acquisition etc., ss. 22 to 24 create a number of summary offences restricting the involvement of people of various ages in their dealings with firearms and ammunition. The table opposite provides a brief summary of some of those provisions. For the full extent of these restrictions and their exemptions, reference should be made to the 1968 Act.

It is a summary offence (punishable by one month's imprisonment and/or a fine) to be in possession of *any* loaded firearm when drunk (Licensing Act 1872, s. 12). There is no requirement that the person be in a public place. This offence carries a power of arrest in relation to any person found committing it. Given the decisions in other cases where similar powers of arrest remain applicable (**see, e.g., chapter 4 and Crime, chapter 10**), that power would appear to be available to police officers.

5.10 Police Powers

Section 47 of the Firearms Act 1968 provides that:

> *(1) A constable may require any person whom he has reasonable cause to suspect—*
> *(a) of having a firearm, with or without ammunition, with him in a public place; or*
> *(b) to be committing or about to commit, elsewhere than in a public place, an offence relevant for the purposes of this section,*
> *to hand over the firearm or any ammunition for examination by the constable.*

Keynote

This power has two distinct elements. The first applies where the officer has reasonable cause to suspect that a person has a firearm with him/her in a public place. The second relates to a situation where the officer has reasonable cause to suspect that the person is committing or is about to commit an offence relevant to this section anywhere else.

An 'offence relevant to this section' appears to be an offence under s. 18(1) and s. 20 (see s. 47(6)).

It is a summary offence to fail to hand over a firearm when required under this section (s. 47(2)).

In order to exercise this power, a police officer may search the person and may detain him/her for that purpose (s. 47(3)). The officer may also enter *any place* (s. 47(4)).

If the officer has reasonable cause to suspect that:

- there is a firearm in a vehicle in a public place, or
- that a vehicle is being/about to be used in connection with the commission of an 'offence relevant to this section' (see above)

he/she may search the vehicle and, for that purpose, may require the person driving or in control of the vehicle to stop it (s. 47(4)).

The provisions of the PACE Codes of Practice, Code A, will apply to the exercise of these powers of stop and search (**see appendix 1**).

For powers of stop and search generally, **see chapter 2**.

Age	Restrictions	Applies to imitation?
Under 14 years	• Having with them air weapon or ammunition for one (s. 22(4) subject to exception*†).	No
	• Possessing any s. 1 firearm or ammunition without lawful authority (except as permitted for sports and shooting clubs etc.).	Yes
	• Giving or lending s. 1 firearm or ammunition or parting with possession to such a person except as permitted (for sports and shooting clubs etc.) (s. 24(2)).	Yes
	• Giving or parting with possession of air weapon to such a person (unless under permitted circumstances*) (s. 24(4)).	Yes
Under 15 years	• Having with them assembled shotgun unless supervised by person aged at least 21 or while shotgun is securely covered (s. 22(3)).	No
	• Giving shotgun or ammunition for one to such a person (s. 24(3)).	No
Under 17 years	• Buying or hiring any firearm or ammunition (s. 22(1)).	No
	• Having with them air weapon in public place except airgun or air rifle securely covered† (s. 22(5)).	No
	• Selling or letting on hire to such a person any firearm or ammunition (s. 24(1)).	No
Under 18 years	• Holder of certificate using firearm for purpose not authorised by European weapons directive (s. 22(1A)).	No

*Section 23 provides that no offence is committed if the person is under the supervision of another who is at least 21 years old. The person under 14 must not use the air weapon for firing missiles beyond the relevant premises and the supervising person must not allow the air weapon to be so used.

†Section 23 goes on to provide that no offence is committed where a person who is a member of an approved rifle club (or miniature rifle club) has with them an air weapon or ammunition while engaged in target shooting as such, nor where he/she is using the weapon at a shooting gallery where the air weapons or miniature rifles being used do not exceed .23 inch calibre.

Note that s. 24 makes a number of defences where the person giving, lending etc. is mistaken about the true age of the other person concerned.

Section 48 provides that:

> *(1)   A constable may demand, from any person whom he believes to be in possession of a firearm or ammunition to which section 1 of this Act applies, or of a shot gun, the production of his firearm certificate or, as the case may be, his shot gun certificate.*

Keynote

The demand for the relevant documentation may be made where the police officer 'believes' that a person is in possession of a section 1 firearm, ammunition or a shotgun. There is no requirement that the officer's belief be reasonable.

Where the person fails to:

- produce the relevant certificate or
- show that he/she is not entitled to be issued with such a certificate or
- show that he/she is in possession of the firearm exclusively in connection with recognised purposes (collecting/historical/cultural) under the law of another EU member State

the officer may demand the production of the relevant valid documentation issued in another member State under any corresponding provisions (s. 48(1A)).

Failing to produce any of the required documents *and* to let the officer read it, or failing to show an entitlement to possess the firearm or ammunition triggers (!) the power of seizure under s. 48(2). It also gives the officer the power to demand the person's name and address. This requirement is similar to the provision under s. 170 of the Road Traffic Act 1998 (duty to give details after an accident; **see Road Traffic, chapter** 4) where it has been held that the name and address of the person's solicitor would suffice (*DPP* v *McCarthy, The Times*, 8 January 1999). That decision was based on the purpose behind the Road Traffic Act requirement, namely to allow the respective parties to the accident to get in touch with each other in the future. It is suggested that the purpose of the Firearms Act power is a very different one of regulating the possession of weapons and that the furnishing of details of some convenient administrative location for correspondence would not be enough to satisfy the requirements of this section.

If the person refuses to give his/her name or address or gives a false name and address, he/she commits a summary offence (s. 48(3)).

A person from another member State who is in possession of a firearm and who fails to comply with a demand under s. 48(1A) also commits a separate summary offence (s. 48(4)).

5.11   Shortening and Conversion of Firearms

Offence — Shortening Barrel of Shotgun to Less than 24 Inches — Firearms Act 1968, s. 4(1)
*Triable either way. Sentence: see sch. 6, **appendix 5**.*
(*Arrestable offence*)

The Firearms Act 1968, s. 4 states:

(1) Subject to this section, it is an offence to shorten the barrel of a shot gun to a length less than 24 inches.

Offence — Shortening Barrel of Other Smooth Bore Section 1 Firearm to Less than 24 Inches — Firearms (Amendment) Act 1988 s. 6(1)
Triable either way. Five years' imprisonment and/or a fine on indictment; six months' imprisonment and/or a fine summarily.
(Arrestable offence)

The Firearms Act 1988, s. 6 states:

(1) Subject to subsection (2) below, it is an offence to shorten to a length less than 24 inches the barrel of any smooth-bore gun to which section 1 of the principal Act applies other than one which has a barrel with a bore exceeding 2 inches in diameter; . . .

Offence — Converting Imitation Firearm — Firearms Act 1968, s. 4(3)
*Triable either way. Sentence: see sch. 6, **appendix 5**.*
(Arrestable offence)

The Firearms Act 1968, s. 4 states:

(3) It is an offence for a person other than a registered firearms dealer to convert into a firearm anything which, though having the appearance of being a firearm, is so constructed as to be incapable of discharging any missile through its barrel.

Keynote

The relevant definitions are considered at **para. 5.4**.

The first two offences are concerned with the shortening of barrels while the third involves conversion of anything which has the appearance of a firearm so that it can be fired. Registered firearms dealers (**see para. 5.5.4**) are excluded from the wording of the conversion offence. They are also exempted by ss. 4(2) and 6(2) from the relevant offences involving shortening barrels provided the shortening is done *for the sole purpose* of replacing a defective part of the barrel *so as to produce a new barrel having an overall length of at least 24 inches.*

The length of the barrel of a weapon will be measured from its muzzle to the point at which the charge is exploded (s. 57(6)(a) of the 1968 Act).

Once the shortening or conversion has taken place, the nature of the firearm will have changed (e.g. from a shotgun into a section 1 firearm or from an imitation into a real firearm), in which case the person will also commit the relevant possession offences unless he/she has the appropriate authorisation.

5.12 Restrictions on Transfer of Firearms

The Firearms (Amendment) Act 1997 created a number of offences concerned with the transfer, lending, hiring etc. of firearms and ammunition.

In brief, a person 'transferring' (that is, selling, letting on hire, lending or giving) a section 1 firearm or ammunition to another must:

- produce a certificate or permit entitling him/her to do so (s. 32(2)(a));
- he/she must comply with all the conditions of that certificate or permit (s. 32(2)(b)); and
- the transferor must personally hand the firearm or ammunition over to the receiver

(s. 32(2)(c)).

The 1997 Act also requires any person who is the holder of a certificate or permit who is involved in such a transfer (which includes a lending of the firearm/ammunition for a period exceeding 72 hours) to give notice to the chief officer of police who granted the certificate or permit (s. 33(2)).

Notice is also required of certificate or permit holders where a firearm is lost, de-activated or destroyed or where ammunition is lost, or where firearms are sold outside Great Britain (see ss. 34 and 35).

Offence — Failing to Comply with Requirements — Firearms (Amendment) Act 1997, ss. 32–35
Section 1 firearm/ammunition: triable either way. Five years' imprisonment and/or fine on indictment; six months' imprisonment and/or fine summarily.
(Arrestable offence)
Shotguns: triable summarily. Six months' imprisonment and/or a fine.
(No specific power of arrest)

Offence — Trade Transactions by Person not Registered as Firearms Dealer — Firearms Act 1968, s. 3(1)
*Triable either way. Sentence: see sch. 6, **appendix 5**.*
(Arrestable offence)

The Firearms Act 1968, s. 3 states:

> (1) A person commits an offence if, by way of trade or business, he—
> (a) manufactures, sells, transfers, repairs, tests or proves any firearm or ammunition to which section 1 of this Act applies, or a shotgun; or
> (b) exposes for sale or transfer, or has in his possession for sale, transfer, repair, test or proof any such firearm or ammunition, or a shotgun,
> without being registered under this Act as a firearms dealer.

Keynote

The various definitions are considered above. A registered firearms dealer is a person who, by way of trade or business, manufactures, sells, transfers, repairs, tests or proofs firearms or ammunition to which s. 1 applies, or shotguns (s. 57(4) of the 1968 Act).

If the person undertakes the repair, proofing etc. of a s. 1 firearm or ammunition or a shotgun otherwise than as a trade or business, he/she commits an offence (carrying the same punishment as the s. 3(1) offence above) under s. 3(3) unless he/she can point to some authorisation under the Act allowing him/her to do so.

Section 3 goes on to create further either way offences of selling or transferring a firearm or ammunition to someone other than a registered firearms dealer or someone otherwise authorised under the Act to buy or acquire them and of falsifying certificates with a view to acquiring firearms. These offences also carry the same punishment as the s. 3(1) offence above.

Registration is under s. 33 of the 1968 Act.

'Transferring' is also defined under s. 57(4) and includes letting on hire, giving, lending and parting with possession.

Section 9(2) of the 1968 Act exempts auctioneers from the restrictions on selling and possessing for the purposes of sale of firearms and ammunition where the auctioneer has a permit from the chief officer of police. There are further defences provided by s. 9 (for carriers and warehouse staff) and also under s. 8 (transfer to people authorised to possess firearms without certificate).

5.13 Other Offences under the Firearms (Amendment) Act 1988

There are two offences under the Firearms (Amendment) Act 1988 introduced to ensure compliance with the European weapons directive; ss. 18(6) and 18A(6). Both are summary offences punishable with three months' imprisonment and/or a fine.

Other summary offences under the 1968 Act include:

- A firearms dealer failing to send the required notification within 48 hours to the chief officer of police, after selling a firearm or shotgun (s. 18(5)).

- The transferor of a shotgun to another failing to notify police of the details of that transfer as required by s. 4 (s. 4(5)).

- Selling certain ammunition to a person who is not a registered firearms dealer and is not permitted to have the relevant weapon for the ammunition (s. 5(2)).

- A pawnbroker taking a section 1 firearm or ammunition as a pawn (s. 3(6)).

- Any person selling or transferring any firearm or ammunition or carrying out repairs or tests on such for another person who is drunk or of unsound mind (s. 25).

5.14 Documentation

The enforcement of the firearms legislation depends heavily on the possession and production of the relevant documents and the Firearms Act 1968, ss. 30A–30D allow for the revocation or partial revocation of certificates by chief officers of police. There are therefore many offences which deal with the application for and obtaining of documents, the falsification of records and documents and the failure to maintain proper records. The offences under the Firearms Act 1968 are under ss. 26(5), 29(3), 30(4), 38(8), 39(1) to (3), 40(5) and 52(2)(c), see sch. 6, **appendix 5**.

There is also an offence under the Firearms (Amendment) Act 1988, s. 12(2) of failing to comply with a notice from the chief officer of police for the surrender of a certificate. This is a summary offence punishable with three months' imprisonment and/or a fine.

There are further summary offences which were created to ensure compliance with the European weapons directive (see the Firearms Act 1968, ss. 32B(5), 32C(6), 42A(3) and 48A(4)).

CHAPTER SIX

WEAPONS

6.1 Introduction

The carrying of weapons has become an issue of considerable concern over recent years. The law has developed in a slightly untidy fashion and, in considering the different offences and restrictions, it is important to look at the *particular weapons* covered by each piece of legislation, together with the *particular activity* which parliament has sought to control.

Although it is convenient to refer to the *possession* of offensive weapons, that word has a wide meaning which goes beyond the expressions used in most offences involving the carrying of weapons.

It is also useful to bear in mind the differences between offensive weapons and *weapons of offence*. The latter are specifically concerned with the entry onto premises as a trespasser and are slightly wider in their definition than offensive weapons.

6.2 Offensive Weapons

Offence — Having Offensive Weapon in Public Place — Prevention of Crime Act 1953, s. 1(1)
Triable either way. Four years' imprisonment and/or a fine on indictment; six months' imprisonment and/or a fine summarily.
(*Arrestable offence*)

The Prevention of Crime Act 1953, s. 1 states:

> (1) *Any person who without lawful authority or reasonable excuse, the proof whereof shall lie on him, has with him in any public place any offensive weapon shall be guilty of an offence.*

Keynote

'Lawful authority' means those occasions where people from time to time are required to carry weapons as a matter of duty, such as police officers or members of the armed forces (*Bryan* v *Mott* (1975) 62 Cr App R 71). Security guards carrying truncheons, even if required to do so by their contracts of employment, are not covered (*R* v *Spanner* [1973] Crim LR 704). If someone does not fall into this — very limited — group, he/she may still have a 'reasonable excuse' for having the weapon with him/her.

'Reasonable excuse' may arise from a number of circumstances. People having tools with them in the course of their trade (e.g. craft knives for fitting carpets or hammers for carpentry) may have a 'reasonable excuse' (see *Ohlson* v *Hylton* [1975] 1 WLR 724). If a person passing the scene of a recent disturbance sees a weapon lying on the ground and he/she picks it up and puts it in his/her car intending to take it to the nearest police station, those circumstances would amount to a reasonable excuse for having the weapon with him/her.

Not being aware that you have an offensive weapon with you (*R* v *Densu* [1998] 1 Cr App R 400) or forgetting that you have one in the car you are driving (*R* v *McCalla* (1988) 87 Cr App 372) are *not* reasonable excuses. However, where the defendant — a taxi driver — was found with a piece of wood and a cosh in the back of his cab where they had been left by passengers earlier in the week, the Court of Appeal held that his forgetting to remove the weapons might have been accepted as a reasonable excuse and the question should have been left for the jury (*R* v *Glidewell*, *The Times*, 14 May 1999).

It is not reasonable to have a weapon with you as *a general precaution* in case you are attacked (*Evans* v *Hughes* [1972] 1 WLR 1452). It may, however, be reasonable to have a weapon if you have good grounds to anticipate an unprovoked or unlawful attack (e.g. for a person guarding cash transits — see *Malnik* v *DPP* [1989] Crim LR 451).

Having a weapon for some other reason may amount to a reasonable excuse and whether or not it does so is a matter of fact for the court/jury to decide (see e.g. *Houghton* v *Chief Constable of Greater Manchester Police* (1986) 84 Cr App R 319 where the defendant was in 'fancy dress' costume as a police officer and had a truncheon with him as part of the costume — held to amount to 'reasonable excuse').

The burden of proving the reasonable excuse or lawful authority rests with the defendant, but only when the prosecution have established that the defendant had an offensive weapon with him/her at the time. That burden of proof will be judged against the balance of probabilities and not 'beyond a reasonable doubt' (**see Evidence and Procedure, chapter 11**).

Note that there is a specific offence relating to the carrying of weapons on school premises (**see para. 6.3.2**).

6.2.1 'Has With Him'

This expression (which is also discussed in relation to firearms, **see chapter 5**), shows that the offence is designed to prevent the carrying of weapons; it is not an offence of *intention* and the reported decisions of the courts have consistently reflected that fact.

This is most apparent where an 'innocent' article is used offensively. In *Ohlson* v *Hylton* [1975] 1 WLR 724 the defendant had a bag of tools with him in the course of his trade. He produced a hammer from the bag and used it to hit someone. The court held that, as he had formed the intention to use the hammer *after* it came into his possession, the offence was not made out. Although the court accepted that there might be times where a later intention to use an innocent article offensively would amount to an offence under the 1953 Act, the main purpose of the law was to prevent people from arming themselves with weapons. Similar decisions have been reached in relation to picking up a discarded knife during a fight (*Bates* v *Bulman* [1979] 1 WLR 1190), brandishing a jack taken from a car (*R* v *Dayle* [1974] 1 WLR 181) and using a penknife — which the defendant happened to be carrying — to stab someone who attacked him (*R* v *Humphreys* [1977] Crim LR 225).

Some confusion has been caused in this area by the different interpretations of the expression 'has with him' in relation to firearms offences (**see chapter 5**).

The fact that the offence is not one of intention is supported by the decisions on 'reasonable excuse' above; the reasonable excuse must relate to the *carrying* of the weapon or article and not the *intention* of the person carrying it (*R* v *Jura* [1954] 1 QB 503).

It is possible for more than one person to have the same weapon 'with them', provided you can show that they knew of its existence in the hands of another at the time (*R* v *Edmonds* [1963] 2 QB 142).

You must show that the defendant knew that he/she had *something* with him/her and that the 'something' was, in fact, an offensive weapon (*R* v *Cugullere* [1961] 1 WLR 858). For a similar situation regarding 'possession' of drugs, **see Crime, chapter 6**.

6.2.2 Public Place

Section 1(4) of the 1953 Act provides that:

> *(4)   In this section 'public place' includes any highway and any other premises or place to which at the material time the public have or are permitted to have access, whether on payment or otherwise . . .*

6.2.3 Offensive Weapon

Section 1(4) of the 1953 Act also provides that:

> *(4)   . . . 'offensive weapon' means any article made or adapted for use for causing injury to the person, or intended by the person having it with him for such use by him or by some other person.*

Keynote

Offensive weapons fall into three categories for the purposes of this offence, namely articles:

- **made** for causing injury (offensive weapons *per se*);
- **adapted** for causing injury; and
- **intended** by the person who has it, for causing injury.

(For the definition of a 'weapon of offence' used in aggravated burglary, **see para. 6.4 and Crime, chapter 12**).

Offensive weapons *per se* are those which have been manufactured for use for causing injury and include truncheons, PR-24 batons and bayonets. A swordstick has been held to be such a weapon (*R* v *Butler* [1988] Crim LR 695) as have flick-knives (*R* v *Simpson* [1983] 1 WLR 1494) and butterfly knives (*DPP* v *Hynde* [1998] 1 WLR 1222). In *Hynde* the court took notice of the fact that butterfly knives were outlawed under the Criminal Justice Act 1988 (**see para. 6.5**) in deciding that such knives were clearly 'made' for causing injury.

Once it has been shown that the article in question was in fact an offensive weapon, there is no need for the prosecution to show any intention to use it for causing injury (*Davis* v *Alexander* (1970) 54 Cr App R 398).

Weapons *adapted* for causing injury can include virtually anything. Whether something has in fact been so adapted is a question of fact for the court/jury to decide in each case. Bottles or glasses which have been broken in order to create a jagged edge have been held to be 'adapted' (*R* v *Simpson* [1983] 1 WLR 1494), so too has a potato with razor blades protruding from it (*R* v *Williamson* (1977) 67 Cr App R 35). If the article itself has not been altered in any physical way (such as by putting ammonia in a 'Jif' lemon to squirt in people's eyes — *R* v *Formosa* [1991] 2 QB 1), it has not been adapted.

It is still unclear whether the adaptation has to be to cause injury to *another* person or whether its capacity for self-inflicted injury (as in a suicide attempt) is enough. It is submitted that, as it is the *adaptation* of the article which is relevant, and not the *intention* of the person carrying it, the ultimate 'victim' is irrelevant (see *Bryan* v *Mott* (1975) 62 Cr App R 71).

Weapons *intended* to be used for causing injury can also include virtually anything. Here the intention of the person carrying it *is relevant* and you must prove an intention to cause injury (as to intention generally, **see Crime, chapter 1**). An intention to cause shock can be enough to satisfy this condition (see *R* v *Rapier* (1979) 70 Cr App R 17) but simply using the article to scare potential attackers away will not (*R* v *Snooks* [1997] Crim LR 230).

6.3   Other Offences involving the Carrying of Weapons

6.3.1   Having Bladed or Pointed Article in Public Place

Offence — Having Bladed or Sharply Pointed Article in Public Place — Criminal Justice Act 1988, s. 139(1)
Triable either way. Two years' imprisonment and/or a fine on indictment; six months' imprisonment and/or a fine summarily.
(***Arrestable offence***)

The Criminal Justice Act 1988, s. 139 states:

(1)   Subject to subsections (4) and (5) below, any person who has an article to which this section applies with him in a public place shall be guilty of an offence.

Keynote

This offence applies to any sharply pointed article or article having a blade. Folding pocket knives are excluded unless the cutting edge of the blade exceeds three inches (7.62 cms). If the knife is a lock-knife and the blade is locked open at the time, it will be covered by this offence (*Harris* v *DPP* (1992) 96 Cr App R 235).

Whether an article falls within the parameters of s. 139 is a question of law for the judge/magistrate(s) to determine (*R v Deegan* [1998] 2 Cr App R 121 — a case that also concerned the carrying of a folding pocket-knife that was locked open). In *R v Davis* [1998] Crim LR 564 the Court of Appeal reiterated that the question of whether an article was 'bladed' or not was a matter of law for the judge to decide. In that case the defendant had been carrying a screwdriver which, the prosecution contended, was a 'bladed' article capable of causing injury. The court decided that the test to be applied in such cases was not whether the 'bladed' article was capable of causing injury, but whether it had a cutting edge. Deciding whether or not an article was caught by the provisions of s. 139 was not a matter of interpreting the ordinary English word 'blade', but required the straightforward construction of the statute. This decision does not mean that a screwdriver can *never* fall within the type of article outlawed under s. 139 and if the screwdriver is pointed or it has been sharpened, it may still be caught by the above offence.

'Has with him' is discussed above.

'Public place' is similar to that under the Prevention of Crime Act 1953 (see **para. 6.2.2**).

Note that there is a specific offence relating, to the carrying of weapons on school premises (**see para. 6.3.2**).

Defences

The defendant may show that he/she had 'good reason' or 'lawful authority' for having the article in a public place. Lawful authority is discussed above; good reason is similar to reasonable excuse, also discussed above. This approach was confirmed by the Court of Appeal in *R v Emmanuel* [1998] Crim LR 347 where it accepted that 'good reason' could include self-defence. Again it will be for the defendant to prove this authority or reason on the balance of probabilities and again, forgetting that you have the article with you is not a general defence (*DPP v Gregson* (1992) 96 Cr App R 240).

A defendant may also show that he/she has the article:

* For use at work, e.g. joiners, chefs, gardeners etc.

* For religious reasons, e.g. members of the Sikh religion having a *kirpan*.

* As part of any national costume — such as someone in Highland Dress with a *skean dhu*.

Strangely, whether or not an article is for the uses or reasons set out above appears to be a question of *fact* (see *R v Manning* [1998] Crim LR 198).

6.3.2   Weapons on School Premises

Offence — Having Bladed or Sharply Pointed Article on School Premises — Criminal Justice Act 1988, s. 139A(1)
Triable either way. Two years' imprisonment and/or a fine on indictment; six months' imprisonment and/or a fine summarily.
(Arrestable offence)

The Criminal Justice Act 1988, s. 139A states:

> *(1) Any person who has an article to which section 139 of this Act applies with him on school premises shall be guilty of an offence.*

Keynote

'Has with him' is much narrower than 'possession', **see chapter 5** and also **Crime, chapter 6**.

'School premises' means land used for the purposes of a school *excluding any land occupied solely as a dwelling by a person employed at the school*. This means that the provisions would not apply to someone found in the garden of a caretakers' house if that house was occupied solely as a dwelling by the school caretaker.

'School' under the Education Act 1996, s. 4, means:

> *(1) . . . an educational institution which is outside the further education sector and the higher education sector and is an institution for providing—*
> *(a) primary education,*
> *(b) secondary education, or*
> *(c) both primary and secondary education,*
> *whether or not the institution also provides part-time education suitable to the requirements of junior pupils or further education.*

This offence applies to the same articles as those covered under s. 139(1), **see para. 6.3.1**.

Defence

The defences are the same as for s. 139(1), **see para. 6.3.1**.

Offence — Having Offensive Weapon on School Premises — Criminal Justice Act 1988, s. 139A(2)
Triable either way. Four years' imprisonment and/or a fine on indictment; six months' imprisonment and/or a fine summarily.
(*Arrestable offence*)

The Criminal Justice Act 1988, s. 139A states:

> *(2) Any person who has an offensive weapon within the meaning of section 1 of the Prevention of Crime Act 1953 with him on school premises shall be guilty of an offence.*

Keynote

For the purposes of this offence, 'offensive weapons' fall into the three categories discussed at **para. 6.2.3**.

'Has with him', 'school premises' and 'school' are all discussed above.

Power of Entry

The Criminal Justice Act 1988, s. 139B states:

(1)   A constable may enter school premises and search those premises and any person on those premises for—

(a)   any article to which section 139 of this Act applies, or

(b)   any offensive weapon within the meaning of section 1 of the Prevention of Crime Act 1953, if he has reasonable grounds for believing that an offence under section 139A of this Act is being, or has been, committed.

(2)   If in the course of a search under this section a constable discovers an article or weapon which he has reasonable grounds for suspecting to be an article or weapon of a kind described in subsection (1) above, he may seize and retain it.

(3)   The constable may use reasonable force, if necessary, in the exercise of the power of entry conferred by this section.

6.4   Trespassing with Weapon of Offence

As a further complication, there is another offence relating to weapons, namely that under the Criminal Law Act 1977. As opposed to the carrying of weapons in public, or the carrying of them on school premises, this offence is concerned with preventing people *trespassing* with weapons in much the same way as aggravated burglary.

Offence — Trespassing with Weapon of Offence — Criminal Law Act 1977, s. 8(1)
Triable summarily. Six months' imprisonment and/or a fine.
(*Statutory power of arrest*)

The Criminal Law Act 1977, s. 8 states:

(1)   A person who is on any premises as a trespasser, after having entered as such, is guilty of an offence if, without lawful authority or reasonable excuse, he has with him on the premises any weapon of offence.

Keynote

The definition of 'weapon of offence' is the same as that for aggravated burglary (**see Crime, chapter 12**), namely any article made or adapted for use for causing injury to or incapacitating a person, or intended by the person having it with him/her for that use (s. 8(2)).

This offence is restricted to a person who has entered the relevant premises as a trespasser. It does not therefore extend to a person who, having entered lawfully, then becomes a trespasser for whatever reason (e.g. because the occupier has told him/her to leave).

'Premises' for this purpose means:

- any building or
- any part of a building under separate occupation
- any land adjacent to and used/intended for use in connection with a building
- the site comprising any building(s) together with ancillary land
- any fixed structure
- any movable structure, vehicle or vessel designed or adapted for residential purposes

(s. 12 of the 1977 Act).

There are specific offences of trespassing on land or in buildings with firearms (**see chapter 5**).

For a further discussion of the meaning of 'has with him', 'trespasser' and 'made, adapted or intended', **see Crime, chapter 12**.

Power of Arrest

Section 8(4) provides that:

> *(4)   A constable in uniform may arrest without warrant anyone who is, or whom he with reasonable cause suspects to be, in the act of committing an offence under this section.*

Keynote

This power of arrest is a 'preserved' power under the Police and Criminal Evidence Act 1984, s. 26 and sch. 2. It is limited to officers in uniform and is drafted in the present tense, that is, it will only apply where there is a reasonable suspicion that the person is in the act of committing this offence.

For a discussion of 'reasonable cause to suspect', **see chapter 2**.

6.5   Manufacture and Sale of Weapons

In addition to the controls on the carrying of weapons, there are also restrictions on the sale, manufacture, hire and buying of some weapons. The legislation is aimed at restricting the supply of such weapons and their availability in England and Wales. As such, they are mainly concerned with manufacture, sale, offering for sale etc. and should not be confused with offences of *carrying* such weapons (which are dealt with above).

Some of the offences relate to *possession* for the purpose of sale, hire etc.; this is a much wider term than that used in the carrying offences ('has with him') and is discussed in greater detail in the context of drugs (**see Crime, chapter 6**) and firearms (**see chapter 5 above**).

Offence — Manufacture, Sale or Hire of Weapons — Restriction of Offensive Weapons Act 1959, s. 1
Triable summarily. Six months' imprisonment and/or a fine.
(No *specific power of arrest*)

The Restriction of Offensive Weapons Act 1959, s. 1 states:

> *(1)   Any person who manufactures, sells or hires or offers for sale or hire or exposes or has in his possession for the purpose of sale or hire, or lends or gives to any other person—*
> *(a)   any knife which has a blade which opens automatically by hand pressure applied to a button, spring or other device in or attached to the handle of the knife, sometimes known as a 'flick knife' or 'flick gun'; or*
> *(b)   any knife which has a blade which is released from the handle or sheath thereof by the force of gravity or the application of centrifugal force and which, when released, is locked in place by means of a button, spring, lever, or other device, sometimes known as a 'gravity knife',*
> *shall be guilty of an offence . . .*

WEAPONS

Offence — Manufacture, Sale and Hire of Offensive Weapons — Criminal Justice Act 1988, s. 141
Triable summarily. Six months' imprisonment and/or a fine.
(No specific power of arrest)

The Criminal Justice Act 1988, s. 141 states:

> (1)   Any person who manufactures, sells or hires or offers for sale or hire, exposes or has in his possession for the purpose of sale or hire, or lends or gives to any other person, a weapon to which this section applies shall be guilty of an offence

Keynote

The importation of the weapons described in these offences is also prohibited (under s. 141(2) and (4) respectively.

The weapons to which the 1988 Act offence applies are set out in the schedule to the Criminal Justice Act 1988 (Offensive Weapons) Order 1988 (SI 1988 No. 2019). The weapons listed include knuckledusters, swordsticks, some telescopic truncheons, butterfly knives and a whole range of martial arts weapons. The complete list is as follows:

> . . .
> (a)   a knuckleduster that is, a band of metal or other hard material worn on one or more fingers, and designed to cause injury, and any weapon incorporating a knuckleduster;
> (b)   a swordstick, that is, a hollow walking-stick or cane containing a blade which may be used as a sword;
> (c)   the weapon sometimes known as a 'handclaw', being a band of metal or other hard material from which a number of sharp spikes protrude, and worn around the hand;
> (d)   the weapon sometimes known as a 'belt buckle knife', being a buckle which incorporates or conceals a knife;
> (e)   the weapon sometimes known as a 'push dagger', being a knife the handle of which fits within a clenched fist and the blade of which protrudes from between two fingers;
> (f)   the weapon sometimes known as a 'hollow kubotan', being a cylindrical container containing a number of sharp spikes;
> (g)   the weapon sometimes known as a 'footclaw', being a bar of metal or other hard material from which a number of sharp spikes protrude, and worn strapped to the foot;
> (h)   the weapon sometimes known as a 'shuriken', 'shaken' or 'death star', being a hard non-flexible plate having three or more sharp radiating points and designed to be thrown;
> (i)   the weapon sometimes known as a 'balisong' or 'butterfly knife', being a blade enclosed by its handle, which is designed to split down the middle, without the operation of a spring or other mechanical means, to reveal the blade;
> (j)   the weapon sometimes known as a 'telescopic truncheon', being a truncheon which extends automatically by hand pressure applied to a button, spring or other device in or attached to its handle;
> (k)   the weapon sometimes known as a 'blowpipe' or 'blow gun' being a hollow tube out of which hard pellets or darts are shot by the use of breath;
> (l)   the weapon sometimes known as a 'kusari gama', being a length of rope, cord, wire or chain fastened at one end to a sickle;
> (m)   the weapon sometimes known as a 'kyoketsu shoge', being a length of rope, cord, wire or chain fastened at one end to a hooked knife;
> (n)   the weapon sometimes known as a 'manrikigusari' or 'kusari', being a length of rope, cord, wire or chain fastened at each end to a hard weight or hand grip.
> For the purposes of the schedule, a weapon is an antique if it was manufactured more than 100 years before the date of any offence alleged to have been committed in respect of the weapon.

The courts will take notice of the fact that a weapon has been outlawed under this legislation in deciding whether or not it is 'made' for causing injury under the Prevention of Crime Act 1953 (**see para. 6.2.3**).

Defences

There are a number of defences which include Crown servants and visiting forces (ss. 141(5)–(7)) and transactions made by or to museums and galleries (ss. 141(8)–(11)).

6.6 Knives

Although some knives will fall into the categories of offence covered above, there are further restrictions which apply to knives generally.

6.6.1 Sale of Knives etc. to Persons under 16

Offence — Selling, Knives and Articles to Under 16's — Criminal Justice Act 1988, s. 141A
Triable summarily. Six months' imprisonment and/or a fine.
(No specific power of arrest)

The Criminal Justice Act 1988, s. 141A states:

> *(1) Any person who sells to a person under the age of sixteen years an article to which this section applies shall be guilty of an offence . . .*
> *(2) Subject to subsection (3) below, this section applies to—*
> *(a) any knife, knife blade or razor blade,*
> *(b) any axe, and*
> *(c) any other article which has a blade or which is sharply pointed and which is made or adapted for use for causing injury to the person.*
> *(3) This section does not apply to any article described in—*
> *(a) section 1 of the Restriction of Offensive Weapons Act 1959,*
> *(b) an order made under section 141(2) of this Act, or*
> *(c) an order made by the Secretary of State under under this section.*

Keynote

This offence does not apply to folding pocket knives with a cutting edge not exceeding three inches (7.62 cms), neither does it apply to certain types of razor blade in a cartridge where not more than 2 mm of blade is exposed (Criminal Justice Act 1988 (Offensive Weapons) (Exemptions) Order 1996 (SI 1996 No. 3064)).

Defence

Section 141A of the 1988 Act states:

> *(4) It shall be a defence for a person charged with an offence under subsection (1) above to prove that he took all reasonable precautions and exercised all due diligence to avoid the commission of the offence.*

6.6.2 Unlawful Marketing of Knives

Offence — Unlawful Marketing of Knives — Knives Act 1997, s. 1
Triable either way. Two years' imprisonment and/or a fine on indictment; six months' imprisonment and/or a fine summarily.
(No specific power of arrest)

The Knives Act 1997, s. 1 states:

> *(1)   A person is guilty of an offence if he markets a knife in a way which—*
> *(a)   indicates, or suggests, that it is suitable for combat; or*
> *(b)   is otherwise likely to stimulate or encourage violent behaviour involving the use of the knife as a weapon.*

Keynote

'Knife' for this purpose means any instrument which has a blade *or* which is sharply pointed (s. 10 of the 1997 Act).

Marketing will include selling, hiring, offering or exposing for sale or hire and possessing it for those purposes (s. 1(4)).

'Indicates or suggests' is a very loose concept requiring no *mens rea* on the part of the defendant (however, see defences below).

'Suitable for combat' means suitable for use as a weapon for inflicting injury to anyone *or causing them to fear injury*, and 'violent behaviour' means an unlawful act inflicting injury *or causing a person to fear injury* (s. 10). The elements in italics (author's emphasis) show that the legislation is intended to address the fear of the use of knives as well as their actual use.

The suggestion that knives are suitable for combat may be express or it may be implied by the name given to a product (e.g. 'commando') or by the packaging or advertisement relating to it (s. 1(3)). Therefore such packaging or advertising material, together with any surrounding advertisements, can be produced in evidence.

Defences

The Knives Act 1997, ss. 3 and 4 state:

> *3.—(1)   It is a defence for a person charged with an offence under section 1 to prove that—*
> *(a)   the knife was marketed—*
> *(i)   for use by the armed forces of any country;*
> *(ii)   as an antique or curio; or*
> *(iii)   as falling within such other category (if any) as may be prescribed;*
> *(b)   it was reasonable for the knife to be marketed in that way; and*
> *(c)   there were no reasonable grounds for suspecting that a person into whose possession the knife might come in consequence of the way in which it was marketed would use it for an unlawful purpose.*
> *(2)   It is a defence for a person charged with an offence under section 2 to prove that—*
> *(a)   the material was published in connection with marketing a knife—*
> *(i)   for use by the armed forces of any country;*
> *(ii)   as an antique or curio; or*
> *(iii)   as falling within such other category (if any) as may be prescribed;*
> *(b)   it was reasonable for the knife to be marketed in that way; and*
> *(c)   there were no reasonable grounds for suspecting that a person into whose possession the knife might come in consequence of the publishing of the material would use it for an unlawful purpose.*
>
> *4.—(1)   It is a defence for a person charged with an offence under section 1 to prove that he did not know or suspect, and had no reasonable grounds for suspecting, that the way in which the knife was marketed—*
> *(a)   amounted to an indication or suggestion that the knife was suitable for combat; or*
> *(b)   was likely to stimulate or encourage violent behaviour involving the use of the knife as a weapon.*

(2) It is a defence for a person charged with an offence under section 2 to prove that he did not know or suspect, and had no reasonable grounds for suspecting, that the material—

(a) amounted to an indication or suggestion that the knife was suitable for combat; or

(b) was likely to stimulate or encourage violent behaviour involving the use of the knife as a weapon.

(3) It is a defence for a person charged with an offence under section 1 or 2 to prove that he took all reasonable precautions and exercised all due diligence to avoid committing the offence.

Keynote

The defences at s. 3 require the person to show that the knife was marketed/the material published:

- for one of the uses at s. 3(1)(a)(i)–(iii) and s. 3(2)(a)(i)–(iii) *and*
- that it was reasonable to market it in that way *and*
- that there were no reasonable grounds for suspecting that a person would use the knife for an unlawful purpose.

The defences at s. 4 require the person to show that he/she:

- did not know or suspect, or
- *have any reasonable grounds to suspect*
- that the marketing/the marketing material amounted to an indication or even a *suggestion* that the knife was suitable for combat *or*
- was likely to stimulate or encourage violent behaviour involving the use of the knife as a weapon.

There is also the general defence under s. 4(3) for the person to show that he/she took *all* reasonable precautions and exercised *all* due diligence to avoid committing the offence.

In each of these cases, the standard of proof will be against the balance of probabilities (**see Evidence and Procedure, chapter 11**).

6.6.3   Publications Relating to Knives

Offence — Publications Relating to Knives — Knives Act 1997, s. 2
Triable either way. Two years' imprisonment and/or a fine on indictment; six months' imprisonment and/or a fine summarily.
(No specific power of arrest)

The Knives Act 1997, s. 2 states:

(1) A person is guilty of an offence if he publishes any written, pictorial or other material in connection with the marketing of any knife and that material—

(a) indicates, or suggests, that the knife is suitable for combat; or

(b) is otherwise likely to stimulate or encourage violent behaviour involving the use of the knife as a weapon.

Keynote

This offence is aimed at the publishers of advertisements rather than those who are involved in the sale and marketing of knives. The defences are shown above.

6.7   Crossbows

Even though they might fit into some of the other offences discussed above, crossbows are also subject to specific legislation.

Offence — Person under 17 Having Crossbow — Crossbows Act 1987, s. 3
Triable summarily. Fine.
(No specific power of arrest)

The Crossbows Act 1987, s. 3 states:

> *A person under the age of seventeen who has with him—*
>   *(a)   a crossbow which is capable of discharging a missile, or*
>   *(b)   parts of a crossbow which together (and without any other parts) can be assembled to form*
> *a crossbow capable of discharging a missile,*
> *is guilty of an offence, unless he is under the supervision of a person who is twenty-one years of age or older.*

Offence — Selling or Letting on Hire Crossbow to Person under 17 — Crossbows Act 1987, s. 1
Triable summarily. Six months' imprisonment and/or a fine.
(No specific power of arrest)

The Crossbows Act 1987, s. 1 states:

> *A person who sells or lets on hire a crossbow or a part of a crossbow to a person under the age of seventeen is guilty of an offence, unless he believes him to be seventeen years of age or older and has reasonable ground for the belief.*

Offence — Purchase or Hire of Crossbow by Person under 17 — Crossbows Act 1987, s. 2
Triable summarily. Fine.
(No specific power of arrest)

The Crossbows Act 1987, s. 2 states:

> *A person under the age of seventeen who buys or hires a crossbow or a part of a crossbow is guilty of an offence.*

Keynote

The offence under s. 3 again relates to a person 'having with him' (**see para. 6.2.1**) and it only applies to a crossbow which is capable of firing a missile or the parts of one which can be assembled to do so. If the crossbow has a 'draw weight' (the force required to pull back the cord to load it) of less than 1.4 kg, the offence does not apply.

In each of the above cases the court may order forfeiture of the crossbow or parts of a crossbow.

Power of Search and Seizure

The Crossbows Act 1987, s. 4

> *(1)   If a constable suspects with reasonable cause that a person is committing or has committed an offence under section 3, the constable may—*
> *(a)   search that person for a crossbow or part of a crossbow;*
> *(b)   search any vehicle, or anything in or on any vehicle, in or on which the constable suspects with reasonable cause there is a crossbow, or part of a crossbow, connected with the offence.*

Keynote

This power of search is governed by PACE Codes of Practice, Code A (**see appendix 1**). For the a full discussion of police powers to stop and search, **see chapter 2**.

A police officer may detain a person or vehicle for the purpose of a search under this power (s. 4(2)).

Anything that appears to be a crossbow or part of a crossbow to the officer found during the search may be seized (s. 4(3)).

For the purposes of exercising the powers above, a police officer may enter any land other than a dwelling house (s. 4(4)).

PART THREE

GENERAL POLICE DUTIES

CHAPTER SEVEN

CIVIL DISPUTES

7.1 Introduction

Although most civil disputes, by definition, do not involve the core functions of the police, there are occasions when the involvement of the police is necessary. The most common are 'domestic' disputes (usually involving close friends, partners and relatives) and trade disputes.

Other common sources of civil dispute are addressed under **chapter 3**.

7.2 Domestic Disputes

A 'domestic' dispute may involve a whole range of infringements of the criminal law, from a breach of the peace (**see chapter 4**), to serious assault and homicide (**see Crime, chapters 8** and **5** respectively).

Each of these is dealt with in other areas of this work, together with any attendant powers of entry and arrest (**see chapter 2**).

There are also occasions where police officers become involved in enforcing what are in effect civil matters in relation to *matrimonial* or *family* domestic disputes. Generally these occasions will come about where one party is subject to a court order preventing them from doing certain acts, acts which they nevertheless go on to carry out.

7.2.1 Court Orders

There are two main sources of court order in relation to matrimonial or family domestic disputes:

- the Family Law Act 1996 — which can be made by any court having jurisdiction over family law matters; and

- the Domestic Proceedings and Magistrates' Courts Act 1978 — which can be made by magistrates.

7.2.2   The Family Law Act 1996

The Family Law Act 1996 consolidates many aspects of the law regulating family proceedings. Part IV of the Act makes provisions for family homes and for dealing with domestic violence.

Non-Molestation Orders

Section 42 of the 1996 Act provides for 'non-molestation' orders. Section 42 states:

> (1)   In this Part a 'non-molestation order' means an order containing either or both of the following provisions—
>
> (a)   provision prohibiting a person ('the respondent') from molesting another person who is associated with the respondent;
>
> (b)   provision prohibiting the respondent from molesting a relevant child.
>
> (2)   The court may make a non-molestation order—
>
> (a)   if an application for the order has been made (whether in other family proceedings or without any other family proceedings being instituted) by a person who is associated with the respondent; or
>
> (b)   if in any family proceedings to which the respondent is a party the court considers that the order should be made for the benefit of any other party to the proceedings or any relevant child even though no such application has been made.

Keynote

Non-molestation orders can be applied for even though no other proceedings have been begun and such orders do not just relate to spouses or former partners; they apply to anyone who is 'associated' with the respondent.

Under s. 62, a person is 'associated' with another person if:

> (3)   . . .
>
> (a)   they are or have been married to each other;
>
> (b)   they are cohabitants or former cohabitants;
>
> (c)   they live or have lived in the same household, otherwise than merely by reason of one of them being the other's employee, tenant, lodger or boarder;
>
> (d)   they are relatives;
>
> (e)   they have agreed to marry one another (whether or not that agreement has been terminated);
>
> (f)   in relation to any child, they are both persons falling within subsection (4); or
>
> (g)   they are parties to the same family proceedings (other than proceedings under this Part).
>
> (4)   A person falls within this subsection in relation to a child if—
>
> (a)   he is a parent of the child; or
>
> (b)   he has or has had parental responsibility for the child.

In deciding whether or not to make such an order, the court must consider all the circumstances including the need to secure the health, safety and well-being of the applicant or any relevant child (s. 42(5)).

A person under 16 cannot apply for a non-molestation order without leave of the court (s. 43(1)) but, if the person satisfies the court that he/she has sufficient understanding to make the application, he/she may be granted leave (s. 43(2)).

Power of Arrest for Breach of the Order

Section 47 of the 1996 Act provides that:

> *(2) If—*
> *(a) the court makes a relevant order; and*
> *(b) it appears to the court that the respondent has used or threatened violence against the applicant or a relevant child,*
> *it shall attach a power of arrest to one or more provisions of the order unless satisfied that in all the circumstances of the case the applicant or child will be adequately protected without such a power of arrest.*
> . . .
> *(6) If, by virtue of subsection (2) or (3), a power of arrest is attached to certain provisions of an order, a constable may arrest without warrant a person whom he has reasonable cause for suspecting to be in breach of any such provision.*

Keynote

Under s. 47(3), the ability to attach a power of arrest will also apply to a non-molestation order which has been made *ex parte*, that is, without telling the other person, but only if:

- the respondent has used or threatened violence against the applicant or a relevant child; or

- there is a risk of significant harm to the applicant or relevant child attributable to the conduct of the respondent if a power of arrest is not attached immediately.

Section 47(7) provides that:

> *(7) If a power of arrest is attached under subsection (2) or (3) to certain provisions of the order and the respondent is arrested under subsection (6)—*
> *(a) he must be brought before the relevant judicial authority within the period of 24 hours beginning at the time of his arrest; and*
> *(b) if the matter is not then disposed of forthwith, the relevant judicial authority before whom he is brought may remand him.*
> *In reckoning for the purposes of this subsection any period of 24 hours, no account is to be taken of Christmas Day, Good Friday or any Sunday.*

Keynote

Where a judge makes a non-molestation order under s. 47(2), he/she is obliged to attach a power of arrest unless there are exceptional circumstances. If the judge considers that to attach such a power would give the applicant an unacceptable amount of influence over the respondent, the appropriate course of action is to refuse to grant the order altogether (*Chechi* v *Bashir, The Times*, 25 March 1999).

If the court does not attach a power of arrest at the time of making an order, it may issue a warrant of arrest if the respondent fails to comply with the terms and conditions of the order (s. 47(8)).

If it is not convenient to take the arrested person before the 'relevant judicial authority' (i.e. the court which made the order) in a courtroom within the 24-hour period, the judge or magistrate can sit at any convenient and suitably open place (*Practice Direction (Domestic Violence: Procedure on Arrest) (No. 2)* [1998] WLR 476).

'Molesting' includes conduct which does not extend to actual physical violence and includes conduct which intentionally causes such a degree of harassment that the intervention of the courts is required (*Johnson* v *Walton* [1990] FCR 568).

For harassment generally, **see chapter 3**.

For malicious communications, **see chapter 3**.

For the offence of 'actual bodily harm' and for powers in relation to the protection of children, **see Crime, chapters 8 and 11**.

7.2.3 Magistrates' Court Order

Section 16 of the Domestic Proceedings and Magistrates' Courts Act 1978 provides:

> *(1) Either party to a marriage may, whether or not an application is made by that party for an order under section 2 of this Act, apply to a magistrates' court for an order under this section.*
> *(2) Where on an application for an order under this section the court is satisfied that the respondent has used, or threatened to use, violence against the person of the applicant or a child of the family and that it is necessary for the protection of the applicant or a child of the family that an order should be made under this subsection, the court may make one or both of the following orders, that is to say—*
> *(a) an order that the respondent shall not use, or threaten to use, violence against the person of the applicant;*
> *(b) an order that the respondent shall not use, or threaten to use, violence against the person of a child of the family.*
> *(3) Where on an application for an order under this section the court is satisfied—*
> *(a) that the respondent has used violence against the person of the applicant or a child of the family, or*
> *(b) that the respondent has threatened to use violence against the person of the applicant or a child of the family and has used violence against some other person, or*
> *(c) that the respondent has in contravention of an order made under subsection (2) above threatened to use violence against the person of the applicant or a child of the family,*
> *and that the applicant or a child of the family is in danger of being physically injured by the respondent (or would be in such danger if the applicant or child were to enter the matrimonial home) the court may make one or both of the following orders, that is to say—*
> *(i) an order requiring the respondent to leave the matrimonial home;*
> *(ii) an order prohibiting the respondent from entering the matrimonial home.*

Keynote

This power is more restrictive than that under the 1996 Act above in that it only applies to parties to a marriage.

The court may also make an order requiring the respondent to allow the applicant to enter the matrimonial home (s. 16(4)).

Power of Arrest

Section 18 of the 1978 Act provides that:

> *(1) Where a magistrates' court makes an order under section 16 of this Act which provides that the respondent—*
> *(a) shall not use violence against the person of the applicant, or*
> *(b) shall not use violence against a child of the family, or*
> *(c) shall not enter the matrimonial home,*
> *the court may, if it is satisfied that the respondent has physically injured the applicant or a child of the family and considers that he is likely to do so again, attach a power of arrest to the order.*

(2)   Where by virtue of subsection (1) above a power of arrest is attached to an order, a constable may arrest without warrant a person whom he has reasonable cause for suspecting of being in breach of any such provision of the order as is mentioned in paragraph (a), (b) or (c) of subsection (1) above by reason of that person's use of violence or, as the case may be, his entry into the matrimonial home.

(3)   Where a power of arrest is attached to an order under subsection (1) above and the respondent is arrested under subsection (2) above—

(a)   he shall be brought before a justice of the peace within a period of 24 hours beginning at the time of his arrest, and

(b)   the justice of the peace before whom he is brought may remand him.

In reckoning for the purposes of this subsection any period of 24 hours, no account shall be taken of Christmas Day, Good Friday, or any Sunday.

Keynote

If the court does not attach a power of arrest to such an order it may issue a warrant under s. 18(4) for the arrest of the person who is in breach. Such a warrant may be executed even if it is not in the officer's possession at the time but it must be shown to the arrested person as soon as practicable afterwards (Magistrates' Courts Act 1980, s. 125).

For warrants generally, **see chapter 2**.

7.3   Trade Disputes

The law regulating trade disputes changed dramatically during the 1980s and 1990s. Over this period the workforce in the community became more disparate and fragmented; working practices changed and there was a general decline in the traditionally unionised industries.

Despite the best intentions of those involved, trade disputes will no doubt continue to arise but the occasions on which they require any significant police involvement will hopefully continue to be rare (see the Home Office Consolidated Circular on Crime and Kindred Matters).

In addition to the provisions discussed in this section you should also consider offences and powers under:

- offences against public order, **see chapter 4**;
- offences against the person, **see Crime, chapter 8**;
- offences involving weapons, **see chapter 6**;
- obstruction and danger to road users, **see Road Traffic, chapter 8**.

Most of the conditions regulating trade disputes can be found in the Trade Union and Labour Relations (Consolidation) Act 1992.

The areas which have historically created the greatest need for police involvement arise from the differences between those who wish to exercise their right to strike and those who wish to continue to work.

7.3.1   Picketing

Section 220 of the 1992 Act provides that:

(1) It is lawful for a person in contemplation or furtherance of a trade dispute to attend—

    (a) at or near his own place of work, or

    (b) if he is an official of a trade union, at or near the place of work of a member of the union whom he is accompanying and whom he represents,

for the purpose only of peacefully obtaining or communicating information, or peacefully persuading any person to work or abstain from working.

(2) If a person works or normally works—

    (a) otherwise than at any one place, or

    (b) at a place the location of which is such that attendance there for a purpose mentioned in subsection (1) is impracticable,

his place of work for the purposes of that subsection shall be any premises of his employer from which he works or from which his work is administered.

(3) In the case of a worker not in employment where—

    (a) his last employment was terminated in connection with a trade dispute, or

    (b) the termination of his employment was one of the circumstances giving rise to a trade dispute,

in relation to that dispute his former place of work shall be treated for the purposes of subsection (1) as being his place of work.

(4) A person who is an official of a trade union by virtue only of having been elected or appointed to be a representative of some of the members of the union shall be regarded for the purposes of subsection (1) as representing only those members; but otherwise an official of a union shall be regarded for those purposes as representing all its members.

Keynote

Section 220 effectively restricts lawful picketing to 'primary' picketing outside the person's own place of work.

If there is a real danger of any offence (such as a public order offence, **see chapter 4**) being committed, then pickets have no right to attend the place in question under s. 220 (*Piddington* v *Bates* [1960] 3 All ER 660).

Although s. 220 does not place any restriction on the numbers of pickets, if they gather in large enough numbers, there may be a presumption that the pickets intend to intimidate others (*Broome* v *DPP* [1974] AC 587).

Section 220 does not authorise pickets to enter onto private land (*British Airports Authority* v *Ashton* [1983] 1 WLR 1079).

A person's place of work does not include new premises of an employer who has moved since dismissing the people picketing (*News Group Newspapers Ltd* v *SOGAT'82 (No. 2)* [1987] ICR 181).

For the Code of Practice on Picketing, see the Code of Practice (Picketing) Order 1992 (SI 1992 No. 476).

7.3.2   Meaning of 'Trade Dispute'

Section 244(1)of the 1992 Act provides that:

(1) In this Part a 'trade dispute' means a dispute between workers and their employer which relates wholly or mainly to one or more of the following—

    (a) terms and conditions of employment, or the physical conditions in which any workers are required to work;

    (b) engagement or non-engagement, or termination or suspension of employment or the duties of employment, of one or more workers;

(c)   *allocation of work or the duties of employment between workers or groups of workers;*
(d)   *matters of discipline;*
(e)   *a worker's membership or non-membership of a trade union;*
(f)   *facilities for officials of trade unions; and*
(g)   *machinery for negotiation or consultation, and other procedures, relating to any of the above matters, including the recognition by employers or employers' associations of the right of a trade union to represent workers in such negotiation or consultation or in the carrying out of such procedures.*

Keynote

If the dispute is between workers in a government department and the relevant minister, the dispute can still come within this section even though he/she is not the workers' 'employer' (s. 244(2)).

Offence — Intimidation or Annoyance by Violence or Otherwise — Trade Union and Labour Relations (Consolidation) Act 1992, s. 241
Triable summarily. Six months' imprisonment and/or a fine.
(Statutory power of arrest)

The Trade Union and Labour Relations (Consolidation) Act 1992, s. 241 states:

(1)   *A person commits an offence who, with a view to compelling another person to abstain from doing or to do any act which that person has a legal right to do or abstain from doing, wrongfully and without legal authority—*
(a)   *uses violence to or intimidates that person or his wife or children, or injures his property,*
(b)   *persistently follows that person about from place to place,*
(c)   *hides any tools, clothes or other property owned or used by that person, or deprives him of or hinders him in the use thereof,*
(d)   *watches or besets the house or other place where that person resides, works, carries on business or happens to be, or the approach to any such house or place, or*
(e)   *follows that person with two or more other persons in a disorderly manner in or through any street or road.*
(2)   . . .
(3)   *A constable may arrest without warrant anyone he reasonably suspects is committing an offence under this section.*

Keynote

'With a view to compelling' means with intent to compel. This is therefore an offence of 'specific intent' (**see Crime, chapter 1**).

'Wrongfully' means a civil wrong.

Although the breach of a contract is generally not a criminal offence, this section imposes a duty on some contracted personnel not to breach their contract under certain conditions.

For this offence you would have to show that the person acted wilfully and maliciously (**see Crime, chapter 1**); you would also have to show knowledge or reasonable cause to believe that the listed consequences would apply. This would clearly create practical difficulties and this offence is likely to be very rare.

For some reason this offence does not apply to 'seamen' (s. 241(4)).

CHAPTER EIGHT

ANIMALS

8.1 Introduction

There is a considerable amount of legislation designed to protect animals or to restrict the way in which they are treated, ranging from the use of animals in public performances to the importation of destructive animals.

This chapter sets out some of the more relevant provisions, particularly those aimed at preventing and punishing acts of cruelty, and those designed to ensure community safety.

Some of the legislation is aimed at particular animals — such as dogs — but there will be times when an incident involving an animal falls under a number of different Acts.

8.2 Dangerous Dogs

8.2.1 Dangerous Dogs Act 1991

The Dangerous Dogs Act 1991 imposes a number of duties on dog owners and people who are in charge of dogs. The main aim of this part of the legislation is to make people responsible for their dogs in public and to avoid any dog presenting a danger to other people.

8.2.2 Failing to Keep Dogs under Proper Control

Offence — Failing to Keep Dogs under Proper Control — Dangerous Dogs Act 1991, s. 3(1)
Aggravated offence: triable either way. Two years' imprisonment and/or a fine on indictment; six months' imprisonment and/or a fine summarily. Otherwise: triable summarily. Six months' imprisonment and/or a fine.
(No specific power of arrest)

The Dangerous Dogs Act 1991, s. 3 states:

> *(1)   If a dog is dangerously out of control in a public place—*
> *(a)   the owner; and*
> *(b)   if different, the person for the time being in charge of the dog,*
> *is guilty of an offence, or, if the dog while so out of control injures any person, an aggravated offence, under this subsection.*
> *(2)   . . .*
> *(3)   If the owner or, if different, the person for the time being in charge of a dog allows it to enter a place which is not a public place but where it is not permitted to be and while it is there—*
> *(a)   it injures any person; or*
> *(b)   there are grounds for reasonable apprehension that it will do so,*
> *he is guilty of an offence, or, if the dog injures any person, an aggravated offence, under this subsection.*

Keynote

For the definition of 'public place', see the Keynote to **para. 8.2.3** below.

The offence under s. 3(1) can be committed by both the owner and the person in charge of the dog, the offence under s. 3(3) applies to either the owner, or the person in charge.

Whether someone is 'in charge' of a dog is a question of fact for a court/jury to determine in each case.

For these offences under s. 3 the type of dog is irrelevant.

Dangerously Out of Control

Under s. 10(3) of the 1991 Act , 'dangerously out of control' means:

> *. . . a dog shall be regarded as dangerously out of control on any occasion on which there are grounds for reasonable apprehension that it will injure any person, whether or not it actually does so, but references to a dog injuring a person or there being grounds for reasonable apprehension that it will do so do not include references to any case in which the dog is being used for a lawful purpose by a constable or a person in the service of the Crown.*

Keynote

'Grounds for reasonable apprehension' that a dog will injure someone may arise even where the dog's behaviour is sudden and unexpected (see *Rafiq* v *DPP* (1997) 161 JP 412); and, although the reasonable apprehension must be that the dog will injure any *person*, an attack on another dog may well give rise to that apprehension (**see below**). See also the Dogs Act 1906, s. 1, which extends the scope of the Dogs Act 1871 giving magistrates a power to make an order in relation to dangerous dogs to cover dogs that injure certain farm animals.

If an offence is committed under s. 3 above and the person who owns the dog is under 16, the 'head of the household' also commits the offence (s. 6 and **see para. 8.2.3**).

The offences are 'strict liability' offences, that is, there is no need to show any particular *mens rea* (state of mind) on the part of the defendant (**see Crime, chapter 1**) and there is no need to prove even an element of negligence by a defendant (*R* v *Bezzina* [1994] 1 WLR 1057).

The proviso relating to the use of police dogs or other dogs in the service of the Crown, would appear to cover properly-conducted training exercises and displays if they could be shown to be 'lawful purposes'.

Defence

Section 3(2) of the 1991 Act provides that:

(2) In proceedings for an offence under subsection (1) above against a person who is the owner of a dog but was not at the material time in charge of it, it shall be a defence for the accused to prove that the dog was at the material time in the charge of a person whom he reasonably believed to be a fit and proper person to be in charge of it.

Keynote

The statutory defence under s. 3(2) does not call for a minute examination as to which member of a family had charge of a dog kept in the home at any one particular moment in time. Therefore, where the wife of an owner of a dog lets it out and it bit someone, the owner could not claim that he had momentarily transferred charge of that dog to her (*R v Huddart*, unreported 24 November 1998). The Court of Appeal held that, in order to avail himself/herself of that defence, there must be evidence to show that the owner had for the time being divested himself/herself of responsibility for the dog in favour of an identifiable person (see also *R v Harter* [1988] Crim LR 336 which was distinguished in this case).

8.2.3 Possessing Dogs under Section 1

Offence — Possessing Dogs of Type Controlled by Section 1 — Dangerous Dogs Act 1991, s. 1(3)
Triable summarily. Six months' imprisonment and/or a fine.
(No specific power of arrest)

The Dangerous Dogs Act 1991, s. 1 states:

(3) After such day as the Secretary of State may by order appoint for the purposes of this subsection no person shall have any dog to which this section applies in his possession or custody except—
 (a) in pursuance of the power of seizure conferred by the subsequent provisions of this Act; or
 (b) in accordance with an order for its destruction made under those provisions;
but the Secretary of State shall by order make a scheme for the payment to the owners of such dogs who arrange for them to be destroyed before that day of sums specified in or determined under the scheme in respect of those dogs and the cost of their destruction.

Offence — Breeding, Selling, Offering etc. Dogs of Type Controlled by Section 1 — Dangerous Dogs Act 1991, s. 1(2)
Triable summarily. Six months' imprisonment and/or a fine.
(No specific power of arrest)

The Dangerous Dogs Act 1991, s. 1 states:

(2) No person shall—
 (a) breed, or breed from, a dog to which this section applies;
 (b) sell or exchange such a dog or offer, advertise or expose such a dog for sale or exchange;
 (c) make or offer to make a gift of such a dog or advertise or expose such a dog as a gift;
 (d) allow such a dog of which he is the owner or of which he is for the time being in charge to be in a public place without being muzzled and kept on a lead; or
 (e) abandon such a dog of which he is the owner or, being the owner or for the time being in charge of such a dog, allow it to stray.

Keynote

The breeding of dogs generally is regulated by the Breeding of Dogs Act 1973. This piece of legislation has been amended in several respects by the Breeding and Sale of Dogs (Welfare) Act 1999. Between them the Acts provide for a system of licensing for breeding establishments and create a number of summary offences for breaching the relevant requirements. The 1999 Act creates a number of new summary offences in respect of the sale of dogs by keepers of licensed breeding establishments (s. 8). The 1999 Act also allows a court to disqualify a person from keeping a licensed breeding establishment upon conviction for a relevant offence.

The above offence, however, relates solely to the breeding etc. of dogs that are of the 'types' specified below.

For the law relating to dog fights, **see para. 8.3**.

The offence under s. 1 is not committed if a person has a certificate of exemption in respect of the dog, or if the person has custody of the dog under the power of seizure provided by the 1991 Act (**see para. 8.2.4**).

The expression used in the legislation is dogs of the 'type' known as pit bull terriers etc. This expression is much wider than 'breed' and will include dogs which have a substantial number of the breed characteristics. Therefore the Act will cover some cross-breeds (see *R* v *Knightsbridge Crown Court, ex parte Dunne* [1994] 1 WLR 296). The statutory controls also apply to the Japanese tosa, the dogo Argentino and the fila Bràziliero.

The offences under s. 1 are 'strict liability' offences (**see Crime, chapter 1**).

'Public place' includes any street, road or other place to which the public have access, whether for payment or otherwise and includes common parts of a building containing two or more separate dwellings (s. 10(2)). Therefore a shared landing or garden within a residential complex could fall within the definition.

A dog locked in a car which is parked in a public place is itself 'in a public place' (*Bates* v *DPP* (1993) 157 JP 1004).

A private path or driveway is *not* necessarily a public place simply because certain people have an implied licence to come to the door (*Fellowes* v *DPP* (1993) 157 JP 936).

In showing that a place is a 'public place' for the purposes of the 1991 Act there is no need to prove *actual use* by the public. A court may infer that an area is a 'public place' from the fact that it is publicly owned (e.g. by the local council), even though the land has been fenced off and is not generally used by the public (*Cummings* v *DPP, The Times*, 26 March 1999).

'Muzzled' means having a muzzle *securely fitted* in a way which prevents the dog from biting anyone (s. 7(1)(a)).

'Kept on a lead' means *securely* held on a lead by a *person who is not less than 16* (s. 7(1)(b)).

'Advertisement' *includes* any means of bringing a matter to the attention of the public (s. 10(2)); but this does necessarily *exclude* any private or restricted advertisement such as in a workplace or club.

If an offence is committed under s. 1(2)(d) or (e) above and the person who owns the dog is under 16, the 'head of the household' also commits the offence (s. 6).

The Secretary of State may add other types of dog to this list (s. 1(1)(c)) and may impose further conditions on any other types of dog (s. 2).

Many cases have been brought where the characteristics of the dog's type are in dispute. Section 5 of the 1991 Act provides that:

> (5)   If in any proceedings it is alleged by the prosecution that a dog is one to which section 1 or an order under section 2 above applies it shall be presumed that it is such a dog unless the contrary is shown by the accused by such evidence as the court considers sufficient; and the accused shall not be permitted to adduce such evidence unless he has given the prosecution notice of his intention to do so not later than the fourteenth day before that on which the evidence is to be adduced.

Keynote

This statutory presumption does not apply in civil cases (*R* v *Walton Street Magistrates' Court, ex parte Crothers* (1996) 160 JP 427).

Some forces have officers who are specifically trained as expert witnesses in giving evidence of a dog's 'type'.

Defence

Section 1(7) of the 1991 Act provides that:

> (7)   Any person who contravenes this section is guilty of an offence . . . except that a person who publishes an advertisement in contravention of subsection (2)(b) or (c)—
> (a)   shall not on being convicted be liable to imprisonment if he shows that he published the advertisement to the order of someone else and did not himself devise it; and
> (b)   shall not be convicted if, in addition, he shows that he did not know and had no reasonable cause to suspect that it related to a dog to which this section applies.

8.2.4   Enforcement

Power of Seizure

Section 5(1) of the Dangerous Dogs Act 1991 provides that:

> (1)   A constable or an officer of a local authority authorised by it to exercise the powers conferred by this subsection may seize—
> (a)   any dog which appears to him to be a dog to which section 1 above applies and which is in a public place—
> (i)   after the time when possession or custody of it has become unlawful by virtue of that section; or
> (ii)   before that time, without being muzzled and kept on a lead;
> (b)   any dog in a public place which appears to him to be a dog to which an order under section 2 above applies and in respect of which an offence against the order has been or is being committed; and

(c)   any dog in a public place (whether or not one to which that section or such an order applies) which appears to him to be dangerously out of control.

Entry and Search

Section 5(2) and (4) provide for the issuing of a warrant to enter and search premises in connection with offences under the 1991 Act, and for the destruction of any dog lawfully seized.

8.2.5   Courts' Powers

The powers of the courts to make orders in relation to dogs under the Dangerous Dogs Act 1991 were amended by the Dangerous Dogs (Amendment) Act 1997.

Those powers are now contained in ss. 4 and 4A which provide that:

4.—(1)   Where a person is convicted of an offence under section 1 or 3(1) or (3) above or of an offence under an order made under section 2 above the court—
(a)   may order the destruction of any dog in respect of which the offence was committed and shall do so in the case of an offence under section 1 or an aggravated offence under section 3(1) or (3) above; and
(b)   may order the offender to be disqualified, for such period as the court thinks fit, for having custody of a dog.

4A.—(1)   Where—
(a)   a person is convicted of an offence under section 1 above or an aggravated offence under section 3(1) or (3) above;
(b)   the court does not order the destruction of the dog under section 4(1)(a) above; and
(c)   in the case of an offence under section 1 above, the dog is subject to the prohibition in section 1(3) above,
the court shall order that, unless the dog is exempted from that prohibition within the requisite period, the dog shall be destroyed.

Keynote

It is a summary offence to have custody of a dog in contravention of s. 4(1)(b) above or to fail to comply with a requirement under s. 4(4)(a) (s. 4(8)).

The courts' powers to make control or destruction orders under the Dogs Act 1871, s. 2 still apply and it is a summary offence to fail to comply with such an order (Dangerous Dogs Act 1989, s. 1(3)). The courts may also order that a person be disqualified from keeping a dog and failure to comply with such an order is also a summary offence (Dangerous Dogs Act 1989, s. 1(6)).

In making an order under the Dangerous dogs Act 1871 magistrates should consider the normal, everyday meaning of the word 'dangerous'. That term is not therefore limited to a dog that presents a threat to humans but could also extend to dogs that attack other dogs (*Briscoe* v *Shattock*, *The Times*, 12 October 1998). Although this decision was made in relation to the 1871 Act, it tends to support the assertion above that a dog's dangerous disposition towards people might be demonstrated, in part, by its behaviour towards other animals.

Section 13(1) of the Protection of Badgers Act 1992 empowers a court to order the destruction of dogs which have been present when certain offences involving badgers have been committed (**see also para. 8.10**).

8.2.6 Control of Dogs on Roads

Section 27 of the Road Traffic Act 1988 creates a summary offence for any person to cause or permit a dog to be on a designated road without being held on a lead. 'Designated' roads for this purpose are roads specified by the relevant local authority. Certain limitations may be imposed on the extent of such an order by the local authority, provided that they have consulted with the relevant chief officer of police (s. 27(3) and (5)).

The provisions do not apply to dogs kept for driving or tending sheep or cattle in the course of a trade or business, nor do they apply to dogs held at the material time to have been in use under proper control for sporting purposes (s. 27(4)).

For the general meaning of 'cause or permit', **see Road Traffic, chapter 1**.

8.3 Animal Fighting

In addition to the offence of cruelty (**see para. 8.8**), there are specific offences relating to animal fighting.

Offence — Attendance at Animal Fights — Protection of Animals Act 1911, s. 5A
Triable summarily. Fine.
(**No specific power of arrest**)

The Protection of Animals Act 1911, s. 5A states:

> *A person who, without reasonable excuse, is present when animals are placed together for the purpose of their fighting each other shall be liable . . .*

Offence — Advertising Animal Fights — Protection of Animals Act 1911, s. 5B
Triable summarily. Fine.
(**No specific power of arrest**)

The Protection of Animals Act 1911, s. 5B states:

> *If a person who publishes or causes to be published an advertisement for a fight between animals knows that it is such an advertisement he shall be liable . . .*

Keynote

The first offence (s. 5A) requires no knowledge by the defendant, and very little in the way of *actus reus* (criminal conduct; **see Crime, chapter 2**). Simply being present is enough.

The second offence (s. 5B) requires proof that the person knew of the nature of the advertisement. Knowledge here will include shutting your eyes to the obvious (*Westminster City Council* v *Croyalgrange Ltd* [1986] 2 All ER 353).

It is also a summary offence to cause, procure or assist at the fighting or baiting of any animal or to keep premises for that purpose (s. 1(1)(c) of the 1911 Act).

8.3.1 Cockfighting

The Cockfighting Act 1952 creates a summary offence of having any instruments for use in cockfighting, while the Town Police Clauses Act 1847, s. 36, and the Metropolitan Police Act 1839, s. 47, create offences of keeping places for the fighting or baiting of animals.

8.4 Guard Dogs

Guard dogs will be covered by much of the legislation above but there is also special provision made for the proper control of such animals.

Offence — Control of Guard Dogs — Guard Dogs Act 1975, s. 1
Triable summarily. Fine.
(*No specific power of arrest*)

The Guard Dogs Act 1975, s. 1 states:

> (1)   A person shall not use or permit the use of a guard dog at any premises unless a person ('the handler') who is capable of controlling the dog is present on the premises and the dog is under the control of the handler at all times while it is being so used except while it is secured so that it is not at liberty to go freely about the premises.
>
> (2)   The handler of a guard dog shall keep the dog under his control at all times while it is being used as a guard dog at any premises except—
>
> (a)   while another handler has control over the dog; or
>
> (b)   while the dog is secured so that it is not at liberty to go freely about premises.
>
> (3)   A person shall not use or permit the use of a guard dog at any premises unless a notice containing a warning that a guard dog is present is clearly exhibited at each entrance to the premises.

Keynote

'Permitting' implies some form of unconditional 'allowing' or condoning of the use (**see Road Traffic, chapter 1**).

If a dog is tied up securely there is no need for the handler to be present (*Hobson* v *Gledhill* [1978] Crim LR 45).

Under s. 7, a 'guard dog' means a dog which is being used to **p**rotect:

- **p**remises,
- **p**roperty kept on the premises, or
- **p**eople guarding the premises or such property.

'Premises' are land (other than agricultural land and land around a dwelling-house) and buildings, including parts of buildings, other than dwelling-houses (s. 7).

Therefore the 1975 Act does not apply to dogs being used to protect houses or agricultural land (which includes fields, pig and poultry farms, allotments, nurseries and orchards).

8.5 Dogs and Livestock

8.5.1 Worrying Livestock

The activities of dogs around livestock is regulated by the Dogs (Protection of Livestock) Act 1953.

Offence — Worrying Livestock — Dogs (Protection of Livestock) Act 1953, s. 1(1)
Triable summarily. Fine.
(No *specific power of arrest*)

The Dogs (Protection of Livestock) Act 1953, s. 1 states:

(1) Subject to the provisions of this section, if a dog worries livestock on any agricultural land, the owner of the dog, and if it is in the charge of a person other than its owner, that person also, shall be guilty of an offence . . .

Keynote

For the purposes of s. 1(2) of the 1953 Act, 'worrying livestock' means:

- attacking livestock, or

- chasing livestock in such a way as may reasonably be expected to cause injury or suffering to the livestock or, in the case of females, abortion, or loss of or diminution in their produce (s. 1(1)(b)), or

- not being on a lead or under close control in a field or enclosure in which there are sheep (s. 1(1)(c)).

The offence under s. 1(1)(c) involving sheep does not apply in relation to:

- a dog owned by, or in the charge of, the occupier of the field or enclosure or the owner of the sheep or a person authorised by either of those people, or

- a police dog, a guide dog, a trained sheep dog, a working gun dog or a pack of hounds (s. 1(2A)).

Defence

Section 1(3) and (4) of the 1953 Act provides that:

(3) A person shall not be guilty of an offence under this Act by reason of anything done by a dog, if at the material time the livestock are trespassing on the land in question and the dog is owned by, or in the charge of, the occupier of that land or a person authorised by him, except in a case where the said person causes the dog to attack the livestock.
(4) The owner of a dog shall not be convicted of an offence under this Act in respect of the worrying of livestock by the dog if he proves that at the time when the dog worried the livestock it was in the charge of some other person, whom he reasonably believed to be a fit and proper person to be in charge of the dog.

Police Powers

Section 2(2) of the 1953 Act provides that:

> *(2)   Where in the case of a dog found on any land—*
>   *(a)   a police officer has reasonable cause to believe that the dog has been worrying livestock on that land, and the land appears to him to be agricultural land, and*
>   *(b)   no person is present who admits to being the owner of the dog or in charge of it,*
> *then for the purpose of ascertaining who is the owner of the dog the police officer may seize it and may detain it until the owner has claimed it and paid all expenses incurred by reason of its detention.*

Keynote

There is a difference between 'reasonable grounds to suspect' and 'reasonable cause to *believe*' (**see chapter 2**). The latter requirement needs more evidence than mere suspicion on the part of the officer concerned.

This power only applies to land which appears to the officer to be agricultural land.

Section 2A provides for the issue of search warrants in connection with dogs suspected of being involved in the worrying of livestock.

A prosecution for an offence involving a dog on agricultural land cannot be brought without the consent of the chief officer of police for that area, the occupier of the land or the owner of the relevant livestock (s. 2(1)).

8.5.2   Killing of or Injury to Dogs Worrying Livestock

It is not uncommon for dogs found to be worrying livestock to be shot by farmers or landowners. Section 9 of the Animals Act 1971 provides that:

> *(1)   In any civil proceedings against a person (in this section referred to as the defendant) for killing or causing injury to a dog it shall be a defence to prove—*
>   *(a)   that the defendant acted for the protection of any livestock and was a person entitled to act for the protection of that livestock; and*
>   *(b)   that within forty-eight hours of the killing or injury notice thereof was given by the defendant to the officer in charge of a police station.*
> *(2)   For the purposes of this section a person is entitled to act for the protection of any livestock if, and only if—*
>   *(a)   the livestock or the land on which it is belongs to him or to any person under whose express or implied authority he is acting; and*
>   *(b)   the circumstances are not such that liability for killing or causing injury to the livestock would be excluded by section 5(4) of this Act.*
> *(3)   Subject to subsection (4) of this section, a person killing or causing injury to a dog shall be deemed for the purposes of this section to act for the protection of any livestock if, and only if, either—*
>   *(a)   the dog is worrying or is about to worry the livestock and there are no other reasonable means of ending or preventing the worrying; or*
>   *(b)   the dog has been worrying livestock, has not left the vicinity and is not under the control of any person and there are no practicable means of ascertaining to whom it belongs.*

Keynote

Notice may be given over the telephone, in writing or, presumably, by fax or e-mail. Its purpose is to provide a record of the incident so that the information can be made available to any court at a later date.

8.6 Rabies

The Animal Health Act 1981 creates a number of provisions for regulating the movement of animals in and around the UK; for controlling and containing outbreaks of diseases; and for the enforcement of powers in relation to rabies.

8.6.1 Police Powers

The Animal Health Act 1981, s. 61 provides that:

(1)   A constable may arrest without warrant any person whom he, with reasonable cause, suspects to be in the act of committing or to have committed an offence to which this section applies.

(2)   The offences to which this section applies are offences against this Act consisting of—

(a)   the landing or attempted landing of any animal in contravention of an order made under this Act and expressed to be made for the purpose of preventing the introduction of rabies into Great Britain; or

(b)   the failure by the person having the charge or control of any vessel, or boat to discharge any obligation imposed on him in that capacity by such order; or

(c)   the movement, in contravention of an order under section 17 or 23 of this Act, of any animal into, within or out of a place or area declared to be infected with rabies.

Keynote

For the purposes of arresting someone under the above provisions, s. 62 provides a power of entry (if need be, by force) and search of any boat, vessel, aircraft or vehicle where the officer has reasonable cause to suspect that person to be. The section goes on to provide similar powers in order to seize animals under the law relating to the spread of rabies.

These powers are governed by the provisions of the Police and Criminal Evidence Act 1984 (**see chapter 2**).

Sections 72 and 73 create offences of doing or failing to do anything in contravention of the provisions of the 1981 Act.

8.7 Dangerous Wild Animals

Just as some types of dog are subject to special legislative control, so too are some species of wild animal. The Dangerous Wild Animals Act 1976 regulates the keeping of those wild animals which are listed in its schedule. The schedule (which reads like Noah's passenger list) contains many exotic and rare wild animals including old-world monkeys, reptiles and birds.

Under s. 1 of the 1976 Act it is necessary to obtain a licence from a local authority before keeping any wild animal. Any such licence will contain details of which specific animals are covered and where they are to be kept. Certain exemptions are made for some zoos, scientific establishments, circuses and some licensed pet shops (s. 5).

Local authorities are given powers to seize animals which are kept in contravention of the Act (s. 4).

8.8   Cruelty

Offence — Cruelty — Protection of Animals Act 1911, s. 1(1)
Triable summarily. Six months' imprisonment and/or a fine.
(*Statutory power of arrest*)

The Protection of Animals Act 1911, s. 1 states:

(1) If any person—

(a) shall cruelly beat, kick, ill-treat, over-ride, over-drive, over-load, torture, infuriate, or terrify any animal, or shall cause or procure, or, being the owner, permit any animal to be so used, or shall, by wantonly or unreasonably doing or omitting to do any act, or causing or procuring the commission or omission of any act, cause any unnecessary suffering, or, being the owner, permit any unnecessary suffering to be so caused to any animal; or

(b) shall convey or carry, or cause or procure, or, being the owner, permit to be conveyed or carried, any animal in such manner or position as to cause that animal any unnecessary suffering; or

(c) shall cause, procure, or assist at the fighting or baiting of any animal; or shall keep, use, manage, or act or assist in the management of, any premises or place for the purpose, or partly for the purpose of fighting or baiting any animal, or shall permit any premises or place to be so kept, managed, or used, or shall receive, or cause or procure any person to receive, money for the admission of any person to such premises or place; or

(d) shall wilfully, without any reasonable cause or excuse, administer, or cause or procure, or being the owner permit, such administration of, any poisonous or injurious drug or substance to any animal, or shall wilfully, without any reasonable cause or excuse, cause any such substance to be taken by any animal; or

(e) shall subject, or cause or procure, or being the owner permit, to be subjected, any animal to any operation which is performed without due care and humanity; or

(f) shall tether any horse, ass or mule under such conditions or in such manner as to cause that animal unnecessary suffering;

such person shall be guilty of an offence of cruelty within the meaning of this Act . . .

Keynote

As can be seen, the legislation anticipates virtually every conceivable example of cruelty which might be inflicted on animals. This offence can be committed by omission as well as by a positive 'action' (**see Crime, chapter 2**). Where an owner of the relevant animal is shown to have failed to have exercised reasonable care for it, he/she will be deemed to have 'permitted' cruelty (s. 1(2)).

Animals are also property under many circumstances and can therefore be 'stolen' or 'damaged' by some of the acts described above. (**See Crime, chapters 12 and 14.**)

An 'animal' for the purposes of this offence means any domestic or captive animal, which will include most forms of farm animal and domestic pets but not invertebrates (s. 15). Animals which are wild but which have become temporarily trapped are not necessarily 'captive' and each case will have to be determined on its own facts.

Unnecessary suffering has been held to be suffering which could have been avoided and the test as to whether an animal has suffered 'unnecessarily' is an objective one, that is, it will depend on the view of a reasonable bystander and not the actual state of mind of the defendant (*RSPCA* v *Isaacs* [1994] Crim LR 517).

8.8.1   Police Powers

A police officer may arrest without warrant anyone who he/she has reasonable cause to believe is guilty of an offence of cruelty which is punishable by imprisonment without the option of a fine. This expression would appear to mean that the power is available in respect of any act of cruelty under s. 1(1) except the offence of an owner permitting cruelty within s. 1(2) (see *Halsbury's Laws of England*, vol. 2, para. 459). The power applies if the officer witnesses the offence himself/herself or if a third person gives his/her name and address and provides information to the effect that such an offence was committed (s. 12(1)).

Section 12(2) of the 1911 Act goes on to provide a power of seizure in respect of any animal or vehicle stopped in connection with an offence of cruelty. Such powers would be governed by the Police and Criminal Evidence Act 1984 (**see chapter 2**).

It is worth remembering that some animals are capable of being damaged or stolen under the Theft Act 1968 and the Criminal Damage Act 1971 (**see Crime, chapters 12 and 14**), both of which create arrestable offences.

8.8.2 Police Powers: Injured Animals

Section 11 of the 1911 Act provides that:

> (1)   If a police constable finds any animal so diseased or so severely injured or in such a physical condition that, in his opinion, having regard to the means available for removing the animal, there is no possibility of removing it without cruelty, he shall, if the owner is absent or refuses to consent to the destruction of the animal, at once summon a duly registered veterinary surgeon, if any such veterinary surgeon resides within a reasonable distance, and, if it appears by the certificate of such veterinary surgeon that the animal is mortally injured, or so severely injured, or so diseased, or in such physical condition, that it is cruel to keep it alive, it shall be lawful for the police constable, without the consent of the owner, to slaughter the animal, or cause or procure it to be slaughtered, with such instruments or appliances, and with such precautions, and in such manner, as to inflict as little suffering as practicable, and, if the slaughter takes place on any public highway, to remove the carcase or cause or procure it to be removed therefrom.
>
> (2)   If any veterinary surgeon summoned under this section certifies that the injured animal can without cruelty be removed, it shall be the duty of the person in charge of the animal to cause it forthwith to be removed with as little suffering as possible, and, if that person fails so to do, the police constable may, without the consent of that person, cause the animal forthwith to be so removed.
>
> (3)   Any expense which may be reasonably incurred by any constable in carrying out the provisions of this section (including the expenses of any veterinary surgeon summoned by the constable, and whether the animal is slaughtered under this section or not) may be recovered from the owner summarily as a civil debt, and, subject thereto, any such expense shall be defrayed out of the fund from which the expenses of the police are payable in the area in which the animal is found.

Keynote

These very broad powers are of limited practical effect as they do not apply to the most frequently-encountered 'injured animals' — cats and dogs. 'Animals' for this purpose are confined to horses, mules, asses, bulls, sheep, goats and pigs (s. 11(4)).

Charitable organisations such as the RSPCA or the PDSA may assist in providing for injured animals.

8.9   Wild Mammals

Given the restrictions on the applicability of the cruelty offence (see **para. 8.8 above**), further protection was provided by the Wild Mammals (Protection) Act 1996.

Offence — Cruelty to Wild Mammals — Wild Mammals (Protection) Act 1996, s. 1

Triable summarily. Six months' imprisonment and/or fine.
(No specific power of arrest)

The Wild Mammals (Protection) Act 1996, s. 1 states:

If, save as permitted by this Act, any person mutilates, kicks, beats, nails or otherwise impales, stabs, burns, stones, crushes, drowns, drags or asphyxiates any wild mammal with intent to inflict unnecessary suffering he shall be guilty of an offence.

Keynote

As its title suggests, this Act only applies to wild mammals which are defined as any mammal which is not a domestic or captive animal within the meaning of the Protection of Animals Act 1911 (or the Protection of Animals (Scotland) Act 1912) (s. 3 of the 1996 Act).

8.9.1 Exceptions

Section 2 of the 1996 Act provides that:

A person shall not be guilty of an offence under this Act by reason of—
(a)   the attempted killing of any such wild mammal as an act of mercy if he shows that the mammal had been so seriously disabled otherwise than by his unlawful act that there was no reasonable chance of its recovering;
(b)   the killing in a reasonably swift and humane manner of any such wild mammal if he shows that the wild mammal had been injured or taken in the course of either lawful shooting, hunting, coursing or pest control activity;
(c)   doing anything which is authorised by or under any enactment;
(d)   any act made unlawful by section 1 if the act was done by means of any snare, trap, dog, or bird lawfully used for the purpose of killing or taking any wild mammal; or
(e)   the lawful use of any poisonous or noxious substance on any wild mammal.

Keynote

These exceptions are fairly wide and allow some acts which might be regarded as 'cruel' by many people to go unchecked. Section 2(a) also provides an opportunity for a defendant to claim that he/she was simply 'putting an animal out of its misery' caused by injuries inflicted by someone else.

8.9.2 Police Powers

Section 4 of the 1996 Act provides that:

Where a constable has reasonable grounds for suspecting that a person has committed an offence under the provisions of this Act and that evidence of the commission of the offence may be found on that person or in or on any vehicle he may have with him, the constable may—
(a)   without warrant, stop and search that person and any vehicle or article he may have with him; and
(b)   seize and detain for the purposes of proceedings under any of those provisions anything which may be evidence of the commission of the offence or may be liable to be confiscated under section 6 of this Act.

Keynote

Unlike the Protection of Animals Act 1911, the 1996 Act does not provide a power of arrest.

Section 6 empowers a court to order the confiscation of any vehicle or equipment used in the commission of the relevant offence.

8.10 Badgers

Because of the particular risk which faces badgers, both as a threatened species, and as a target of certain 'blood sports', there is specific legislation designed to protect them.

Offence — Taking, Injuring or Killing Badgers — Protection of Badgers Act 1992, s. 1(1)
Triable summarily. Six months' imprisonment and/or a fine.
(No specific power of arrest)

The Protection of Badgers Act 1992, s. 1 states:

A person is guilty of an offence if, except as permitted by or under this Act, he wilfully kills, injures or takes, or attempts to kill, injure or take, a badger.

Keynote

Section 1(2) creates a statutory presumption that a defendant was trying to kill, injure or take a badger if there is evidence from which that fact might reasonably be concluded. Such evidence might include any equipment which the defendant had with him/her or the presence of blood, hair etc. in a vehicle.

Sections 2 and 3 go on to create summary offences (punishable as for s. 1) of cruelty to badgers, digging for badgers and of interfering with badger setts.

Offence — Selling or Possessing a Live Badger — Protection of Badgers Act 1992, s. 4
Triable summarily. Fine.
(No specific power of arrest)

The Protection of Badgers Act 1992, s. 4 states:

A person is guilty of an offence if, except as permitted by or under this Act, he sells a live badger or offers one for sale or has a live badger in his possession or under his control.

8.10.1 Police Powers

Section 11 of the 1992 Act provides that:

Where a constable has reasonable grounds for suspecting that a person is committing an offence under the foregoing provisions of this Act, or has committed an offence under those provisions or those of the Badgers Act 1973 and that evidence of the commission of the offence is to be found on that person or any vehicle or article he may have with him, the constable may—
   (a)   without warrant stop and search that person and any vehicle or article he may have with him;

(b)   seize and detain for the purposes of proceedings under any of those provisions anything which may be evidence of the commission of the offence . . .

Keynote

These powers are governed by the Police and Criminal Evidence Act 1984 (**see chapter 2**).

The Badgers Act 1973 referred to has been repealed but presumably the inclusion of it in this section is to deal with any offences committed during the transitional period of the two Acts.

8.10.2   Defence

Section 7 of the 1992 Act provides that:

(1)   Subject to subsection (2) below, a person is not guilty of an offence under section 1(1) above by reason of—
    (a)   killing or taking, or attempting to kill or take, a badger; or
    (b)   injuring a badger in the course of taking it or attempting to kill or take it,
if he shows that his action was necessary for the purpose of preventing serious damage to land, crops, poultry or any other form of property.
    (2)   The defence provided by subsection (1) above does not apply in relation to any action taken at any time if it had become apparent, before that time, that the action would prove necessary for the purpose there mentioned and either—
    (a)   a licence under section 10 below authorising that action had not been applied for as soon as reasonably practicable after that fact had become apparent; or
    (b)   an application for such a licence had been determined.

Sections 8 and 9 create further exceptions from the provisions of the 1992 Act for people such as carriers or people taking injured badgers for treatment, while s. 10 provides for a system of licensing in relation to the possession etc. of badgers.

8.11   Pet Shops

Under the Pet Animals Act 1951 pet shops must be licensed by a local authority (s. 1(1)). The local authority will need to be satisfied about the cleanliness and suitability of any premises, together with the applicants' precautions for preventing the spread of disease (s. 1(2)).

It is a summary offence to sell pet animals in the street (s. 2) and it is also an offence to sell an animal as a pet to a person where there is reasonable cause to believe that the person is under 12 (s. 3).

CHAPTER NINE

OFFENCES RELATING TO PREMISES

9.1 Introduction

The law regulating the relationship between landlord and occupier falls largely within the province of 'civil' law. There are, however, a number of occasions and circumstances where the interests of landowners and occupiers conflict. Under some such circumstances the threat to public order, property or proprietary rights are considered to need the protection of the criminal law.

9.2 Criminal Trespass

The law of trespass, as with that of landlord and tenant, is generally dealt with a civil law and, contrary to the many notices that appear on premises, trespass is not usually a matter for prosecution. However, there are an increasing number of occasions where trespass to property can attract criminal liability. Some examples considered elsewhere would include:

- burglary (**see Crime, chapter 12**)
- trespassing with a firearm (**see chapter 5**)
- trespassing with a weapon (**see chapter 6**).

These occasions can apply to most types of premises and usually depend on the actions or intentions of the trespasser. Other examples can be found in relation to poaching (e.g. under the Game Act 1831 or the Night Poaching Acts).

Some offences of criminal trespass only apply to certain types of premises such as railways (**see chapter 13**) or areas of special protection under the Wildlife and Countryside Act 1981 and in such cases there is usually no need to prove any intention or specific behaviour on the part of the trespasser.

Whatever the remedy, whether it be civil or criminal, trespass involves an interference with someone's occupation of land or premises. This chapter is concerned with four main aspects of such interference, namely:

- aggravated trespass (which can include common as well as private land)
- interfering with the rights of occupiers/intending occupiers
- trespassing during court order
- nuisances on educational premises.

9.3 Aggravated Trespass

In the wake of several well-publicised encounters between police officers and groups of people who either had, or intended to trespass on someone else's land, parliament created a number of criminal offences (in the Criminal Justice and Public Order Act 1994). It also created specific police powers to deal with such occasions.

The types of trespass addressed by the 1994 Act can be categorised into four main groups:

- trespassing with the intention of disrupting or obstructing a lawful activity, or intimidating those engaged in it;
- two or more people trespassing with the purpose of residing on the land;
- 100 or more people attending a 'rave';
- residing in vehicles on land.

9.3.1 Trespass Intending to Obstruct, Disrupt or Intimidate

Offence — Trespass Intending to Obstruct, Disrupt or Intimidate — Criminal Justice and Public Order Act 1994, s. 68
Triable summarily. Three months' imprisonment and/or a fine.
(Statutory power of arrest)

The Criminal Justice and Public Order Act 1994, s. 68 states:

> *(1)   A person commits the offence of aggravated trespass if he trespasses on land in the open air and, in relation to any lawful activity which persons are engaging in or are about to engage in on that or adjoining land in the open air, does there anything which is intended by him to have the effect—*
> *(a)   of intimidating those persons or any of them so as to deter them or any of them from engaging in that activity,*
> *(b)   of obstructing that activity, or*
> *(c)   of disrupting that activity.*
> *(2)   Activity on any occasion on the part of a person or persons on land is 'lawful' for the purposes of this section if he or they may engage in the activity on the land on that occasion without committing an offence or trespassing on the land.*

Keynote

Examples of the sort of conduct envisaged would be 'eco-warriors' disrupting a building programme or saboteurs disrupting a fox hunt (see *Winder* v *DPP* (1996) 160 JP 713).

This is an offence of specific intent (**see Crime, chapter 1**) rather than consequence. Therefore what must be shown is the defendant's intention to bring about the effects set out at s. 68(1)(a)–(c). There is no need to specify which of the intended activities (i.e. deterring, obstructing or disrupting) in any charge and use of all three expressions is not bad for duplicity (*Nelder* v *DPP*, *The Times*, 11 June 1998).

The activity of the defendant can include 'anything' provided it was accompanied by the relevant intention. Before there can be an offence under s. 68, however, it must first be proved that the defendant was a trespasser on land in the open air.

The lawful activity that people are engaging in (or are about to engage in) must also take place (be proposed to take place) on the same land in the open air or on adjoining land in the open air.

Land does not include land forming part of a highway unless it is:

- a footpath, bridleway or byway open to all traffic or road used as a public path (as defined by s. 54 of the Wildlife and Countryside Act 1981) or
- a cycle track under the Highways Act 1980 or the Cycle Tracks Act 1984

(s. 68(5)).

Lawful activity is defined at s. 68(2) and is a very wide concept. Given the general permissive nature of our legal system (**see chapter 2**) a good rule of thumb in assessing the lawfulness of an activity might be to ask whether the activity in question is definitely 'unlawful'.

Power of Arrest

The Criminal Justice and Public Order Act 1994, s. 68 states:

(4)   A constable in uniform who reasonably suspects that a person is committing an offence under this section may arrest him without a warrant.

Keynote

This power of arrest is restricted to officers in uniform and only applies where the person is reasonably suspected of being in the act of committing the offence. It is not a pre-requisite that the person *is* actually committing the offence, only that the officer reasonably suspects him/her of doing so (see *Capon* v *DPP*, *The Independent*, 23 March 1998).

For a discussion of 'reasonable suspicion', **see chapter 2**.

Police Powers

The Criminal Justice and Public Order Act 1994, s. 69 states:

(1)   If the senior police officer present at the scene reasonably believes—
(a)   that a person is committing, has committed or intends to commit the offence of aggravated trespass on land in the open air; or
(b)   that two or more persons are trespassing on land in the open air and are present there with the common purpose of intimidating persons so as to deter them from engaging in a lawful activity or of obstructing or disrupting a lawful activity,
he may direct that person or (as the case may be) those persons (or any of them) to leave the land.
(2)   A direction under subsection (1) above, if not communicated to the persons referred to in subsection (1) by the police officer giving the direction, may be communicated to them by any constable at the scene.

Keynote

Although this power requires the senior officer present at the scene to have a reasonable *belief* (a narrower concept than mere suspicion) as to the circumstances set out at s. 69(1)(a) or (b), the power is available as a preventive measure and as a means of dealing with the incident after it has happened. In this respect it is far wider than the power of arrest above.

The direction to leave the land may be communicated to the relevant people by any police officer at the scene and there is no requirement for either officer to be in uniform.

Offence — Failure to Leave or Re-entry when Directed to Leave — Criminal Justice and Public Order Act 1994, s. 69(3)
Triable summarily. Three months' imprisonment and/or a fine.
(*Statutory power of arrest*)

The Criminal Justice and Public Order Act 1994, s. 69 states:

> *(3) If a person knowing that a direction under subsection (1) above has been given which applies to him—*
> *(a)   fails to leave the land as soon as practicable, or*
> *(b)   having left again enters the land as a trespasser within the period of three months beginning with the day on which the direction was given,*
> *he commits an offence . . .*

Keynote

In order to prove this offence it must be shown that the person knew of the direction and that it applied to him/her. Clearly the easiest way of ensuring both elements would be to serve a written notice on the person at the same time as communicating the direction to leave and to record any response.

Defence

The Criminal Justice and Public Order Act 1994, s. 69 states:

> *(4) In proceedings for an offence under subsection (3) it is a defence for the accused to show—*
> *(a)   that he was not trespassing on the land, or*
> *(b)   that he had a reasonable excuse for failing to leave the land as soon as practicable or, as the case may be, for again entering the land as a trespasser.*

Power of Arrest

The Criminal Justice and Public Order Act 1994, s. 69 states:

> *(5) A constable in uniform who reasonably suspects that a person is committing an offence under this section may arrest him without a warrant.*

Keynote

Although the direction to leave may be communicated by any police officer at the scene, the power of arrest is limited to officers in uniform. This power is subject to the same conditions as that at s. 68(4) above.

9.3.2 Two or More People Trespassing for Purpose of Residence

Offence — Two or More People Trespassing for Purpose of Residence — Criminal Justice and Public Order Act 1994, s. 61
Triable summarily. Three months' imprisonment and/or a fine.
(Statutory power of arrest)

The Criminal Justice and Public Order Act 1994, s. 61 states:

(1)   If the senior police officer present at the scene reasonably believes that two or more persons are trespassing on land and are present there with the common purpose of residing there for any period, that reasonable steps have been taken by or on behalf of the occupier to ask them to leave and—

(a)   that any of those persons has caused damage to the land or to property on the land or used threatening, abusive or insulting words or behaviour towards the occupier, a member of his family or an employee or agent of his, or

(b)   that those persons have between them six or more vehicles on the land,

he may direct those persons, or any of them, to leave the land and to remove any vehicles or other property they have with them on the land.

(2)   Where the persons in question are reasonably believed by the senior police officer to be persons who were not originally trespassers but have become trespassers on the land, the officer must reasonably believe that the other conditions specified in subsection (1) are satisfied after those persons became trespassers before he can exercise the power conferred by that subsection.

(3)   A direction under subsection (1) above, if not communicated to the persons referred to in subsection (1) by the police officer giving the direction, may be communicated to them by any constable at the scene.

Keynote

The key features of this section can be broken down into two parts. First, the senior officer present at the scene must have a reasonable belief that:

- at least two people *are trespassing* on land *and*
- that they are there with the common purpose of residing there *and*
- that reasonable (though not *all* reasonable) steps have been taken by/on behalf of the occupier to ask them to leave.

If this is the case, the senior officer must also have a reasonable belief that:

- *any* of those people have caused damage to the land or to property on the land *or*
- *any* of those people have used threatening, abusive or insulting words or behaviour towards the occupier or a member of the occupier's family or staff or one of his/her agents *or*
- those people have between them six or more vehicles on the land.

If all the conditions under the first heading, together with any of the conditions under the second are met, the officer may direct the people to leave the land and to take their vehicles and other property with them.

Most of the terms used in this section are defined under s. 61(9). 'Land' does not include buildings other than agricultural buildings or scheduled monument. It also has the same restrictions in relation to highways as those set out under s. 68 above.

The damaging of property includes the deposit of any substance capable of polluting the land and property for the purposes of damage has the same meaning as under the Criminal Damage Act 1971 (**see Crime, chapter 14**).

'Vehicles' do not have to be in a fit state for use on a road and can include a chassis or body (with or without wheels) appearing to have formed part of a vehicle. They also include caravans (as defined under the Caravan Sites and Control of Development Act 1960).

A person may be regarded as having a purpose of residing on land even though he/she has a home elsewhere.

Where the land concerned is 'common land', any references to trespassing will be construed as acts that are an infringement of the rights of the occupier or 'commoners' rights'. Where the public has access to that common land, references to the occupier will include the local authority (s. 61(7)).

If the people concerned were not originally trespassers (e.g. because they were given limited permission to be there), the senior officer present must have a reasonable belief that the relevant conditions above came about after the people became trespassers.

Again, the direction to leave the land may be communicated to the relevant parties by any police officer at the scene and there is no requirement for either officer to be in uniform.

Offence — Failure to Leave when Directed — Criminal Justice and Public Order Act 1994, s. 61(4)
Triable summarily. Three months' imprisonment and/or a fine.
(Statutory power of arrest)

The Criminal Justice and Public Order Act 1994, s. 61 states:

> (4)   If a person knowing that a direction under subsection (1) above has been given which applies to him—
> (a)   fails to leave the land as soon as reasonably practicable, or
> (b)   having left again enters the land as a trespasser within the period of three months beginning with the day on which the direction was given,
> he commits an offence . . .

Keynote

The requirements as to proof of knowledge here are the same as those under s. 69 above. This offence is the same as that under s. 69 with the exception of the word *reasonably* before practicable. This suggests that the law provides more latitude to people directed to leave the land under s. 61 than under s. 69, a suggestion that is also borne out by the wording of the respective defences.

Defence

The Criminal Justice and Public Order Act 1994, s. 61 states:

> (6)   In proceedings for an offence under this section it is a defence for the accused to show—
> (a)   that he was not trespassing on the land, or
> (b)   that he had a reasonable excuse for failing to leave the land as soon as reasonably practicable or, as the case may be, for again entering the land as a trespasser.

246

Power of Arrest

The Criminal Justice and Public Order Act 1994, s. 61 states:

> *(5)   A constable in uniform who reasonably suspects that a person is committing an offence under this section may arrest him without a warrant.*

Keynote

Although the direction to leave may be communicated by any police officer at the scene, the power of arrest is limited to officers in uniform. This power is subject to the same conditions as those at s. 68(4) and s. 69(5) above.

Power of Seizure

If a direction has been given under s. 61 and a police officer reasonably suspects that any person to whom it applies has, without reasonable excuse:

- failed to remove any vehicle on the land which appears to the officer to belong to him/her or to be in his/her possession or under his/her control; or
- entered the land as a trespasser with a vehicle within the period of three months beginning with the day when the direction was given

the officer may seize and remove the vehicle (s. 62).

9.3.3   One Hundred or More People Attending a Rave

Offence — Failing to Leave Land when Directed: 'Raves' — Criminal Justice and Public Order Act 1994, s. 63
Triable summarily. Three months' imprisonment and/or a fine.
(Statutory power of arrest)

The Criminal Justice and Public Order Act 1994, s. 63 states:

> *(2)   If, as respects any land in the open air, a police officer of at least the rank of superintendent reasonably believes that—*
> *(a)   two or more persons are making preparations for the holding there of a gathering to which this section applies,*
> *(b)   ten or more persons are waiting for such a gathering to begin there, or*
> *(c)   ten or more persons are attending such a gathering which is in progress,*
> *he may give a direction that those persons and any other persons who come to prepare or wait for or to attend the gathering are to leave the land and remove any vehicles or other property which they have with them on the land.*
> *(3)   A direction under subsection (2) above, if not communicated to the persons referred to in subsection (2) by the police officer giving the direction, may be communicated to them by any constable at the scene.*
> *(4)   Persons shall be treated as having had a direction under subsection (2) above communicated to them if reasonable steps have been taken to bring it to their attention.*
> *(5)   . . .*
> *(6)   If a person knowing that a direction has been given which applies to him—*
> *(a)   fails to leave the land as soon as reasonably practicable, or*
> *(b)   having left again enters the land within the period of 7 days beginning with the day on which the direction was given,*
> *he commits an offence . . .*

Keynote

Whereas the powers to direct people to leave land above can be exercised by the senior police officer present at the scene, the power under s. 63 is restricted to an officer of at least superintendent rank.

Again, the officer must have a reasonable belief that one of the circumstances set out in s. 63(2) applies in respect of any land in the open air. Those circumstances are that:

- at least two people are making preparations for the holding of a relevant gathering *or*
- at least ten people are waiting for such a gathering to begin or are attending such a gathering which is in progress.

Where this is the case, the officer may direct those people, together with any others who come to prepare, wait for or attend the gathering, to leave the land and to take their property with them.

Given the practical constraints on communicating with people at an open air 'rave', s. 63 makes provision for the communication of a direction to leave. If reasonable steps have been taken to bring the direction to the attention of the people concerned, s. 63(4) provides that the relevant person will be taken to have received it. Therefore a person cannot later argue that he/she had not been able to hear or understand the direction when it was given.

In common with the other sections above, the direction to leave the land may be communicated to the relevant people by any police officer at the scene and there is no requirement for either officer to be in uniform.

The elements of the type of gathering to which s. 63 applies are set out at s. 63(1):

> *(1)   This section applies to a gathering on land in the open air of 100 or more persons (whether or not trespassers) at which amplified music is played during the night (with or without intermissions) and is such as, by reason of its loudness and duration and the time at which it is played, is likely to cause serious distress to the inhabitants of the locality; and for this purpose—*
> *(a)   such a gathering continues during intermissions in the music and, where the gathering extends over several days, throughout the period during which amplified music is played at night (with or without intermissions); and*
> *(b)   'music' includes sounds wholly or predominantly characterised by the emission of a succession of repetitive beats.*

Keynote

This offence does not apply to gatherings licensed by an entertainment licence (s. 63(9)). 'Land in the open air' includes a place partly open to the air (s. 63(10)).

Defence

The Criminal Justice and Public Order Act 1994, s. 63 states:

> *(7)   In proceedings for an offence under this section it is a defence for the accused to show that he had a reasonable excuse for failing to leave the land as soon as reasonably practicable or, as the case may be, for again entering the land.*

Powers of Arrest

The Criminal Justice and Public Order Act 1994, s. 63 states:

(8)   A constable in uniform who reasonably suspects that a person is committing an offence under this section may arrest him without a warrant.

Keynote

In common with the other powers of arrest above, this power is limited to officers in uniform. It is also drafted in the present tense and is subject to the same conditions as those under ss. 61, 68 and 69 above.

In addition to these powers, raves have been held to amount to a public nuisance at common law and therefore the powers applicable to arrestable offences may be available (**see chapter 3**).

Power of Entry

If a superintendent or above reasonably believes that circumstances justifying the giving of a direction under s.63 above exist, he/she may authorise any police officer to enter the relevant land for the purposes of:

*   ascertaining whether such circumstances exist and
*   to exercise any power conferred by s. 63 or
*   to exercise the power of seizure below

(s. 64).

The power of seizure arises if a direction has been given under s. 63 and a police officer reasonably suspects that any person to whom it applies has, without reasonable excuse:

*   failed to remove any vehicle or sound equipment on the land which appears to the officer to belong to him/her or to be in his/her possession or under his/her control; or
*   entered the land as a trespasser with a vehicle within the period of seven days beginning with the day when the direction was given

the officer may seize and remove the vehicle or equipment (provided it does not belong to an exempt person) (s. 64(4) and (5)).

Exemptions

The directions will not apply to 'exempt persons' (s. 63(5) of the 1994 Act). Such people include the occupier of the land, any member of his/her family or his/her employees/agents, or anyone whose home is situated on the land (s. 63(10)).

The directions will not apply to a gathering covered by an entertainment licence (s. 63(9)(a)).

Powers to Stop People from Proceeding to 'Raves'

Under s. 65 of the 1994 Act, if a police officer in uniform reasonably believes that a person is on his/her way to a relevant gathering (as defined above) in relation to which a direction under s. 63(2) is in force, the officer may stop that person and direct him/her not to proceed in the direction of the gathering.

Offence — Failing to Comply with Direction not to Proceed — Criminal Justice and Public Order Act 1994, s. 65(4)
Triable summarily. Fine.
(*Statutory power of arrest*)

The Criminal Justice and Public Order Act 1994, s. 65 states:

> *(4) If a person knowing that a direction under [s. 65(1)] has been given to him fails to comply with that direction, he commits an offence.*

Keynote

This power may only be exercised at a place within five miles of the boundary of the site of the gathering (s. 65(2)).

Unlike the other directions discussed above, this one must be given by a police officer in uniform. The power does not appear to authorise the stopping of vehicles and therefore the general power under the Road Traffic Act 1988 would need to be used (**see Road Traffic, chapter 10**).

For the general provisions in relation to the stopping of people and vehicles, **see chapter 2.**

Power of Arrest

The Criminal Justice and Public Order Act 1994, s. 65 states:

> *(5) A constable in uniform who reasonably suspects that a person is committing an offence under this section may arrest him without warrant.*

9.3.4 Residing in Vehicles on Land

In addition to the powers set out above, the Criminal Justice and Public Order Act 1994 gives local authorities powers to deal with people living in vehicles on certain land.

Offence — Failure to Leave Land when Directed: Residing in Vehicles — Criminal Justice and Public Order Act 1994, s. 77
Triable summarily. Fine.
(*No specific power of arrest*)

The Criminal Justice and Public Order Act 1994, s. 77 states:

> *(1) If it appears to a local authority that persons are for the time being residing in a vehicle or vehicles within that authority's area—*
> *(a) on any land forming part of a highway;*
> *(b) on any other unoccupied land; or*
> *(c) on any occupied land without the consent of the occupier,*
> *the authority may give a direction that those persons and any others with them are to leave the land and remove the vehicle or vehicles and any other property they have with them on the land.*
> *(2) Notice of a direction under subsection (1) must be served on the persons to whom the direction applies, but it shall be sufficient for this purpose for the direction to specify the land and (except where the direction applies to only one person) to be addressed to all occupants of the vehicles on the land, without naming them.*

(3)   If a person knowing that a direction under subsection (1) above has been given which applies to him—

(a)   fails, as soon as practicable, to leave the land or remove from the land any vehicle or other property which is the subject of the direction, or

(b)   having removed any such vehicle or property again enters the land with a vehicle within the period of three months beginning with the day on which the direction was given,

he commits an offence . . .

Keynote

This offence is committed after notice has been served by a local authority. Sections 77 to 79 make provision for the manner in which the notices are to be served. A direction in the notice is operative in relation to people who return to the land with their vehicles within three months of the serving of the notice (s. 77(4)).

A person can be regarded as 'residing' on land notwithstanding that he/she has a home elsewhere (s. 77(6)).

Defence

The Criminal Justice and Public Order Act 1994, s. 77 states:

(5)   In proceedings for an offence under this section it is a defence for the accused to show that his failure to leave or to remove the vehicle or other property as soon as practicable or his re-entry with a vehicle was due to illness, mechanical breakdown or other immediate emergency.

Removal Order

A local authority may apply to a magistrates' court for a removal order if people continue to reside in their vehicles on land in contravention of a notice under s. 77 of the 1994 Act (s. 78(1)).

The local authority can enforce the order by entering onto the land in question and taking such steps as are mentioned in the order. Before doing so, however, the local authority must give the owner of the land, and the occupiers 24 hours' notice of its intention (unless the names and addresses cannot be ascertained after reasonable enquiries) (s. 78(3)).

Interim Possession Orders

Wilful obstruction of anyone executing such an order is a summary offence, punishable by a fine.

Under certain circumstances, a court may make an interim possession order when land is occupied by trespassers. Any person who is in occupation of those premises at the time such an order is served is, by the Criminal Justice and Public Order Act 1994, s. 76(6) to be treated for the purposes of the following offences as 'trespassers'.

Offence — Trespassing During Interim Possession Order — Criminal Justice and Public Order Act 1994, s. 76
Triable summarily. Six months' imprisonment and/or a fine.
(*Statutory power of arrest*)

OFFENCES RELATING TO PREMISES

The Criminal Justice and Public Order Act 1994, s. 76 states:

(1)   This section applies where an interim possession order has been made in respect of any premises and served in accordance with rules of court; and references to 'the order' and 'the premises' shall be construed accordingly.

(2)   Subject to subsection (3), a person who is present on the premises as a trespasser at any time during the currency of the order commits an offence.

(3)   No offence under subsection (2) is committed by a person if—

(a)   he leaves the premises within 24 hours of the time of service of the order and does not return; or

(b)   a copy of the order was not fixed to the premises in accordance with rules of court.

(4)   A person who was in occupation of the premises at the time of service of the order but leaves them commits an offence if he re-enters the premises as a trespasser or attempts to do so after the expiry of the order but within the period of one year beginning with the day on which it was served.

Keynote

For the power of entry without warrant for this offence, **see chapter 2**.

This offence is complete when the person is present as a trespasser during the currency of the order. There is no need to prove any further *actus reus* and there is no requirement for any *mens rea* (**see Crime, chapter 1**). Therefore, in practice, the person has got 24 hours from the time of service of the order to get out and stay out to avoid committing this offence. If the copy of the notice was not fixed to the premises as required, there will be no offence.

Power of Arrest

(7)   A constable in uniform may arrest without a warrant anyone who is, or whom he reasonably suspects to be, guilty of an offence under this section.

Keynote

This power of arrest is not restricted to someone who is reasonably suspected of being in the act of committing an offence, but applies to anyone who has, or who is reasonably suspected to have, committed the offence.

Section 75 creates several either way offences in relation to the making of false or misleading statements in order to obtain or resist the making of an interim possession order.

Offence — Making False Statement to Obtain Interim Possession Order — Criminal Justice and Public Order Act 1994, s. 75

Triable either way. Two years' imprisonment and/or a fine on indictment; six months' imprisonment and/or a fine summarily.

(No specific power of arrest)

The Criminal Justice and Public Order Act 1994, s. 75 states:

(1)   A person commits an offence if, for the purpose of obtaining an interim possession order, he—

(a)   makes a statement which he knows to be false or misleading in a material particular; or

(b)   recklessly makes a statement which is false or misleading in a material particular.

(2)   *A person commits an offence if, for the purpose of resisting the making of an interim possession order, he—*

   (a)   *makes a statement which he knows to be false or misleading in a material particular; or*

   (b)   *recklessly makes a statement which is false or misleading in a material particular.*

9.4   Other Offences Involving Premises

9.4.1   Depriving Residential Occupier

Offence — Depriving Residential Occupier — Protection from Eviction Act 1977, s. 1

Triable either way. Two years' imprisonment and/or a fine on indictment; six months' imprisonment and/or a fine summarily.

(No specific power of arrest)

The Protection from Eviction Act 1977, s. 1 states:

(1)   . . .

(2)   *If any person unlawfully deprives the residential occupier of any premises of his occupation of the premises or any part thereof, or attempts to do so, he shall be guilty of an offence unless he proves that he believed, and had reasonable cause to believe, that the residential occupier had ceased to reside in the premises.*

(3)   *If any person with intent to cause the residential occupier of any premises—*

   (a)   *to give up the occupation of the premises or any part thereof; or*

   (b)   *to refrain from exercising any right or pursuing any remedy in respect of the premises or part thereof;*

does acts likely to interfere with the peace or comfort of the residential occupier or members of his household, or persistently withdraws or withholds services reasonably required for the occupation of the premises as a residence, he shall be guilty of an offence.

(3A)   *Subject to subsection (3B) below, the landlord of a residential occupier or an agent of the landlord shall be guilty of an offence if—*

   (a)   *he does acts likely to interfere with the peace or comfort of the residential occupier or members of his household, or*

   (b)   *he persistently withdraws or withholds services reasonably required for the occupation of the premises in question as a residence,*

and (in either case) he knows, or has reasonable cause to believe, that that conduct is likely to cause the residential occupier to give up the occupation of the whole or part of the premises or to refrain from exercising any right or pursuing any remedy in respect of the whole or part of the premises.

Keynote

The first two offences can be committed by 'any person', whereas the offence under s. 1(3A) can only be committed by a landlord or his/her agent.

Where these offences are committed by a 'body corporate' (e.g. a company), then the company's officers may be guilty as well as the company itself (s. 1(6)).

The actions envisaged by s. 1(2) are those which amount to an eviction for any length of time (*R v Yuthiwattana* (1984) 80 Cr App R 55), while anything less (e.g. changing the locks of an entrance door while the residential occupier is out) would amount to an offence under s. 1(3) (*Costelloe v London Borough of Camden* [1986] Crim LR 249).

A caravan may amount to 'premises' for these offences (*Norton v Knowles* [1969] 1 QB 572).

Under s. 1 of the 1977 Act 'residential occupier' means:

> *(1)   . . . in relation to any premises, . . . a person occupying the premises as a residence, whether under a contract or by virtue of any enactment or rule of law giving him the right to remain in occupation or restricting the right of any other person to recover possession of the premises.*

Defence

In addition to the defence provided by s. 1(2) above, there is a specific defence to an offence under s. 1(3A):

> *(3B)   A person shall not be guilty of an offence under subsection (3A) above if he proves that he had reasonable grounds for doing the acts or withdrawing or withholding the services in question.*

9.4.2   Using or Threatening Violence to Secure Entry

Offence — Using or Threatening Violence to Secure Entry to Premises — Criminal Law Act 1977, s. 6(1)
Triable summarily. Six months' imprisonment and/or a fine.
(Preserved power of arrest)

The Criminal Law Act 1977, s. 6 states:

> *(1)   Subject to the following provisions of this section, any person who, without lawful authority, uses or threatens violence for the purpose of securing entry into any premises for himself or for any other person is guilty of an offence, provided that—*
> *(a)   there is someone present on those premises at the time who is opposed to the entry which the violence is intended to secure; and*
> *(b)   the person using or threatening the violence knows that that is the case.*

Keynote

This offence is not restricted to occasions involving 'residential occupiers'.

It is immaterial whether the violence used/threatened is against a person or property, or whether the purpose of the entry is to gain possession of the premises or any other purpose (s. 6(4)).

The fact that a person has any right or interest in premises will not constitute 'lawful authority' to use violence to secure entry into those premises (s. 6(2)).

For the power of entry for this offence, **see chapter 2**.

Defence

The Criminal Law Act 1977, s. 6(1A) states:

> *(1A)   Subsection (1) above does not apply to a person who is a displaced residential occupier or a protected intending occupier of the premises in question or who is acting on behalf of such an occupier; and if the accused adduces sufficient evidence that he was, or was acting on behalf of, such an occupier he shall be presumed to be, or to be acting on behalf of, such an occupier unless the contrary is proved by the prosecution.*

(2)   Subject to subsection (1A) above, the fact that a person has any interest in or right to possession or occupation of any premises shall not for the purposes of subsection (1) above constitute lawful authority for the use or threat of violence by him or anyone else for the purpose of securing his entry into those premises.

A 'displaced residential occupier' is defined at s. 12(3), which states:

(3)   Subject to subsection (4) below, any person who was occupying any premises as a residence immediately before being excluded from occupation by anyone who entered those premises, or any access to those premises, as a trespasser is a displaced residential occupier of the premises for the purposes of this Part of this Act so long as he continues to be excluded from occupation of the premises by the original trespasser or by any subsequent trespasser.

(4)   A person who was himself occupying the premises in question as a trespasser immediately before being excluded from occupation shall not by virtue of subsection (3) above be a displaced residential occupier of the premises for the purposes of this Part of this Act.

Keynote

The definition of a 'protected intending occupier' (s. 12A) must be one of the longest definitions in criminal law (if not criminal history) and takes up an entire page of the Act! The gist of it is that it will include someone with a freehold or leasehold interest in the premises which has at least two years left to run; where the person needs the premises for his/her own occupation as a residence; where he/she is excluded from those premises by a trespasser and where he/she has documentation to prove his/her right to occupy the premises. (For a full discussion, see *Blackstone's Criminal Practice*, 1999, section B13.27.)

Power of Arrest

The Criminal Law Act 1977, s. 6 states:

(6)   A constable in uniform may arrest without warrant anyone who is, or whom he, with reasonable cause, suspects to be, guilty of an offence under this section.

9.4.3   Failing to Leave

Offence — Failing to Leave Premises — Criminal Law Act 1977, s. 7
Triable summarily. Six months' imprisonment and/or a fine.
(*Preserved power of arrest*)

The Criminal Law Act 1977, s. 7 states:

(1)   Subject to the following provisions of this section and to section 12A(9) below, any person who is on any premises as a trespasser after having entered as such is guilty of an offence if he fails to leave those premises on being required to do so by or on behalf of—
(a)   a displaced residential occupier of the premises; or
(b)   an individual who is a protected intending occupier of the premises.

Power of Arrest

(6)   A constable in uniform may arrest without warrant anyone who is, or whom he, with reasonable cause, suspects to be, guilty of an offence under this section.

Defence

Section 7 of the 1977 Act provides the following defences:

(2)   In any proceedings for an offence under this section it shall be a defence for the accused to prove that he believed that the person requiring him to leave the premises was not a displaced residential occupier or protected intending occupier of the premises or a person acting on behalf of a displaced residential occupier or protected intending occupier.

(3)   In any proceedings for an offence under this section it shall be a defence for the accused to prove—

(a)   that the premises in question are or form part of premises used mainly for non-residential purposes; and

(b)   that he was not on any part of the premises used wholly or mainly for residential purposes.

Section 12A(9) of the 1977 Act provides:

(9)   In any proceedings for an offence under section 7 of this Act where the accused was requested to leave the premises by a person claiming to be or to act on behalf of a protected intending occupier of the premises—

(a)   it shall be a defence for the accused to prove that, although asked to do so by the accused at the time the accused was requested to leave, that person failed at that time to produce to the accused such a statement as is referred to in subsection (2)(d) or (4)(d) above or such a certificate as is referred to in subsection (6)(d) above; and

(b)   any document purporting to be a certificate under subsection (6)(d) above shall be received in evidence and, unless the contrary is proved, shall be deemed to have been issued by or on behalf of the authority stated in the certificate.

9.4.4   Found on Enclosed Premises

It is a summary offence under the Vagrancy Act 1824, s. 4 for any person to be found in or upon any dwelling house, warehouse, coach house, stable or outhouse or in any enclosed yard, garden or area for *any unlawful purpose*. The unlawful purpose must be to commit some specific criminal offence as opposed to simply trespassing and a purely immoral purpose, and without more, will not suffice (*Hayes v Stevenson* (1860) 3 LT 296).

Where the defendant is found on the enclosed premises, he/she can be arrested elsewhere (*R v Lumsden* [1951] 2 KB 513). Where a defendant was found in the garden of a house peering through the window at a woman inside intending to frighten her, his conduct was held to amount to an 'unlawful purpose' (*Smith v Chief Superintendent of Woking Police Station* (1983) 76 Cr App R 234). Had there not been any intention to frighten, the 'unlawful' purpose would probably not have been made out.

An area may still be 'enclosed' even though there are spaces left in-between buildings, arches etc. for access (*Goodhew v Morton* [1962] 2 All ER 771. Railway sidings have been held not to amount to 'enclosed' premises and the essential feature of yards and similar enclosed areas for the purposes of this offence would appear to be that they are small pieces of land ancillary to a building (see *Quatromini v Peck* [1972] 3 All ER 521).

There is no need to show that the person intended to carry out the relevant criminal offence at the time or at that particular place. If the person is found in a building and either intends to commit certain offences there or had that intention when entering, the relevant offences of burglary may well apply (**see Crime, chapter 12**).

Power of Arrest

Section 6 of the 1824 Act provides any person with a power to apprehend any other person found committing an offence against the Act and to take them to a justice of the peace or to deliver them to a constable.

There was some confusion as to the extent of this power in relation to police officers. This has now been clarified by the decision in *Gapper* v *Chief Constable of Avon & Somerset* [1998] 4 All ER 248 where it was held that the general power of arrest under s. 6 did apply to police officers.

9.4.5 Housing Act 1996

Under the Housing Act 1996 the High Court or a county court can grant an injunction to a local authority. Such an injunction, made under s. 152, can prohibit the respondent from:

- engaging in or threatening
- conduct that causes/is likely to cause
- nuisance or annoyance to
- a person residing in, visiting or otherwise engaged in lawful activity in
- 'residential premises' or their locality

The injunction can also prevent a person from entering residential premises or from using such premises for an immoral or illegal purpose.

The injunction is only available in relation to dwelling houses held under tenancies from a local authority or accommodation provided by such a local authority.

The court cannot grant an injunction unless it is of the opinion that:

- the respondent has used/threatened violence against someone residing in, visiting or otherwise engaged in lawful activity in relevant premises; and
- there is a significant risk of harm to that person or to a person of a similar description if the injunction is not granted.

Under s. 155(1) of the 1996 Act, the court may attach a power for a constable to arrest without warrant a person whom he/she has reasonable cause to suspect to be in breach of any of the provisions of the injunction.

Further, more limited powers, to apply for an injunction are available to local housing authorities, housing action trusts and charitable housing trusts under s. 153.

Although the availability of all such injunctions is restricted to the relevant local or housing authority, liaison between the police and such agencies now has a firm statutory basis (under ss. 5 and 6 of the Crime and Disorder Act 1998) and the Housing Act 1996 may provide a further option to police and local authorities in tackling crime and the fear of it. (For other measures to restrain anti-social or disturbing behaviour, **see chapters 3 and 7**.)

9.4.6 Nuisance on Educational Premises

There has been increasing concern over recent years that schools and the their premises are particularly vulnerable to crime and the fear of crime. There are two main areas of behaviour in relation to school premises which the law seeks to regulate; the carrying of certain weapons and the creation of nuisance or disturbance.

For the law relating to the carrying of weapons on school premises, **see chapter 6**.

There are virtually identical provisions made by two Acts in relation to nuisances on educational premises. The first Act, the Local Government (Miscellaneous Provisions) Act 1982, applies to premises that provide further or higher education and which are maintained by a local education authority. The second Act, the Education Act 1996, applies to premises that provide primary or secondary education (or both) and which are maintained by a local education authority or are grant-maintained.

Offence — Causing or Permitting Nuisance — Local Government (Miscellaneous Provisions) Act 1982, s. 40(1) and Education Act 1996, s. 547(1)
Triable summarily. Fine.
(No specific power of arrest. Statutory power of removal)

The Local Government (Miscellaneous Provisions) Act 1982, s. 40 and the Education Act 1996, s. 547 state:

> *(1)   Any person who without lawful authority is present on premises to which this section applies and causes or permits nuisance or disturbance to the annoyance of persons who lawfully use those premises (whether or not any such persons are present at the time) [shall be guilty of an offence].*

Keynote

These offences are designed to deal with many types of nuisance, from using school playing fields inappropriately to interrupting lessons and lectures.

To be guilty of the above offences the defendant must be on the relevant premises without lawful authority and to have caused (been directly responsible for bringing about) or permitted a nuisance or disturbance.

Both sections apply to playing fields and other premises for outdoor recreation of the relevant institution. In the case of schools, the Education Act 1996 provisions extend to playgrounds as well (s. 547(2)).

Compare this with the definition in relation to carrying weapons on school premises (**see chapter 6**).

Police Powers

Subsection (3) of each Act provides that:

> *(3)   If—*
> *(a)   a police constable or*
> *(b)   subject to subsection (5) . . ., a person whom a local education authority have authorised to exercise the power conferred by this subsection,*
> *has reasonable cause to suspect that any person is committing or has committed an offence under this section, he may remove him from the premises.*

Keynote

The nuisance or disturbance may have finished by the time the police officer gets to the premises but the wording of the subsection allows for the removal of the offender provided there is reasonable cause to suspect that he/she committed the offence.

The reference to subsection (5) is to a limitation on the appointment of such 'authorised' people in the case of certain types of school/establishment.

CHAPTER TEN

LICENSED PREMISES

10.1　Introduction

This chapter deals with the main provisions of the Licensing Act 1964, together with several related pieces of legislation. There are many other offences and powers which, though they involve intoxicating liquor and the behaviour of those who either wish to drink (or, as the 1964 Act terms it, 'consume') it or who have done so, are dealt with in other chapters (**see particularly chapter 4**).

Many other offences are committed by people who are drunk at the time; for the effects of this on culpability, **see Crime, chapter 4**.

The law in relation to licensed premises is under review and can be expected to change in the near future.

10.2　Definitions

10.2.1　Intoxicating Liquor

Section 201 of the Licensing Act 1964 defines intoxicating liquor as: 'spirits, wine, beer, cider and any fermented, distilled or spirituous liquor'.

Excluded from this definition are:

- any liquor which is of a strength not exceeding 0.5 per cent at the time of the sale or other relevant conduct;
- flavouring essences recognised as not being intended for consumption as, or with, alcoholic liquor;
- spirits or wine intended for use as a medicine and not as a drink;
- perfumes.

In determining the status of flavouring essences or medicinal wine, the opinion of HM Customs and Excise may be sought.

10.2.2 Low Alcohol Drinks and Shandy

The definition above was amended because of the problems in relation to low alcohol drinks which, at the time of their original manufacture, exceeded the permitted alcohol content and so attracted all the relevant provisions of the Licensing Act 1964. The amended definition was added by the Licensing (Low Alcohol Drinks) Act 1990.

Clearly drinks which have been *alcohol-free* throughout their manufacture are not included.

Another problematic area is whether or not the mixture of lemonade and beer is a intoxicating liquor. It has been held that shandy is 'intoxicating liquor' if mixed by barstaff at the time of the sale, even if its overall strength is below that of proprietary shandy sold by retailers (*Hall* v *Hyder* [1966] 1 All ER 661). Such a sale is treated as two separate sales of the different constituents. Shandy sold in cans or bottles will be below the prescribed strength at the time of sale and will not therefore count as intoxicating liquor.

10.2.3 Licensed Premises

Section 200 of the Licensing Act 1964 defines any reference to licensed premises as being:

> *A reference to premises for which a justices' licence [or occasional licence . . .] is in force and including a reference to any premises in respect of which a notice under section 199(c) of this Act is for the time being in force.*

This definition clearly includes both on and off licences together with other premises such as theatres which enjoy a notice under s. 199(c) of the 1964 Act.

10.2.4 Bars

The Licensing Act 1964, s. 201(1) defines a bar as including any place exclusively or mainly used for the *sale and consumption* of intoxicating liquor.

Certain places become excluded from this definition (by s. 171) when they are set apart for the service of table meals which are accompanied by intoxicating liquor. As long as the sale of such liquor is confined to people having those table meals, the definition will not apply provided also that:

- those parts of the premises are usually set aside for the service of table meals; and
- the intoxicating liquor is *ancillary* to the meals being served, i.e. the food and not the drink, is the primary purpose of that particular part of the premises.

The second requirement does *not* mean that drink can only be served to people who are seated at a table.

For these purposes a table meal will be a meal eaten by someone seated at a table (or at a counter or other structure which serves the purpose of a table) which is not used for the service of refreshments for consumption by other people.

The type of meal envisaged will include a substantial sandwich or ploughman's lunch but each case will be decided by the relevant court as a question of fact.

A 'bar counter' will always be 'a bar' (*Carter* v *Bradbeer* [1975] 2 All ER 571).

Whether a place is exclusively or mainly used for the sale *and* consumption of intoxicating liquor is a question of fact and you will need to prove both elements in any offence involving bars.

10.3 Justices' Licences

A licence issued by the licensing justices authorises the retail sale of intoxicating liquor. It also authorises the supply of intoxicating liquor to, or to the order of members of a club otherwise than by way of sale.

10.3.1 On-licence

An on-licence is a justices' licence authorising sale for consumption either on or off the relevant premises (s. 1(2)(a) of the Licensing Act 1964).

Under s. 1(3), it may authorise the sale of:

- intoxicating liquor of all descriptions; or
- beer, cider and wine only; or
- beer and cider only; or
- cider only; or
- wine only.

10.3.2 Off-licence

An off-licence is a justices' licence authorising sale for consumption off the relevant premises (s. 1(2)(b) of the 1964 Act).

Under s. 1(3)(b), it may authorise the sale of:

- intoxicating liquor of all descriptions; or
- beer, cider and wine only.

10.4 Other Types of Licence

10.4.1 Occasional Permissions

The Licensing (Occasional Permissions) Act 1983 allows licensing justices to grant 'occasional permissions' — that is, temporary authorities for the sale of intoxicating liquor — to organisations not operating for profit or private gain.

An example would be a church committee wishing to hold a fund-raising event for the rebuilding of a community centre.

Application and the granting of such occasional permissions is regulated in the 1983 Act, which also sets out in its schedule offences such as the making of false statements in connection with an application, breaching any conditions imposed, the illegal sale of intoxicating liquor and failing to allow a constable admission to premises where the permission is in force. (See particularly para. 9 of the schedule for the power of entry by a constable for the purpose of preventing or detecting these offences.)

10.4.2 Occasional Licences

The holder of an on-licence may apply for an occasional licence which allows the sale of intoxicants at a place other than the licensee's usual premises (s. 180 of the Licensing Act 1964).

Occasional licences are issued by a magistrates' court as opposed to licensing justices. They authorise the sale of intoxicants by the licensee at places such as dance halls, fêtes and exhibitions.

An occasional licence sets out the hours during which sale is permitted and runs for a period not exceeding three weeks. These licences will not apply on Christmas Day or Good Friday (s. 180(1)(b) of the 1964 Act).

The application procedure is set out under s. 180(7) of the 1964 Act. If applying in person an applicant must:

- give at least 24 hours' notice to his/her chief officer of police of his/her intention to apply;

- provide his/her name and address;

- provide details of the place and the occasion(s) for which the licence is required;

- state the period for which the licence is required; and

- specify the hours during which the licence is required.

Justices may grant an occasional licence without having a hearing.

In order to apply, an applicant must submit to the justices' clerk two copies of his/her written application within a period which is not less than one month before the licence is required. On receipt of the application the clerk will ordinarily send a copy to the chief officer of police. The police — or indeed anyone else — may object in writing within seven days of the justices' clerk sending that copy. In the event that someone does lodge an objection, the justices must hold a hearing.

If such a licence is granted and intoxicants are then sold outside the specified hours *but during the period when the occasional licence is still valid*, there is no offence of selling intoxicating liquor without a justices' licence contrary to s. 160 of the Licensing Act 1964 (*Southall* v *Haime* [1979] Crim LR 249).

The offence of selling liquor without a licence (s. 160(1)(b)) would be committed where intoxicating liquor is sold after the occasional licence has expired as the defendant would no longer be the holder of a licence in respect of those premises.

In practice, as most occasional licences are for one short function, e.g. dinners, dances, fêtes, etc., s. 160 will still apply to most cases where a sale takes place after the licence has expired.

The drinking of intoxicants outside permitted hours is dealt with under s. 59 of the 1964 Act. Section 59(3), however, states that the provisions preventing the sale of intoxicants outside permitted hours will not apply to intoxicants sold under an occasional licence.

Occasional Licences and 'Licensed Premises'

Although premises for which an occasional licence is in force will be classed as 'licensed premises' during the currency of that licence, they cease to be such when the licence expires. Therefore, drinking intoxicants after the hours specified in the occasional licence, even when the licence has expired, will not amount to an offence under s. 59 of the 1964 Act which only applies to 'licensed premises'.

In the case of a licensee permitting such behaviour, the police could object to any future application by that person (or for those premises), using evidence of non-conformity with the licensing conditions to support their objection.

Occasional Licences and Children under 14

Section 168 of the 1964 Act prohibits anyone under 14 years from being in bars of 'licensed premises' during permitted hours.

Because there are no 'permitted hours' for occasional licences, it would seem that there is no restriction in respect of children under 14 on premises which are the subject of such a licence.

Again, any evidence of the presence of children on such premises could be used by the police — or others — in opposing any future application for an occasional licence in respect of those premises or that applicant.

Note that the offence of selling intoxicating liquor to a person under 18 years (**see para. 10.6.3**), and the drinking of intoxicating liquor by such a person can be committed at premises licensed under an occasional licence.

10.5   Permitted Hours

'Permitted hours' are the general licensing hours for a district. These hours can be increased by a general order of exemption, a special order of exemption, a restaurant certificate (or 'supper hour extension'), a special hours certificate, and an extended hours order.

10.5.1   Permitted Hours in Licensed Premises

The Licensing Act 1964, s. 60(1) (as amended by s. 1 of the Licensing Act 1988 and the Licensing (Sunday Hours) Act 1995) states that:

> *(1)   Subject to the following provisions of this Part of this Act, the permitted hours in licensed premises shall be—*
> *(a)   on weekdays, other than Christmas Day or Good Friday, the hours from 11 am to 11 pm, and*
> *(b)   on Sundays, other than Christmas Day, and on Good Friday, the hours from 12 noon to 10.30 pm,*
> *(c)   on Christmas Day, the hours from 12 noon to 10.30 pm, with a break of four hours beginning at 3 pm.*

Section 60(4) of the 1964 Act states that:

(4) The licensing justices for any licensing district, if satisfied that the requirements of the district make it desirable, may by order modify for the district the hours specified in subsection (1)(a) of this section [so that the permitted hours begin at a time earlier than 11 am, but not earlier than 10 am].

Keynote

Permitted hours for licensed premises generally will be 11 am to 11 pm on weekdays; 12 noon to 10.30 pm on Sundays and Good Fridays; and 12 noon to 3 pm and 7 pm to 10.30 pm on Christmas Day.

These hours may be modified in accordance with s. 60(4) above.

The permitted hours for registered clubs are the same as the general licensing hours with the exception that, on Christmas Day, the hours are determined by the rules of the club in accordance with the conditions set out in s. 62(1).

'General licensing hours' means, in relation to any licensing district, the hours specified in s. 60(1)(a) to (b), with any modification applying in the district by virtue of s. 60(4) (s. 60(5)).

10.5.2 Off-licences

In premises licensed for the sale of intoxicating liquor for consumption off the premises only, the permitted hours on weekdays, other than Christmas Day shall begin at 8 am, and the permitted hours on Sundays, other than Christmas Day, shall begin at 10 am (s. 60(6) of the 1964 Act).

References to permitted hours shall (except in so far as the context otherwise requires), be construed in relation to any licensed premises where the permitted hours are restricted by any conditions attached to the licence, as referring to the hours as so restricted (s. 60(7)).

10.5.3 Offences

Offence — Selling Intoxicating Liquor Outside Permitted Hours — Licensing Act 1964, s. 59(1)
Triable summarily. Fine.
(No specific power of arrest)

The Licensing Act 1964, s. 59 states:

(1) Subject to the provision of this Act, no person shall, except during the permitted hours—
(a) himself or by his servant or agent sell or supply to any person in licensed premises in respect of which a club is registered any intoxicating liquor, whether to be consumed on or off the premises; or
(b) consume in or take from such premises any intoxicating liquor.

Keynote

The exceptions to s. 59 are shown below.

Section 59 does not apply in relation to intoxicating liquor sold under an occasional licence (s. 59(3)).

Exceptions

Section 63 of the Licensing Act 1964 (as amended by s. 2 of the Licensing Act 1988) states that:

(1)   Where any intoxicating liquor is supplied in any premises during the permitted hours, section 59 of this Act does not prohibit or restrict—

(a)   during the first 20 minutes after the end of any period forming part of those hours, the consumption of the liquor on the premises, nor, unless the liquor was supplied or is taken away in an open vessel, the taking of the liquor from the premises;

(b)   during the first half hour after the end of such a period, the consumption of the liquor on the premises by persons taking meals there, if the liquor was supplied for consumption as an ancillary to their meals.

(2)   Section 59 of this Act does not prohibit or restrict—

(a)   the sale or supply to, or consumption by, any person of intoxicating liquor in any premises where he is residing;

(b)   the ordering of intoxicating liquor to be consumed off the premises, or the despatch by the vendor of liquor so ordered;

(c)   the sale of intoxicating liquor to a trader for the purposes of his trade, or to a registered club for the purposes of the club; or

(d)   the sale or supply of intoxicating liquor to any canteen or mess.

(3)   Section 59 of this Act does not prohibit or restrict—

(a)   the taking of intoxicating liquor from the premises by a person residing there; or

(b)   the supply of intoxicating liquor for consumption on the premises to any private friends of a person residing there who are bona fide entertained by him at his own expense, or the consumption of intoxicating liquor by persons so supplied; or

(c)   the supply of intoxicating liquor for consumption on the premises to persons employed there for the purposes of the business carried on by the holder of the licence, or the consumption of liquor so supplied, if the liquor is supplied at the expense of their employer or of the person carrying on or in charge of the business on the premises.

(4)   In subsection (2) of this section, as it applies to licensed premises, and in subsection (3) of this section, references to a person residing in the premises shall be construed as including a person not residing there but carrying on or in charge of the business on the premises.

Keynote

The exceptions involving 'drinking-up' time under ss. 63(1)(a) and (b) are those most commonly encountered.

Where the licensee takes advantage of this exception and *bona fide* entertains private friends, he/she must not do so with his/her ordinary customers. A licensee cannot transform regular customers into private friends to evade the effects of s. 59(1).

Whether a person is a private friend is a question of fact for the justices in each case. The onus is on the defendant to prove that the people concerned were friends (*Atkins v Agar* [1914] 1 KB 26). These exemptions do not extend to other offences and if the friends are drunk on licensed premises they still commit an offence.

Offence — Failing to Abide by Terms of Off-Licence — Licensing Act 1964, s. 164(1)
Triable summarily. Fine.
(No specific power of arrest)

The Licensing Act 1964, s. 164 states:

(1)   Where a person, having purchased intoxicating liquor from the holder of a justices' licence which does not cover the sale of that liquor for consumption on the premises, drinks the liquor—

(a) in the licensed premises, or

(b) in premises which adjoin or are near the licensed premises and which belong to the holder of the licence or are under his control or used by his permission, or

(c) on a highway adjoining or near those premises,

then, if the drinking is with the privity or consent of the holder of the licence, the holder of the licence shall be liable . . .

Keynote

This offence can be committed in the off-licence premises, in premises adjoining them or on the highway near the premises. In all cases the privity or consent of the licensee must be proved.

To prove this offence you will also need to show more than mere knowledge by the licensee of the drinking. Evidence that the licensee provided glasses for drinking or set aside tables and chairs would support such proof.

10.6 Under Age Drinking

10.6.1 Children's Certificates

Under s. 168A(1) of the Licensing Act 1964 the holder of a justices' licence may apply to the licensing justices for a certificate in relation to any area of his/her premises which consists of, or includes a bar.

Under s. 168A(2), the licensing justices may grant an application for a certificate if it appears to them to be appropriate to do so, but shall not do so unless they are satisfied:

- that the area to which the application relates constitutes an environment in which it is suitable for people under 14 to be present; and

- that meals and drinks other than intoxicating liquor will be available for sale for consumption in that area.

Under s. 168A(3), where a children's certificate is in force, the holder of the justices' licence must keep posted, in some conspicuous place in the area to which the certificate relates, a notice which both:

- states that a children's certificate is in force in relation to the area; and

- explains the effect of the certificate and of any conditions attached to it.

**Offence — Failing to Conform to Conditions of Children's Certificate —
Licensing Act 1964, s. 168A(4)**
Triable summarily. Fine.
(No *specific power of arrest*)

The Licensing Act 1964, s. 168A states:

(4)   A person who fails to perform the duty imposed on him by subsection (3) of this section shall be guilty of an offence.

Keynote

Under s. 168(8), where it is alleged that a person was under 14 years, and he/she appears to the court to have been under that age, he/she shall be deemed to have been under that age, unless the contrary is shown.

Defence

Section 168A(5) of the 1964 Act provides that:

(5)   In any proceedings for an offence under subsection (4) of this section, it shall be a defence for the accused to prove that he took all reasonable precautions, and exercised all due diligence, to avoid the commission of the offence.

10.6.2   Person under 14 in Bar

Offence — Holder of Justices' Licence Allowing Person under 14 in Bar — Licensing Act 1964, s. 168(3)
Triable summarily. Fine.
(No specific power of arrest)

The Licensing Act 1964, s. 168 states:

(1)   The holder of a justices' licence shall not allow a person under fourteen to be in the bar of the licensed premises during the permitted hours.
(2)   No person shall cause or procure, or attempt to cause or procure, any person under fourteen to be in the bar of licensed premises during the permitted hours.
(3)   Where it is shown that a person under fourteen was in the bar of any licensed premises during the permitted hours, the holder of the justices' licence shall be guilty of an offence under this section unless he proves either—
(a)   that he exercised all due diligence to prevent the person under fourteen from being admitted to the bar, or
(b)   that the person under fourteen had apparently attained that age.

Keynote

To avoid liability under this section the licensee must prove that he/she exercised *all* due diligence to prevent the commission of the offence *or* that the person had apparently reached the age of 14.

Section 168 applies where:

- the person under 14, or a person in whose company he/she is, is eating a meal bought before the certificate ceased to be operational; and

- no more than 30 minutes have elapsed since the certificate ceased to be operational.

Defence

Section 168(3A) of the 1964 Act provides that:

(3A)   No offence shall be committed under subsection (1) of this section if—
(a)   the person under fourteen is in the bar in the company of a person who is eighteen or over,
(b)   there is in force a certificate under section 168A(1) of this Act relating to the bar, and
(c)   the certificate is operational or subsection (3B) of this section applies.

Section 168(3C) provides that:

(3C) No offence shall be committed under subsection (2) of this section if the person causes or procures, or attempts to cause or procure, the person under fourteen to be in the bar in the circumstances mentioned in paragraphs (a) to (c) of subsection (3A) of this section.

Keynote

Section 168(4) provides a defence if the person under 14 is:

• is the licence holder's child;

• resides in the premises, but is not employed there; or

• is in the bar solely for the purpose of passing to or from some part of the premises which is not a bar and to or from which there is no other convenient means of access (or exit).

Section 168(5) provides that:

(5) No offence shall be committed under this section if the bar is in any railway refreshment-rooms or other premises constructed, fitted and intended to be used bona fide for any purpose to which the holding of a justices' licence is merely ancillary.

10.6.3 Offences Involving a Person under 18

Offence — Providing Intoxicating Liquor for Person under 18 — Licensing Act 1964, s. 169(1)
Triable summarily. Fine. Discretionary forfeiture of licence on second offence.
(No specific power of arrest)

The Licensing Act 1964, s. 169 states:

(1) Subject to subsection (4) of this section, in licensed premises the holder of the licence or his servant shall not sell intoxicating liquor to a person under eighteen or knowingly allow a person under eighteen to consume intoxicating liquor in a bar nor shall the holder of the licence knowingly allow any person to sell intoxicating liquor to a person under eighteen.

Keynote

To prove the last two elements of this offence you must show *knowledge* on the part of the licensee (**see Crime, chapter 1**). Knowledge can include turning a blind eye (see *Buxton* v *Chief Constable of Northumbria* (1983) 148 JP 9).

Such proof is not needed in respect of offences of *selling* to a person under 18.

Defence

Section 169(4A) and (4B) provides that:

(4A) Where a person is charged under subsection (1) of this section with the offence of selling intoxicating liquor to a person under eighteen and he is charged by reason of his own act, it shall be a defence for him to prove—
(a) that he exercised all due diligence to avoid the commission of such an offence; or

(b)   that he had no reason to suspect that the person was under eighteen.

(4B)   Where the person charged with an offence under subsection (1) of this section is the licence holder and he is charged by reason of the act or default of some other person, it shall be a defence for him to prove that he exercised all due diligence to avoid the commission of an offence under that subsection.

Keynote

A licensee can be liable for an offence under this section, where he/she has delegated control to his servant, even though the licensee has no actual knowledge of the offence. A spouse is not necessarily a 'servant' for this purpose and this offence does not apply to a licensee's 'agent' (unlike the offence of selling outside permitted hours, **see para. 10.5.3**). A trainee branch manager of a brewery which also employs the licensee is the 'servant' of *that company* and not of the licensee for this purpose (*Russell* v *DPP* (1997) 161 JP 184).

Offence — Person under 18 Buying or Drinking Intoxicating Liquor in a Bar — Licensing Act 1964, s. 169(2)
Triable summarily. Fine.
(No specific power of arrest)

The Licensing Act 1964, s. 169 states:

(2)   Subject to subsection (4) of this section, a person under eighteen shall not in licensed premises buy or attempt to buy intoxicating liquor, nor consume intoxicating liquor in a bar.

Keynote

This is probably the most commonly encountered offence under the 1964 Act.

Note that you must prove that the relevant part of the offence took place in a 'bar' and you should consider the occasions where such drinking with a table meal may be permitted (**see para. 10.2.4**).

Offence — Buying Intoxicating Liquor for a Person under 18 — Licensing Act 1964, s. 169(3)
Triable summarily. Fine.
(No specific power of arrest)

The Licensing Act 1964, s. 169 states:

(3)   No person shall buy or attempt to buy intoxicating liquor for consumption in a bar in licensed premises by a person under eighteen.

Keynote

This offence only relates to drinking which is going to take place in a bar. If the drinking takes place, or is intended to take place elsewhere than in a bar, this offence would not be made out.

Offence — Delivery of Intoxicating Liquor to a Person Under 18 — Licensing Act 1964, s. 169(5)
Triable summarily. Fine.
(No specific power of arrest)

The Licensing Act 1964, s. 169 states:

> *(5)   Subject to subsection (7) of this section, the holder of the licence or his servant shall not knowingly deliver, nor shall the holder of the licence knowingly allow any person to deliver, to a person under eighteen intoxicating liquor sold in licensed premises for consumption off the premises, except where the delivery is made at the residence or working place of the purchaser.*

Keynote

See an exception to this offence, below.

Offence — Sending a Person under 18 for Intoxicating Liquor — Licensing Act 1964, s. 169(6)
Triable summarily. Fine.
(No specific power of arrest)

The Licensing Act 1964, s. 169 states:

> *(6)   Subject to subsection (7) of this section, a person shall not knowingly send a person under eighteen for the purpose of obtaining intoxicating liquor sold or to be sold in licensed premises for consumption off the premises, whether the liquor is to be obtained from the licensed premises or other premises from which it is delivered in pursuance of the sale.*

Keynote

This offence includes both on and off-licence premises; sending someone who is under 18 to either type of premises to buy drink would amount to an offence under this section.

Where the person under 18 is a member of the licensee's family or his/her servant and is employed as a messenger to deliver intoxicating liquor, no offence under s. 169(6), nor s. 169(5) above, is committed (s. 169(7)).

Approved Training Schemes

Section 170A of the Licensing Act 1964 allows the Secretary of State to make regulations for approval of training schemes. Under such a scheme, a person under 18 may be permitted to work behind a bar provided certain conditions in relation to his/her training and supervision are met. For information relating to such training schemes for the purpose of employing 16 and 17 years old in bars, see Home Office Circular 16/99.

10.6.4   Confiscation of Alcohol

The Confiscation of Alcohol (Young Persons) Act 1997, s. 1(1) states that:

> *(1)   Where a constable reasonably suspects that a person in a relevant place is in possession of intoxicating liquor and that either—*
> *(a)   he is under the age of 18; or*
> *(b)   he intends that any of the liquor should be consumed by a person under the age of 18 in that or any other relevant place; or*
> *(c)   a person under the age of 18 who is, or has recently been, with him has recently consumed intoxicating liquor in that or any other relevant place,*
> *the constable may require him to surrender anything in his possession which is, or which the constable reasonably believes to be, intoxicating liquor and to state his name and address.*

Keynote

It was made quite clear during the passage of the 1997 Act that it did not impose a *duty* on police officers to confiscate intoxicating liquor (see HC Official Report, 6th series, 24 January 1977, 288). This is a discretionary power for police officers to exercise as they deem fit.

It is unusual that the wording of the section says 'either', then goes on to give *three* instances where the power will be available. However, if one of the instances at s. 1(1)(a)–(c) applies the police officer may require the person concerned to:

- surrender anything that is, or that the officer reasonably *believes* (a narrower expression that 'suspects') to be intoxicating liquor; and
- state his/her name and address.

The requirement for the person to state his/her name and *his/her own address* appears to be quite specific. However, a similar provision under s. 170 of the Road Traffic Act 1998 (duty to give details after an accident; **see Road Traffic, chapter 4**) has been held to be satisfied where the person concerned gave the name and address of his/her solicitor (*DPP* v *McCarthy*, *The Times*, 8 January 1999). Given that the above power relates principally to young people, it would seem unlikely that anything less than their own personal details would satisfy the requirements of this section. It is an important point, however, because failure to comply with either requirement under s. 1(1) triggers the power of arrest under s. 1(5) (see below).

Under s. 1(2), the officer may dispose of *anything* surrendered to him/her in answer to the making of such a requirement. This wide discretionary power is not limited to intoxicating liquor and the officer could dispose of any other drink surrendered under this section (see HC Official Report SC C, 12 February 1997).

Offence — Failing to Surrender Intoxicating Liquor — Confiscation of Alcohol (Young Persons) Act 1997, s. 1(3)
Triable summarily. Fine.
(*Statutory power of arrest*)

The Confiscation of Alcohol (Young Persons) Act 1997, s. 1 states:

> (3) *A person who fails without reasonable excuse to comply with a requirement imposed on him under subsection (1) commits an offence.*

Keynote

Where a constable imposes a requirement on a person under s. 1(1) above, he/she must inform that person of his/her suspicion and that to fail without reasonable excuse to comply with such a requirement is an offence (s. 1(4)).

Under s. 1(6), a 'relevant place' is:

- any public place, other than licensed premises; or

- any place, other than a public place, to which that person has unlawfully gained access;

and for this purpose a place is a public place if, at the material time, the public or any section of the public has access to it — on payment or otherwise — as of right or by virtue of express or implied permission. Therefore the power may be exercised in any public place (as defined above) not being 'licensed premises', an expression that includes off-licenses (**see para. 10.2.3**). It may also be exercised in any other place that is not a public place to which the person has gained access unlawfully. This second expression suggests that the person must, as a matter of fact, have gained access to the place unlawfully — as opposed to the officer simply 'suspecting' or 'believing' that to be the case. It also suggests that, if the person was originally in the place lawfully but was later asked to leave, the power would not apply as the person's access would not have been 'unlawfully gained'. The section does not provide the police officer with a power of entry, nor a power to search.

The 1997 Act provides a useful power which might be considered in relation to events such as parties and 'raves' (**see chapter 9**).

Intoxicating liquor and licensed premises have the same meaning as in the Licensing Act 1964 (s. 1(7) of the 1997 Act).

Power of Arrest

Under s. 1(5) of the 1997 Act a constable may arrest without warrant a person who fails to comply with a requirement imposed on him/her under s. 1(1).

Perhaps unusually, this power is not restricted to police officers in uniform. It is triggered when the person fails to comply with either of the requirements under s. 1(1). Although the *offence* states that the failure must be without reasonable excuse, there is no such restriction on the power of arrest which becomes available once the person fails to comply with the requirement apparently whether that failure is supported by a reasonable excuse or not.

10.7 Drunkenness

Offence — Permitting Drunkenness — Licensing Act 1964, s. 172(1)
Triable summarily. Fine.
(*No specific power of arrest*)

The Licensing Act 1964, s. 172 states:

(1) The holder of a justices' licence shall not permit drunkenness or any violent, quarrelsome or riotous conduct to take place in the licensed premises.

Keynote

As this offence applies only to the licensee, you would usually need to show that he/she was aware of the drunken person's presence or that he/she was negligent in that regard.

If charged with permitting drunkenness, the onus is on the licensee to prove that he/she took all reasonable steps to prevent it happening.

Offence — Selling Intoxicating Liquor to a Drunk Person — Licensing Act 1964, s. 172(3)
Triable summarily. Fine.
(**No specific power of arrest**)

The Licensing Act 1964, s. 172 states:

> *(3) The holder of a justices' licence shall not sell intoxicating liquor to a drunken person.*

Offence — Procuring Intoxicating Liquor for a Drunk Person — Licensing Act 1964, s. 173(1)
Triable summarily. Fine.
(**No specific power of arrest**)

The Licensing Act 1964, s. 173 states:

> *If any person in licensed premises procures or attempts to procure any intoxicating liquor for consumption by a drunken person he shall be guilty of an offence . . .*

Offence — Aiding a Drunk Person to Obtain Intoxicating Liquor — Licensing Act 1964, s. 173(2)
Triable summarily. Fine.
(**No specific power of arrest**)

The Licensing Act 1964, s. 173 states:

> *(2) If any person aids a drunken person in obtaining or consuming intoxicating liquor in licensed premises he shall be guilty of an offence . . .*

Keynote

Where a licensee sells drink to someone who is drunk (s. 172(3)), it is an offence of absolute liability (**see Crime, chapter 1**). Therefore it is no defence to show that the licensee or his/her servants did not in fact know that the person was drunk. There is no requirement that the relevant liquor must be consumed for this offence to be complete.

The offence under s. 173 (procuring etc. for a person who is drunk) will apply to all licensed premises, including theatre bars and premises for which there is an occasional licence in force (**see para. 10.4.2**).

10.7.1   Power to Exclude Drunks

Section 174 of the Licensing Act 1964 provides that:

> *(1) Without prejudice to any other right to refuse a person admission to premises or to expel a person from premises, the holder of a justices' licence may refuse to admit to, or may expel from the licensed premises any person who is drunken, violent, quarrelsome or disorderly, or whose presence in the licensed premises would subject the licence holder to a penalty under this Act.*

Offence — Failing to Leave Premises when Required — Licensing Act 1964, s. 174(2)
Triable summarily. Fine.
(**No specific power of arrest**)

The Licensing Act 1964, s. 174 states:

> *(2)   If any person liable to be expelled from licensed premises under this section, when requested by the holder of the justices' licence or his agent or servant or any constable to leave the premises, fails to do so, he shall be liable . . .*

Keynote

Other rights to refuse admission would include a person's common law right to revoke an otherwise open invitation or 'licence' to enter his/her premises.

Examples of situations where the presence of someone would make the licensee liable to a penalty would include people who were drunk or children under 14 (subject to the exceptions above).

In proving the offence under s. 174(2) you must show:

- that the defendant was drunk, violent, quarrelsome or disorderly; and

- that a request to leave had been made by the licensee, servant or constable; and

- that the defendant failed to leave.

Note that the constable is there to help the licensee or servant, not to expel the person of his/her own volition.

10.7.2   Found Drunk

Offence — Being Found Drunk — Licensing Act 1872, s. 12
Triable summarily. Fine.
(Statutory power of arrest)

The Licensing Act 1872, s. 12 states:

> *Every person found drunk in any highway or other public place, whether a building or not, or on any licensed premises, shall be liable . . .*

Keynote

This offence is committed if a person is on the highway or public place and shown to be drunk. It does not matter that person is only there briefly or of his/her own volition.

'Other public place' will include all places to which the public have access (whether on payment or otherwise).

The offence has held to apply to the licensee when found drunk on the licensed premises, even when those premises were not open to the public (see *Evans* v *Fletcher* (1926) 135 LT 153).

The drunkenness must be as a result of excessive consumption of *alcohol*; if the person's state is caused by some other intoxicant, e.g. glue solvents, the offence is not made out (*Lanham* v *Rickwood* (1984) 148 JP 737). The same ruling applies to a person who is disorderly whilst drunk (**see chapter 4**).

Under the Licensing Act 1902, s. 1 a person found drunk in a highway or public place is liable to arrest if he/she is incapable of taking care of himself/herself. The power is not restricted to police officers and may be used where there is an honest belief based on reasonable grounds that the person is committing this offence (see *Trebeck* v *Croudace* [1918] 1 KB 158).

On arresting a person for this offence, a police officer may, if he/she thinks fit, take the person to an approved treatment centre under s. 34 of the Criminal Justice Act 1972. During the journey to such a treatment centre the person will be deemed to be in lawful custody. Section 34 does not allow a person to be detained at the centre and does not preclude any charge being brought in relation to the offence.

For the offence of being drunk in charge of a carriage (under s. 12 of the Licensing Act 1872), **see Road Traffic, chapter 5**.

10.8 Licensed Premises

10.8.1 Failing to Produce a Licence

Offence — Failing to Produce a Licence — Licensing Act 1964, s. 185
Triable summarily. Fine.
(No specific power of arrest)

The Licensing Act 1964, s. 185 states:

> *If the holder of a justices' licence, an occasional licence, a canteen licence, an order under section 87A of this Act or a general or special order of exemption, on being ordered by a justice of the peace or constable to produce it for examination, fails to do so within a reasonable time he shall be liable . . .*

Keynote

Section 87A is unlikely to be relevant on many occasions — it relates to on-licences at vineyards. There appears to be no restriction on the time or place when such a demand can be made. However, for a power of entry onto licensed premises, see below.

10.8.2 Power of Constable to Enter Licensed Premises

The Licensing Act 1964, s. 186(1) provides that:

> *(1)   For the purpose of preventing or detecting the commission of any offence against this Act, a constable may enter licensed premises, a licensed canteen or premises for which or any part of which a special hours certificate is in force under section 78 or 78ZA of this Act—*
> *(a)   at any time within the hours specified in relation to the premises in subsection (1A) of this section, and*
> *(b)   in the case of premises for which a justices' licence is in force or a licensed canteen, at any time outside those hours when he suspects, with some reasonable cause, that such an offence is being or is about to be committed there.*

Keynote

The power to enter under the circumstances in s. 186(1)(b) has a preventive element and may be exercised where the officer has reasonable cause to suspect that an offence is about to be committed.

The order under s. 78ZA is another rare one — it relates to special hours certificates to registered clubs undergoing alteration.

Under s. 186(1A), the hours referred to above are:

- in the case of licensed premises (other than premises which are licensed premises by virtue only of an occasional licence) or a licensed canteen, the permitted hours and the first half hour after the end of any period forming part of those hours;

- in the case of premises for which an occasional licence is in force, the hours specified in the licence;

- in the case of premises for which (or for any part of which), a special hours certificate is in force under s. 78 (or s. 78ZA) of the 1964 Act, the hours beginning at 11 pm and ending 30 minutes after the end of the permitted hours fixed by s. 76 of the Act.

Offence — Failing to Admit a Constable — Licensing Act 1964, s. 186(2)
Triable summarily. Fine.
(No specific power of arrest)

The Licensing Act 1964, s. 186 states:

> (2)   *If any person, himself or by any person in his employ or acting with his consent, fails to admit a constable who demands entry to premises in pursuance of this section he shall be liable.*

Keynote

The effect of the above is that a constable may enter:

- **Licensed premises** (other than premises covered only by an occasional licence) — including licensed canteens — at any time during permitted hours and during the first half hour following the end of any period forming part of those hours.

- **Premises for which an occasional licence is in force** — during the hours specified in that licence.

- **Premises for which (or for any part of which), a special hours certificate is in force** — during the hours beginning at 11 pm and ending 30 minutes after the end of the permitted hours.

- **Any licensed premises for which a justices' licence is in force** (including a licensed canteen) — at any time outside the permitted hours where the constable reasonably suspects that an offence against the Licensing Act 1964 is being, or is about to be committed.

A constable seeking admission must identify himself/herself and demand admission (*Alexander* v *Rankin* [1899] 1 F 58).

The power to enter licensed premises during and immediately after permitted hours does not require any suspicion of an offence being committed. Although the offence under s. 186(2) carries no power of arrest, there is a power of arrest in relation to the obstruction of a police officer under circumstances where a breach of the peace is likely to be occasioned (see **Crime, chapter 8**).

Section 187 makes provision for a warrant to enter and search licensed premises to be issued by a magistrate.

10.8.3 Exclusion of People from Licensed Premises

Under the Licensed Premises (Exclusion of Certain Persons) Act 1980, courts may exclude people from licensed premises.

The power applies where any offence involving violence, or the threat of violence is committed on licensed premises. In such cases, a court may make an order that the offender cannot enter those licensed premises (or any other licensed premises specified) without the express consent of the licensee or his/her agent. Such an order may remain in force for any period between three months and two years.

Power to Expel

The Licensed Premises (Exclusion of Certain Persons) Act 1980, s. 3 provides that:

Without prejudice to any other right to expel a person from premises, the licensee of licensed premises or his servant or agent may expel from those premises any person who has entered or whom he reasonably suspects of having entered the premises in breach of an exclusion order; and a constable shall on the demand of the licensee or his servant or agent help to expel from licensed premises any person whom the constable reasonably suspects of having entered in breach of an exclusion order.

Keynote

This power is similar to that above (see **para. 10.7.1**) in that the constable is obliged to help the licensee etc. to expel the person.

Offence — Entering Licensed Premises in Breach of Exclusion Order — Licensed Premises (Exclusion of Certain Persons) Act 1980, s. 2(1)
Triable summarily. One month's imprisonment and/or fine.
(No specific power of arrest)

The Licensed Premises (Exclusion of Certain Persons) Act 1980, s. 2 states:

(1)   A person who enters any premises in breach of an exclusion order shall be guilty of an offence.

Keynote

In addition to exclusion, a person who has been charged with an offence may be subject to certain bail conditions which also prevent him/her from entering particular premises (for bail generally, **see Evidence and Procedure, chapter 5**).

10.9   Betting and Gaming on Premises

The legislation regulating betting and gaming can be found in:

- the Betting, Gaming and Lotteries Act 1963; and
- the Gaming Act 1968.

10.9.1   Betting

Betting is not defined in the Betting, Gaming and Lotteries Act 1963 but is usually taken to mean the staking of money or something of value on the forecast outcome of an event which is in doubt at the time the stake is made.

Generally betting is not prohibited but it does become unlawful under certain circumstances:

- If it takes place on premises other than authorised premises, such as licensed dog-tracks and betting offices (s. 1). If everyone involved in the betting either lives or works on the premises concerned, the provisions of the 1963 Act do not apply.

- If it takes place in a street or public place (other than places such as licensed racetracks on race days) (s. 8).

- If it involves a person under 18 (s. 21).

Bookmakers and Betting Offices

A bookmaker is a person who receives or negotiates bets, whether on his/her own account or as a servant or agent to another (s. 55 of the 1963 Act). Bookmakers working for themselves or for others require a permit (unless they are registered pools promoters) (s. 2). Carrying on a business as a bookmaker without a permit to do so is a summary offence (s. 21).

Betting offices must be licensed and s. 10 and sch. 4 to the 1963 Act set out the conditions which must be adhered to by betting offices. These conditions include the opening hours (between 7 am and 6.30 pm), the posting of certain notices in betting offices and the provision of entertainment and refreshment. They also include strict regulation of any advertising of or in a betting office. At the time of writing, betting offices must remain closed on Christmas Day, Good Friday and Sundays.

Enforcement

Under s. 10(2) of the 1963 Act the licensee (or servant) may refuse to admit or may expel anyone who is drunk, quarrelsome or violent or whose presence on the premises is likely to attract a penalty for the licensee (e.g. children). These provisions are similar to those relating to bars and pubs under the Licensing Act 1964 (**see para. 10.7**).

Police Powers

Sections 10 of the 1963 Act provides that:

> *(3)   Any constable may, on the request of the licensee or any servant or agent of the licensee, help to expel from a licensed betting office any person whom the constable has reasonable cause to believe to be liable to be expelled therefrom under subsection (2) of this section; and the constable may use such force as may be required for that purpose.*
> *(4)   Any constable may enter any licensed betting office for the purpose of ascertaining whether the provisions of subsection (1) of this section are being complied with, and any person who obstructs any constable in the exercise of his powers under this subsection shall be liable on summary conviction to a fine.*

Keynote

As with the corresponding provisions for licensed premises, the power given to police officers is to assist the licensee (or servant) to remove people from the relevant premises.

A person convicted of an ofence under s. 10(1) (failing to manage the premises in accordance with the provisions of sch. 4) may have his/her betting office licence cancelled by the court (s. 10A).

10.9.2 Gaming

The main piece of legislation regulating gaming is the Gaming Act 1968. Divided into four parts, the Act regulates:

- gaming elsewhere other than on licensed or registered premises (Part I);
- gaming on premises which are licensed or registered (Part II);
- gaming machines (Part III);
- gaming at functions and parties (Part IV).

Unlike betting, 'gaming' is defined and means the playing of a game of chance for winnings in money (or money's worth) whether anyone playing the game is at risk of losing any such money/money's worth or not (Gaming Act 1968, s. 52(1)).

This definition means that even 'rigged' games or purely social games where there is no risk of losing money/money's worth are covered.

'Games of chance' do not include athletic games or sports; they do however include hybrid games of mixed chance and skill (such as many card games).

Gaming other than on Authorised Premises

As with betting, there are restrictions on gaming in some premises and public places. Where the people playing the game are all residents in a private dwelling or a similar place which is not used as a place of business, gaming may be permitted under certain conditions (see s. 2 of the 1968 Act). For such games to be permitted, no charges must be levied, either on people taking part in such games or on their stakes/winnings (ss. 3 and 4).

It is a summary offence to take part in gaming in a street or public place (s. 5). It is however permissible to play games of cribbage and dominoes and other games approved by the licensing justices on licensed premises (**see above**) (s. 6). Under s. 6(4) justices may impose restrictions on the playing of those games as far as they consider it necessary to ensure that such gaming does not involve high stakes or does not become an inducement to people to come to the premises.

Gaming using some types of gaming machines with limited payouts may also be approved by the licensing justices in respect of licensed premises (see s. 34 and sch. 9).

Gaming on Authorised Premises

Gaming on premises which are licensed or registered is subject to strict regulations under the 1968 Act. The most important of those regulations relate to the age and status of the people taking part (i.e. they must be at least 18 years old and club members/guests).

Section 43 provides a power for police officers to enter premises licensed under the 1968 Act at any reasonable time to ascertain whether the Act has been contravened (**see below**).

The use of gaming machines is regulated by the 1968 Act which generally creates two main types of machine:

- Jackpot machines which:

  - have a charge limit for playing;
  - cannot be used when the relevant premises are open to the public;
  - must only have prizes in coins from that machine; and
  - for which premises must have a licence or be registered (under sch. 7).

- Amusements with prize machines which:

  - have a charge limit for playing;
  - have restrictions on prize money/tokens;
  - have restrictions on non-money prizes; and
  - for which premises must: have a permit (under sch. 9); have a licence or be registered and have no jackpot machines; form part of a travelling showman's 'pleasure fair'.

The respective amounts that can be charged and won by machine owners and players changes frequently and the most recent regulations should be referred to when dealing with gaming offences under the Act.

There are, however, general exemptions for all gaming machines when they are used in connection with non-commercial entertainment on unlicensed or unregistered premises where all proceeds after expenses have been deducted are used other than for private gain (e.g. dinner-dances, garden fêtes etc.) (s. 33).

Further concessions are made for gaming (by machines or otherwise) at charitable and not-for-profit events (Part IV). The 1968 Act imposes certain restrictions on admission charges, the type of gaming which may take place and the total value of any prizes. As might be expected, all proceeds after the deduction of reasonable costs must be used other than for private gain.

Casinos

Casinos must have a gaming licence. Such licences are only issued after a very thorough process which includes an examination of the suitability of both the applicant and the location of the premises. Applicants must specify which of the permitted games (see sch. 2 of the 1968 Act) will be played at the club; they must also obtain a Certificate of Consent from the Gaming Board of Great Britain to support their application. The certificate will specify the period for which the licence may be requested. Applicants will then have to appear before a hearing held by the justices four times a year. The Gaming Board are very influential in the process of licensing and renewal and should be consulted in any cases involving impropriety by a licence holder or on premises licensed for gaming.

Police Powers

Section 43 of the 1968 Act provides that:

> *(2)   Any . . . constable may at any reasonable time enter any premises in respect of which a licence under this Act is for the time being in force, and while on the premises may—*
>
> *(a)   inspect the premises and any machine or other equipment on the premises, and any book or document on the premises, which he reasonably requires to inspect for the purpose of ascertaining whether a contravention of this Act or of any regulations made under it is being or has been committed;*
>
> *(b)   take copies of any such book or document or of any entry in it; and*
>
> *(c)   if any information reasonably required by him for that purpose is contained in a computer and is accessible from the premises, require it to be produced in a form in which it can be taken away and in which it is visible and legible.*
>
> *(3)   If any person, being the holder of a licence under this Act in respect of any premises or a person acting on behalf of the holder of such a licence—*
>
> *(a)   fails without reasonable excuse to admit . . . [a] constable who demands admission to the premises in pursuance of subsection (2) of this section, or*
>
> *(b)   on being required by . . . [a] constable to do so, fails without reasonable excuse to permit the . . . constable to inspect the premises or any machine or other equipment on the premises, or*
>
> *(c)   on being required by . . . [a] constable to produce any book or document in his possession or under his control which relates to those premises and which the . . . constable reasonably requires to inspect for the purpose specified in subsection (2) of this section, fails without reasonable excuse to produce it to the . . . constable and to permit the . . . constable (if he so desires) to take copies of it or of an entry in it, or*
>
> *(ca)   fails without reasonable excuse to comply with a requirement imposed in relation to those premises under subsection (2)(c) of this section; or*
>
> *(d)   . . .*
>
> *the holder of the licence shall be guilty of an offence.*

Keynote

These powers also apply to Gaming Board inspectors. Section 43(5) provides a power for magistrates to issue a search warrant in respect of premises licensed for gaming; it also creates offences of failing to comply with requirements made under such a warrant.

For a full discussion of the law relating to betting, gaming and lotteries, together with the functions of the Gaming Board of Great Britain, see *Paterson's Licensing Acts* published annually by Butterworths.

For general police powers of entry, search and seizure, **see chapter 2.**

CHAPTER ELEVEN

OFFENCES INVOLVING INFORMATION

11.1 Introduction

Although not capable of being 'stolen' or 'damaged' (**see Crime, chapters 12 and 14**), information can be both extremely valuable and damaging. The Official Secrets Acts cover many of the situations involving information relating to the State (see *Blackstone's Criminal Practice*, 1999, section B9).

The Prevention of Terrorism (Temporary Provisions) Act 1989 creates arrestable offences covering the unlawful collection of information likely to be useful to those planning acts of terrorism (s. 16B) and failing to disclose information relating to terrorism or its investigation (s. 18) (see **chapter 4** and also *Blackstone's Criminal Practice*, 1999, section B10).

This chapter considers the offences concerned with accessing computer programs and also the handling of personal data held on such programs.

11.2 Offences under the Computer Misuse Act 1990

Offence — Unauthorised Access to Computer ('Hacking') — Computer Misuse Act 1990, s. 1
Triable summarily. Six months' imprisonment and/or a fine.
(**No specific power of arrest**)

The Computer Misuse Act 1990, s. 1 states:

> (1) A person is guilty of an offence if—
> (a) he causes a computer to perform any function with intent to secure access to any program or data held in any computer;
> (b) the access he intends to secure is unauthorised; and
> (c) he knows at the time when he causes the computer to perform the function that that is the case.

(2) *The intent a person has to have to commit an offence under this section need not be directed at—*

    (a) *any particular program or data;*

    (b) *a program or data of any particular kind; or*

    (c) *a program or data held in any particular computer.*

Keynote

This offence involves 'causing a computer to perform any function', which means more than simply looking at material on a screen or having any physical contact with computer hardware. In the latter case an offence of criminal damage may be appropriate. Any attempt to log on would involve getting the computer to perform a function (even if the function is to deny you access!).

As this is a summary offence it cannot be 'attempted' in the sense of the Criminal Attempts Act 1981 (**see Crime, chapter 3**). However, the wording of the substantive offence covers virtually every activity from the switching on of the computer, including many activities which would ordinarily be classed as 'merely preparatory'.

Any access must be 'unauthorised'. If the defendant is authorised to *access* a computer, albeit for restricted purposes, then he/she does not commit this offence if he/she then *uses* any information gained for some other unauthorised purpose (e.g. police officers using data from the Police National Computer for private gain (*DPP* v *Bignell* [1998] 1 Cr App R 1)). It is the *access* which the 1990 Act seeks to control not the subsequent use to which any data is put (for offences covering the protection of data, **see para. 11.3**).

In order to prove the offence under s. 1 you must show that the defendant intended to secure access to the program or data. This is therefore an offence of 'specific intent' (**see Crime, chapter 1**) and lesser forms of *mens rea* such as recklessness will not do.

You must also show that the defendant knew the access was unauthorised.

Section 11(2) of the 1990 Act states that proceedings for an offence under s. 1 must be brought within a period of six months from the date on which evidence sufficient in the opinion of the prosecutor to warrant the proceedings comes to his/her knowledge. It has been held that anyone actively involved in the making or prosecuting of a charge (e.g. the officer in charge of the investigation) can be 'the prosecutor' for this purpose and that the expression is not restricted to the Crown Prosecution Service (*Morgans* v *DPP*, *The Times*, 29 December 1998). It was also held that the time limit began from the date when sufficient evidence to warrant a prosecution had actually come to the knowledge of the prosecutor, i.e. when the evidence was assembled by the officer in charge of the case. It did not mean the point at which the prosecutor *formed the opinion* that the evidence was sufficient. This meant that, where the papers from the case had been assembled but the officer in charge had gone sick, leaving a long delay before the Crown Prosecution Service were able to form the opinion that there was sufficient evidence to warrant proceedings, the proceedings were 'out of time' and the defendant's conviction was quashed.

The 1990 Act defines a number of its terms at s. 17 which provides:

(2) *A person secures access to any program or data held in a computer if by causing a computer to perform any function he—*

    (a) *alters or erases the program or data;*

(b)   copies or moves it to any storage medium other than that in which it is held or to a different location in the storage medium in which it is held;

(c)   uses it; or

(d)   has it output from the computer in which it is held (whether by having it displayed or in any other manner);

and references to access to a program or data (and to an intent to secure such access) shall be read accordingly.

(3)   For the purposes of subsection (2)(c) above a person uses a program if the function he causes the computer to perform—

(a)   causes the program to be executed; or

(b)   is itself a function of the program.

(4)   For the purposes of subsection (2)(d) above—

(a)   a program is output if the instructions of which it consists are output; and

(b)   the form in which any such instructions or any other data is output (and in particular whether or not it represents a form in which, in the case of instructions, they are capable of being executed or, in the case of data, it is capable of being processed by a computer) is immaterial.

(5)   Access of any kind by any person to any program or data held in a computer is unauthorised if—

(a)   he is not himself entitled to control access of the kind in question to the program or data; and

(b)   he does not have consent to access by him of the kind in question to the program or data from any person who is so entitled

but this subsection is subject to section 10.

(6)   References to any program or data held in a computer include references to any program or data held in any removable storage medium which is for the time being in the computer; and a computer is to be regarded as containing any program or data held in any such medium.

(7)   A modification of the contents of any computer takes place if, by the operation of any function of the computer concerned or any other computer—

(a)   any program or data held in the computer concerned is altered or erased; or

(b)   any program or data is added to its contents;

and any act which contributes towards causing such a modification shall be regarded as causing it.

(8)   Such a modification is unauthorised if—

(a)   the person whose act causes it is not himself entitled to determine whether the modification should be made; and

(b)   he does not have consent to the modification from any person who is so entitled.

Keynote

Securing access will therefore include:

* altering or erasing a program or data;
* copying or moving a program or data to a new storage medium;
* using data or having it displayed or 'output' in any form from the computer in which it is held.

Access is 'unauthorised' if the person is neither entitled to control that type of access to a program or data, nor does he/she have the consent of any person who is so entitled. This definition does not affect the powers available to any 'enforcement officers', i.e. police officers or other people charged with a duty of investigating offences (s. 10).

For the powers of a police officer to seize data contained on a computer, **see chapter 2**.

A modification will also take place if, by the operation of *any* computer (not just the one being 'misused') any program or data in the computer concerned is altered, erased or added. A modification is 'unauthorised' if the person whose act causes it is neither entitled to determine whether that modification should be made, nor has the consent of anyone who is so entitled.

Offence — Unauthorised Access with Intent to Commit Arrestable Offence — Computer Misuse Act 1990, s. 2

Triable either way. Five years' imprisonment and/or a fine on indictment; six months' imprisonment and/or a fine summarily.
(Arrestable offence)

The Computer Misuse Act 1990, s. 2 states:

> *(1)   A person is guilty of an offence under this section if he commits an offence under section 1 above ('the unauthorised access offence') with intent—*
> *(a)   to commit an offence to which this section applies; or*
> *(b)   to facilitate the commission of such an offence (whether by himself or by any other person);*
> *and the offence he intends to commit or facilitate is referred to below in this section as the further offence.*
> *(2)   This section applies to offences—*
> *(a)   for which the sentence is fixed by law; or*
> *(b)   for which a person of twenty-one years of age or over (not previously convicted) may be sentenced to imprisonment for a term of five years (or, in England and Wales, might be so sentenced but for the restrictions imposed by section 33 of the Magistrates' Courts Act 1980).*
> *(3)   It is immaterial for the purposes of this section whether the further offence is to be committed on the same occasion as the unauthorised access offence or on any future occasion.*
> *(4)   A person may be guilty of an offence under this section even though the facts are such that the commission of the further offence is impossible.*

Keynote

The defendant must be shown to have had the required intent at the time of the access or other *actus reus* (**see Crime, chapter 2**).

The 'further' offences must come under the particular classes of arrestable offence set out under s. 24 of the Police and Criminal Evidence Act 1984. This does not include offences that are made 'arrestable' by virtue only of their inclusion in the list under s. 24(2) of PACE (**see chapter 2**). The intended further offence does not have to be committed at the same time, but may be committed in the future (e.g. where the data is used to commit an offence of blackmail or to secure the transfer of funds from a bank account).

The provision as to impossibility (s. 2(4)) means that a person would still commit the offence if he/she tried, say, to access the bank account of a person who did not in fact exist (for impossibility generally, **see Crime, chapter 3**).

Offence — Unauthorised Modification of Computer Material — Computer Misuse Act 1990, s. 3

Triable either way. Five years' imprisonment and/or a fine on indictment; six months' imprisonment and/or a fine summarily.
(Arrestable offence)

The Computer Misuse Act 1990, s. 3 states:

> *(1)   A person is guilty of an offence if—*
> *(a)   he does any act which causes an unauthorised modification of the contents of any computer;* *and*
> *(b)   at the time when he does the act he has the requisite intent and the requisite knowledge.*
> *(2)   For the purposes of subsection (1)(b) above the requisite intent is an intent to cause a modification of the contents of any computer and by so doing—*
> *(a)   to impair the operation of any computer;*

> (b) to prevent or hinder access to any program or data held in any computer; or
> (c) to impair the operation of any such program or the reliability of any such data.
> (3) The intent need not be directed at—
> (a) any particular computer;
> (b) any particular program or data or a program or data of any particular kind; or
> (c) any particular modification or a modification of any particular kind.
> (4) For the purposes of subsection (1)(b) above the requisite knowledge is knowledge that any modification he intends to cause is unauthorised.
> (5) It is immaterial for the purposes of this section whether an unauthorised modification or any intended effect of it of a kind mentioned in subsection (2) above is, or is intended to be, permanent or merely temporary.
> (6) For the purposes of the Criminal Damage Act 1971 a modification of the contents of a computer shall not be regarded as damaging any computer or computer storage medium unless its effect on that computer or computer storage medium impairs its physical condition.

Keynote

This offence covers a whole range of behaviour provided that the defendant is shown to have had the required intent *and* knowledge at the time.

Implanting viruses would be caught by s. 3.

The purpose of s. 3(6) was to avoid future convictions such as that in *Cox* v *Riley* (1986) 83 Cr App R 54 where the defendant deleted information from a computer card and was convicted of criminal damage (as to which, **see Crime, chapter 14**).

11.3 The Data Protection Act 1998

The Data Protection Act 1984 restricted the use made of some data stored in computer programs. The new Data Protection Act 1998 is intended to implement Council Directive 95/46 in relation to the protection of individuals with regard to the processing and free movement of personal data (see [1995] OJ L281/31). Member States of the European Union were required to implement the provisions of that Directive by 1998.

The 1998 Act will eventually repeal the 1984 Act in its entirety with s. 55 replacing the relevant offences that currently appear under s. 5. Although retaining many of the same provisions and penalties as its predecessor, the 1998 Act represents a far more complex piece of legislation. Among its key changes are:

- the introduction of the Data Protection Commissioner (in place of the Registrar);
- the change in definition from data user to data controller; and
- the extension of the Act's provisions to cover some manual records.

This last provision will extend some of the restrictions on the storage of, and access to certain data to 'relevant filing systems'. This will mean that structured sets of information filed manually — as opposed to being stored on a computer — may fall within the provisions of the Act, although there is still some debate as to just which records will eventually be covered. The 1998 Act provides for Regulations to be made in relation to a number of its sections and until those Regulations are finalised there will be some uncertainty as to the precise extent and ambit of the legislation.

Part II of the 1998 Act provides a number of fundamental rights relating to records containing personal data about them. Section 7 entitles the individual to be given information and explanation by the relevant 'data controller' (**see below**) about some of that data, to identify the source of it and, under certain circumstances, to be informed as to some decision-making processes involved in its use. Part II makes specific provisions in relation to credit reference agencies and the use of personal data in direct marketing. Provision is made for the compensation of individuals where the requirements of the Act have not been complied with.

It is important to note that some of the 1998 Act came into force on the day it was passed (16 July 1998), other sections will come into force on a day to be appointed by the Secretary of State. Some provisions of the Act are subject to a transitional period which extends to 23 October 2007.

The 1998 Act places many duties on data users who have to register their systems and the use for which data is held. Most police organisations have Data Protection Officers whose advice should be sought in every case and particularly in relation to the commencement dates and application of the Act's provisions.

Section 1 of the 1998 Act provides that:

> *(1)   In this Act, unless the context otherwise requires—*
> *'data' means information which—*
> *(a)   is being processed by means of equipment operating automatically in response to instructions given for that purpose,*
> *(b)   is recorded with the intention that it should be processed by means of such equipment,*
> *(c)   is recorded as part of a relevant filing system or with the intention that it should form part of a relevant filing system, or*
> *(d)   does not fall with paragraph (a), (b) or (c) but forms part of an accessible record as defined by section 68.*

Accessible records as defined by s. 68(1) include a health record, an educational record and an accessible public record.

> *'Relevant filing system' means any set of information relating to individuals to the extent that, although the information is not processed by means of equipment operating automatically in response to instructions given for that purpose, the set is structured, either by reference to individuals or by reference to criteria relating to individuals, in such a way that specific information relating to a particular individual is readily accessible ((s. 1(1)).*

The Data Protection Act 1998 seeks to protect 'personal data', that is,

> *'data which relate to a living individual who can be identified — (a) from those data, or (b) from those data and other information which is in the possession of, or is likely to come into the possession of, the data controller, and includes any expression of opinion about the individual and any indication of the intentions of the data controller or any other person in respect of the individual' (s. 1(1)).*

Keynote

The definition of personal data would clearly apply to data held on police computers about suspected and convicted offenders and may well apply to other similar paper records.

The 1998 Act makes special provision in relation to 'sensitive personal data' which it defines (at s. 2) as:

. . . personal data consisting of information as to—

    (a)   the racial or ethnic origin of the data subject,

    (b)   his political opinions,

    (c)   his religious beliefs or other beliefs of a similar nature,

    (d)   whether he is a member of a trade union (within the meaning of the Trade Union and Labour Relations (Consolidation) Act 1992),

    (e)   his physical or mental health or condition,

    (f)   his sexual life,

    (g)   the commission or alleged commission by him of any offence, or

    (h)   any proceedings for any offence committed or alleged to have been committed by him, the disposal of such proceedings or the sentence of any court in such proceedings.

11.3.1   Data Protection Principles and Schedules

A crucial element in the 1998 Act is the data protection principles set out at sch. 1. As well as introducing the principles, s. 4 makes it clear that it is the duty of the relevant 'data controller' (**see para. 11.3.2**) to comply with those principles wherever they apply. Part I of sch. 1 sets out the principles as being:

1.   Personal data shall be processed fairly and lawfully and, in particular, shall not be processed unless—

    (a)   at least one of the conditions in Schedule 2 is met, and

    (b)   in the case of sensitive personal data, at least one of the conditions in Schedule 3 is also met.

2.   Personal data shall be obtained only for one or more specified and lawful purposes, and shall not be further processed in any manner incompatible with that purpose or those purposes.

3.   Personal data shall be adequate, relevant and not excessive in relation to the purpose or purposes for which they are processed.

4.   Personal data shall be accurate and, where necessary, kept up to date.

5.   Personal data processed for any purpose or purposes shall not be kept for longer than is necessary for that purpose or those purposes.

6.   Personal data shall be processed in accordance with the rights of data subjects under this Act.

7.   Appropriate technical and organisational measures shall be taken against unauthorised or unlawful processing of personal data and against accidental loss or destruction of, or damage to, personal data.

8.   Personal data shall not be transferred to a country or territory outside the European Economic Area unless that country or territory ensures an adequate level of protection for the rights and freedoms of data subjects in relation to the processing of personal data.

Part II of sch. 1 contains further detail on the interpretation of these principles.

Schedule 2 sets out further conditions that apply to the first principle above, while sch. 3 deals specifically with sensitive personal data.

Schedule 4 sets out occasions where the eighth principle above will not apply.

Schedules 5 and 6 make provision for the Data Protection Commissioner and the Data Protection Tribunal, together with a system for hearing appeals.

Schedule 7 makes a number of exemptions from some of the Act's provisions (**see para. 11.3.2**) while sch. 8 sets out a number of transitional exemptions — especially in relation to manual data — between various dates up to 24 October 2007.

Schedule 9 gives powers and directions for the issuing and executing of search warrants.

Schedule 10 provides for the giving of assistance by the Commissioner in relation to someone bringing an action in connection with 'the special purposes', that is journalistic, artistic or literary purposes.

Schedule 11 deals with educational records, while sch. 12 sets out the authorities in relation to accessible public records.

The other schedules make transitional savings, modifications and repeals.

11.3.2 Other Duties and Responsibilities

Part III of the 1998 Act sets out the responsibilities of data controllers, defined as the people who (alone or jointly) determine the purposes for which and the manner in which any personal data are, or are to be processed (see s. 1(1)).

Personal data must not be processed unless and until the relevant data controller has registered the details ('registrable particulars') set out at s. 16.

Part II imposes responsibility on data controllers to register with the Commissioner and to notify him/her of any changes in the registrable particulars above.

Processing personal data without registration and failing to notify the Commissioner of any relevant changes are offences, triable either way and punishable on indictment with unlimited fines.

Part III of the 1998 Act makes certain limited exemptions from the first data protection principle and from the provisions of s. 7 (**see above**). These exemptions apply to some occasions where personal data is processed for:

- the prevention or detection of crime
- the apprehension or prosecution of offenders
- the assessment or collection of tax or duty.

There is also an exemption from complying with the data protection principles and some other parts of the Act where that exemption is required for the purposes of safeguarding national security.

Regulatory activity (i.e. lawful activities that exist to protect people and organisations from fraud, malpractice or incompetence or to regulate some public bodies) is also exempt from many of the Act's provisions.

Further specific exemptions are made in relation to:

- journalism, literature and art (s. 32);
- research, history and statistics (s. 33);
- information that the data controller is obliged to make available to the public (s. 34);
- personal data processed by an individual for the purposes of his/her personal, family or household affairs (s. 36); and
- matters included in sch. 7 (examination marks and papers, armed forces, judicial appointments, employment by the Crown, corporate finance and forecasts, legal professional privilege and self-incrimination).

Offences under the 1998 Act may not be prosecuted by anyone other than the Data Protection Commissioner or with the consent of the Director of Public Prosecutions.

CHAPTER TWELVE

DISCRIMINATION AND EQUALITY

12.1   Introduction

This chapter sets out in brief summary the law relating to equality and discrimination in the workplace. This area of employment law is very specialised and, on occasions, very sensitive. Most police organisations have employee relations or human resources departments to help both managers and employees in these fields. The police staff associations, together with other groups such as the Black Police Association will also provide help in ensuring that the spirit of this legislation is observed at work.

Most police organisations also have grievance procedures to deal with issues of equality in an informal setting. Although there is a growing array of legislative provisions to protect the rights of various groups within the workplace, recourse to the law is not the only — or even the best — solution to issues of diversity. The government has introduced further legislation aimed at averting litigation through the courts and industrial tribunals and encouraging local resolution.

It is worth noting that, on some occasions, a chief officer will be liable for some, though not all (see *R* v *Farah*, *The Times*, 17 October 1996), of the actions of his/her staff in the course of their duties (**see chapter 1**) It is also worth noting that discrimination and victimisation are included in the new Code of Conduct for police officers (**see chapter 1**). Where acts amounting to discrimination take place outside the workplace, the employer and employees may still be caught within the framework of the legislation. So, for instance, where police officers engage in inappropriate sexual behaviour towards a colleague at a work-related social function, a tribunal may be entitled to hold that the function was an extension of the workplace and so hold the chief officer liable for the acts of his/her officers at that function (see *Chief Constable of Lincolnshire* v *Stubbs* [1999] IRLR 81).

12.2   The Law

There are four main sources of legislation which deal with equality and discrimination:

- Race Relations Act 1976
- Sex Discrimination Act 1975

- Equal Pay Act 1970
- Disability Discrimination Act 1995.

All of these Acts deal with matters which fall under the heading of employment law as that is the main area of their concern. It should be noted that, other than the 1995 Act, these Acts have been around for over 20 years — equality of opportunity and the prohibition of discrimination is not 'new'!

In addition to these statutes, the role of European law in this area is of considerable significance — and is growing all the time. Most important among the various pieces of European legislation are:

- the Equal Treatment Directive (76/207)
- the Equal Pay Directive (75/117)
- case law from the European Court of Justice.

This is a complex area of law and is outside the scope of this Manual.

There are other pieces of legislation, such as those specific offences under the Public Order Acts (**see chapter** 4) which are aimed at discriminatory behaviour by anyone under certain circumstances. There are also offences under the Discipline Code (**see chapter** 1) which deal with other forms of discriminatory behaviour by police officers in the course of their duties.

Generally, however, there is no overall legal restriction on discriminatory behaviour. There is no 'Equal Opportunities Act' as is widely believed and the UK has no written constitution protecting the individual from being discriminated against other than in the circumstances described in this chapter. One of the cornerstones of the European Community, however, is the achievement of equality of treatment for individuals of each member State within the Community and European law has had a significant influence on the impact of equal opportunities and discrimination (at least on the grounds of sex) in England and Wales.

The purpose of the two main Acts, the Race Relations Act 1976 and the Sex Discrimination Act 1975, was summed up by Waite LJ in *Jones* v *Tower Boot Company Ltd* [1997] ICR 254:

> The legislation . . . broke new ground in seeking to work upon the minds of men and women and thus affect their attitude to the social consequences of differences between the sexes or the distinction of skin colour. Its general thrust was educative, persuasive, and where necessary coercive. . .

His Lordship went to on to say how, against this background, the courts would not adopt a technical or restrictive approach when interpreting the law in this area.

12.2.1 Procedure

The procedure relating to claims made against employers has been significantly altered by the Employment Rights (Dispute Resolution) Act 1998. The 1998 Act has re-named industrial tribunals 'employment tribunals' to convey their function more clearly. The Act goes on to make provision for regulations permitting tribunals to determine cases without a full hearing or, at times, without a hearing at all under certain circumstances.

It also makes provisions for 'compromise agreements' made by relevant independent advisers — as opposed to qualified lawyers — and sets out a new class of individuals, to be known as 'legal officers' who may carry out some of the more straightforward functions currently carried out by tribunal chair people.

At the time of writing, no specific Regulations in this regard have been made under the 1998 Act.

12.3 The Race Relations Act 1976

The Race Relations Act 1976 deals with racial discrimination, the first type of discrimination to be prohibited in England and Wales. It follows the same definitions as those used in the Sex Discrimination Act 1975 and has a Code of Practice to support it. Matters falling within its parameters are overseen by the Commission for Racial Equality.

Under s. 3, the 1976 Act aims to control discrimination (**see para. 12.8**) on grounds of:

* colour
* race
* nationality
* ethnic or national origins.

Ethnic group is a broad definition which may include any group with a shared culture or history (**see chapter 3**). It does not include Rastafarians (*Crown Suppliers* v *Dawkins* [1993] ICR 517). Speakers of a particular language (e.g. Welsh) are not an 'ethnic' group *per se* (*Gwynedd County Council* v *Jones* [1986] ICR 833); it would need to be shown that such people belonged to a group with a shared culture or history before they come under the provisions of the 1976 Act.

12.4 The Sex Discrimination Act 1975

The Sex Discrimination Act 1975 is aimed at preventing discrimination on the grounds of sex or marital status.

This Act also has a Code of Practice to support it and matters falling within its parameters are overseen by the Equal Opportunities Commission.

The 1975 Act makes it unlawful to discriminate on the grounds of a person's sex (s. 1) or marital status (s. 3). The provisions apply in favour of both men and women equally (s. 2); they do not however, operate equally in respect of married and single people and an employer may provide greater benefits for employees who are married.

12.5 The Equal Pay Act 1970

The Equal Pay Act 1970 requires that men and women who do the same type of work receive the same rewards. Originally enacted to come into force with the Sex Discrimination Act 1975, the first Act failed to satisfy the requirements of the relevant European directive and had to be amended.

Unlike the 1975 and 1976 Acts, this Act only relates to issues within the field of employment.

12.6 The Disability Discrimination Act 1995

The Disability Discrimination Act 1995, which also goes beyond the field of employment, introduces a relatively new area of discrimination, that of disability. The 1995 Act is supported by a Code of Practice, together with other materials and regulations to help with the complexity of its application.

A person is 'disabled' for the purposes of the Act if they have a physical or mental impairment which has a substantial and long term adverse effect on their ability to carry out normal day-to-day functions (s. 1).

Again there are exceptions which may be justified. However, under the 1995 Act employers and others are required to make 'reasonable adjustments' to prevent disabled people from being put at a substantial disadvantage when compared with others (s. 6). This means that entry and exit points will need to be adapted for wheelchairs, and provisions made for those who are visually or aurally disadvantaged.

12.7 Areas Not Covered

Areas which are often thought to be subject to protection from discrimination but are not directly covered by the law are:

- age
- sexual orientation
- religious belief.

However, in a recent case before the Court of Appeal it was held that discrimination against a man based on his homosexuality could amount to discrimination against him *as a man*, which would therefore be discrimination on grounds of sex (*Smith* v *Gardner Merchant*, *The Times*, 21 July 1998).

12.8 Gender Reassignment

Many of the provisions of the Sex Discrimination Act 1975 have been extended to cover discrimination on the grounds of gender reassignment in employment and vocational training. These extensions were made by the Sex Discrimination (Gender Reassignment) Regulations 1999 (SI 1999 No. 1102) in response to a case in the European Court of Justice (*P* v *S and Cornwall County Council* (case C–13/94) [1996] All ER (EC) 397). Gender reassignment means a process which is undertaken under medical supervision for the purpose of reassigning a person's sex by changing physiological or other characteristics of sex (reg. 2(3)). The Regulations only extend the provisions of some sections of the 1975 Act and include a number of concessions and exemptions.

12.9 Discrimination

Discrimination under the 1975 and 1976 Acts may come about in three ways:

- directly
- indirectly
- by victimisation.

12.9.1 Direct Discrimination

This type of discrimination happens when one person is directly treated less favourably than another on the grounds of or by reason of his/her racial origin, marital status or sex. The key elements here are the 'treatment' of the person and the fact that such treatment was 'less favourable' than it would have been had the person not fallen into that particular group. Treatment will generally involve dealing with or behaving towards someone — as opposed to simply talking in a derogatory fashion *about* them (see e.g. *De Souza* v *Automobile Association* [1986] ICR 514). Treatment can be shown by a continuing state of affairs as well as a particular act (*Owusu* v *London Fire & Civil Defence Authority* [1995] IRLR 574 — employer continually failing to re-grade appellant's post).

It must be shown that the treatment was made *on the grounds* of or *by reason* of the person's belonging to a protected group. Like the test of 'causation' in criminal law (as to which, **see Crime, chapter 2**), the 'but for' test is helpful here, i.e. asking whether the person would have received the same treatment as others *but for* their sex or race. In determining whether a person has been so treated the courts will not look at the motive of an employer or individual, only at the cause of the treatment (see *R* v *Birmingham City Council, ex parte Equal Opportunities Commission* [1989] IRLR 173 — more boys than girls allocated places at a school).

If an employer introduces rules restricting the times when employees may take holidays and that rule operates to the detriment of a group of people who are protected by the legislation (e.g. Muslim employees whose observance of religious festivals was affected by those restrictions), the introduction of those rules may be unlawful (see *Walker Ltd* v *Hussain* [1996] IRLR 11).

Other examples would include:

- getting someone to carry out unpleasant tasks or duties (*Ministry of Defence* v *Jeremiah* [1978] IRLR 436)
- personal harassment (*Strathclyde Regional Council* v *Porcelli* [1986] IRLR 134)
- refusing to employ someone (*Grieg* v *Community Industries* [1979] IRLR 159)

in each case as a result of their membership of a protected group.

12.9.2 Indirect Discrimination

Indirect discrimination involves applying the same conditions to all relevant people (e.g. job applicants), but under circumstances where those criteria have a different and adverse effect on members of a protected group because the proportion of people from that group *who can comply* with the condition(s) are considerably smaller. As with other expressions in the legislation, 'compliance' will be broadly interpreted by the courts. The fact that someone can *physically* comply with a requirement (e.g. a woman could decide not to have children in order to comply with an age requirement in a promotion system) does not mean that it falls outside the legislation. What the courts will look at is the person's *practical* ability to comply with a condition. Therefore, in *Mandla* v *Dowell Lee* [1983] ICR 385, the fact that the complainant could physically remove his turban and cut his hair in order to comply with his chosen school's admission policy did not prevent that policy from being indirectly discriminatory. The House of Lords said that the test of whether someone could comply with a condition would be taken to mean could he/she comply in practice or in a way that was consistent with the customs and cultural conditions of the group.

A further example of indirect discrimination can be seen in the recent case of *London Underground Ltd* v *Edwards*, *The Times*, 1 June 1998. Despite the fact that a managerial policy only had an adverse effect on one woman train driver among a total of 24, the fact that *all* 2,023 male drivers could comply with it made the policy discriminatory. While 100% of males could comply with the policy, which related to rostering of duties, only 95.2% of females were able to do so. Accordingly, the Court of Appeal held that the policy discriminated indirectly against the applicant who was unable to continue in her job as a result.

Other examples would include:

- requiring all employees to work within 'normal office hours' (*Bhudi* v *IMI Refiners* [1994] IRLR 10)
- requiring all workers to have short hair — thereby making it more difficult for some groups such as Sikhs to comply (*Mandla* v *Dowell Lee*).

12.9.3 Victimisation

Victimisation is a type of discrimination and therefore only attracts protection in the same circumstances as the other discrimination provisions of the various Acts.

A person is discriminated against by way of 'victimisation' under s. 2 of the Race Relations Act 1976, s. 3 of the Sex Discrimination Act 1975 and s. 55 of the Disability Discrimination Act 1995, if they are treated less favourably than another person is (or would be) treated in the same circumstances with regard to any action covered by any of those Acts because the person:

- brought proceedings against any person under any of those Acts;

- have given evidence or information in connection with proceedings brought by any person under any of those Acts;

- otherwise did anything under or by reference to the Acts with regard to any person (e.g. provided advice to someone as to his/her rights);

- have alleged that any person has done anything which would amount to a contravention of those Acts (whether or not the allegation specifically so states); or

- because the discriminator knows or suspects that the person victimised has done or intends to do any of the things set out above.

The protection from victimisation does not extend to treatment of a person by reason of any allegation that the person makes falsely and not in good faith.

Where the person victimised has (or had) a disability, that disability is to be disregarded when deciding whether or not he/she has been treated 'less favourably' than another person in the same circumstances.

In proving victimisation, the person must show that less favourable treatment occurred as a result of his/her involvement in the action described that is, applying the 'but for' test (see *Aziz* v *Trinity Street Taxis Ltd* [1988] ICR 534).

12.10 Exceptions and Defences

There are a number of exceptions and defences to the provisions of the Race Relations Act 1976 and Sex Discrimination Act 1975. As with other defences and exceptions, not all of them apply to all types of behaviour and it is necessary to refer to the relevant legislation in each case. Below are some of the more common exceptions and defences.

12.10.1 Genuine Occupational Qualification

The most frequently encountered defence to acts made unlawful by the Race Relations Act 1976 and the Sex Discrimination Act 1975 is that of 'genuine occupational qualification' (GOQ).

In each case the GOQ defence only applies to:

- recruitment
- refusing employment, and
- affording access to promotion, training etc.

The principle behind the GOQ defence is that, in certain jobs and roles, there may well be a legitimate reason demanded by that job/role for the relevant person to be a particular sex or to belong to a particular racial group. Such occasions are generally concerned with:

- preserving decency and privacy (e.g. public lavatory attendants)
- authenticity (e.g. actors/actresses in plays), or
- the provision of personal services

Exceptions to unlawful discrimination can be found in a number of areas under the relevant Acts, though there are far more exceptions to discrimination on the grounds of sex than for reasons of race.

12.10.2 Positive Action

In order to encourage members of particular groups to follow training courses, employers and other bodies may discriminate in their provision of training opportunities under certain circumstances. They may discriminate in this regard if, within the 12-month period preceding the act of discrimination:

- there are no people or
- only a small number of people
- from a particular racial group or of a particular sex
- doing that work in Great Britain or in a specific locality.

Efforts made under these circumstances are positive *action* and should not be confused with positive *discrimination* or *affirmative* action as used in the United States and elsewhere. Affirmative action in that sense (whereby people are selected in preference to others solely on the basis of their membership of a certain minority group) is unlawful in England and Wales.

12.11 Sexual Harassment

Sexual harassment is unwanted conduct of a sexual nature, or other conduct based on sex affecting the dignity of women and men at work (see *Wardman* v *Carpenter Farrar* [1993] IRLR 374).

It can include verbal remarks. Most equal opportunities policies include some reference to this type of behaviour and grievance procedures take account of it. Harassment is also a criminal offence (**see chapter 3**) and, if anxiety or shock caused to another person is sufficiently serious, a charge of assault may be brought (**see Crime, chapter 8**).

12.12 Maternity

In addition to the protection which appears in the above enactments, women have other statutory protection in relation to pregnancy and childbirth. These include:

- rights to unpaid time off work
- protection against dismissal
- rights to maternity pay
- rights to maternity leave
- rights to return to work.

These and other protections are contained in the Employment Rights Act 1996.

CHAPTER THIRTEEN

RAILWAYS

13.1 | Introduction

Responsibility for providing police services to the railway network — including the London underground — in England and Wales (and Scotland) lies primarily with the British Transport Police (BTP). Owing to geographical factors, however, there are occasions where the assistance of other police forces may be required or requested. There is a considerable amount of legislation that relates to the railway network, together with many operational policies. These are properly the concern of the BTP and, where officers from other forces are called upon to deal with incidents involving railways, it is suggested that they confer with their colleagues at BTP.

This chapter sets out some of the legislation that is relevant to police officers in general.

13.2 | Powers of Entry

Although much railway property is now owned by private commercial companies, railway stations and platforms are generally public places for most purposes. Where there is any doubt as to the existence of a power of entry or an implied permission to enter (as to which, **see chapter 2**), the guidance of the BTP should be sought.

There are some specific offences concerned with trespassing on railway property — including the running lines — and this is one of the few areas of criminal law where there is a direct sanction imposed for a simple trespassory act (see the Regulation of Railways Act 1868, s. 23, as amended). For trespass generally, **see chapter 9**.

13.3 | Offences

There are many offences that relate specifically to railways; in particular those set out under the relevant by-laws. Many of these are summary offences and often require proof of certain facts or circumstances that existed at the time.

Among the more serious offences are:

Offence — Obstruction with Intent to Cause Damage etc. — Malicious Damage Act 1861, s. 35
Triable on indictment. Life imprisonment.
(*Arrestable offence*)

The Malicious Damage Act 1861, s. 35 provides that:

Whosoever shall unlawfully and maliciously put, place, cast, or throw upon or across any railway any wood, stone, or other matter or thing, or shall unlawfully and maliciously take up, remove, or displace any rail, sleeper, or other matter or thing belonging to any railway, or shall unlawfully and maliciously turn, move, or divert any points or other machinery belonging to any railway, or shall unlawfully and maliciously make or show, hide or remove, any signal or light upon or near to any railway, or shall unlawfully and maliciously do or cause to be done any matter or thing, with intent, in any of the cases aforesaid, to obstruct, upset, overthrow, injure, or destroy any engine, tender, carriage, or truck using such railway, shall be guilty of an offence . . .

Keynote

For the meaning of 'maliciously' here, **see Crime, chapter 2**.

This offence extends to privately-owned railways that are not constructed under statute. This offence requires proof of 'specific intent' (**see Crime, chapter 2**). Where there is no such intent, the lesser offence under s. 36 (triable either way and carrying two years' imprisonment) may be charged.

Offence — Obstruction with Intent to Endanger Safety — Offences Against the Person Act 1861, s. 32
Triable on indictment. Life imprisonment.
(*Arrestable offence*)

The Offences Against the Person Act 1861, s. 32 provides that:

Whosoever shall unlawfully and maliciously put or throw upon or across any railway any wood, stone, or other matter or thing, or shall unlawfully and maliciously take up, remove, or displace any rail, sleeper, or other matter or thing belonging to any railway, or shall unlawfully and maliciously turn, move or divert any points or other machinery belonging to any railway, or shall unlawfully and maliciously make or show, hide or remove, any signal or light upon or near to any railway, or shall unlawfully and maliciously do or cause to be done any other matter or thing, with intent, in any of the cases aforesaid, to endanger the safety of any person travelling or being upon such railway, shall be guilty of an offence . . .

Keynote

This is also an offence of 'specific intent' and has a lesser alternative charge where no such intent was present (under s. 33).

The intention necessary is an intention to endanger the safety (not necessarily the *life*) of any person travelling or being upon the railway concerned.

It is an either way offence for any person, by any unlawful act or wilful omission, to endanger the safety of any person on the railway (s. 34). That an offence is committed where there is a potential danger caused, even though the threat is removed by the intervention of a third party (*R v Pearce* [1967] 1 QB 150).

13.4 Offences Involving Drink and Drugs

Given the potential safety risks presented by railway operations, there are a number of legislative provisions aimed at regulating the behaviour of people on railway or similar transport systems where those people have taken drink or drugs. In addition to these provisions, which are set out below, many if not all employment contracts for people working on railway systems will contain some clauses dealing with the effects of drink/drugs when 'on duty'. Again, in cases of doubt, the guidance of the BTP should be sought.

13.4.1 The Transport and Works Act 1992

Modelled largely on the provisions of the Road Traffic Act 1988 (**see Road Traffic, chapter 5**), the Transport and Works Act 1992 gives the police certain powers in relation to suspected offences involving drink or drugs by staff on railway or similar transport systems. The provisions of the 1992 Act are not restricted to railways but also extend to tramways and systems using a mode of guided transport that have been designated by the Secretary of State (e.g. the 'people movers' operated at Gatwick airport).

The 1992 Act will not apply unless the transport system concerned is used or intended to be used wholly or partly for the carriages of members of the public. It need not be shown that a particular part of the system or an individual carriage was so used or intended; it is the use/intended use of the system as a whole that will be considered in determining whether or not the Act applies.

13.4.2 Staff

Unlike the road traffic legislation, the Transport and Works Act 1992 is not only concerned with those people who are driving, attempting to drive or in charge of vehicles. The 1992 Act will apply to any relevant worker whose duties or job description bring him/her into the categories set out under s. 27. These relevant workers will include:

- train drivers
- guards
- signalmen/women
- any other worker who can, in their capacity as such, control or affect the movement of a vehicle
- maintenance workers employed to work on the tracks and lines, signalling equipment or the electricity supply to the vehicles or their guidance systems
- supervisors and look-outs for such maintenance workers

Offence — Relevant Worker Unfit through Drink or Drugs — Transport and Works Act 1992, s. 27(1)
Triable summarily. Six months' imprisonment and/or fine.
(Statutory power of arrest)

The Transport and Works Act 1992, s. 27(1) provides that:

(1) If a person works on a transport system to which this chapter applies as a relevant worker when he is unfit to carry out that work through drink or drugs, he shall be guilty of an offence.

Offence —Relevant Worker Over the Prescribed Limit — Transport and Works Act 1992, s. 27(2)
Triable summarily. Six months' imprisonment and/or fine.
(*No specific power of arrest*)

The Transport and Works Act 1992, s. 27(2) provides that:

> (2)   *If a person works on a transport system to which this chapter applies as a relevant worker after consuming so much alcohol that the proportion of it in his breath, blood or urine exceeds the prescribed limit, he shall be guilty of an offence.*

Keynote

The prescribed limits are the same as those set out in relation to road traffic offences; so too are the relevant provisions in relation to approved breath test devices and police station procedure (**see Road Traffic, chapter 5**).

'Drug' includes intoxicants other than alcohol.

A constable may arrest a person without warrant if he/she has reasonable cause to suspect that the person is, or has been committing an offence under s. 27(1) (s. 30). For a discussion of the requirements for 'reasonable cause to suspect', **see chapter 2**. In order to arrest a person under this section a constable may enter (if need be by force) any place where that person is or where the constable, with reasonable cause, suspects him/her to be (s. 30(3)).

Under s. 29 a constable in uniform may require a person to provide a specimen of breath for a breath test where the constable has reasonable cause to suspect that:

- the person is working on a transport system in any capacity mentioned under s. 27 (i.e. a relevant worker) and that he/she has alcohol in his/her body; or

- the person has been working in such a capacity with alcohol in his/her body and that he/she still has alcohol in his/her body.

In addition, where an accident or an incident which *in the constable's opinion* involved a danger of death or personal injury (to anyone) occurs on a relevant transport system, a constable in uniform may also require a specimen of breath if he/she has reasonable cause to suspect that:

- at the time of the accident or dangerous incident, the person was working on the transport system in the capacity of a 'relevant worker'; and

- that an act or omission of that person while so working *may have been a cause* of the accident/dangerous incident.

It is not necessary that the person's act/omission may have been the *only*, or even a substantial cause of the accident/dangerous incident.

For the purposes of:

- requiring a person to provide a specimen of breath under s. 29(2) where the constable reasonably suspects that the accident/dangerous incident involved the death of or personal injury to another person, or

- arresting a person in such a case

the constable may enter (if need by force) any place where that person is or where the constable, with reasonable cause, suspects him/her to be (s. 30(4)).

The requirement for the provision of the breath specimen may be made at or near the place where the requirement is made or, if it is made under s. 27(2) and the constable thinks fit, at a police station (s. 29(4)).

Failing or refusing to provide a specimen under s. 29 is a summary offence (s. 29(5)).

If, as a result of a breath test under s. 29 a constable has reasonable cause to suspect that the proportion of alcohol in the person's breath or blood exceeds the prescribed limit, he/she may arrest the person without warrant (s. 30(2)(a)).

If the person fails or refuses to provide a specimen under s. 29 and the constable has reasonable cause to suspect that that person has alcohol in his/her body, he/she may arrest them without warrant (s. 30(2)(b)).

Further offences are committed by the operator of the transport system if a person working on that system commits an offence under s. 27 (s. 28). There is however a general defence open to the 'responsible operators' if they can show that they exercised all due diligence to prevent the commission of a s. 27 offence on their system.

APPENDIX ONE

PACE CODE OF PRACTICE FOR THE EXERCISE BY POLICE OFFICERS OF STATUTORY POWERS OF STOP AND SEARCH (CODE A)

1. General

1.1   This code of practice must be readily available at all police stations for consultation by police officers, detained persons and members of the public.

1.2   The notes for guidance included are not provisions of this code, but are guidance to police officers and others about its application and interpretation. Provisions in the annexes to the code are provisions of this code.

1.3   This code governs the exercise by police officers of statutory powers to search a person without first arresting him or to search a vehicle without making an arrest. The main stop and search powers to which this code applies at the time the code was prepared are set out in Annex A, but that list should not be regarded as definitive.

1.4   This code does not apply to the following powers of stop and search:
    (i)   Aviation Security Act 1982, s. 27(2);
    (ii)   Police and Criminal Evidence Act 1984, s. 6(1) (which relates specifically to powers of constables employed by statutory undertakers on the premises of the statutory undertakers).

1.5   This code applies to stops and searches under powers:
    (a)   requiring reasonable grounds for suspicion that articles unlawfully obtained or possessed are being carried;
    (b)   authorised under section 60 of the Criminal Justice and Public Order Act 1994, (as amended by section 8 of the Knives Act 1997), based upon a reasonable belief that incidents involving serious violence may take place or that people are carrying dangerous instruments or offensive weapons within any locality in the police area [See Note 1A];
    (c)   authorised under section 13A of the Prevention of Terrorism (Temporary Provisions) Act 1989, (as amended by section 81 of the Criminal Justice and Public Order Act 1994 and section 1 of the Prevention of Terrorism (Additional Powers) Act 1996);
    (d)   authorised under section 13B of the Prevention of Terrorism (Temporary Provisions) Act 1989, (as inserted by section 1 of the Prevention of Terrorism (Additional Powers) Act 1996);

(e) exercised under paragraph 4(2) of Schedule 5 to the Prevention of Terrorism (Temporary Provisions) Act 1989.
[See Note 1AA]

(a)   Powers requiring reasonable suspicion

1.6   Whether a reasonable ground for suspicion exists will depend on the circumstances in each case, but there must be some objective basis for it. An officer will need to consider the nature of the article suspected of being carried in the context of other factors such as the time and the place, and the behaviour of the person concerned or those with him. Reasonable suspicion may exist, for example, where information has been received such as a description of an article being carried or of a suspected offender; a person is seen acting covertly or warily or attempting to hide something; or a person is carrying a certain type of article at an unusual time or in a place where a number of burglaries or thefts are known to have taken place recently. But the decision to stop and search must be based on all the facts which bear on the likelihood that an article of a certain kind will be found.

1.6A   For example, reasonable suspicion may be based upon reliable information or intelligence which indicates that members of a particular group or gang, or their associates, habitually carry knives unlawfully or weapons or controlled drugs.

1.7   Subject to the provision in paragraph 1.7AA below, reasonable suspicion can never be supported on the basis of personal factors alone without supporting intelligence or information. For example, a person's colour, age, hairstyle or manner of dress, or the fact that he is known to have a previous conviction for possession of an unlawful article, cannot be used alone or in combination with each other as the sole basis on which to search that person. Nor may it be founded on the basis of stereotyped images of certain persons or groups as more likely to be committing offences.

1.7AA   However, where there is reliable information or intelligence that members of a group or gang who habitually carry knives unlawfully or weapons or controlled drugs, and wear a distinctive item of clothing or other means of identification to indicate membership of it, the members may be identified by means of that distinctive item of clothing or other means of identification. [See Note 1H]

1.7A   Where a police officer has reasonable grounds to suspect that a person is in innocent possession of a stolen or prohibited article or other item for which he is empowered to search, the power of stop and search exists notwithstanding that there would be no power of arrest. However every effort should be made to secure the person's co-operation in the production of the article before resorting to the use of force.

(b)   Authorisation under section 60 of the Criminal Justice and Public Order Act 1994, as amended by section 8 of the Knives Act 1997

1.8   Authority to exercise the powers of stop and search under section 60 of the Criminal Justice and Public Order Act 1994, as amended by section 8 of the Knives Act 1997, may be given where it is reasonably believed that incidents involving serious violence may take place in any locality in the police area, and it is expedient to use these powers to prevent their occurrence, or that persons are carrying dangerous instruments or offensive weapons without good reason in any locality in any police area. Authorisation may only be given by an officer of the rank of inspector or above, in writing, specifying the grounds on which it was given, the locality in which the powers may be exercised and the period of time for which they are in force. The period authorised shall be no longer than appears reasonably necessary to prevent, or try to prevent incidents of serious violence, or to deal with the problem of carrying dangerous instruments or offensive weapons and it may not exceed 24 hours. If an inspector gives an authorisation, he must, as soon as practicable, inform an officer of or above the rank of superintendent. An officer of or above the rank of superintendent may direct that the period shall be extended for a further 24 hours if violence or the carrying of dangerous instruments or offensive weapons has occurred or is suspected to have occurred and the continued use of the powers is considered necessary to prevent or deal with further such activity. That direction must also be given in writing at the time or as soon as practicable afterwards. [See Notes 1A, 1F and 1G]

(c)   Authorisation under section 13A of the Prevention of Terrorism (Temporary Provisions) Act 1989, as inserted by section 81 of the Criminal Justice and Public Order Act 1994 and amended by the Prevention of Terrorism (Additional Powers) Act 1996

1.8A   (Removed)

1.9   An authorisation given under section 13A of the Prevention of Terrorism (Temporary Provisions) Act 1989 gives a constable in uniform the power to stop and search any vehicle, its driver and any passengers for articles which could be used for terrorist purposes. A constable may exercise the power whether or not he has any grounds for suspecting the presence of such articles.

1.10   Authority for the use of the power may be given where it appears expedient to do so to prevent acts of terrorism. The authorisation must:

(i)   be given by an officer of the rank of assistant chief constable (or equivalent or above);

(ii)   be in writing (it may be given orally at first but should be confirmed in writing by the officer who gave it as soon as reasonably practicable);

(iii)   be signed, dated and timed by the officer giving the authorisation;

(iv)   state the geographical area in which the power may be used (i.e. whether it applies to the whole or only a specific part of his force area); and

(v)   specify the time and date that the authorisation starts and ends (up to a, maximum of 28 days from the time the authorisation was given).

1.11   Further use of the power requires anew authorisation.

[See Notes 1F, 1G and 1I]

(d)   Authorisation under section 13B of the Prevention of Terrorism (Temporary Provisions) Act 1989, as inserted by section 1 of the Prevention of Terrorism (Additional Powers) Act 1996

1.12   An authorisation given under section 13B of the Prevention of Terrorism (Temporary Provisions) Act 1989 gives a constable in uniform the power to stop a pedestrian and search him, or anything carried by him, for articles which could be used for terrorist purposes. A constable may exercise the power whether or not he has any grounds for suspecting the presence of such articles.

1.13   Authority for the use of the power may be given where it appears expedient to do so to prevent acts of terrorism. The authorisation must be given in exactly the same way as explained in paragraph 1.10 (and may in fact be combined with a section 13A authorisation). However, the officer giving an authorisation under section 13B must cause the Secretary of State to be informed, as soon as reasonably practicable, that such an authorisation has been given. The authorisation may take effect before the Secretary of State has decided whether to confirm it. But it ceases to have effect if it is not confirmed by the Secretary of State within 48 hours of its having been given.

1.14   Following notification of the authorisation, the Secretary of State may:

(i)   cancel the authorisation with immediate effect or with effect from such other time as he may direct;

(ii)   confirm it but for a shorter period than that specified in the authorisation (which may not be more than 28 days); or

(iii)   confirm the authorisation as given.

1.15   Further use of the power requires a new authorisation.

1.16   The selection of persons stopped under sections 13A and 13B of the Prevention of Terrorism (Temporary Provision) Act 1989 should reflect an objective assessment of the threat posed by the various terrorist groups active in Great Britain. The powers should not be used to stop and search for reasons unconnected with terrorism. Officers should take particular care not to discriminate against members of ethnic minorities in the exercise of these powers. There may be circumstances, however, where it is appropriate for officers to take account of a person's ethnic origin in selecting persons to be stopped in response to a specific terrorist threat (for example, some international terrorist groups are associated with particular ethnic identities).

[See Notes 1F, 1G and 1I]

Notes for Guidance

1A   Section 60 is amended by section 25 of the Crime and Disorder Act 1998 to provide a power to demand the removal of face coverings where an authority referred to in paragraph 1.8 above is given. The officer exercising the power must reasonably believe that someone is wearing the face covering wholly or mainly for the purpose of concealing identity. There is also a power to seize face coverings where the officer believes that a person intends to wear them for this purpose. **There is not a power to stop and search for face coverings.** An officer may seize any face covering which he comes across when exercising a power of search for something else, or which he sees being carried, and which he reasonably believes is intended to be used for concealing anyone's identity.

1AA   It is important to ensure that powers of stop and search are used responsibly by those who exercise them and those who authorise their use. An officer should bear in mind that he may be required to justify the authorisation or use of the powers to a senior officer and in court, and that misuse of the powers is likely to be harmful to the police effort in the long term and can lead to mistrust of the police by the community. Regardless of the power exercised, all police officers should be careful to ensure that the selection and treatment of those questioned or searched is based upon objective factors and not upon personal prejudice. It is also particularly important to ensure that any person searched is treated courteously and considerately. Where there may be religious sensitivities about asking someone to remove a face covering using the powers in section 25 of the Crime and Disorder Act 1998, for example in the case of a Muslim woman wearing a face covering for religious purposes, the officer should permit the item to be removed out of public view. Where practicable, the item should be removed in the presence of an officer of the same sex as the person and out of sight of anyone of the opposite sex. In all cases, the officer must reasonably believe that the person is wearing the item in question *wholly or mainly* to conceal his or her identity.

1B   This code does not affect the ability of an officer to speak to or question a person in the ordinary course of his duties (and in the absence of reasonable suspicion) without detaining him or exercising any element of compulsion. It is not the purpose of the code to prohibit such encounters between the police and the community with the co-operation of the person concerned and neither does it affect the principle that all citizens have a duty to help police officers to prevent crime and discover offenders.

1C   (Not Used)

1D   Nothing in this code affects

(a)   the routine searching of persons entering sports grounds or other premises with their consent, or as a condition of entry; or

(b)   the ability of an officer to search a person in the street with his consent where no search power exists. In these circumstances, an officer should always make it clear that he is seeking the consent of the person concerned to the search being carried out by telling the person that he need not consent and that without his consent he will not be searched.

1E   If an officer acts in an improper manner this will invalidate a voluntary search. Juveniles, people suffering from a mental handicap or mental disorder and others who appear not to be capable of giving an informed consent should not be subject to a voluntary search.

1F   It is for the authorising officer to determine the period of time during which the powers mentioned in paragraph 1.5(b), (c) and (d) may be exercised. The officer should set the minimum period he considers necessary to deal with the risk of violence, the carrying of knives or offensive weapons, or terrorism. A direction to extend the period authorised under the powers mentioned in paragraph 1.5(b) may be given only once. Thereafter further use of the powers requires a new authorisation. There is no provision to extend an authorisation of the powers mentioned in paragraph 1.5(c) and (d); further use of the powers requires a new authorisation.

1G   It is for the authorising officer to determine the geographical area in which the use of the powers are to be authorised. In doing so he may wish to take into account factors such as the nature and venue of the anticipated incident, the numbers of people who may be in the immediate area of any possible incident, their access to surrounding areas and the anticipated level of violence. The officer should not set a geographical area which is wider than that he believes necessary for the purpose of preventing anticipated violence, the carrying of knives or offensive weapons, or terrorism. It is particularly important to ensure that constables exercising such powers are fully aware of where they may be used. If the area specified is smaller than the whole force area, the officer giving the authorisation should specify either the streets which form the boundary of the area or a divisional boundary within the force area. If the power is to be used in response to a threat or incident that straddles police force areas, an officer from each of the forces concerned will need to give an authorisation.

1H   Other means of identification might include jewellery, insignias, tattoos or other features which are known to identify members of the particular gang or group.

1I   An officer who has authorised the use of powers under section 13B of the Prevention of Terrorism (Temporary Provisions) Act 1989 must take immediate steps to send a copy of the authorisation to the National Joint Unit, Metropolitan Police Special Branch, who will forward it to the Secretary of State. The Secretary of State should be informed of the reasons for the authorisation. The National Joint Unit will inform the force concerned, within 48 hours of the authorisation being made, whether the Secretary of State has confirmed or cancelled or altered the authorisation. The National Joint Unit should also be sent a copy of all section 13A authorisations for national monitoring purposes.

2.   Action before a search is carried out

(a)   Searches requiring reasonable suspicion

2.1   Where an officer has the reasonable grounds for suspicion necessary to exercise a power of stop and search, he may detain the person concerned for the purposes of and with a view to searching him. There is no power to stop or detain a person against his will in order to find grounds for a search.

2.2   Before carrying out a search the officer may question the person about his behaviour or his presence in circumstances which gave rise to the suspicion, since he may have a satisfactory explanation which will make a search unnecessary. If, as a result of any questioning preparatory to a search, or other circumstances which come to the attention of the officer, there cease to be reasonable grounds for suspecting that an article is being carried of a kind for which there is a power of stop and search, no search may take place. [See Note 2A]

2.3   The reasonable grounds for suspicion which are necessary for the exercise of the initial power to detain may be confirmed or eliminated as a result of the questioning of a person detained for the purposes of a search (or such questioning may reveal reasonable grounds to suspect the possession of a different kind of unlawful article from that originally suspected); but the reasonable grounds for suspicion without which any search or detention for the purposes of a search is unlawful cannot be retrospectively provided by such questioning during his detention or by his refusal to answer any question put to him.

(b)   All searches

2.4   Before any search of a detained person or attended vehicle takes place the officer must take reasonable steps to give the person to be searched or in charge of the vehicle the following information:

(i)   his name (except in the case of enquiries linked to the investigation of terrorism, in which case he shall give his warrant or other identification number) and the name of the police station to which he is attached;
(ii)   the object of the search; and
(iii)   his grounds or authorisation for undertaking it.

2.5   If the officer is not in uniform he must show his warrant card. In doing so in the case of enquiries linked to the investigation of terrorism, the officer need not reveal his name. Stops and searches under the powers mentioned in paragraphs 1.5 (b) and (c) may be undertaken only by a constable in uniform.

2.6   Unless it appears to the officer that it will not be practicable to make a record of the search, he must also inform the person to be searched (or the owner or person in charge of a vehicle that is to be searched, as the case may be) that he is entitled to a copy of the record of the search if he asks for it within a year. If the person wishes to have a copy and is not given one on the spot, he shall be advised to which police station he should apply.

2.7   If the person to be searched, or in charge of a vehicle to be searched, does not appear to understand what is being said, or there is any doubt about his ability to understand English, the officer must take reasonable steps to bring the information in paragraphs 2.4 and 2.6 to his attention. If the person is deaf or cannot understand English and has someone with him then the officer must try to establish whether the person can interpret or otherwise help him to give the required information.

Note for Guidance

2A   In some circumstances preparatory questioning may be unnecessary, but in general a brief conversation or exchange will be desirable, not only as a means of avoiding unsuccessful searches but to explain the grounds for the stop/search, to gain co-operation and reduce any tension there might be surrounding the stop/search. Where a person is lawfully detained for the purpose of a search, but no search in the event takes place, the detention will not thereby have been rendered unlawful.

3.   Conduct of the search

3.1   Every reasonable effort must be made to reduce to the minimum the embarrassment that a person being searched may experience.

3.2   The co-operation of the person to be searched shall be sought in every case, even if he initially objects to the search. A forcible search may be made only if it has been established that the person is unwilling to co-operate (e.g. by opening a bag) or resists. Although force may only be used as a last resort, reasonable force may be used if necessary to conduct a search or to detain a person or vehicle for the purposes of a search.

3.3   The length of time for which a person or vehicle may be detained will depend on the circumstances, but must in all circumstances, be reasonable and not extend beyond the time taken for the search. Where the exercise of the power requires reasonable suspicion, the thoroughness and extent of a search must depend on what is suspected of being carried, and by whom. If the suspicion relates to a particular article which is seen to be slipped into a person's pocket, then, in the absence of other grounds for suspicion or an opportunity for the article to be moved elsewhere, the search must be confined to that pocket. In the case of a small article which can readily be concealed, such as a drug, and which might be concealed anywhere on the person, a more extensive search may be necessary. In the case of searches mentioned in paragraph 1.5(b), (c), (d) and (e), which do not require reasonable grounds for suspicion, the officer may make any reasonable search to find what he is empowered to search for. [See Note 3B]

3.4   The search must be conducted at or nearby the place where the person or vehicle was first detained.

3.5   Searches in public must be restricted to superficial examination of outer clothing. There is no power to require a person to remove any clothing in public other than an outer coat, jacket or gloves (other than under sections 13A and 13B of the Prevention of Terrorism (Temporary Provisions) Act 1989, which grant a constable in addition the power to require a person to remove in public any headgear and footwear, or under section 60 of the Criminal Justice and Public Order Act 1994 as amended by the Crime and Disorder Act 1998, which grants a constable power to require the removal of any item worn to conceal identity). Where on reasonable grounds it is considered necessary to conduct a more thorough search (e.g. by requiring a person to take off a T-shirt), this shall be done out of public view for example, in a police van or police station if there is one nearby. Any search involving the removal of more than an outer coat, jacket, gloves, headgear or footwear, or any other item concealing identity, may only be made by an officer of the same sex as the person searched and may not be made in the presence of anyone of the opposite sex unless the person being searched specifically requests it. [See Note 3A and 3C]. No search involving exposure of intimate parts of the body may take place in a police van. All searches involving exposure of intimate parts of the body shall be conducted in accordance with paragraph 11 of Annex A to Code C. The other provisions of Code C do not apply to persons at police stations for the purposes of searches under stop and search powers.

3.5A   The powers under sections 13A and 13B of the Prevention of Terrorism (Temporary Provisions) Act 1989 allow a constable to search only for articles which could be used for terrorist purposes. The powers must not be used for any other purpose (for example to search for drugs in the absence of reasonable grounds for suspicion). However, this would not prevent a search being carried out under other powers if, in course of exercising powers under sections 13A or 13B, the police officer formed reasonable grounds for suspicion.

Notes for Guidance

3A   A search in the street itself should be regarded as being in public for the purposes of paragraph 3.5 above, even though it may be empty at the time a search begins. Although there is no power to require a person to do so, there is nothing to prevent an officer from asking a person to voluntarily remove more than an outer coat, jacket or gloves (and headgear or footwear under section 13A and 13B of the Prevention of Terrorism (Temporary Provisions) Act 1989) in public.

3B   As a search of a person in public should be superficial examination of outer clothing, such searches should be completed as soon as possible.

3C   Where there may be religious sensitivities about asking someone to remove headgear using a power under section 13A or 13B of the Prevention of Terrorism (Temporary Provisions) Act 1989, the police officer should offer to carry out the search out of public view (for example, in a police van or police station if there is one nearby).

4.   Action after a search is carried out

(a)   General

4.1   An officer who has carried out a search must make a written record unless it is not practicable to do so, on account of the numbers to be searched or for some other operational reason, e.g. in situations involving public disorder.

4.2   The records must be completed as soon as practicable – on the spot unless circumstances (e.g. other immediate duties or very bad weather) make this impracticable.

4.3   The record must be made on the form provided for this purpose (the national search record).

4.4   In order to complete the search record the officer shall normally seek the name, address and date of birth of the person searched, but under the search procedures there is no obligation on a person to provide these details and no power to detain him if he is unwilling to do so.

4.5   The following information must always be included in the record of a search even if the person does not wish to identify himself or give his date of birth:
    (i)   the name of the person searched, or (if he withholds it) a description of him;
    (ii)   a note of the person's ethnic origin; [See Note 4DA]
    (iii)   when a vehicle is searched, a description of it, including its registration number; [See Note 4B]
    (iv)   the object of the search;
    (v)   the grounds for making it;
    (vi)   the date and time it was made;
    (vii)   the place where it was made;
    (viii) its results;
    (ix)   a note of any injury or damage to property resulting from it;
    (x)   the identity of the officer making it (except in the case of enquiries linked to the investigation of terrorism, in which case the record shall state the officer's warrant or other identification number and duty station). [See Note 4A]

4.6   A record is required for each person and each vehicle searched. However, if a person is in a vehicle and both are searched, and the object and grounds of the search are the same, only one record need be completed.

4.7   The record of the grounds for making a search must, briefly but informatively, explain the reason for suspecting the person concerned, whether by reference to his behaviour or other circumstances; or in the case of those searches mentioned in paragraph 1.5 (b), (c), (d) and (e) by stating the authority provided to carry out such a search. [See Note 4D]

4.7A   The driver of a vehicle which is stopped in accordance with the powers mentioned in paragraphs 1.5 (b) and (c) may obtain a written statement to that effect within twelve months from the day the vehicle was stopped. A written statement may be similarly obtained by any person if he is searched in accordance with the powers mentioned in paragraph 1.5 (b) and (d) (see paragraph 2.6). The statement may form part of the national search record or be supplied on a separate document. [See Note 4C]

(b)   Unattended vehicles

4.8   After searching an unattended vehicle, or anything in or on it, an officer must leave a notice in it (or on it, if things in or on it have been searched without opening it) recording the fact that it has been searched.

4.9   The notice should include the name of the police station to which the officer concerned is attached and state where a copy of the record of the search may be obtained and where any application for compensation should be directed.

4.10   The vehicle must if practicable be left secure.

Notes for Guidance

4A   Where a search is conducted by more than one officer the identity of all the officers engaged in the search must be recorded on the search record.

4B   Where a vehicle has not been allocated a registration number (e.g. a rally car or a trials motorbike) that part of the requirements under 4.5 (iii) does not apply.

4C   In paragraph 4.7A, a written statement means a record that a person or vehicle was stopped under the powers contained in paragraph 1.5 (b), (c) or (d) of this code.

4D   It is important for national monitoring purposes to specify in the record whether a stop and search under the Prevention of Terrorism (Temporary Provisions) Act 1989 were made under section 13A or section 13B powers.

4DA   Supervising officers, in monitoring the exercise of officers' stop and search powers, should consider in particular whether there is any evidence that officers are exercising their discretion on the basis of stereotyped images of certain persons or groups contrary to the provisions of this code. It is important that any such evidence should be addressed. Supervising officers should take account of the information about the ethnic origin of those stopped and searched which is collected and published under section 95 of the Criminal Justice Act 1991.

ANNEX A

SUMMARY OF MAIN STOP AND SEARCH POWERS [See paragraph 1.3]

POWER	OBJECT OF SEARCH	EXTENT OF SEARCH	WHERE EXERCISABLE
Unlawful articles general			
1. Public Stores Act 1875, s. 6	HM Stores stolen or unlawfully obtained	Persons, vehicles and vessels	Anywhere where the constabulary powers are exercisable
2. Firearms Act 1968, s. 47	Firearms	Persons and vehicles	A public place, or anywhere in the case of reasonable suspicion of offences of carrying firearms with criminal intent or trespassing with firearms
3. Misuse of Drugs Act 1971, s. 23	Controlled drugs	Persons and vehicles	Anywhere
4. Customs and Excise Management Act 1979, s. 163	Goods: (a) on which duty has not been paid; (b) being unlawfully removed, imported or exported; (c) otherwise liable to forfeiture to HM Customs and Excise	Vehicles and vessels only	Anywhere
5. Aviation Security Act 1982, s. 27(1)	Stolen or unlawfully obtained goods	Airport employees and vehicles carrying airport employees or aircraft or any vehicle in a cargo area whether or not carrying an employee	Any designated airport
6. Police and Criminal Evidence Act 1984, s. 1	Stolen goods; articles for use in certain Theft Act offences; offensive weapons, including bladed or sharply-pointed articles (except folding pocket knives with a bladed cutting edge not exceeding 3 inches)	Persons and vehicles	Where there is public access
Police and Criminal Evidence Act 1984, s. 6(3) (by a constable of the United Kingdom Atomic Energy Authority Constabulary in respect of property owned or controlled by British Nuclear Fuels plc)	HM Stores (in the form of goods and chattels belonging to British Nuclear Fuels plc)	Persons, vehicles and vessels	Anywhere where the constabulary powers are exercisable

POWER	OBJECT OF SEARCH	EXTENT OF SEARCH	WHERE EXERCISABLE
7. Sporting Events (Control of Alcohol etc.) Act 1985, s. 7	Intoxicating liquor	Persons, coaches and trains	Designated sports grounds or coaches and trains travelling to or from a designated sporting event
8. Crossbows Act 1987, s. 4	Crossbows or parts of crossbows (except crossbows with a draw weight of less than 1.4 kilograms)	Persons and vehicles	Anywhere except dwellings
Evidence of game and wildlife offences			
9. Poaching Prevention Act 1862, s. 2	Game or poaching equipment	Persons and vehicles	A public place
10. Deer Act 1991, s. 12	Evidence of offences under the Act	Persons and vehicles	Anywhere except dwellings
11. Conservation of Seals Act 1970, s. 4	Seals or hunting equipment	Vehicles only	Anywhere
12. Badgers Act 1992, s. 11	Evidence of offences under the Act	Persons and vehicles	Anywhere
13. Wildlife and Countryside Act 1981, s. 19	Evidence of wildlife offences	Persons and vehicles	Anywhere except dwellings
Other			
14. Prevention of Terrorism (Temporary Provisions) Act 1989, s. 15(3)	Evidence of liability to arrest under section 14 of the Act	Persons	Anywhere
15. Section 13A of the Prevention of Terrorism (Temporary Provisions) Act 1989	Articles which could be used for a purpose connected with the commission, preparation or instigation of acts of terrorism	Vehicles, drivers and passengers	Anywhere within the area or locality authorised under subsection (1)
16. Section 13B of the Prevention of Terrorism (Temporary Provisions) Act 1989	Articles which could be used for a purpose connected with the commission, preparation or instigation of acts of terrorism	Pedestrians	Anywhere within the area of locality authorised
17. Paragraph 4.2 of Schedule 5 to the Prevention of Terrorism (Temporary Provisions) Act 1989	Anything relevant to determining if a person being examined falls within paragraph 2(1)(a) to (c) of Schedule 5	Persons, vehicles, vessels etc	Ports and airports
18. Section 60 Criminal Justice and Public Order Act 1994, as amended by s.8 of the Knives Act 1997	Offensive weapons or dangerous instruments to prevent incidents of serious violence or to deal with the carrying of such items	Persons and vehicles	Anywhere within a locality authorised under subsection (1)

APPENDIX TWO

PACE CODE OF PRACTICE FOR THE SEARCHING OF PREMISES BY POLICE OFFICERS AND THE SEIZURE OF PROPERTY FOUND BY POLICE OFFICERS ON PERSONS OR PREMISES (CODE B)

1. General

1.1 This code of practice must be readily available at all police stations for consultation by police officers, detained persons and members of the public.

1.2 The notes for guidance included are not provisions of this code, but are guidance to police officers and others about its application and interpretation.

1.3 This code applies to searches of premises:
   (a) undertaken for the purposes of an investigation into an alleged offence, with the occupier's consent, other than searches made in the following circumstances:
      – routine scenes of crime searches
      – calls to a fire or a burglary made by or on behalf of an occupier or searches following the activation of fire or burglar alarms
      – searches to which paragraph 4.4 applies
      – bomb threat calls;
   (b) under powers conferred by sections 17, 18 and 32 of the Police and Criminal Evidence Act 1984;
   (c) undertaken in pursuance of a search warrant issued in accordance with section 15 of, or schedule 1 to the Police and Criminal Evidence Act 1984, or section 15 of, or schedule 7 to the Prevention of Terrorism (Temporary Provisions) Act 1989.
'Premises' for the purpose of this code is defined in section 23 of the Police and Criminal Evidence Act 1984. It includes any place and, in particular, any vehicle, vessel, aircraft, hovercraft, tent or movable structure. It also includes any offshore installation as defined in section 1 of the Mineral Workings (Offshore Installations) Act 1971.

1.3A Any search of a person who has not been arrested which is carried out during a search of premises shall be carried out in accordance with Code A.

1.3B   This code does not apply to the exercise of a statutory power to enter premises or to inspect goods, equipment or procedures if the exercise of that power is not dependent on the existence of grounds for suspecting that an offence may have been committed and the person exercising the power has no reasonable grounds for such suspicion.

2.   Search warrants and production orders

(a)   Action to be taken before an application is made

2.1   Where information is received which appears to justify an application, the officer concerned must take reasonable steps to check that the information is accurate, recent and has not been provided maliciously or irresponsibly. An application may not be made on the basis of information from an anonymous source where corroboration has not been sought. [See Note 2A]

2.2   The officer shall ascertain as specifically as is possible in the circumstances the nature of the articles concerned and their location.

2.3   The officer shall also make reasonable enquiries to establish what, if anything, is known about the likely occupier of the premises and the nature of the premises themselves; and whether they have been previously searched and if so how recently; and to obtain any other information relevant to the application.

2.4   No application for a search warrant may be made without the authority of an officer of at least the rank of inspector (or, in the case of urgency where no officer of this rank is readily available, the senior officer on duty). No application for a production order or warrant under schedule 7 to the Prevention of Terrorism (Temporary Provisions) Act 1989, may be made without the authority of an officer of at least the rank of superintendent.

2.5   Except in a case of urgency, if there is reason to believe that a search might have an adverse effect on relations between the police and the community then the local police/community liaison officer shall be consulted before it takes place. In urgent cases, the local police/community liaison officer should be informed of the search as soon as practicable after it has been made. [See Note 2B]

(b)   Making an application

2.6   An application for a search warrant must be supported by an information in writing, specifying:
    (i)   the enactment under which the application is made;
    (ii)   the premises to be searched and the object of the search; and
    (iii)   the grounds on which the application is made (including, where the purpose of the proposed search is to find evidence of an alleged offence, an indication of how the evidence relates to the investigation).

2.7   An application for a search warrant under paragraph 12(a) of Schedule 1 to the Police and Criminal Evidence Act 1984, or under Schedule 7 to the Prevention of Terrorism (Temporary Provisions) Act 1989, shall also, where appropriate, indicate why it is believed that service of notice of an application for a production order may seriously prejudice the investigation.

2.8   If an application is refused, no further application may be made for a warrant to search those premises unless supported by additional grounds.

Notes for Guidance

2A   The identity of an informant need not be disclosed when making an application, but the officer concerned should be prepared to deal with any questions the magistrate or judge may have about the accuracy of previous information provided by that source or other related matters.

2B   The local police/community consultative group, where it exists, or its equivalent, should be informed as soon as practicable after a search has taken place where there is reason to believe that it might have had an adverse effect on relations between the police and the community.

3. Entry without warrant

(a) Making an arrest etc.

3.1 The conditions under which an officer may enter and search premises without a warrant are set out in section 17 of the Police and Criminal Evidence Act 1984.

(b) Search after arrest of premises in which arrest takes place or in which the arrested person was present immediately prior to arrest

3.2 The powers of an officer to search premises in which he has arrested a person or where the person was immediately before he was arrested are as set out in section 32 of the Police and Criminal Evidence Act 1984.

(c) Search after arrest of premises other than those in which arrest takes place

3.3 The specific powers of an officer to search premises occupied or controlled by a person who has been arrested for an arrestable offence are as set out in section 18 of the Police and Criminal Evidence Act 1984. They may not (unless subsection (5) of section 18 applies) be exercised unless an officer of the rank of inspector or above has given authority in writing. That authority shall (unless wholly impracticable) be given on the Notice of Powers and Rights (see paragraph 5.7(i)). The record of the search required by section 18(7) of the Act shall be made in the custody record, where there is one. In the case of enquiries linked to the investigation of terrorism, the authorising officer shall use his warrant or other identification number.

4. Search with consent

4.1 Subject to paragraph 4.4 below, if it is proposed to search premises with the consent of a person entitled to grant entry to the premises the consent must, if practicable, be given in writing on the Notice of Powers and Rights before the search takes place. The officer must make enquiries to satisfy himself that the person is in a position to give such consent. [See Notes 4A and 4B and paragraph 5.7(i)]

4.2 Before seeking consent the officer in charge of the search shall state the purpose of the proposed search and inform the person concerned that he is not obliged to consent and that anything seized may be produced in evidence. If at the time the person is not suspected of an offence, the officer shall tell him so when stating the purpose of the search.

4.3 An officer cannot enter and search premises or continue to search premises under 4.1 above if the consent has been given under duress or is withdrawn before the search is completed.

4.4 It is unnecessary to seek consent under paragraphs 4.1 and 4.2 above where in the circumstances this would cause disproportionate inconvenience to the person concerned. [Note 4C]

Notes for Guidance

4A In the case of a lodging house or similar accommodation a search should not be made on the basis solely of the landlord's consent unless the tenant, lodger or occupier is unavailable and the matter is urgent.

4B Where it is intended to search premises under the authority of a warrant or a power of entry and search without warrant, and the co-operation of the occupier of the premises is obtained in accordance with paragraph 5.4 below, there is no additional requirement to obtain written consent as at paragraph 4.1 above.

4C Paragraph 4.4 is intended in particular to apply to circumstances where it is reasonable to assume that innocent occupiers would agree to, and expect that, police should take the proposed action. Examples are where a suspect has fled from the scene of a crime or to evade arrest and it is necessary quickly to check surrounding gardens and readily accessible places to see whether he is hiding; or where police have arrested someone in the night after a pursuit and it is necessary to make a brief check of gardens along the route of the pursuit to see whether stolen or incriminating articles have been discarded.

5. Searching of premises: general considerations

(a) Time of searches

5.1 Searches made under warrant must be made within one calendar month from the date of issue of the warrant.

5.2   Searches must be made at a reasonable hour unless this might frustrate the purpose of the search. [See Note 5A]

5.3   A warrant authorises an entry on one occasion only.

(b)   Entry other than with consent

5.4   The officer in charge shall first attempt to communicate with the occupier or any other person entitled to grant access to the premises by explaining the authority under which he seeks entry to the premises and ask the occupier to allow him to enter, unless:

(i)   the premises to be searched are known to be unoccupied;

(ii)   the occupier and any other person entitled to grant access are known to be absent; or

(iii)   there are reasonable grounds for believing that to alert the occupier or any other person entitled to grant access by attempting to communicate with him would frustrate the object of the search or endanger the officers concerned or other people.

5.5   Where the premises are occupied the officer shall identify himself (by warrant or other identification number in the case of inquiries linked to the investigation of terrorism) and, if not in uniform, show his warrant card (but in so doing in the case of enquiries linked to the investigation of terrorism, the officer need not reveal his name); and state the purpose of the search and the grounds for undertaking it, before a search begins, unless sub-paragraph 5.4 (iii) applies.

5.6   Reasonable force may be used if necessary to enter premises if the officer in charge is satisfied that the premises are those specified in any warrant, or in exercise of the powers described in 3.1 to 3.3 above, and where:

(i)   the occupier or any other person entitled to grant access has refused a request to allow entry to his premises;

(ii)   it is impossible to communicate with the occupier or any other person entitled to grant access; or

(iii)   any of the provisions of 5.4(i) to (iii) apply.

(c)   Notice of powers and rights

5.7   If an officer conducts a search to which this code applies he shall, unless it is impracticable to do so, provide the occupier with a copy of a notice in a standard format:

(i)   specifying whether the search is made under warrant, or with consent, or in the exercise of the powers described in 3.1 to 3.3 above (the format of the notice shall provide for authority or consent to be indicated where appropriate – see 3.3 and 4.1 above);

(ii)   summarising the extent of the powers of search and seizure conferred in the Act;

(iii)   explaining the rights of the occupier, and of the owner of property seized in accordance with the provisions of 6.1 to 6.5 below, set out in the Act and in this code;

(iv)   explaining that compensation may be payable in appropriate cases for damages caused in entering and searching premises, and giving the address to which an application for compensation should be directed; and

(v)   stating that a copy of this code is available to be consulted at any police station.

5.8   If the occupier is present, copies of the notice mentioned above, and of the warrant (if the search is made under warrant) should if practicable be given to the occupier before the search begins, unless the officer in charge of the search reasonably believes that to do so would frustrate the object of the search or endanger the officers concerned or other people. If the occupier is not present, copies of the notice, and of the warrant where appropriate, should be left in a prominent place on the premises or appropriate part of the premises and endorsed with the name of the officer in charge of the search (except in the case of inquiries linked to the investigation of terrorism, in which case the officer's warrant or other identification number shall be given), the name of the police station to which he is attached and the date and time of the search. The warrant itself shall be endorsed to show that this has been done.

(d)   Conduct of searches

5.9   Premises may be searched only to the extent necessary to achieve the object of the search, having regard to the size and nature of whatever is sought. A search under warrant may not continue under the authority of that warrant once all the things specified in it have been found, or the officer in charge of the search is satisfied that they are not on the premises.

5.10 Searches must be conducted with due consideration for the property and privacy of the occupier of the premises searched, and with no more disturbance than necessary. Reasonable force may be used only where this is necessary because the co-operation of the occupier cannot be obtained or is insufficient for the purpose.

5.11 If the occupier wishes to ask a friend, neighbour or other person to witness the search then he must be allowed to do so, unless the officer in charge has reasonable grounds for believing that this would seriously hinder the investigation or endanger the officers concerned or other people. A search need not be unreasonably delayed for this purpose.

(e) Leaving premises

5.12 If premises have been entered by force the officer in charge shall before leaving them, satisfy himself that they are secure either by arranging for the occupier or his agent to be present or by any other appropriate means.

(f) Search under Schedule 1 to the Police and Criminal Evidence Act 1984

5.13 An officer of the rank of inspector or above shall take charge of and be present at any search made under a warrant issued under schedule 1 to the Police and Criminal Evidence Act 1984 or under schedule 7 to the Prevention of Terrorism (Temporary Provisions) Act 1989. He is responsible for ensuring that the search is conducted with discretion and in such a manner as to cause the least possible disruption to any business or other activities carried on in the premises.

5.14 After satisfying himself that material may not be taken from the premises without his knowledge, the officer in charge of the search shall ask for the documents or other records concerned to be produced. He may also, if he considers it to be necessary, ask to see the index to files held on the premises, if there is one; and the officers conducting the search may inspect any files which, according to the index, appear to contain any of the material sought. A more extensive search of the premises may be made only if the person responsible for them refuses to produce the material sought, or to allow access to the index; if it appears that the index is inaccurate or incomplete; or if for any other reason the officer in charge has reasonable grounds for believing that such a search is necessary in order to find the material sought. [See Note 5B]

Notes for Guidance

5A In determining at what time to make a search, the officer in charge should have regard, among other considerations, to the time of day at which the occupier of the premises is likely to be present, and should not search at a time when he, or any other person on the premises, is likely to be asleep unless not doing so is likely to frustrate the purpose of the search.

5B In asking for documents to be produced in accordance with paragraph 5.14 above, officers should direct the request to a person in authority and with responsibility for the documents.

5C If the wrong premises are searched by mistake, everything possible should be done at the earliest opportunity to allay any sense of grievance. In appropriate cases assistance should be given to obtain compensation.

6. Seizure and retention of property

(a) Seizure

6.1 Subject to paragraph 6.2 below, an officer who is searching any premises under any statutory power or with the consent of the occupier may seize:
   (a) anything covered by a warrant; and
   (b) anything which he has reasonable grounds for believing is evidence of an offence or has been obtained in consequence of the commission of an offence.
Items under (b) may only be seized where this is necessary to prevent their concealment, alteration, loss, damage or destruction.

6.2   No item may be seized which is subject to legal privilege (as defined in section 10 of the Police and Criminal Evidence Act 1984).

6.3   An officer who decides that it is not appropriate to seize property because of an explanation given by the person holding it, but who has reasonable grounds for believing that it has been obtained in consequence of the commission of an offence by some person, shall inform the holder of his suspicions and shall explain that, if he disposes of the property, he may be liable to civil or criminal proceedings.

6.4   An officer may photograph or copy, or have photographed or copied, any document or other article which he has power to seize in accordance with paragraph 6.1 above.

6.5   Where an officer considers that a computer may contain information which could be used in evidence, he may require the information to be produced in a form which can be taken away and in which it is visible and legible.

(b)   Retention

6.6   Subject to paragraph 6.7 below, anything which has been seized in accordance with the above provisions may be retained only for as long as is necessary in the circumstances. It may be retained, among other purposes:
    (i)   for use as evidence at a trial for an offence;
    (ii)   for forensic examination or for other investigation in connection with an offence; or
    (iii)   where there are reasonable grounds for believing that it has been stolen or obtained by the commission of an offence, in order to establish its lawful owner.

6.7   Property shall not be retained in accordance with 6.6(i) and (ii) (i.e. for use as evidence or for the purposes of investigation) if a photograph or copy would suffice for those purposes.

(c)   Rights of owners etc.

6.8   If property is retained the person who had custody or control of it immediately prior to its seizure must on request be provided with a list or description of the property within a reasonable time.

6.9   He or his representative must be allowed supervised access to the property to examine it or have it photographed or copied, or must be provided with a photograph or copy, in either case within a reasonable time of any request and at his own expense, unless the officer in charge of an investigation has reasonable grounds for believing that this would prejudice the investigation of an offence or any criminal proceedings. In this case a record of the grounds must be made.

Note for Guidance

6A   Any person claiming property seized by the police may apply to a magistrates' court under the Police (Property) Act 1897 for its possession, and should, where appropriate, be advised of this procedure.

7.   Action to be taken after searches

7.1   Where premises have been searched in circumstances to which this code applies, other than in the circumstances covered by the exceptions to paragraph 1.3(a), the officer in charge of the search shall, on arrival at a police station, make or have made a record of the search. The record shall include:
    (i)   the address of the premises searched;
    (ii)   the date, time and duration of the search;
    (iii)   the authority under which the search was made. Where the search was made in the exercise of a statutory power to search premises without warrant, the record shall include the power under which the search was made; and where the search was made under warrant, or with written consent, a copy of the warrant or consent shall be appended to the record or kept in a place identified in the record;
    (iv)   the names of all the officers who conducted the search (except in the case of enquiries linked to the investigation of terrorism, in which case the record shall state the warrant or other identification number and duty station of each officer concerned);
    (v)   the names of any people on the premises if they are known;
    (vi)   either a list of any articles seized or a note of where such a list is kept and, if not covered by a warrant, the reason for their seizure;

(vii)   whether force was used, and, if so, the reason why it was used;

(viii)   details of any damage caused during the search, and the circumstances in which it was caused.

7.2   Where premises have been searched under warrant, the warrant shall be endorsed to show:

(i)   whether any articles specified in the warrant were found;

(ii)   whether any other articles were seized;

(iii)   the date and time at which it was executed;

(iv)   the names of the officers who executed it (except in the case of enquiries linked to the investigation of terrorism, in which case the warrant or other identification number and duty station of each officer concerned shall be shown);

(v)   whether a copy, together with a copy of the Notice of Powers and Rights was handed to the occupier; or whether it was endorsed as requested by paragraph 5.8, and left on the premises together with the copy notice and, if so, where.

7.3   Any warrant which has been executed or which has not been executed within one calendar month of its issue shall be returned, if it was issued by a justice of the peace, to the clerk to the justices for the petty sessions area concerned or, if issued by a judge, to the appropriate officer of the court from which he issued it.

8. Search registers

8.1   A search register shall be maintained at each sub-divisional police station. All records which are required to be made by this code shall be made, copied, or referred to in the register.

APPENDIX THREE

CPS PUBLIC ORDER OFFENCES CHARGING STANDARD

AGREED BY THE POLICE AND THE CROWN PROSECUTION SERVICE

PUBLIC ORDER OFFENCES CHARGING STANDARD

INDEX

PUBLIC ORDER OFFENCES CHARGING STANDARD AGREED BY THE POLICE AND CROWN PROSECUTION SERVICE

1 Charging Standard — Purpose

1.1 The purpose of joint charging standards is to make sure that the most appropriate charge is selected, in the light of the evidence which can be proved, at the earliest possible opportunity. This will help the police and Crown Prosecutors in preparing the case. Adoption of this joint standard should lead to a reduction in the number of times charges have to be amended which in turn should lead to an increase in efficiency and a reduction in avoidable extra work for the police and the Crown Prosecution Service.

1.2 This joint charging standard offers guidance to police officers who have responsibility for charging and to Crown Prosecutors on the most appropriate charge to be preferred in cases relating to public order offences. The guidance:

- **should not be used** in the determination of any **pre-charge** decision, such as the decision to arrest;

- **does not** override any guidance issued on the use of appropriate alternative forms of disposal **short of charge**, such as cautioning;

- **does not** override the principles set out in the Code for Crown Prosecutors;

- **does not** override the need for consideration to be given in every case as to whether a charge/prosecution is in the public interest;

- **does not** remove the need for each case to be considered on its individual merits or fetter the discretion of the police to charge and the CPS to prosecute the most appropriate offence depending on the particular facts of the case in question.

2 Introduction

2.1 The criminal law in respect of public order offences is intended to penalise the use of violence and/or intimidation by individuals or groups. The principal public order offences are contained in Part I of the Public Order Act 1986 ('the Act'). Further offences are found in Part III of the Act which deals with public disorder designed to stir up racial hatred. Other public order offences are set out in the Football Offences Act 1991, and reference is also made to the offence of drunk and disorderly behaviour. This joint standard gives guidance about the charge which should be preferred if the criteria set out in the Code for Crown Prosecutors are met.

2.2 This standard covers the following offences:

- using threatening, abusive or insulting words or behaviour, or disorderly behaviour likely to cause harassment, alarm or distress — **section 5 of the Act**;

- using threatening, abusive or insulting words or behaviour, or disorderly behaviour **intending to and causing** harassment, alarm or distress **section 4A of the Act**;

- using threatening, abusive or insulting words or behaviour causing fear of or provoking violence — **section 4 of the Act**;

- using threatening, abusive or insulting words or behaviour **intended or likely to stir up racial hatred** — **section 18 of the Act**;

- publishing or distributing material which is threatening, abusive or insulting and **intended or likely to stir up racial hatred** — **section 19 of the Act**;

- possessing racially inflammatory material — **section 23 of the Act**;

- affray — **section 3 of the Act**;

- violent disorder — **section 2 of the Act**;

- riot — **section 1 of the Act**;

- drunk and disorderly behaviour — **section 91 Criminal Justice Act 1967**;

- offences contrary to **sections 2, 3, and 4 of the Football (Offences) Act 1991**.

2.3   Offences involving public disorder are often a precursor to, or part of, the commission of other offences. An offence under the Act may, for example, also lead to or involve an assault, unlawful possession of a weapon or the causing of criminal damage. Paragraph 10 below gives guidance on the selection of the appropriate number and type of charges in such cases.

3   General Principles: Charging Practice

3.1   You should always have in mind the following general principles when selecting the appropriate charge(s):

(i)   the charge(s) should accurately reflect the extent of the defendant's alleged involvement and responsibility, thereby allowing the courts the discretion to sentence appropriately;

(ii)   the choice of charges should ensure the clear and simple presentation of the case, particularly where there is more than one defendant;

(iii)   it is wrong to encourage a defendant to plead guilty to a few charges by selecting more charges than are necessary;

(iv)   it is wrong to select a more serious charge which is not supported by the evidence in order to encourage a plea of guilty to a lesser allegation.

4   General Principle: Public Order Act offences

4.1   The purpose of public order law is to ensure that individual rights to freedom of speech and freedom of assembly are balanced against the rights of others to go about their daily lives unhindered.

5   Offences contrary to sections 5, 4A, 4, 18, 19 and 23 of the Act and section 91 Criminal Justice Act 1967

5.1   There is an overlap in the conduct required to commit any one of these offences.

5.2   To use this section of the Charging Standard you should:

- consider which category the behaviour complained of falls into; and

- refer to the relevant paragraphs to identify which offence may be appropriate to charge and prosecute.

5.3   The categories of conduct are:

- disorderly behaviour (paragraph 5.5–5.18);

- using threatening, abusive or insulting words or behaviour (paragraph 5.19–5.28); and

- publishing, distributing or displaying any writing, sign or other visible representation which is threatening, abusive or insulting (paragraph 5.29–5.33).

5.4   Not all the offences cover each type of behaviour.

Disorderly Behaviour

5.5   Whether behaviour can be properly categorised as disorderly is a question of fact. Disorderly behaviour does not require any element of violence, actual or threatened; and it includes conduct that is not necessarily threatening, abusive or insulting. It is not necessary to prove any feeling of insecurity, in an apprehensive sense, on the part of a member of the public: *Chambers and Edwards* v *DPP* [1995] Crim LR 896. The following types of conduct are examples which may at least be capable of amounting to disorderly behaviour:

- causing a disturbance in a residential area or common part of a block of flats by, for example:

    — persistently shouting;
    — knocking over dustbins;
    — putting refuse through letter-boxes;
    — banging on doors;
    — blockading entrances;
    — throwing things down the stairs;
    — peering in windows;

- persistently shouting abuse or obscenities at passers-by;

- pestering people waiting to catch public transport or otherwise waiting lawfully in a queue;

- rowdy behaviour in a street late at night which might alarm residents or passers-by, especially those who may be vulnerable, such as the elderly or members of an ethnic minority group;

- causing a disturbance in a shopping precinct or other area to which the public have access or might otherwise gather;

- the use of placards, slogans or language aimed at causing distress.

5.6   Where you are satisfied that you are dealing with an offence amounting to disorderly behaviour, the choice of charge is between the following:

- drunk and disorderly behaviour — **section 91 of the Criminal Justice Act 1967**;
- **section 5 of the Act**;
- **section 4A of the Act**.

5.7   The following table sets out what has to be proved in respect of each offence:

TABLE I: ELEMENTS REQUIRED TO PROVE OFFENCES CONTRARY TO S. 91 CJA 1967, S. 5 AND S. 4A OF THE PUBLIC ORDER ACT — DISORDERLY BEHAVIOUR.

Drunk and Disorderly contrary to Section 91 CJA 1967	Section 5 of the Act	Section 4A of the Act
disorderly behaviour	disorderly behaviour	disorderly behaviour
in any public place	in a public or private place (but not when confined to a dwelling house — See paragraph 5.11)	in a public or private place (but not when confined to a dwelling house — see paragraph 5.11)
while drunk		
	with intention or awareness that behaviour may be disorderly; **or** with intention or awareness that such behaviour may be threatening, abusive or insulting	with intent to cause and thereby causing
	within the hearing or sight of a person likely to be caused	
	harassment, alarm or distress	harassment, alarm or distress

5.8   An offence under **section 5** should be charged where there is **disorderly behaviour**, together with evidence that:

- the suspect intended his behaviour to be or was aware that it may be disorderly;

- and it was likely that harassment, alarm or distress would occur as a result: section 6 of the Act.

5.9   There must be a person within the sight or hearing of the suspect who is likely to be caused harassment, alarm or distress by the conduct in question. A police officer may be such a person, but remember that this is a question of fact to be decided in each case by the magistrates. In determining this, the magistrates may take into account the familiarity which police officers have with the words and conduct typically seen in incidents of disorderly conduct. (*DPP* v *Orum* [1988] Crim LR 848.)

5.10   Although the existence of a person who is caused harassment alarm and distress must be proved, there is no requirement that they actually give evidence. In appropriate cases, the offence may be proved on a police officer's evidence alone.

5.11   The conduct may take place in a public or private place. No offence is committed under this section, however, if such conduct takes place inside a dwelling and the other person is also inside that or another dwelling.

5.12   Police officers are aware of the difficult balance to be struck in dealing with those whose behaviour may be perceived by some as exuberant high spirits but by others as disorderly. In such cases informal methods of disposal may be appropriate and effective; but if this approach fails and the disorderly conduct continues then criminal proceedings may be necessary. Section 5 should be used in cases which amount to less serious incidents of anti-social behaviour. Where violence has been used, it is not normally appropriate to charge an offence under section 5.

5.13   In deciding whether a charge under section 5 is appropriate, the nature of the conduct must be considered in light of the penalty that the suspect is likely to receive on conviction.

5.14   As a prerequisite to the execution of a lawful arrest for an offence under section 5, the accused must have been warned by the arresting police officer to refrain from continuing with the disorderly behaviour: *DPP* v *Hancock and Tuttle* [1995] Crim LR 139. (**NB** Any officer may exercise the power of arrest so long as the warning has been given by a police officer on or after 17 October 1996 — Public Order (Amendment) Act 1996.)

5.15   Where there is reliable evidence that the accused was drunk in a public place at the time of the alleged offence to the extent that the accused had lost the power of self control, a charge of drunk and disorderly behaviour should be preferred where otherwise a section 5 charge would be appropriate.

5.16   A charge under section 4A will **only** be appropriate if:

i   the accused **intended** to cause harassment alarm or distress

and

ii   the accused actually **caused** harassment alarm or distress.

If **either** one or both of these additional features is **not** present, a charge under section 5 or, if appropriate, a charge of drunk and disorderly will be the only alternatives available.

5.17   Section 4A may be appropriate where there is evidence of a persistent course of conduct causing harassment, alarm and distress; for example, in cases of racial harassment or 'stalking' behaviour.

5.18   The offence may take place in a public or private place. No offence under this section is committed, however, if such conduct takes place inside a dwelling and the person to whom it is directed is inside that or another dwelling.

Using threatening, abusive or insulting words or behaviour

5.19   The following types of conduct are examples which may at least be capable of amounting to threatening, abusive or insulting words or behaviour:

- threats made or abuse directed towards individuals carrying out public service duties or jobs, such as ambulance workers, fire fighters or bus or train drivers;

- the throwing of missiles by a person taking part in a demonstration or other public gathering where no injury is caused;

- scuffles or incidents of minor violence or threats of violence committed in the context of a brawl (such as in or in the vicinity of a public house);

- incidents between neighbours or within domestic relationships which do not justify a charge of assault;

- incidents which do not justify a charge of assault where an individual is picked on by a gang.

5.20   Where you are satisfied that you are dealing with an offence of using threatening, abusive or insulting words or behaviour, the choice of charge is between the following:

- **section 5**;
- **section 4A**;
- **section 4**;
- **section 18**.

5.21   The following table sets out what has to be proved in respect of each offence:

TABLE II: ELEMENTS REQUIRED TO PROVE OFFENCES CONTRARY TO S. 5, S. 4A, S. 4(1)(a) OR S. 18 OF THE PUBLIC ORDER ACT — THREATENING, ABUSIVE OR INSULTING WORDS OR BEHAVIOUR.

Section 5	Section 4A	Section 4(1)(a)	Section 18*
threatening, abusive or insulting words or behaviour	threatening, abusive or insulting words or behaviour	threatening, abusive or insulting words or behaviour	uses threatening, abusive or insulting words or behaviour
		towards another person	
within the hearing or sight of person likely to be caused	with intent to cause and thereby causing	*either:* with intent to cause that person to believe that immediate unlawful violence will be used against him or another by any person *or:* with intent to provoke the immediate use of unlawful violence by that person or another	with intent to stir up racial hatred or by which racial hatred is likely to be stirred up
harassment, alarm or distress	harassment, alarm or distress	*or:* whereby that person is likely to believe that such violence will be used *or:* it is likely that such violence will be provoked	
with intention or awareness that such behaviour may be threatening, abusive or insulting			*requires AG's consent.

5.22   Conduct which may be capable of amounting to threatening, abusive or insulting words or behaviour for the purposes of an offence under section 4 will be more serious than that required under section 5 or section 4A.

5.23   A charge under section 4 will only be appropriate where there is evidence that the accused **intended** or was aware that his words or behaviour — **being directed towards another person** — were or may have been threatening, abusive or insulting **and** either:

- the accused intended the person against whom the conduct was directed to believe that immediate unlawful violence would be used against him or another by any person; **or**

- the accused intended to provoke the immediate use of unlawful violence by that person or another; **or**

- the person against whom the conduct was directed was likely to believe that violence would be used; **or**

- it was likely that such violence would be provoked.

5.24   The offence may take place in a public or private place. No offence under this section is committed, however, if such conduct takes place inside a dwelling and the other person is also inside that or another dwelling.

5.25   Where there is insufficient evidence to establish any of the elements specified in paragraph 5.23:

either:

a charge under **section 4A** may be appropriate if:
— the suspect had an **intent** to cause harassment alarm or distress **and**
— actually **caused** harassment alarm or distress;

or:

a charge under **section 5** may be appropriate if:
— the prohibited conduct took place within the hearing or sight of a person **likely** to be caused harassment alarm or distress.

5.26   In deciding upon the correct charge as between section 5, section 4A and section 4, it will be necessary to consider the nature of the conduct and the likely penalty that the suspect would receive on conviction.

5.27   If you think that a charge under section 18 may be appropriate, you must refer to the guidance given in paragraphs 5.34–5.48. Please note in particular that a prosecution may not be instituted for an offence under section 18 of the Act, without the consent of the Attorney General.

5.28   The offence under section 18 may be committed in a public or private place. No offence is committed, however, if such conduct takes place inside a dwelling and the person to whom it is directed is inside that or another dwelling.

Publishing, distributing or displaying any writing, sign or other visible representation

5.29   Where you are satisfied that you are dealing with an offence amounting to the publishing, distributing or displaying of any writing, sign or other visible representation, the choice of charge is between the following:

- section 5;
- section 4A;
- section 4;
- section 18;
- section 19.

5.30   The following table sets out what has to be proved in respect of each offence:

TABLE III: ELEMENTS REQUIRED TO PROVE OFFENCES CONTRARY TO S. 5, S. 4A, S. 4, S. 18 OR S. 19 OF THE PUBLIC ORDER ACT — PUBLISHING, DISTRIBUTING OR DISPLAYING ANY WRITING, SIGN ETC.

Section 5	Section 4A	Section 4	Section 18*	Section 19*
		distributes or		publishes/ distributes
displays	displays	displays	displays	
any writing sign or other visible repres.	any writing sign or other visible representation	any writing sign or other visible representation		
which is threatening, abusive or insulting	which is threatening, abusive or insulting	which is threatening, abusive or insulting	which is threatening, abusive or insulting	which is threatening, abusive or insulting
within the hearing or sight of a person likely to be caused	with intent to cause and thereby causing	*either:* with intent to cause that person to believe that immediate unlawful violence will be used against him or another by any person; *or:* with intent to provoke the immediate use of unlawful violence by that person or another; *or:* whereby that person is likely to believe that such violence will be used; *or:* it is likely that such violence will be provoked	with intent to stir up racial hatred or racial hatred is likely to be stirred up	with intent to stire up racial hatred or racial hatred is likely to be stirred up
harassment, alarm or distress thereby	harassment, alarm or distress thereby			
with intention or awareness			* requires AG's consent.	* requires AG's consent

5.31   If you think that a charge under section 18 or 19 may be appropriate, **you must refer to the guidance given in paragraphs 5.34–5.48**. Please note in particular that a prosecution may not be instituted for an offence under section 18 or 19 of the Act, without the consent of the Attorney General.

5.32   Section 1 of the Malicious Communications Act 1988 may be a useful charge if a letter or other article has been sent to a person or persons to cause distress or anxiety. In particular, you may use it as an alternative to section 18 where the material in question is sent to a selected individual or individuals with a hostile intent which is racially motivated but the more general intention to stir up racial hatred required by section 18 is not present.

5.33   For the purposes of section 19, it must be proved that there was a publication or distribution to the public or to a section of the public. Written matter includes any sign or other visible representation.

Racially motivated crimes: Relationship between offences contrary to Part I of the Act and Part III of the Act

5.34   Part III Public Order Act 1986 (sections 17 to 29) creates a number of offences concerned with inciting racial hatred. The offences involve:

- conduct (using words or behaviour, publishing, displaying etc);

- which is threatening, abusive or insulting; and

which is either intended or likely to stir up racial hatred.

Part III offences involve **incitement to racial hatred**. Conduct which is contrary to offences set out in Part I of the Act (sections 1 to 5) may be racially motivated but may not involve incitement to racial hatred. If that is the case, you should charge the appropriate Part I offence. Remember that racial motivation, whether a Part I or Part III offence is involved, is recognised as a public interest factor weighing in favour of prosecution in the Code for Crown Prosecutors. Thus, the public interest will always tend to favour a prosecution in these cases when there is sufficient evidence.

5.35   'Racial hatred' is defined as 'hatred against a group of persons in Great Britain defined by reference to colour, race, nationality . . . or ethnic or national origins': section 17.

5.36   'Hatred' is not defined by the Act. It is much stronger than ridicule or contempt; it is not enough to cause offence or to mock a racial group. 'Hatred' connotes an element of hostility.

5.37   It is an offence to use words or behaviour, or display any written material, which is threatening, abusive or insulting and either intended or likely in all the circumstances to stir up racial hatred: section 18.

5.38   **Part III offences require the consent of the Attorney General to be prosecuted**: section 27. Consent need not be obtained pre-charge (section 25 Prosecution of Offences Act 1985) but must be obtained before the case proceeds to mode of trial proceedings. Generally, however, you should submit the case for consent prior to charging. Police should therefore submit such cases to the CPS for pre-charge advice, with a view to seeking consent if that it appropriate.

5.39   The Attorney General's consent must be sought by the CPS Area through CPS Central Casework (Prosecutions). CPS Central Casework will be responsible for reviewing the evidence and applying for consent in appropriate cases. Whenever there is sufficient evidence to support a Part III charge the case must be referred by the CPS Area to CPS Central Casework (Prosecutions).

5.40   It is important to distinguish between conduct which amounts to an offence under Part I of the Act (particularly sections 5, 4A and 4) and conduct which amounts to an offence under Part III (particularly section 18). The distinction is in the effect the conduct has on the audience (person or persons) who sees/hears the conduct.

5.41   The effect of Part I conduct is to cause offence to the audience of that conduct, by being threatening, abusive or insulting towards the audience. The effect, likely or intended, of Part III conduct is not to offend the audience but to incite them to hatred of a racial group other than that of the audience.

5.42   The general guide is that a charge under Part I should be considered when the conduct is motivated by the audience's race; and a charge under Part III should be considered when the conduct is motivated by the race of a group other than that of the audience.

5.43   A practical example may help: a person uses language which is abusive of a racial group.

- If the audience is exclusively made up of that racial group then it is unlikely that the speaker either intends or is likely to stir up the audience to hatred of the audience's own racial group: a Part III charge will be inappropriate; a Part I charge may be appropriate, aggravated by the racial motivation.

- If the audience is exclusively made up of some other racial group (for example, the same racial group as the speaker) then it may be that there is an intention or likelihood of the speaker stirring up racial hatred in the audience, in which instance a charge under Part III may be appropriate.

5.44   There may be instances when the defendant's conduct does amount to an offence under Part I and Part III of the Act. This is likely to occur when the audience is not exclusively made up of one racial group but is made up of individuals of more than one racial group, each affected by the conduct in different ways, such as in the following circumstances:

- when members of the abused racial group and the defendant's supporters (of a different racial group) are both present and the defendant's conduct, or individual parts of the conduct, is aimed at both groups;

- when there are two or more defendants acting together in a racially motivated attack (verbal and/or physical) upon a victim; as well as the conduct towards the victim of the attack, there may be some conduct, either express or implied, between the defendants amounting to mutual encouragement; and

- when bystanders unconnected with either the defendant or the victim witness the defendant racially attacking (verbally and/or physically) a victim.

5.45   In each instance the conduct must be considered both as a whole and by its constituent parts. The appropriate charge(s) must reflect the seriousness of the conduct. The following should be in mind:

- when there are two or more defendants acting together in a racially motivated attack, as equal partners, it will be more appropriate to pursue a non-Part III offence and to emphasise the racial motivation as an aggravating feature;

- when there are two or more defendants acting together in a racially motivated attack, and one defendant takes a lead role, encouraging and directing others to commit a racially motivated crime while standing apart from the actual attack on the victim, a Part III charge should be considered: such a Part III charge will attach to the conduct of the defendant towards others within his group, not to the conduct of the defendant towards the victim of the racially motivated crime;

- when there are bystanders, unconnected with either the defendant(s) or the victim of a racially motivated attack, a Part III charge may follow if there is some explicit act on the part of the defendant, intended or likely to incite the bystanders. Otherwise, a Part I offence, aggravated by the racial motivation, should be charged. In cases where bystanders make statements expressing sympathy for the victim it will be difficult to support a Part III offence.

5.46   When the evidence supports an offence contrary to sections 5, 4A or 4 of the Act and section 18 of the Act, the section 18 offence should be preferred.

5.47   When the evidence supports an offence contrary to sections 1, 2 or 3 of the Act and section 18, both the Part I and Part III offence should be charged.

5.48   When there is evidence of any other offence linked to the section 18 offence, you should refer to paragraph 10 for further guidance.

Possessing Racially Inflammatory Material

5.49   A charge under section 23 of the Act may be appropriate where there is evidence that a person:

— was in possession of written material
— which is threatening, abusive or insulting
— with a view to its being displayed, published, distributed broadcast or included in a cable programme service
— intending racial hatred to be stirred up thereby; or where,
— having regard to all the circumstances, racial hatred is likely to be stirred up thereby.

5.50   A prosecution may not be instituted for an offence under section 23 of the Act without the consent of the Attorney General.

5.51   For the purposes of section 23, it is not necessary to prove that the accused had physical custody of the material, provided it can be established that he exercised control over it.

5.52   It is a defence for the accused to prove that he was not aware of the content of the material and neither suspected nor had reason to suspect that it was threatening, abusive or insulting.

Penalties and Venue for all offences in paragraph 5

5.53   Table IV sets out details of the mode of prosecution and the penalties for all offences referred to in paragraph 5.

TABLE IV: PROSECUTION AND PUNISHMENT OF OFFENCES REFERRED TO IN PARAGRAPH 5

Offence	General Nature of Offence	Mode of Prosecution	Punishment	Additional Provisions
S. 91 CJA 1967	Drunk and disorderly	Summary	Level 3 fine	
S. 5 POA 1986	Harassment, alarm or distress	Summary	Level 3 fine	
S. 4A POA 1986	Intentional harassment, alarm or distress	Summary	6 months and/or level 5 fine	
S. 4 POA 1986	Fear or provocation of violence	Summary	6 months and/or level 5 fine	
S. 18 POA 1986	Acts intended or likely to stir up racial hatred — use of words or behaviour or display of written material	Either way	(a) Summary: 6 months and/or level 5 fine (b) On indictment: 2 years and/or a fine	Requires AG's consent
S. 19 POA 1986	Acts likely to stir up racial hatred — publishing or distributing written material	Either way	(a) Summary: 6 months and/or level 5 fine (b) On indictment: 2 years and/or a fine	Requires AG's consent
S. 23 POA 1986	Possession of racially inflammatory material	Either way	(a) Summary: 6 months and/or level 5 fine (b) On indictment: 2 years and/or a fine	Requires AG's consent
S. 1 Malicious Communications Act 1988	Offence of sending letters etc. with intent to cause distress or anxiety	Summary	Level 4 fine	

6 Affray

6.1   Under section 3 of the Act, it must be proved that a person has used or threatened:

— unlawful violence
— towards another
— and his conduct is such as would cause
— a person of reasonable firmness
— present at the scene
— to fear for his personal safety.

6.2   The seriousness of the offence lies in the effect that the behaviour of the accused has on members of the public who may have been put in **fear**. There must be some conduct, **beyond the use of words**, which is threatening and directed towards a person or persons. Mere words are not enough. Violent conduct towards property alone is not sufficient for the purposes of an offence under section 3. The offence is **not** confined to group disorder.

6.3   An offence under section 3 is triable either way. The maximum penalty on conviction on indictment is three years' imprisonment and/or a fine of unlimited amount. On summary conviction the maximum penalty is six months' imprisonment and/or a fine not exceeding level 5.

6.4   The offence may be committed in a **public or private place**.

6.5   Examples of the type of conduct appropriate for a section 3 offence include:

- a fight between two people in a place where members of the general public are present (for example, in a public house, discotheque, restaurant or street) and are put in fear for their safety (although the fighting is not directed towards them);

- a person who, on being refused entry to a nightclub, throws objects at the staff whilst at the same time issuing threats towards them;

- a person armed with a knife or other weapon who, when approached by police officers, brandishes the weapon and threatens to use it against them;

- a person who brandishes a knife or other weapon and issues threats of violence towards another while both are on private property (for example inside a dwelling).

6.6   Affray should be charged where there is relevant conduct and it can be proved that the accused:

- used or threatened unlawful violence **towards another**; **and**

- his conduct was such that it would cause a person of reasonable firmness present at the scene **to fear for his personal safety**. No person of reasonable firmness need actually be, or be likely to be, present at the scene however: **section 3(4)**.

R v *Sanchez* (1996) *The Times*, 3 March, makes it clear that the two persons — the 'victim' of the affray and the 'person of reasonable firmness present at the scene' — must be distinguished. It was necessary to show that a notional third person at the scene would have feared for his personal safety, not that the victim was put in fear. Were it otherwise, the definition of affray would be extended to include every common assault.

6.7   The accused must have **intended** to use or threaten violence; or have been **aware** that his conduct may be violent or may threaten violence.

6.8   In cases where an offence under section 3 is a precursor to, or part of, the commission of an offence of **assault**, the question of selecting the number and type of appropriate charge arises. Generally, the more serious the injury, the less likely the need to charge a section 3 offence. For further guidance on charge selection see paragraph 10 below.

7   Violent disorder

7.1   Under section 2 of the Act, it must be proved that:

— three or more persons
— present together
— used or threatened
— unlawful violence
— so that the conduct of them (taken together) would cause
— a person of reasonable firmness
— present at the scene
— to fear for his or her personal safety.

7.2   This offence should only be charged in relation to instances of serious disorder. It will be an especially appropriate charge where such disorder has been planned, although the violence does not have to be premeditated. The offence should **not** be charged simply because three or more persons are involved in minor disorder.

7.1   An offence under section 2 is triable either way. The maximum penalty on conviction on indictment is five years' imprisonment and/or a fine of unlimited amount. On summary conviction the maximum penalty is six months' imprisonment and/or a fine not exceeding level 5.

7.1   The offence may be committed in a **public or private place**. The relevant conduct may be directed against a person or persons or against property.

7.5   Examples of the type of conduct appropriate for a section 2 offence include:

- fighting, involving the use of weapons, between large groups of rival football supporters in a street or town centre;

- fighting, including the use of weapons, between rival groups in a place to which members of the public have access (for example a restaurant, discotheque, public house, street or town centre);

- disorder causing major disruption at a public demonstration where missiles are thrown and other violence is used against and directed towards the police.

7.6   There must be evidence which shows that:

- three or more people (including the accused), while present together, used or threatened unlawful violence; **and**

- their conduct (taken together) was such that it would have caused a person of reasonable firmness present at the scene to fear for his personal safety.

7.7   There must also be evidence which shows that the accused intended to use or threaten violence, or was aware that his conduct may be violentor threaten violence.

7.8   Whilst three or more persons must have been present and used or threatened unlawful violence, it is not necessary that three or more persons should actually be charged and prosecuted: *R* v *Mahroof* (1988) 88 Cr App R 317. The charge must make clear, however, that the defendant was one of the three or more involved in the commission of the offence.

7.9   A charge under section 2 will reflect the potential danger that existed to innocent members of the public. Accordingly, an offence under section 2 should almost always be charged (where there is sufficient evidence) **in addition** to any offence(s) which may also be made out under section 20 or 18 of the Offences Against the Person Act 1861. For further guidance on charge selection see paragraph 10 below.

8   Riot

8.1   Under section 1 of the Act, it must be proved that

— twelve or more persons
— present together
— used or threatened unlawful violence
— for a common purpose; and that
— the conduct of them (taken together)
— was such as to cause
— a person of reasonable firmness
— present at the scene
— to fear for his personal safety.

8.2   An offence under section 1 will be an appropriate charge **only** in wholly exceptional circumstances, where the most serious outbreaks of violence have occurred. Such circumstances will be **rare**.

8.3   A prosecution for riot or incitement to riot may be commenced **only** by, or with the consent of, the Director of Public Prosecutions.

8.4   An offence under section 1 is triable on indictment only. The maximum penalty on conviction is ten years' imprisonment and/or a fine of unlimited amount.

8.5   A charge of riot should be confined to the most serious outbreaks of public disorder. These can be distinguished from other examples of group disorder by virtue of:

- the **scale** of the disruption;

- the **violence** used;

- the **number** of individuals involved;

- the element of **common purpose**.

8.6   Conduct which falls within the scope of this offence includes:

- exceptionally serious acts of violence against public order committed in furtherance of industrial disputes;

- public disturbance on a wide scale involving serious acts of violence, serious damage to property and looting;

- organised attacks on people and property in the context of marches and demonstrations;

- large scale acts of football violence which have an element of organisation;

- serious and organised violent attacks on the police or other public servants.

8.7   The defendant must intend to use violence, or be aware that his conduct may be violent.

8.8   Where there is sufficient evidence for a charge under section 1 of the Act, and an offence under section 20 or 18 of the Offences Against the Person Act 1861 can also be made out, it will almost always be appropriate to continue with the section 1 offence, **in addition** to the assault charge. For further guidance on charge selection see paragraph 10 below.

9   Alternative Verdicts

9.1   The Act recognises that there may be some overlap between some public disorder offences by providing for the return of an alternative verdict where the offences of **affray** or **violent disorder** have been tried on indictment. In these circumstances, the jury may, in finding the defendant not guilty as charged, find him guilty of an offence under section 4. It is important to emphasise, however, that the offence which is most appropriate to the circumstances of the case should **always** be charged. An offence of affray or violent disorder should **never** be charged with a view to obtaining a guilty verdict under section 4.

9.2   The operation of **section 6(3) Criminal Law Act 1967** is not affected by the Act. Hence, a jury may on an indictment for riot, return an alternative verdict of guilty of violent disorder or guilty of affray: *R* v *Fleming* (1989) 153 JP 517. Section 6(3) may also be used where a defendant faced with an indictment charging either violent disorder or affray wishes to plead not guilty as charged, but guilty to an offence contrary to section 4: *R* v *O'Brien* (1992) 156 JP 925.

9.3   Similar provisions do not exist for the return of alternative verdicts in the magistrates' courts.

10   Additional Charges and Charge Selection

10.1   It is a common feature of public order incidents that sufficient evidence exists to charge the accused with offences other than those under the Act, for example, unlawful possession of an offensive weapon, assault and/or criminal damage.

10.2   It is difficult to give general guidance in this area, because each course of conduct should be considered in the light of the facts of the particular case. However, the following general factors may help in deciding which combination of offences should be charged where more than one is possible.

- Is the offence basically one of public disorder in which there has been some minor assault; or vice versa? If the former, concentrate on the public disorder aspect.

- Where there are aggravating features to an assault, such as the use of a weapon, it is likely that an assault charge should be preferred.

- Where there is an allied assault or act of criminal damage, is it one in which compensation is an issue? If so, an assault charge or criminal damage charge may **also** be appropriate. But remember compensation may be payable to a victim in respect of offences of affray and violent disorder. This will be so, if the loss, damage or personal injury arose from the group activity in which the offender took part, and there is sufficient connection between his participation in the offence and the injury to support the making of a compensation order.

10.3 A charge under the Football (Offences) Act 1991 ('F(O)A') will be more suitable where the following types of conduct have occurred at a designated football match:

- throwing missiles onto the playing area, or any area adjacent to the playing area to which spectators are not usually admitted: section 2, F(O)A;

- racialist or indecent chanting: section 3, F(O)A;

- going onto the playing area or any area adjacent to the playing area to which spectators are not usually admitted without lawful authority or lawful excuse: section 4, F(O)A.

10.4 The choice of charge will ultimately be made on the facts of individual cases and in accordance with paragraphs 1.2 and 3.1 above. Paragraph 3.1 (ii) has particular
relevance to public order offences. Where the additional factors listed in paragraph
10.2 are not present, the following paragraphs offer **general guidance** about the correct combination of offences to charge where there is sufficient evidence to proceed on each of them.

Assaults

10.5 If there is sufficient evidence to justify a charge under section 1 of the Public Order Act and an assault contrary to:

- section 18 of the Offences Against the Person Act 1861 (OAPA); or
- section 20 OAPA

it will usually be appropriate to **charge both**. It will not normally be appropriate to charge section 47 or common assault contrary to section 39 of the Criminal Justice Act 1988 together with an offence contrary to section 1 of the Act.

10.6 If there is sufficient evidence to justify a charge under sections 2 or 3 of the Public Order Act and an assault contrary to

- section 18 OAPA; or
- section 20 OAPA; or
- section 47 OAPA

it will usually be appropriate to **charge both**. It will not normally be appropriate to charge common assault (section 39 of the CJA 1988) together with an offence contrary to sections 2 or 13 of the Act.

10.7 If there is sufficient evidence to justify a charge under section 4, 4A, or 5 of the Act and an assault contrary to

- section 18 OAPA;
- or section 20 OAPA; or
- section 47 OAPA

it will usually be appropriate to **charge the assault alone**. In cases of section 4 conduct, if other victims have not been assaulted, it will usually be appropriate to charge section 4 **in addition to the assault**.

10.8 Where you have evidence to prove conduct contrary to section 4, 4A or 5, together with a common assault (section 39 of the CJA 1988), it will usually be appropriate to proceed on the common assault alone. But if the conduct contrary to section 4, 4A or 5 was directed at others who were not victims of common assault, **consider charging both**.

Section 18 — conduct intended to or likely to stir up racial hatred

10.9   Where the evidence supports a charge under section 18 of the Act and there is evidence of an assault, and/or criminal damage, and/or unlawful possession of an offensive weapon, the section 18 offence should always be charged in addition to the other offence(s). Refer to paragraph 5.34–5.48, especially 5.38.

Offensive Weapons

10.10   Generally, the more serious the outbreak of public disorder — when the defendant is also in possession of an offensive or bladed weapon — the more likely it will be to add a further charge to reflect that fact.

10.11   Where any type of weapon is carried by those involved in public disorder, this is an aggravating factor to be taken into account in the presentation of the case. The approach to be taken will depend on the following factors:

- the type of weapon concerned;

- whether the weapon was used or its use threatened;

- how the weapon was used;

- the potential for serious injury;

- the time when the weapon was discovered or produced (i.e. was it produced during the incident or found on arrest).

10.12   Where a summary only public order offence is appropriate, but where the defendant is in unlawful possession of an offensive weapon, police officers and prosecutors should consider carefully whether it might be more appropriate to focus on the possession of the offensive weapon (which is an offence triable either way) and recount the circumstances of the disorder in presenting the case to the relevant tribunal. If, however, the summary public order offence is itself serious, such as, for example, racially motivated harassment or 'stalking', consider charging **both** offences.

10.13   You should reflect the possession of a bladed weapon in a separate charge when the appropriate public disorder offence is summary only.

10.14   You should reflect the unlawful possession of an offensive weapon in a separate charge when the appropriate public order offence is triable either way or only triable on indictment.

Criminal Damage

10.15   Acts of criminal damage are frequently committed during public disorder. Where there is sufficient evidence to support both offences, consider charging both. if, however, offences contrary to section 1 or 2 of the Public Order Act are being charged and the criminal damage is minor, charge the section 1 or 2 offence alone. (Paragraph 10.2 — last bullet point deals with the issue of compensation.) If the criminal damage is serious and the public order act offence is minor, then you should consider charging the criminal damage alone.

11   Alternative Disposal — Bind Over

11.1   Both the Crown Court and magistrates' courts may make an order binding over an individual to keep the peace. An application for a bind over should never be made as a matter of convenience and should not be made in the Crown Court except in exceptional circumstances. A court may be asked to exercise its power to bind over where:

- there has been an outbreak of bad behaviour which is not sufficiently serious to prefer a charge under the Act but which amounts to a **breach of the peace**; and

- there is a danger that the conduct complained of will be **repeated**; and

- the accused **consents** to the proposed course of action.

11.2   For conduct to constitute a breach of the peace, the conduct must involve violence or the threat of violence. The violence need not be perpetrated by the defendant, provided that the natural consequence of his conduct, was that others would be provoked to violence (*Percy* v *DPP* [1995] Crim LR 714).

11.3   It will be appropriate to seek a bind over where conduct falling short of that required for a substantive offence under the Act has been committed. If you have identified the case as one which should proceed by way of bindover, then you should pursue the case on the basis of a complaint rather than charge for an offence.

11.4   Where a decision has been made to prosecute in accordance with the Code for Crown Prosecutors, the circumstances in which it will be appropriate to dispose of the case by way of a bind over will be rare. There must have been a significant change in circumstances; for example, where a witness refuses to give evidence against the defendant, but there remains sufficient evidence that the defendant was involved in a disturbance.

APPENDIX FOUR

FOOTBALL SPECTATORS ACT 1989, SCHEDULE 1

The offences relevant for the purposes of sections 7(2) and 15(1) of this Act are the following—

(a)   any offence under section 2(1) or 5(7) of this Act;

(b)   any offence under section 2 of the Sporting Events (Control of Alcohol etc) Act 1985 (alcohol containers at sports grounds) committed by the accused at any designated football match or while entering or trying to enter the ground;

(c)   any offence under section 5 of the Public Order Act 1986 (harassment, alarm or distress) or any provision of Part III of that Act (racial hatred) committed during a period relevant to a designated football match at any premises while the accused was at, or was entering or leaving or trying to enter or leave, the premises;

(d)   any offence involving the use or threat of violence by the accused towards another person committed during a period relevant to a designated football match at any premises while the accused was at, or was entering or leaving or trying to enter or leave, the premises;

(e)   any offence involving the use or threat of violence towards property committed during a period relevant to a designated football match at any premises while the accused was at, or was entering or leaving or trying to enter or leave, the premises;

(f)   any offence under section 12 of the Licensing Act 1872 (persons found drunk in public places, etc) of being found drunk in a highway or other public place committed while the accused was on a journey to or from a designated football match being an offence as respects which the court makes a declaration of relevance;

(g)   any offence under section 91(1) of the Criminal justice Act 1967 (disorderly behaviour while drunk in a public place) committed in a highway or other public place while the accused was on a journey to or from a designated football match being an offence as respects which the court makes a declaration of relevance;

(h)   any offence under section 1 of the Sporting Events (Control of Alcohol etc) Act 1985 (alcohol on coaches or trains to or from sporting events) committed while the accused was on a journey to or from a designated football match being an offence as respects which the court makes a declaration of relevance;

(i)   any offence under section 5 of the Public Order Act 1986 (harassment, alarm or distress) or any provision of Part III of that Act (racial hatred) committed while the accused was on a journey to or from a designated football match being an offence as respects which the court makes a declaration of relevance;

(j)   any offence under section 4 or 5 of the Road Traffic Act 1988 (driving etc when under the influence of drink or drugs or with an alcohol concentration above the prescribed limit) committed while the accused was on a journey to or from a designated football match being an offence as respects which the court makes a declaration of relevance;

(k)   any offence involving the use or threat of violence by the accused towards another person committed while one or each of them was on a journey to or from a designated football match being an offence as respects which the court makes a declaration of relevance;

(l) any offence involving the use or threat of violence towards property committed while the accused was on a journey to or from a designated football match being an offence as respects which the court makes a declaration of relevance

[(m) any offence under the Football (Offences) Act 1991].

FIREARMS ACT 1968, SCHEDULE 6

FIREARMS ACT 1968, SCHEDULE 6

PART I TABLE OF PUNISHMENTS

Section of this Act creating offence	General nature of offence	Mode of prosecution	Punishment	Additional provisions
Section 1(1)	Possessing etc. firearm or ammunition without certificate.	(a) Summary	6 months or a fine of the prescribed sum; or both.	
		(b) On indictment	(i) where the offence is committed in an aggravated form within the meaning of section 4(4) of this Act, 7 years, or a fine; or both. (ii) in any other case, 5 years or a fine; or both.	[Applies to Scotland only.]
Section 1(2)	Non-compliance with condition of firearm certificate.	Summary	6 months or a fine of level 5 on the standard scale; or both.	
Section 2(1)	Possessing, etc. shot gun without shot gun certificate.	(a) Summary	6 months or the statutory maximum or both.	[Applies to Scotland only.]
		(b) On indictment	5 years or a fine or both.	
Section 2(2)	Non-compliance with condition of shot gun certificate.	Summary	6 months or a fine of level 5 on the standard scale; or both.	[Applies to Scotland only.]
Section 3(1)	Trading in firearms without being registered as firearms dealer.	(a) Summary	6 months or a fine of the prescribed sum; or both.	
		(b) On indictment	5 years or a fine; or both.	
Section 3(2)	Selling firearm to person without a certificate.	(a) Summary	6 months or a fine of the prescribed sum, or both.	
		(b) On indictment.	5 years or a fine; or both.	
Section 3(3)	Repairing, testing etc. firearm for person without a certificate.	(a) Summary	6 months or a fine of the prescribed sum; or both.	
		(b) On indictment	5 years or a fine; or both.	
Section 3(5)	Falsifying certificate, etc. with view to acquisition of firearm.	(a) Summary	6 months or a fine of the prescribed sum; or both.	
		(b) On indictment	5 years or a fine; or both.	

Section of this Act creating offence	General nature of offence	Mode of prosecution		Punishment	Additional provisions
Section 3(6)	Pawnbroker taking firearm in pawn.	Summary		3 months or a fine of level 3 on the standard scale; or both.	
Section 4(1) (3)	Shortening a shot gun; conversion of firearms.	(a) Summary		6 months or a fine of the prescribed sum; or both.	
		(b) On indictment		7 years or a fine; or both.	
Section 5(1)	Possessing or distributing prohibited weapons or ammunition.	(a) Summary		6 months or a fine of the prescribed sum; or both.	
		(b) On indictment		10 years or a fine; or both.	
Section 5(1A)	Possessing or distributing other prohibited weapons or ammunition.	(a) Summary		6 months or a fine of the statutory maximum; or both.	
		(b) On indictment		10 years or a fine; or both.	
Section 5(5)	Non-compliance with condition of Defence Council authority.	Summary		6 months or a fine of level 5 on the standard scale; or both.	
Section 5(6)	Non-compliance with requirement to surrender authority to possess, etc. prohibited weapon or ammunition.	Summary		A fine of level 3 on the standard scale.	
Section 6(3)	Contravention of order under s. 6 (or corresponding Northern Irish order) restricting removal of arms.	Summary		3 months or, for each firearm or parcel of ammunition in respect of which the offence is committed, a fine of level 3 on the standard scale; or both.	Para. 2 of part II of this schedule applies.
Section 7(2)	Making false statement in order to obtain police permit.	Summary		6 months or a fine of level 5 on the standard scale; or both.	
Section 9(3)	Making false statement in order to obtain permit for auction of firearms etc.	Summary		6 months or a fine not exceeding level 5 on the standard scale; or both.	
Section 13(2)	Making false statement in order to obtain permit for removal of signalling apparatus.	Summary		6 months or a fine of level 5 on the standard scale; or both.	

Section of this Act creating offence	General nature of offence	Mode of prosecution	Punishment	Additional provisions
Section 16	Possession of firearm with intent to endanger life or injure property.	On indictment	Life imprisonment or a fine; or both.	
Section 16A	Possession of firearm or imitation firearm with intent to cause fear of violence.	On indictment	10 years or a fine, or both.	
Section 17(1)	Use of firearm or imitation firearm to resist arrest.	On indictment	Life imprisonment or a fine; or both.	Paras 3 to 5 of part II of this schedule apply.
Section 17(2)	Possessing firearm or imitation firearm while committing an offence specified in schedule 1 or, in Scotland, an offence specified in schedule 2.	On indictment	Life imprisonment or a fine; or both.	Paras 3 and 6 of part II of this schedule apply.
Section 18(1)	Carrying firearm or imitation firearm with intent to commit indictable offence (or, in Scotland, an offence specified in schedule 2) or to resist arrest.	On indictment	Life imprisonment or a fine; or both.	
Section 19	Carrying loaded firearm in public place.	(a) Summary	6 months or a fine of the prescribed sum; or both.	
		(b) On indictment (but not if the firearm is an air weapon).	7 years or a fine; or both.	
Section 20(1)	Trespassing with firearm or imitation firearm in a building.	(a) Summary	6 months or a fine of the prescribed sum; or both.	
		(b) On indictment (but not in the case of an imitation firearm or if the firearm is an air weapon).	7 years or a fine; or both.	
Section 20(2)	Trespassing with firearm or imitation firearm on land.	Summary	3 months or a fine of level 4 on the standard scale; or both.	
Section 21(4)	Contravention of provisions denying firearms to ex-prisoners and the like.	(a) Summary	6 months or a fine of the prescribed sum; or both.	
		(b) On indictment	5 years or a fine; or both.	

Section of this Act creating offence	General nature of offence	Mode of prosecution	Punishment	Additional provisions
Section 21(5)	Supplying firearms to person denied them under section 21.	(a) Summary	6 months or a fine of the prescribed sum; or both.	
		(b) On indictment	5 years or a fine; or both.	
Section 22(1)	Person under 17 acquiring firearm.	Summary	6 months or a fine of level 5 on the standard scale; or both.	
Section 22(1A)	Person under 18 using certificated firearm for unauthorised purpose.	Summary	3 months or a fine of level 5 on the standard scale or both.	
Section 22(2)	Person under 14 having firearm in his possession without lawful authority.	Summary	6 months or a fine of level 5 on the standard scale; or both.	
Section 22(3)	Person under 15 having with him a shot gun without adult supervision.	Summary	A fine of level 3 on the standard scale.	Para. 8 of part II of this schedule applies.
Section 22(4)	Person under 14 having with him an air weapon or ammunition therefor.	Summary	A fine of level 3 on the standard scale.	Paras 7 and 8 of part II of this schedule apply.
Section 22(5)	Person under 17 having with him an air weapon in a public place.	Summary	A fine of level 3 on the standard scale.	Paras 7 and 8 of part II of this schedule apply.
Section 23(1)	Person under 14 making improper use of air weapon when under supervision; person supervising him permitting such use.	Summary	A fine of level 3 on the standard scale.	Paras 7 and 8 of part II of this schedule apply.
Section 24(1)	Selling or letting on hire a firearm to person under 17.	Summary	6 months or a fine of level 5 on the standard scale; or both.	
Section 24(2)	Supplying firearm or ammunition (being of a kind to which section 1 of this Act applies) to person under 14.	Summary	6 months or a fine of level 5 on the standard scale; or both.	
Section 24(3)	Making gift of shot gun to person under 15.	Summary	A fine of level 3 on the standard scale.	Para. 9 of part II of this schedule applies.
Section 24(4)	Supplying air weapon to person under 14.	Summary	A fine of level 3 on the standard scale.	Paras 7 and 8 of part II of this schedule apply.

Section of this Act creating offence	General nature of offence	Mode of prosecution	Punishment	Additional provisions
Section 25	Supplying firearm to person drunk or insane.	Summary	3 months or a fine of level 3 on the standard scale; or both.	
Section 26(5)	Making false statement in order to procure grant or renewal of a firearm or shot gun certificate.	Summary	6 months or a fine of level 5 on the standard scale; or both.	
Section 29(3)	Making false statement in order to procure variation of a firearm certificate.	Summary	6 months or a fine of level 5 on the standard scale; or both.	
Section 30D(3)	Failing to surrender certificate on revocation.	Summary	A fine of level 3 on the standard scale.	
Section 32B(5)	Failure to surrender expired European firearms pass.	Summary	A fine of level 3 on the standard scale.	
Section 32C(6)	Failure to produce European firearms pass or Article 7 authority for variation or cancellation etc.; failure to notify loss or theft of firearm identified in pass or to produce pass for endorsement.	Summary	3 months or a fine of level 5 on the standard scale; or both.	
Section 38(8)	Failure to surrender certificate of registration [or register of transactions] on removal of firearms dealer's name from register.	Summary	A fine of level 3 on the standard scale.	
Section 39(1)	Making false statement in order to secure registration or entry in register of a place of business.	Summary	6 months or a fine of level 5 on the standard scale; or both.	
Section 39(2)	Registered firearms dealer having place of business not entered in the register.	Summary	6 months or a fine of level 5 on the standard scale; or both.	
Section 39(3)	Non-compliance with condition of registration.	Summary	6 months or a fine of level 5 on the standard scale; or both.	

Section of this Act creating offence	General nature of offence	Mode of prosecution	Punishment	Additional provisions
Section 40(5)	Non-compliance by firearms dealer with provisions as to register of transactions; making false entry in register.	Summary	6 months or a fine of level 5 on the standard scale; or both.	
Section 42A	Failure to report transaction authorised by visitor's shot gun permit.	Summary	3 months or a fine of level 5 on the standard scale or both.	
Section 46	Obstructing constable or civilian officer in exercise of search powers.	Summary	6 months or a fine of level 5 on the standard scale; or both.	
Section 47(2)	Failure to hand over firearm or ammunition on demand by constable.	Summary	3 months, or a fine of level 4 on the standard scale; or both.	
Section 48(3)	Failure to comply with requirement of a constable that a person shall declare his name and address.	Summary	A fine of level 3 on the standard scale.	
Section 48A(4)	Failure to produce firearms pass issued in another Member State.	Summary	A fine of level 3 on the standard scale.	
Section 49(3)	Failure to give constable facilities for examination of firearms in transit, or to produce papers.	Summary	3 months or, for each firearm or parcel of ammunition in respect of which the offence is committed, a fine of level 3 on the standard scale; or both.	Para. 2 of part II of this schedule applies.
Section 52(2)(c)	Failure to surrender firearm or shot gun certificate cancelled by court on conviction.	Summary	A fine of level 3 on the standard scale.	

APPENDIX SIX

CODE OF PRACTICE ON INTRUSIVE SURVEILLANCE

pursuant to Section 101(3) of the Police Act 1997

Commencement

This code applies to any authorisation of intrusive surveillance (under Part III of the Police Act 1997) by the police, Her Majesty's Customs & Excise, the National Criminal Intelligence Service or the National Crime Squad which begins on or after the day on which this code comes into effect. (22nd February 1999)

Contents
1. GENERAL
2. AUTHORISATION UNDER PART III OF THE POLICE ACT 1997
3. THE CHIEF COMMISSIONER AND COMMISSIONERS
4. APPEALS
5. INFORMATION LEAFLET

1 GENERAL

1.1   This code of practice must be readily available at all operational police premises and offices of HM & Customs Excise, the National Criminal Intelligence Service (NCIS) and the National Crime Squad for consultation and reference by police officers, customs officers, civilian employees of a police authority, persons detained in police or Customs' custody and their representatives. Copies should also be made available for reference by members of the public at all police stations and public offices of HM Customs & Excise.

1.2   Notes for guidance printed in this code are not part of the code but are designed to assist police officers and others in its application.

1.3   This code governs intrusive surveillance operations conducted within the United Kingdom by the police, NCIS, the National Crime Squad and HM Customs & Excise which are authorised under Part III of the Police Act 1997 ('the Act'). References in the code to a police force or police authority include references to NCIS and the National Crime Squad and their Service Authorities, as appropriate.

1.4   Section 101(8) of the Act requires that all persons, other than a Commissioner, shall have regard to this code in the performance of their responsibilities and functions under the Act.

1.5   The Act provides that the code is admissible as evidence in criminal and civil proceedings. If any provision of the code appears relevant to any court or tribunal considering any such proceedings, it can be taken into account.

1.6   The interception of communications sent by post or by means of public telecommunications systems may be authorised only by the Secretary of State personally, in accordance with the terms of the Interception of Communications Act 1985. Nothing in this code should be taken as granting dispensation from the requirements of that Act. [See *Note 1A*].

Interpretation

1.7   For the purpose of this code, 'intrusive surveillance' means surveillance activity which involves entry on or interference with property or with wireless telegraphy within the meaning of section 92 of the Act.

1.8   In this Code:
   — 'authorising officer' means:
- the chief constable of a police force in England or Wales or Scotland as listed in sections 93(5)(a) and 93(5)(d) of the Act, who may authorise operations on application by members of his/her police force in his/her own force area;
- the Commissioner or an Assistant Commissioner of the Metropolitan Police force who may authorise operations on application by members of his/her force in the Metropolitan Police District;
- the Commissioner of the City of London Police force who may authorise operations on application by members of his/her force in the City of London Police area;
- the chief constable or a deputy chief constable of the Royal Ulster Constabulary who may authorise operations on application by members of the Royal Ulster Constabulary in Northern Ireland;
- the Director General of the National Crime Squad, who may authorise operations on application by members of the National Crime Squad in England and Wales;
- the Director General of NCIS who may authorise operations on application by members of NCIS in the United Kingdom; or
- the customs officer designated by the Commissioners of HM Customs & Excise under Section 93(5)(h) of the Act who may authorise operations on application by Customs officers in the United Kingdom. [See *Note 1B*];
   —'designated deputy' means:
- the person holding the rank of assistant chief constable designated to act in the absence of the chief constable under section 12(4) of the Police Act 1996 or section 5(4) of the Police (Scotland) Act 1967;
- the person designated to act in the absence of the Commissioner of the City of London Police under section 25 of the City of London Police Act 1839. [See *Note 1C*];
- the person designated to act in the absence of the Director General of the National Criminal Intelligence Service under section 8 of the Act;
- the person designated to act in the absence of the Director General of the National Crime Squad under section 54 of the Act;
- the customs officer designated to act in the absence of the Chief Investigation Officer by the Commissioners of HM Customs & Excise under section 94(4)(d) of the Act. [see *Note 1D*].
- the expressions 'Chief Commissioner' and 'Commissioner' refer to persons who hold or have held high judicial office and who have been appointed by the Prime Minister for a term of three years to undertake functions specified in Part III of the Act.
- 'serious crime' is defined as conduct which constitutes one or more offences if, and only if:
- it involves the use of violence, results in substantial financial gain or is conduct by a large number of persons in pursuit of a common purpose, or
- the offence or one of the offences is an offence for which a person who has attained the age of twenty-one and has no previous convictions could reasonably be expected to be sentenced to imprisonment for a term of three years or more.

1.9   The 'designated deputy' is empowered to act as 'authorising officer' *only* in the circumstances outlined in section 12(4) of the Police Act 1996, section 5(4) of the Police (Scotland) Act 1967, section 25 of the City of London Police Act 1839, or sections 8 and 54 of the Act.

1.10   In addition, paragraph 2.14 below sets out circumstances where authorisations can be given in the absence of the authorising officers or designated deputies in urgent cases.

Notes for Guidance

1A   The question will frequently arise whether a surveillance device may legitimately be used in circumstances where the incidental effect will be to enable the overhearing of what is said by a party to a telephone conversation who is speaking from a location where a device is installed. The use of a surveillance device should *not* be ruled out simply because it may incidentally pick up one end of a telephone conversation. However, its use would not be appropriate where its purpose is to overhear speech which is being transmitted by a public telecommunications system. In such cases an application must be made for a warrant under the Interception of Communications Act 1985.

There is nothing in the Act comparable to section 9 of the Interception of Communications Act 1985, the effect of which is to exclude intercept material from being adduced as evidence in court proceedings.

1B   This will be the Chief Investigation Officer of the National Investigation Service, HM Customs & Excise.

1C   This will be the Assistant Commissioner of the City of London Police.

1D   This will be a Deputy Chief Investigation Officer of the National Investigation Service, HM Customs & Excise.

2   AUTHORISATION UNDER PART III OF THE POLICE ACT 1997

Criteria

2.1   Responsibility for the authorisation of all intrusive surveillance operations requiring interference with property or with wireless telegraphy rests with the authorising officer. Authorisations require the personal authority of the authorising officer except in circumstances set out in paragraph 2.14 of this code. Authorisations under Part III will not be necessary where the police, the National Crime Squad, NCIS or HM Customs & Excise are acting with the consent of a person able to give permission in respect of relevant property.

2.2   Any person giving an authorisation for intrusive surveillance must believe that:

- the investigation concerns serious crime as defined in the Act;
- the action proposed is necessary because it is likely to be of substantial value in the prevention or detection of serious crime; and
- what the action seeks to achieve cannot reasonably be achieved by other means [see *Note 2A*].

2.3   Any person giving an authorisation should first satisfy him/herself that the degree of intrusion into the privacy of those affected by the surveillance is commensurate with the seriousness of the offence. That is to say, no intrusion should be authorised which is out of proportion to the crime committed or planned. This is especially the case where the subjects of the surveillance might reasonably assume a high degree of privacy, for instance in their homes, or where there are special sensitivities, such as where the intrusion might affect communications between a Minister of any religion or faith and an individual relating to that individual's spiritual welfare or where medical or journalistic confidentiality or legal privilege could be affected. Similar considerations should be given to situations where confidential social services records are involved.

2.4   In this connection, any person giving an authorisation is reminded that police forces in England, Wales, Scotland and Northern Ireland, NCIS, the National Crime Squad and HM Customs & Excise have given an undertaking not to mount surveillance operations in circumstances covered by the Seal of Confession. In addition, where they are satisfied that a Minister of Religion is not himself involved in criminal activity, and they believe that surveillance will lead to them intruding on spiritual counselling between the Minister and a member of his faith, they should, in preparing the case for prior approval by a Commissioner, give serious consideration to discussing the matter first with a relevant senior representative of the religious authority. The views of the senior representative would be included in the request for approval. In this respect, 'spiritual counselling' is defined as conversations with a Minister of Religion acting in his official capacity, which does not amount to a sacramental confession, but where the person being counselled is seeking or the Minister is imparting forgiveness, absolution and the resolution of conscience with the authority of the Divine Being of their faith.

2.5   Collateral intrusion or interference is a matter of particular concern, especially in the case of premises used for any form of medical or professional counselling or therapy. Particular thought should therefore be given to any collateral intrusion on or interference with the privacy of people other than the subject of surveillance. Notifications to a Commissioner should include an assessment of the potential for any such collateral intrusion or interference (see paragraph 2.19).

2.6   Any person giving an authorisation will also need to be aware of particular sensitivities in the local community where the surveillance is taking place or particular local police operations which could impact on the deployment of the surveillance equipment. It is therefore recommended that the authorising officers in NCIS, the National Crime Squad and HM Customs & Excise consult the local chief constable where the authorising officers consider such conflicts might arise.

Cases requiring approval of Commissioner

2.7   In certain cases, the authorisation will not take effect and intrusive surveillance must not begin until it has been approved by a Commissioner and the authorising officer has been notified (but see paragraph 2.13 regarding cases of urgency). These cases are where the person giving the authorisation believes that:

- any of the property specified in the authorisation:
- is used wholly or mainly as a dwelling or as a bedroom in a hotel; or
- constitutes office premises; or
- the action authorised is likely to result in any person acquiring knowledge of:
- matters subject to legal privilege;
- confidential personal information; or
- confidential journalistic material.

2.8   'Office premises' are defined, by reference to section 1(2) of the Offices, Shops and Railway Premises Act 1963 as, any building or part of a building whose sole or principal use is as an office or for office purposes (which means purposes of administration, clerical work, handling money and telephone or telegraph operation).

2.9   Matters subject to legal privilege includes both oral and written communications between a professional legal adviser and his/her client or any person representing his/her client made in connection with the giving of legal advice to the client or in contemplation of legal proceedings and for the purposes of such proceedings, as well as items enclosed with or referred to in such communications. Communications and items held with the intention of furthering a criminal purpose are not matters subject to legal privilege [see *Note 2B*].

2.10   Confidential personal information is information held in confidence concerning an individual (whether living or dead) who can be identified from it, and relating:

a)   to his/her physical or mental health; or
b)   to spiritual counselling or other assistance given or to be given, and

which a person has acquired or created in the course of any trade, business, profession or other occupation, or for the purposes of any paid or unpaid office [see *Note 2C*]. It includes both oral and written information and also communications as a result of which personal information is acquired or created. Under the Act, information is held in confidence if:

- it is held subject to an express or implied undertaking to hold it in confidence; or
- it is subject to a restriction on disclosure or an obligation of secrecy contained in existing or future legislation.

2.11   Confidential journalistic material includes material acquired or created for the purposes of journalism and held subject to an undertaking to hold it in confidence, as well as communications resulting in information being acquired for the purposes of journalism and held subject to such an undertaking.

2.12   The procedures to be adopted for seeking the approval of a Commissioner are the responsibility of the Chief Commissioner.

2.13   Where the case is urgent, the authorisation can take effect immediately and intrusive surveillance begin without the prior approval of the Commissioner. Much will depend on the circumstances of the individual operation, but the urgency provisions should *not* be used routinely. However, it must be recognised that there may be exceptional circumstances, for example where it is impractical in the timescale needed to carry out the operation, to obtain the prior approval of a Commissioner to the authorisation. In such cases, the authorising officer must include his/her reasons for considering the case to be urgent in the notification of the authorisation which he/she sends to the Commissioner (see section 2.19).

Authorisation procedures

2.14   Authorisations will generally be given in writing by the authorising officer. However, in urgent cases, they may be given orally by the authorising officer. In such cases, a statement that the authorising officer has expressly authorised the action should be recorded in writing as soon as is reasonably practicable. This should be done by the person with whom the authorising officer spoke. If the authorising officer is absent as provided for in section 12(4) of the Police Act 1996, section 5(4) of the Police (Scotland) Act 1967, section 25 of the City of London Police Act 1839, or sections 8 or 54 of the Police Act 1997, an authorisation can be given in writing or, in urgent cases, orally by the designated deputy. Where, however, in an urgent case, it is not reasonably practicable for the designated deputy to consider an application, then written authorisation may be given:

- in the case of the police, by an assistant chief constable (other than a designated deputy);
- in the case of the Metropolitan Police and City of London Police, by a commander;
- in the case of NCIS and the National Crime Squad, by the person designated by the relevant Director General [see *Note 2D*];
- in the case of HM Customs & Excise, by the person designated by the Commissioners of Customs & Excise. [See *Note 2E*].

2.15   Applications to the authorising officer for authorisation must be made in writing by a police or customs officer or a member of NCIS or the National Crime Squad (within the terms of section 93(3) of the Act) and should specify:

- the identity or identities of those to be targeted (where known);
- the property which the intrusive surveillance will affect;
- the identity of individuals and/or categories of people, where known, who are likely to be affected by collateral surveillance;
- details of the offence planned or committed; and of the intrusive surveillance involved;
- how the authorisation criteria (as set out in paragraph 2.2) have been met;
- any action which may be necessary to retrieve any equipment used in the surveillance;
- in case of a renewal, the results obtained so far, or a full explanation of the failure to obtain any results;

and subsequently record whether authority was given or refused, by whom and the time and date.

2.16   Additionally, in urgent cases, the authorisation should record (as the case may be):

- reasons why the authorising officer or designated deputy considered the case so urgent that an oral instead of a written authorisation was given;
- reasons why the authorising officer or the designated deputy was not available to give an authorisation.

Notifications

2.17   Where a person gives, renews or cancels an authorisation, he/she must, as soon as is reasonably practicable, give notice of it in writing to a Commissioner, in accordance with arrangements made by the Chief Commissioner. In urgent cases which would otherwise have required the approval of the Commissioner, the notification must specify the grounds on which the case is believed to be one of urgency.

2.18   There may be cases which become urgent after approval has been sought but before a response has been received from a Commissioner. In such a case, the authorising officer should give a fresh authorisation and notify the Commissioner that the case is urgent (pointing out that it has become urgent since the previous notification). In these cases, the authorisation will take effect immediately.

2.19   The information to be included in the notification to the Commissioner of the authorisation is set out in [title of statutory instrument]. All notifications must record:

- whether it is a case for which the approval of a Commissioner is required;
- if it is a case which would otherwise require the approval of a Commissioner but in which intrusive surveillance has started because of urgency, the grounds on which the case is believed to be urgent;
- how the authorisation criteria have been met (for example, how the case fits within the definition of serious crime and why the purpose which the action seeks to achieve cannot reasonably be achieved by other means);

- the identity or identities, where known, of those to be targeted;
- the property against which any intrusive surveillance is to take place;
- the nature of the surveillance authorised and the reason why the intrusive surveillance in question is necessary;
- whether the intrusive surveillance is considered likely to lead to collateral intrusion on or interference with persons other than the person being targeted by the authorisation;
- whether or not it will be necessary to retrieve any equipment used in the surveillance.

Duration of authorisations

2.20 Written authorisations given by authorising officers or designated deputies will cease to have effect at the end of a period of three months beginning with the day on which they took effect. In cases requiring prior approval by a Commissioner this means from the time the Commissioner has approved the authorisation and the person who gave the authorisation has been notified. In cases not requiring prior approval, this means from the time the authorisation was given.

2.21 Oral authorisations given in urgent cases by

- authorising officers; or
- designated deputies

and written authorisations given by:

- assistant chief constables (other than a designated deputy);
- commanders in the Metropolitan Police and City of London Police;
- the person designated to act by the relevant Director General of NCIS and National Crime Squad;
- the person designated for the purpose by the Commissioners of Customs & Excise;

will cease at the end of the period of 72 hours beginning with the time when they took effect.

Renewals

2.22 If at any time before the day on which an authorisation expires the authorising officer or, in his/her absence, the designated deputy considers the authorisation should continue to have effect for the purpose for which it was issued, he/she may renew it in writing for a period of three months beginning with the day on which the authorisation would otherwise have ceased to have effect. Authorisations may be renewed more than once, if necessary, and the renewal should be recorded on the authorisation record (see paragraph 2.30).

2.23 Commissioners must be notified of renewals of authorisations. The information to be included in the notification is set out in [title of statutory instrument]. All notifications must record:

- whether this is the first renewal or every occasion on which the authorisation has been renewed previously;
- the information required in a notification of authorisation - as listed in paragraph 2.19; plus
- every respect in which the information in the previous authorisation has changed;
- why it is necessary to continue with the authorisation;
- the content and value to the investigation of the product so far obtained through the surveillance;
- the results of periodic reviews of the authorisation by the authorising officer;
- an estimate of the length of time the authorisation will continue to be necessary.

2.24 If, at the time of renewal, the criteria in paragraph 2.7 exist, then the approval of a Commissioner must be sought before the renewal can take effect. The fact that the initial authorisation required the approval of a Commissioner before taking effect does not mean that its renewal will automatically require such approval. It will only do so if, at the time of the renewal, it falls into one of the categories requiring approval (and is not urgent).

Reviews and cancellations

2.25 A person who has given an authorisation must cancel it (or one given in his/her absence) if satisfied that the action authorised by it is no longer necessary. An authorising officer must cancel an authorisation given in his/her absence if satisfied that the action authorised is no longer necessary. This could be because an investigation has been completed or discontinued or because the surveillance no longer fulfils the criteria set out in section 2.2. Authorising officers should therefore regularly review authorisations to assess the need for the intrusive surveillance operation to continue. This should be recorded on the 'authorisation record' [see paragraphs 2.30–2.32 below and *Note 2F*]. Particular attention is drawn to the need to regularly and frequently review authorisations or renewals where the surveillance gives access to confidential information or involves collateral surveillance on persons other than those being targeted.

2.26 Commissioners must be notified of cancellations of authorisations. The information to be included in the notification is set out in the Police Act 1997 (Notifications of Authorisations etc) Order 1998. All notifications must record:

- the time and date when the instruction was given by the authorising officer to cease surveillance;
- the reason why the authorisation was cancelled;
- the outcome of the investigation and the nature of any criminal proceedings contemplated;
- the arrangements made for the storage of material obtained as a result of surveillance, for its review and destruction when it is no longer of use and for the immediate destruction of unrelated material.

2.27 The Commissioner has the power to cancel an authorisation if he/she is satisfied that, at any time after an authorisation was given or renewed, there were no reasonable grounds for believing the matters set out in paragraph 2.2 above. In such circumstances, the Commissioner may order the destruction of records, in whole or in part, other than those required for pending criminal or civil proceedings, and award compensation to a complainant, where the authorisation is the subject of a complaint.

Ceasing of surveillance activity

2.28 Once an authorisation or renewal expires or is cancelled or quashed, the authorising officer must immediately instruct those carrying out the surveillance to stop listening, watching or recording the activities of the subject of the authorisation or interfering with wireless telegraphy. The time and date when such an instruction was given should be recorded on the authorisation record (see paragraphs 2.30–2.32).

Retrieval of equipment

2.29 Where a Commissioner quashes or cancels an authorisation or renewal, he/she will, if there are reasonable grounds for doing so, order that the authorisation will remain effective for a specified period, to enable officers to retrieve anything left on the property by virtue of the authorisation. They can only do so if the authorisation or renewal makes provision for this. A decision by the Commissioner not to give such an order can be the subject of an appeal to the Chief Commissioner.

Authorisation record

2.30 An 'authorisation record' should be created which records:

- the time and date when an authorisation is given;
- whether an authorisation is in written or oral form;
- the time and date when it was notified to the Commissioner; and
- the time and date when the Commissioner notified his/her approval (where appropriate).

2.31 The authorisation record should also record:

- every occasion when interference with property or wireless telegraphy has occurred;
- the result of periodic reviews of the authorisation; and
- the date of every renewal.

2.32 Finally, it should record the time and date when any instruction was given by the authorising officer to cease surveillance or interference with wireless telegraphy.

Retention and destruction of the product and records of surveillance

2.33 There should be a central record held in each force/service of all authorisations. These records should be retained for a period of at least five years from the ending of the authorisation. Where the records relate to a case in which the product leads to criminal or civil proceedings or appeal, they should be retained for a suitable period commensurate to any subsequent review.

2.34   If there is any reason to believe that the product obtained during the course of an investigation by intrusive surveillance might be relevant to that investigation or to another investigation or to pending or future civil or criminal proceedings then it should not be destroyed but retained in accordance with established disclosure requirements. Particular attention is drawn to the requirements of the Code of Practice issued under the Criminal Procedure and Investigations Act 1996 which requires that material should be retained if it forms part of the unused prosecution material gained in the course of a criminal investigation, or which may be relevant to an investigation. In Scotland, if a report has been submitted to the Procurator Fiscal in relation to the crime under investigation, he/she must be told of the intrusive surveillance in the subsequent police report and the product of the surveillance should be retained and made available if he/she requests it. Where the police or HM Customs & Excise believe that intrusive surveillance material might be relevant to future civil or criminal proceedings, and there is a possibility that a Commissioner might order the destruction of such material, they should inform the Commissioner of their belief and the reasons for it.

2.35   Authorising officers are reminded of the importance of safeguarding confidential and sensitive information. They must also ensure compliance with appropriate data protection requirements and the ACPO code of practice on data protection in the handling and storage of any material resulting from the conduct of intrusive surveillance. Where material is obtained by intrusive surveillance which is wholly unrelated to a criminal investigation or to any person who is the subject of the investigation, and there is no reason to believe it will be relevant to future civil or criminal proceedings, it should be destroyed immediately. Consideration on whether or not unrelated material should be destroyed is the responsibility of the authorising officer. It is essential that this responsibility should be managed at a senior level in the relevant organisation and that officers are clearly identified and are held accountable for carrying out this function.

2.36   There is nothing in the Act which prevents material obtained through the proper use of the authorisation procedures from being used in other investigations. However, the use outside law enforcement agencies or the courts of any material obtained by means of intrusive surveillance and other than in pursuance of the prevention and detection of serious crime, should be authorised only in the most exceptional circumstances.

Complaints

2.37   The Act creates a complaints procedure for Commissioners to deal with complaints alleging that there has been improperly authorised interference with property or wireless telegraphy. More general complaints about the actions of police officers, civilians working for the police, customs officers and members of NCIS or the National Crime Squad are primarily a matter for the head of the organisation concerned.

Notes for Guidance

2A   For example, intrusive surveillance should not be used as a means of circumventing the need for a warrant under the Interception of Communications Act 1985, or of carrying out operations within the responsibilities of the Security and Intelligence Services which properly fall to be authorised by a warrant issued by the Secretary of State under the Intelligence Services Act 1994.

2B   Legally privileged communications will lose their protection if there is evidence, for example, that the professional legal adviser is intending to hold or use them for a criminal purpose; privilege is not lost if a professional legal adviser is properly advising a person who is suspected of having committed a criminal offence. The concept of legal privilege shall apply to the provision of professional legal advice by any agency or organisation.

2C   Confidential personal information might, for example, include consultations between a health professional or a professional counsellor and a patient or client, or information from a patient's medical records.

2D   For police members of the National Criminal Intelligence Service or the National Crime Squad, this will be an officer who holds the rank of assistant chief constable in that Service or Squad. Additionally, in the case of NCIS, this may be an assistant chief investigation officer of Customs & Excise.

2E   This will be an officer of the rank of assistant chief investigation officer.

2F   The authorising officer should determine how often a review should take place when giving an authorisation. This should be as frequently as is considered necessary and practicable and at no greater interval than one month.

3   THE CHIEF COMMISSIONER AND COMMISSIONERS

3.1   Part III of the Act creates the posts of Commissioner and Chief Commissioner.

3.2   It will be the duty of any person having functions under Part III and any person taking action in relation to which an authorisation was given, to comply with any request of a Commissioner for documents or information as required by him/her for the purpose of enabling him/her to discharge his/her functions.

Functions of the Commissioners

3.3   Each Commissioner will be responsible, *inter alia*, for:

- scrutinising as soon as is reasonably practicable every notice of authorisation received;
- deciding whether to give or refuse approval of authorisations which the authorising officer believes involves dwellings, hotel bedrooms or an office or matters subject to legal privilege, confidential personal information or confidential journalistic material;
- considering whether there are reasonable grounds for believing that the action proposed comes within the criteria for authorisation (those matters detailed in paragraph 2.2);
- notifying the authorising officer whether or not an authorisation, which the authorising officer believes requires approval, is approved;
- investigating under the provisions of the Act any complaint alleging that anything has been done under an authorisation in relation to the complainant's property, which for these purposes includes a place where the complainant works or resides;
- notifying the complainant when a complaint is upheld and reporting the findings to the authorising officer who gave the authorisation, or in whose absence it was given, and to the Chief Commissioner;
- notifying the complainant when no determination has been made in the complainant's favour;
- quashing an authorisation or renewal where the Commissioner is, at any time, satisfied that there were no reasonable grounds for believing that it met the criteria for authorisation (those matters detailed in paragraph 2.2) or for believing the case to be one of urgency (see paragraph 2.13) or cancelling an authorisation where the Commissioner is satisfied that, at any time, there were no reasonable grounds for continuing to believe that it met the criteria;
- reporting the findings to the authorising officer and to the Chief Commissioner when the Commissioner decides to cancel or quash an authorisation;
- deciding whether to order the destruction of records, wholly or in part (other than those required for pending criminal or civil proceedings);
- ordering, in appropriate cases, that an authorisation remain effective for a specified period to retrieve anything from the property;
- ordering, in appropriate cases, compensation if an authorisation is quashed or cancelled and a complaint upheld.

3.4   Where a determination has been made upholding a complaint the Commissioner will notify the complainant and report the findings to the authorising officer who gave the authorisation (or in whose absence it was given) and to the Chief Commissioner. Except in such reports a Commissioner will not give reasons.

Functions of the Chief Commissioner

3.5   The Chief Commissioner will be responsible, *inter alia*, for:

- keeping under review the performance of functions by authorising officers and Commissioners under Part III of the Act;

- considering appeals by authorising officers, and notifying the outcome as required by the Act;
- considering appeals by complainants, and notifying the outcome as required by the Act;
- making an annual report to the Prime Minister on the discharge of functions under this Act and reporting at any other time on any matter relating to those functions.

3.6 The Chief Commissioner will not give reasons for a determination, except, if he/she dismisses an appeal, to the authorising officer, the Commissioner who made the decision and the Prime Minister.

4 APPEALS

4.1 Authorising officers may appeal to the Chief Commissioner within a period of 7 days against any decision made by a Commissioner:

- to refuse to approve an authorisation or its renewal;
- to quash an authorisation or renewal;
- to cancel an authorisation;
- to order the destruction of records when cancelling or on expiry of an authorisation (other than those required for pending civil or criminal proceedings);
- to refuse to order that the authorisation remain effective for a specified period to allow the retrieval of anything left on the premises by virtue of the authorisation;
- to uphold a complaint.

4.2 Complainants who have been notified that a complaint has not been found in their favour may also appeal to the Chief Commissioner against that decision within a period of 7 days.

4.3 Any decision by a Commissioner to order the destruction of records or to direct the payment of compensation will not become operative until the period for appealing against the decision has expired and, where there is an appeal, a decision dismissing it has been made by the Chief Commissioner.

4.4 The decisions of the Chief Commissioner and (with the exception of the appeals process under the provisions of the Act) of the Commissioners are not subject to appeal or liable to be questioned in any court.

5 INFORMATION LEAFLET

5.1 Authorising officers should ensure that the information leaflet 'The Police Act 1997: Complaints about the use of intrusive surveillance' is readily available at any police station or public office of HM Customs & Excise.

INDEX